40 Years of Ups & Downs

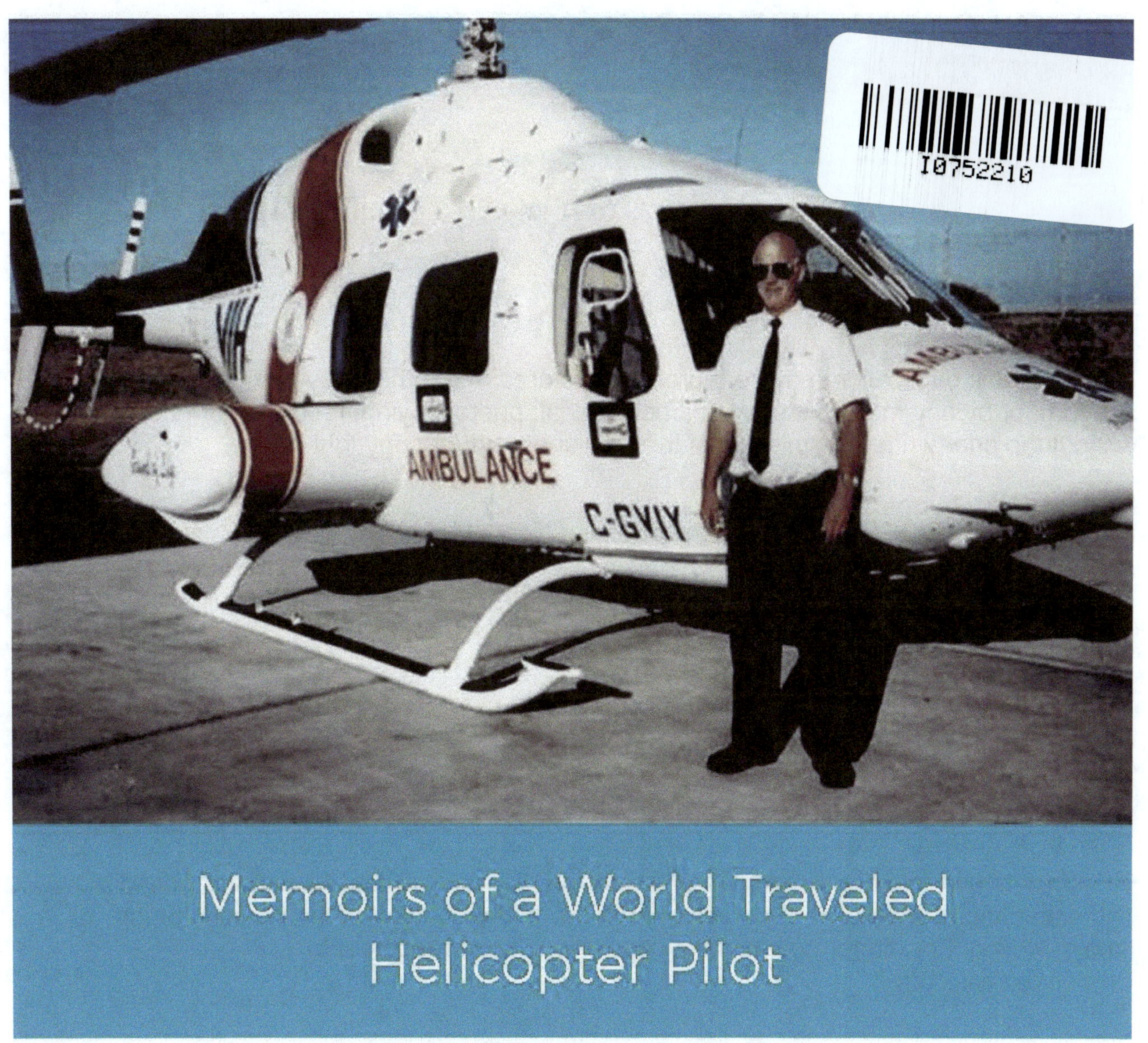

Memoirs of a World Traveled Helicopter Pilot

By **William D. (Bill) Buhr**

Copyright

ISBN: 978-1-7389725-2-4 (Hardcover)
ISBN: 978-1-7389725-3-1 (Electronic)
ISBN: 978-1-7389725-0-0 (Softcover)

40 Years Ups & Downs Memoirs of a World Traveled Helicopter Pilot

Printed in Canada

First Edition: 27 June 2023
Formats:

- E-book for Kindle
- Hardcopy
- Softcopy
- PDF

Additional Copies may be purchased from your favorite retailer including Amazon

Notice

This book is a memoir of William D. (Bill) Buhr of Alberta, Canada. All names, locations and experiences are real, and names are used with the consent of the persons at the time of writing. For further questions or concerns, please reach out to wdbuhr@gmail.com

Dedications

I want to dedicate this journal to my wife, Connie and my three kids; Dean, Chad and Michelle.

I'd also like to express my appreciation to a long-time school-hood friend, Reuben Loewen. He called and inspired me to write about my aviation career. His daughter Angela then gave me excellent foresight as to the direction I should go to record my experiences.

Special Dedication

After relating a story about having heavily armed Thai police on board to settle a rig uprising in the south China Sea, my son, Dean, said, 'Dad, you've never told me that story before!"

So I decided to relate some of my aviation experiences from start to end, highlighting the more interesting events. They might be meant to take on the format of a published book. However, I think many events might be interesting and are in chronological order. At the very least, I enjoyed recalling the events of a memorable career.

His daughter Angela then gave me excellent foresight as to the direction I should go to record my experiences. She also deserves the credit for creating the shared titles of my book: '40 Years of Ups & Downs' and 'Memoirs of a World Traveled Helicopter Pilot'.

My Aviation Career

September 27th, 1966.

My first flight and first time in the air proved to be a significant milestone and a beginning. I had spotted an ad in a local Nanaimo newspaper promoting Pacific Coastal's program for flight training. You could go on a twenty- minute flight for five dollars. I jumped at the opportunity and couldn't get out to Cassidy airport fast enough! I was 20 years old, and it was a thrill to be in the air. The second thrill happened when the instructor gave me a few basic instructions and actually gave me control!

Until that date, and especially in the previous 12 months, I had been increasingly distraught about what I would do for a career. All the way through high school, I was going to be a lawyer. Almost on the day of graduation, I suddenly realized that wasn't for me. So after a year of working on the BC ferries, my future was more and more on my mind to the point of great consternation. I was not really interested in anything, but one of the things I considered was buying a motel. I also contacted a local accounting firm and actually started a home study that could lead to an apprenticeship as an accountant.

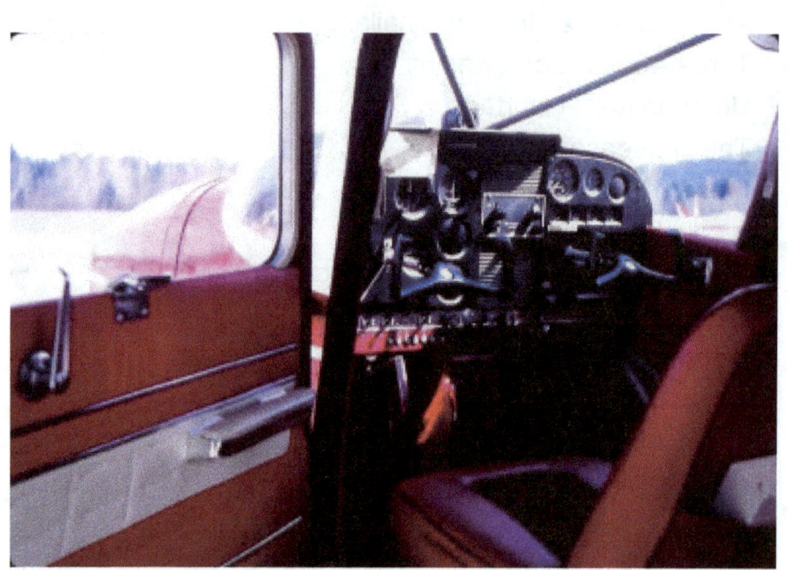

Cessna 172 - cockpit

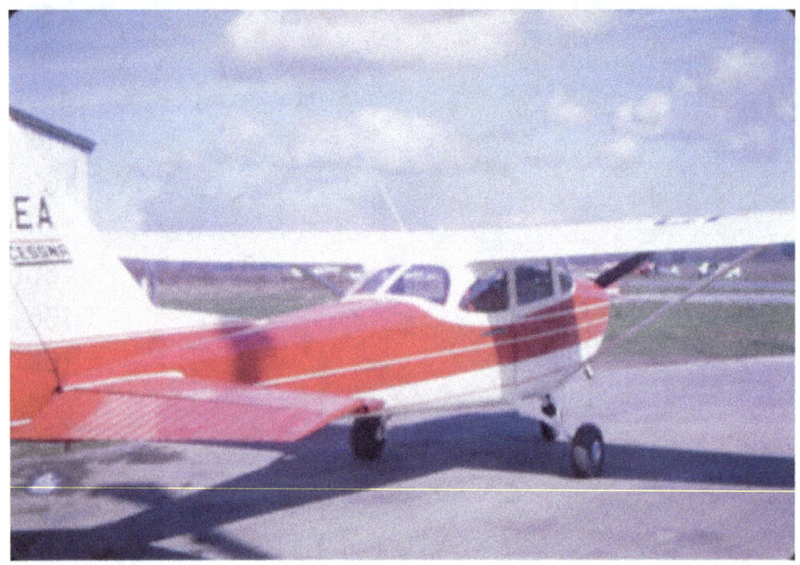

Cessna 172 - CF-XEA

So, when I took that first flight, I was absolutely hooked! I remember looking back to when I was seven and gazing up at the airplanes flying over our farm. It was a practice area north of Saskatoon for the local flying school.
So as an adult just having taken that first flight, I started wondering, could I actually start pursuing the dream of that 7-year-old kid? In my mind, becoming a commercial pilot would be similar in today's terms to wanting to be an astronaut!

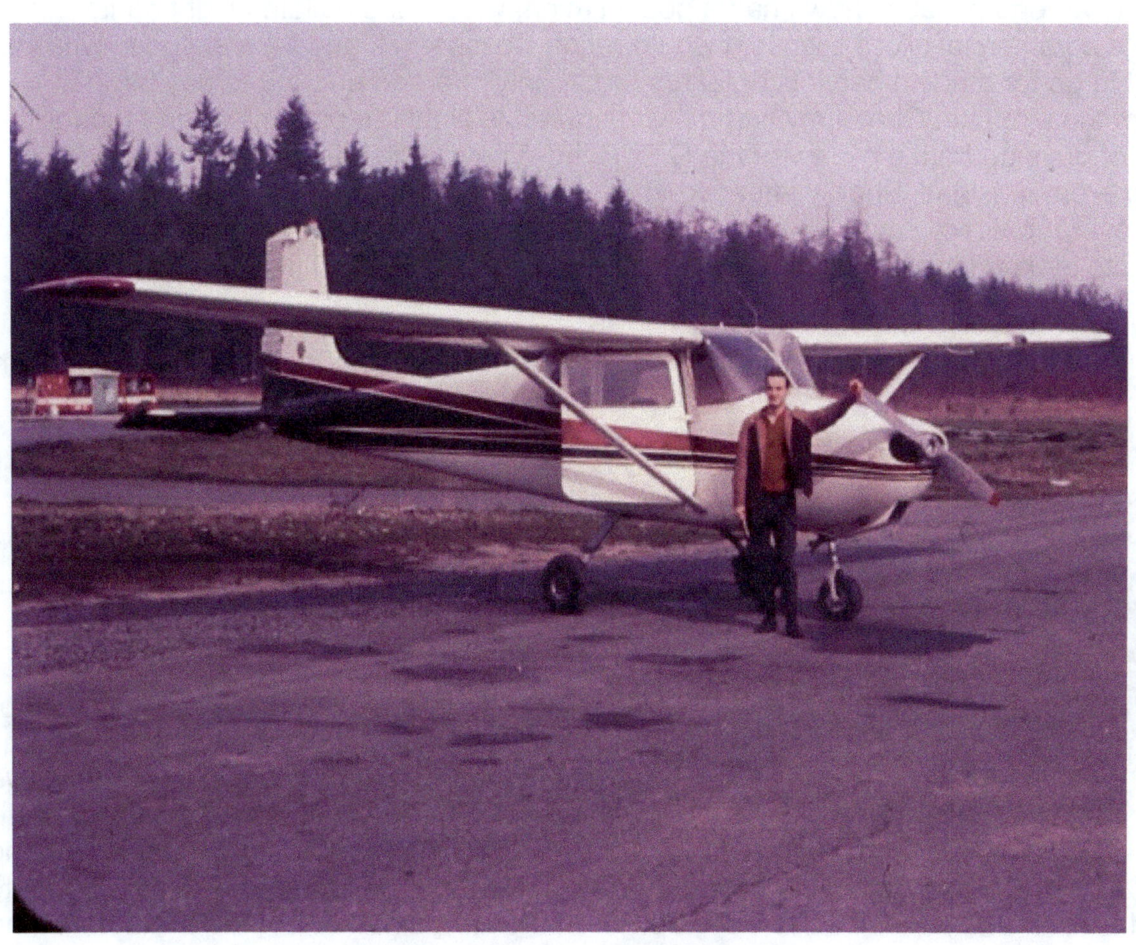

Cessna 150 - 1st trainer

I was elated and started flight training within the month. I was in my element and soloed after just 8 hours of dual instruction. That first solo would be the most exciting event of my career. That included all the type checkouts and endorsements in subsequent years, no matter how exhilarating. By today's standards, the hourly rates were incredibly low. Dual instruction was $12/hr, and the solo was $9/hr. However, I was only making $300/month as a steward on the B.C. ferries. Consequently, it was a big expense for me to accumulate the required 35 hours of flight time for my license. So, basically, the instructor got about $3 per flight hour and $9.00 to the company. I assume they also received some kind of base salary. However, instructors weren't that preoccupied with their salaries. It was primarily a stepping stone to build flight time toward an airline job. As soon as they had sufficient hours and the right endorsements, they were gone.

Building flight hours-

About that time, I left the BC Ferries for a new steward's job on the G.B.Reed, a fisheries research ship based out of Nanaimo. This was a means to an end because now I had a goal in mind, which was building flight hours toward a commercial pilot's license. I would rent a Cessna 172 and take anybody who wanted to go for a ride. I had lots of takers, and I only charged enough to pay for the rental of the airplane. One of my first more memorable flights happened when I took a couple of guys up from the crew of the G.B. Reed. They wanted to see a potential duck hunting area up Island. Shortly after taking off, I noticed a heavy layer of cumulus cloud ahead over me directly over Nanaimo. I started to climb to go over the top of the clouds, but due to inexperience, I miscalculated the height of the layer and flew right into it.

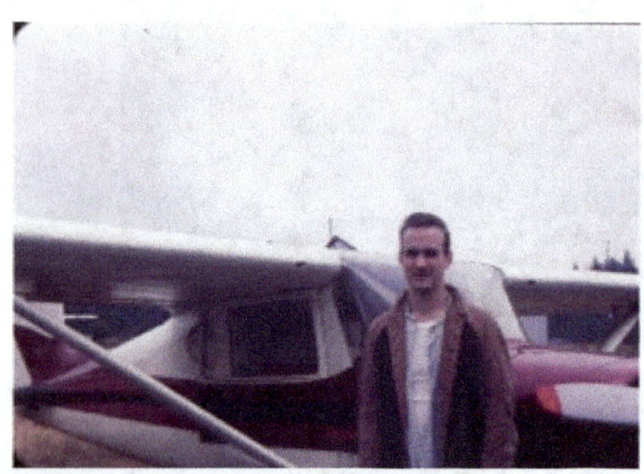

Private licence

I was suddenly having to go entirely on instruments with very minimal training in flying solely by instruments. After getting my private license, I had 2 hours on a fixed trainer called a Frasca simulator. You were introduced to the absolute basics of instrument flight. So there I was, and the first thing I realized when I figured out the instruments was that I was in a steep turn and descending.

Quickly to basics, I levelled the wings and stopped the descent. I mentally calculated the variation and a heading that would take me toward Vancouver and away from the mountains. I put the aircraft into a gentle descent and suddenly broke out to find myself directly over the only high-rise in downtown Nanaimo. I was at only about 800 feet, so I started a climb and turned back on course. This time I remained below the cloud bank and carried on towards Campbell River. When we returned to Nanaimo a couple of hours later and landed, I asked the duck hunters how they enjoyed the ride. They said, "That was great except for the part when we were in the cloud and couldn't see." With a straight face, I said, "Oh yeah, completely normal, we do that all the time."

My first flight carrying a passenger happened to be Connie Gibbs, now my wife of 54 years. She had her little dog 'Smarty' in her arms on take off. I had given her this cute little Cocker Spaniel /Maltese cross because they had an acreage, and I couldn't keep her at my uncle and aunt's where I was staying. She was securely holding the dog, but as I applied power and just before lifting off, the dog panicked and jumped into my lap, obstructing the controls. I quickly one-armed the dog back onto Connie's lap and carried on with the take off. Needless to say, a lesson learned early on about securing pets in an aircraft!

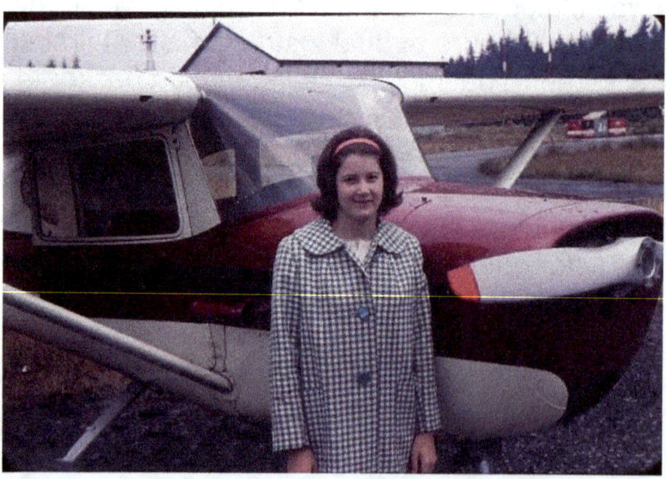

Connie Gibbs - 1st passenger

Another memorable flight early on, as I was gaining experience, was a flight over to Tofino on the west coast of Vancouver Island. It was 3 days before my wedding, and my brother Bob and sister-in-law Janice flew out to attend our wedding. It was a beautiful clear day as I took off from Nanaimo with Bob, Jan and my fiancé Connie on board. The clear day facilitated me filing a flight plan direct to Tofino at 10,000 feet. I had just levelled off at 10,000 feet, and the air was smooth with no turbulence. It was like being motionless and suspended in space. We had an extraordinary view of the mountains below us, the Georgia Straits behind us, and the Pacific Ocean in the distance.

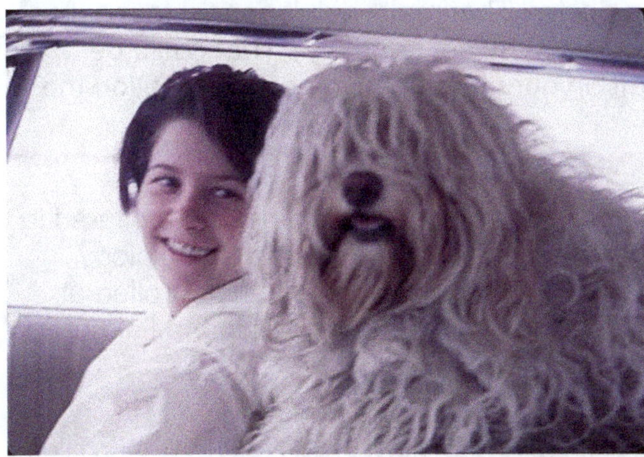

Connie & "Smarty" Nanaimo to Niagara Falls

Suddenly without any warning, the engine quit! I immediately put the plane into a gliding attitude and put out a 'Mayday' call. Because of my altitude, I had excellent line-of-sight communications with Air Traffic Control. Vancouver, Nanaimo and Comox ATC responded immediately. They acknowledged my position and intentions. The only place for a forced landing would be a logging road I had picked out, but it would have a questionable chance of a successful landing. Fortunately, Comox ATC asked if I had tried the carburetor heat. I quickly turned it on, and the engine caught immediately. Up until then, checking carb heat after taking off and occasionally en route had been purely academic. The ground school instructors knew what they were talking about!

Even though it was completely clear, the relative humidity was ideal for carburetor icing choking the engine. That day had one more dramatic twist. We were all out on Long Beach, throwing the ball around. I was batting flies out when suddenly Smarty jumped up to get the ball just as I was in full swing. I caught her right in the back of her head with a sickening sound. She was knocked out cold! My brother, the doctor, checked her vitals but said without an X-ray, it was hard to tell. So we did a quick flight back to Nanaimo and took the dog straight to a veterinarian. It was a huge relief when Smarty regained consciousness and recovered completely. That dog ended up going on our honeymoon and lived with us for many more years.

After the examination

At about that time, I was due for my annual pilot's medical. After the examination, I asked the doctor if there would be any problem with my slight nearsightedness going forward. He said, "You probably won't have a problem passing a private medical, but I doubt you could hold a commercial medical for very long because of your eyes." I was devastated! My dream to fly commercially was suddenly crushed!

So just as I was about to be married, there was an even greater pressure to figure out a career. My parents tried to be helpful with various suggestions. My mother thought I might want to follow in my brother Bob's footsteps and become a doctor. That really didn't appeal to me, but I felt I should do something professionally. So, I thought, "Why not dentistry? That could be interesting, plus good hours and money!" So we left on our short honeymoon, destination the University of Saskatchewan in Saskatoon.

I had to initially go to summer school to take the 4 years of biology that had not been offered in high school. This was a requirement for pre-dentistry. I received high marks for the biology course that summer and found it somewhat interesting. I was then accepted and enrolled at the University that Fall. I actually hated all the classes since my heart was still in the field of aviation, which I thought was no longer available.

I was due for my annual private pilot's medical. The designated Ministry of Transport doctor was a specialist as well. He did a thorough medical including an eye exam. I wasn't really aware that I had talked that much about flying until the doctor made a surprising comment. He said, "Obviously, you'd really like to be flying, so why aren't you doing that?" I explained what the Nanaimo doctor had said. He then went on to say, "Yes, your right eye is a bit nearsighted, but it's fully correctable to 20/20. I get airline pilots in here with worse profiles than that. If you're ever grounded some day, it won't be because of your eyes." I was ecstatic and went straight over to the university to talk to the Dean. I said to him with a bit of a grin, "Excuse me, I was wondering if I could make a few course changes?" He said, "Oh, for sure, that's a common request early on in the year for new students." "Ok, I'd like to drop math and physics." He said, "Well you kind of need physics, but ok." "I'd also like to drop chemistry." "Wait, you really need that for pre-dent!" I went on to say, "Yep, I'd also like to drop, etc." At that point, he laid his pencil down and said, "Ok, what's going on here?" I started smiling and told him I was quitting university and was enrolled in ground school. I'd be starting my commercial aviation training the following week. He smiled and wished me luck!

I enrolled in the commercial fixed-wing course

Initially, my parents were disappointed that I had dropped out of university but realized how relieved and excited I was to be pursuing a career in aviation. I enrolled in the commercial fixed-wing course at Mitchinson's Flying Services at the Saskatoon city airport. October 3rd, 1968, was my first dual flight with the chief pilot, B Flath. I really didn't need an airplane; I was flying high all by myself, realizing I had potentially an exciting career ahead of me! I enjoyed the excellent instruction and every minute of ground school. I think when you are enthusiastic about something, everything makes sense, and even technical aspects are much more comprehensible.

As the training progressed, including building up the required hours, things took an unexpected twist. I was so sure I was headed in the right direction, but I was gradually getting bored with every flight. It just seemed that after taking off and everything trimmed up, there should be more to flying than this. I had never been near a helicopter, but the more I thought about it, the more I liked the idea.

I'll never forget taxiing on that day and parking the airplane. I went into the hangar and approached the chief pilot. "Hey Bill, what do you think the chances are of getting a job as a helicopter pilot?" He said, "Oh, excellent!" I said, "Oh really?!" He said, "Oh yeah, they're killin' them off every other day!" Obviously, he was joking to some extent, but that didn't deter me a bit! I finished off my commercial fixed-wing license in a little less than 6 months on March 13th, 1969. Less than 2 weeks later, Connie and I (and Smarty) were on our way to Niagara Falls. I was enrolled in a commercial course for helicopter training!

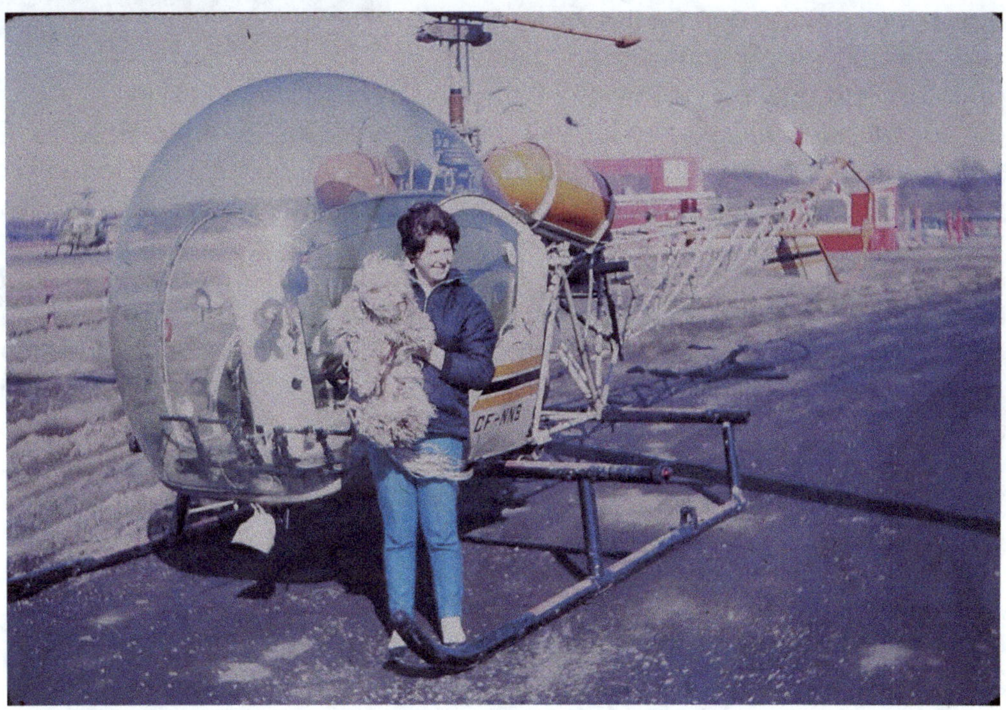

Wife Connie - 1st Helicopter

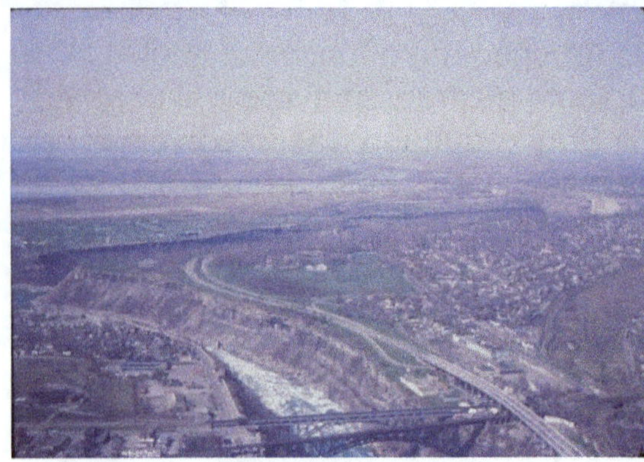
Niagara Falls

In those days, helicopters were still pretty much in a pioneering phase.

Military use had been developed and found to have useful applications in the Korean conflict. This was largely experimental but with some very positive results. There seemed to be some very promising applications that could really be of value in the commercial field as well. Things like aerial photography, pipeline & power line patrol, cattle round ups, traffic patrol, etc., etc., in those early days. Obviously, the slow speeds, maneuverability, and no runway requirements would prove to have tremendous applications in many areas in the future.

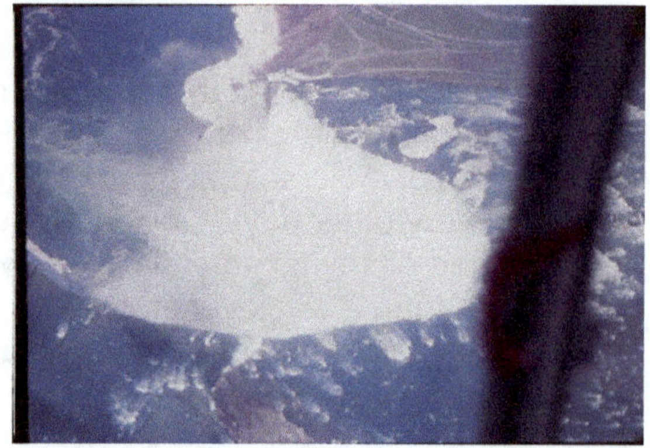
Niagara Falls

My parents weren't too thrilled about my aspirations to be a helicopter pilot. My mom said, "They're probably fun to fly, but can you really make a living at that?" However, they backed me and co-signed the flying loan. Mom even signed over her homestead rights as a guarantee. The flight training was $3800 plus the money we needed for the cost of living for 2 months. So the total loan was for $10,000, which was like a hundred thousand in today's dollars. Flight training alone would be well over $100,000 for the same training today. I realized what a commitment this was on their part and the faith they had in me. So we rented a small U-haul trailer, loaded our few possessions which were largely wedding presents, and struck off for Ontario. My excitement was palpable, and just trying to imagine what it would be like to learn how to fly a helicopter.

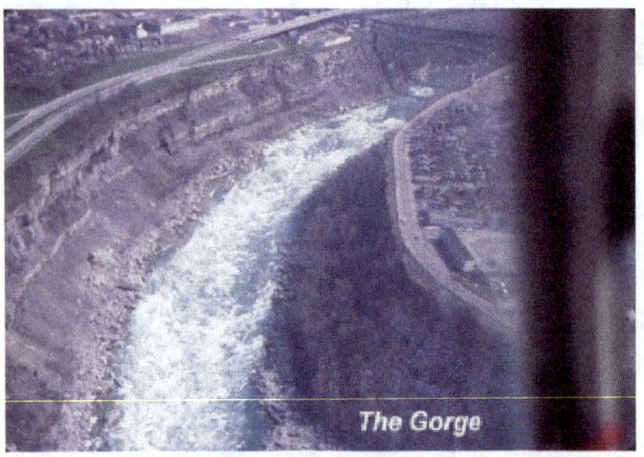
The Gorge

We had a somewhat unnerving incident en route as we were passing through Detroit City. Somewhere coming into Detroit, I took a wrong turn, and we ended up in a very poorly lit and questionable part of the city. It was just after midnight, and I stopped to check the seemingly loose trailer hitch.

As I was tightening the hitch assembly, a car full of African Americans drove by. They then turned around and came back very slowly, yelling obscenities. We took off and lost them, but we were now more lost than ever. I finally found an all-night gas station. I got out of the car, and the black attendant looked at us like we had come from another planet! He gave us great directions, which took us to the Detroit/Windsor bridge and a large feeling of relief.

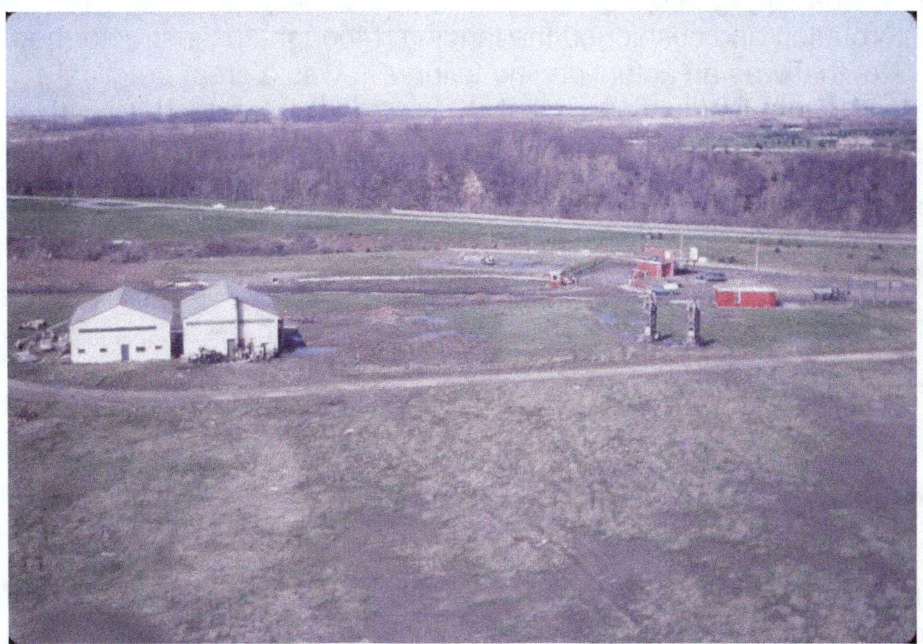

The next day we reached Niagara Falls and checked in with Niagara Helicopters at their hangar near the Falls. In the field beside their hangar, we saw a helicopter doing what looked like extreme maneuvers all over the area. So I met the chief instructor and asked him if I'd be able to fly like that when I got my license. He said, "Hell no, the student is trying to hover in one spot!"

Niagara Helicopters training

I'll never forget that first training flight. I was in a 4- foot hover in front of the hangar. We were absolutely stationary like a hummingbird and could go backwards, sideways or forward. This was real flying and any previous feelings of boredom completely vanished!

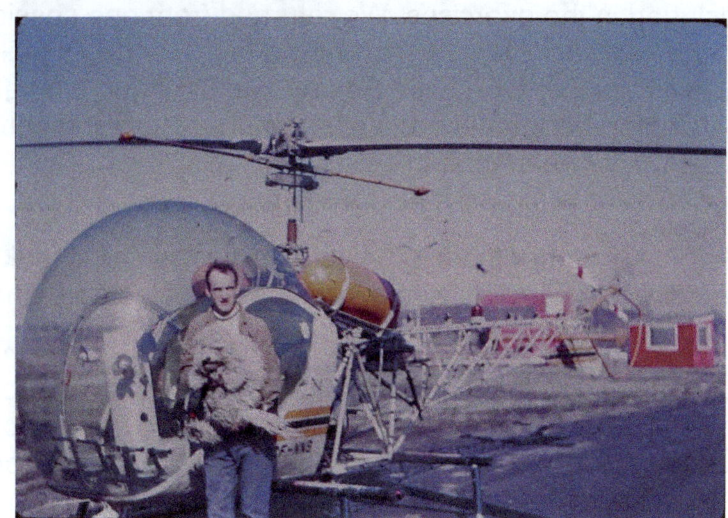

First day of training

The training was exciting and fulfilling.

We had an interesting incident one day. The instructor demonstrated some hovering autorotations and then had me try a few. A hovering autorotation simulates an engine failure. The throttle is cut, and as the aircraft settles to the ground, you fully increase the pitch on the main rotor. This is controlled by a lever on the left side of the pilot called a 'collective.' So I was successfully completing these exercises when suddenly there was a large loss of power. There was a magneto malfunction which was basically an engine failure. I just did the normal autorotation and cushioned the landing. I thought the instructor had done something, but he said, "No, that was an actual engine failure!" It was a great practical exercise to have an engine failure in real-time.

Since I already had a commercial fixed- wing licence, I was only required to have a 50-hour rotary endorsement. The cost of training was $3800. If I was willing to pay $6000, I had a guaranteed job flying tourists over the Falls. I wanted some real 'bush' experience, so I turned down that option.

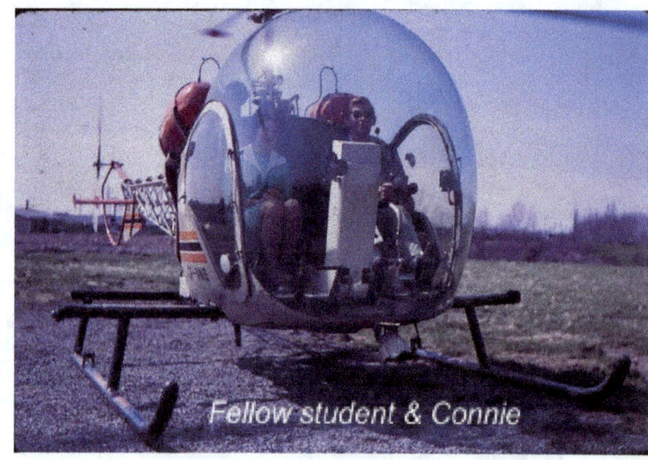
Fellow student & Connie

The training was comprehensive and fascinating. Reconnaissance of confined areas, autorotations, simulated engine failures, restricted control problems, rotor,fire, transmission, etc., and other emergencies were included in the exercises. We returned from one session, and one of the instructors told me I had a very lucky dog. Apparently, a tail rotor has a high frequency that really attracts dogs, sort of like a dog whistle. Little Smarty had been jumping at the tail rotor of another running helicopter. Fortunately, she was small enough and couldn't quite reach it. One touch and she would have been destroyed!

So 6 weeks after the beginning of initial training, I took the Transport Canada flight test. Needless to say, this was a tremendous milestone, and I was on my way!

During my training, I mailed out applications to helicopter companies across Canada. Now that I had a commercial license, I could follow up on my applications in person. The first stop was a company in Arnprior, Ontario. They were very polite, but no, they didn't need a 50-hour pilot. So we headed off to Montreal for my next stop. That night we slept in the car because our finances were getting very low.

The next morning we were trying to find our way to the south side of Dorval airport, where Canadian Helicopters was located at the Atlantic Aviation hangar. Near the airport, we were trying to navigate the Decarie traffic circle. Taking a wrong turn, we ended up on the industrial side of the airport. I remember saying, "Let's forget it; they probably won't hire an English-speaking pilot anyhow. Let's just follow up on the other applications farther west and closer to home." Connie said, "Let's just try one more time." We finally found it, and I went into the building and introduced myself to the president of Canadian Helicopters. The interview barely started when surprisingly, he wanted to know if my wife was outside. I told him she was out in the car, and he said he'd like to meet her. I went out and asked her if she would come in, and of course,she was a bit reluctant. She had slept in the car overnight and quickly pulled a brush through her hair. Of course, Smarty followed us back in. They both went into L Ayer's office, and he closed the door. They were in there for a long time, and meanwhile, his secretary and I talked about the weather or something. They finally came out, and Ayers shook my hand and said, "Welcome to Canadian Helicopters!" A year later, I asked him what that was all about. He said he always got the best feel for a new pilot by meeting the wife or girlfriend first. To this day, my wife says she landed me my first flying job!

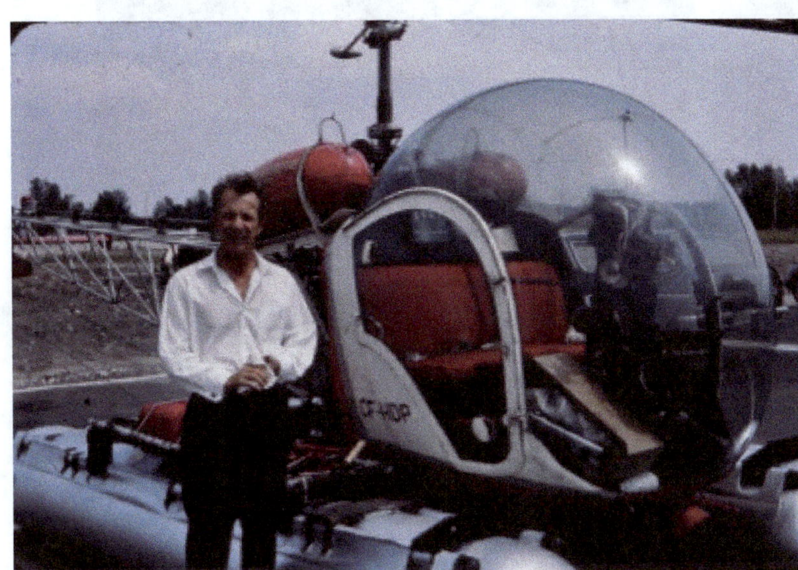

L Ayers - President Canadian Helicopters

Needless to say, I was pretty excited and further to that when my new boss put us up in the Airport Hilton for the night. He was giving me a couple of weeks before I would start. At that point, he wanted me to take the mountain course with the parent company, Okanagan Helicopters, at their Penticton base. Of course, they were paying for this 25- hour course on techniques of mountain flying.

Even though the Laurentian Mountains in the east were not as high or complicated as the Rockies, he wanted all his pilots to have this training. The basics of that course proved to be invaluable in later years.

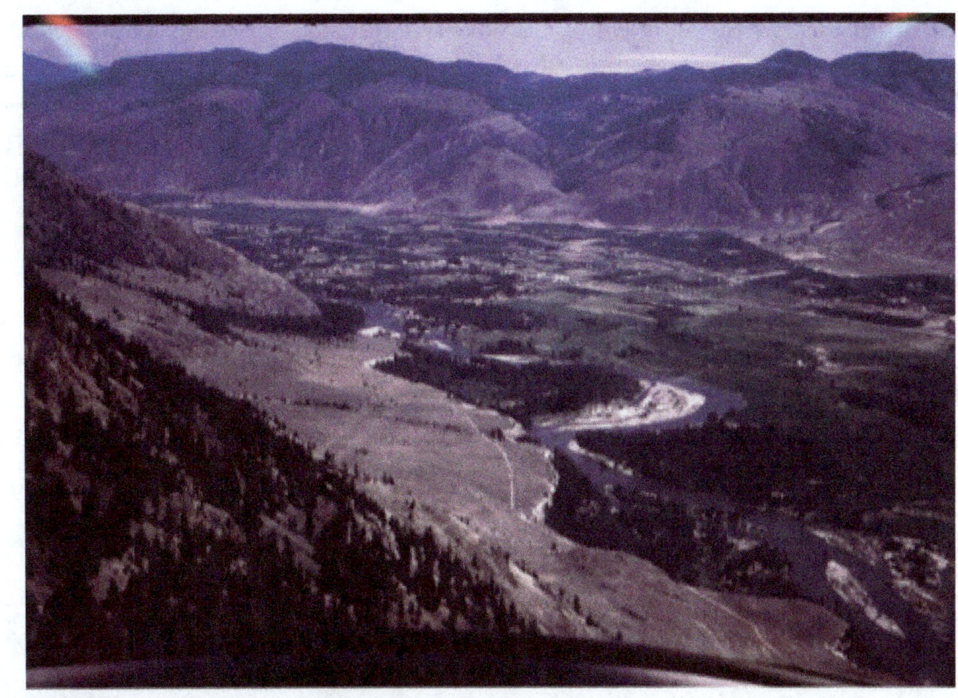
Keremeos BC

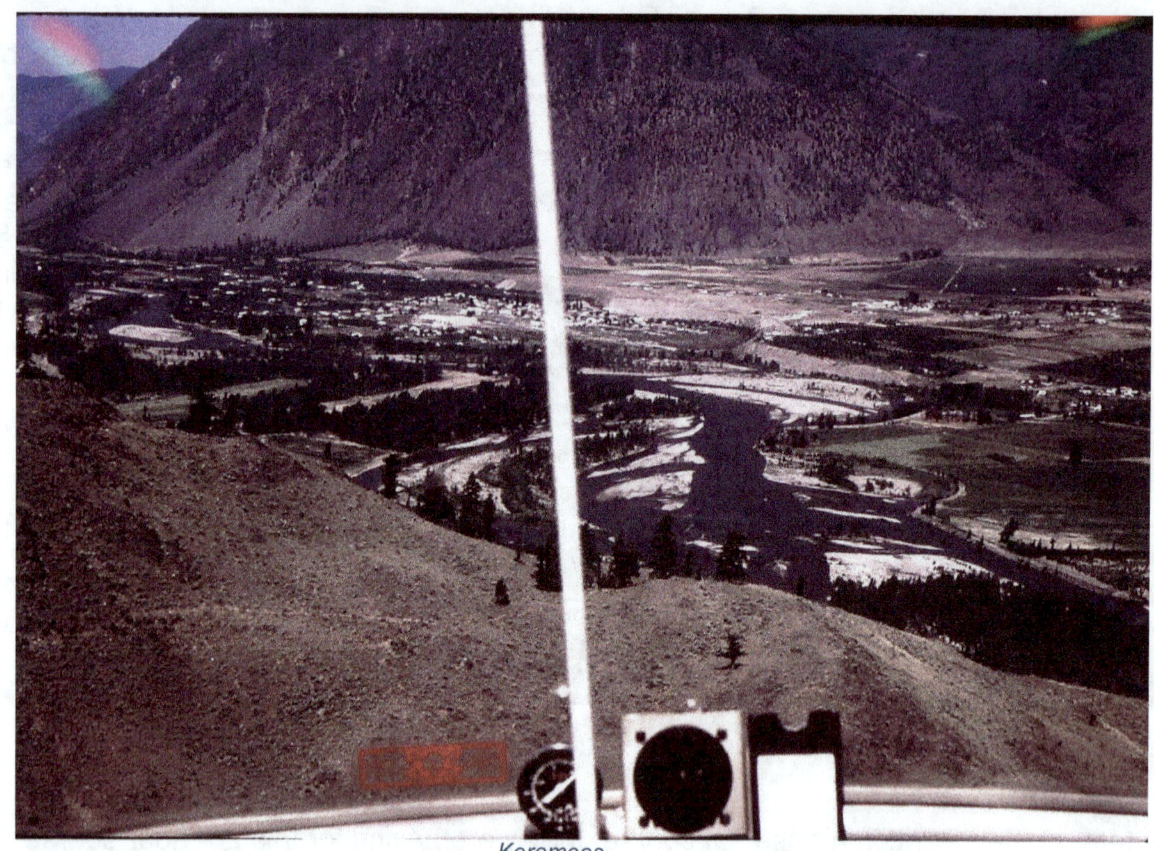

Keremeos

So I thought that was fairly easy, so why not get a job further west. It turned out there were no other job offers largely because of my inexperience and low flying time. So I was very thankful for the only job I was offered as I checked into Penticton. It was exciting to have an opportunity to go on an Okanagan Helicopters mountain course in Penticton. Civilian and military pilots from all over the world were lined up to take this acclaimed mountain course. The techniques for flying in the mountains were taught by very experienced Okanagan pilots. You learned how to determine the wind direction in converging valleys, as it is critical to land and take off into the wind. Assessing suitable landing spots in everchanging terrain or whether or not a landing area is level enough to land on can be a complete optical illusion. Available power as it decreases with altitude and operates in very turbulent conditions on the lee side of mountains.

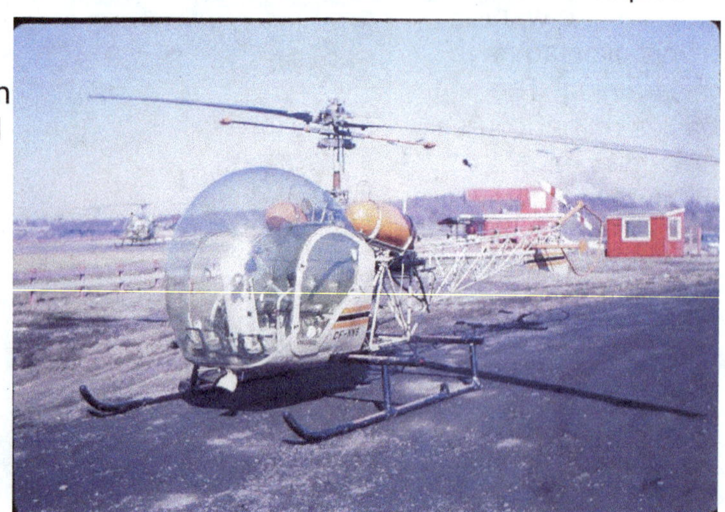

Bell 47 - Training Helicopter

The chief instructor,

B Tillotson, was an old seasoned pilot and very experienced in mountain flying.

Pilots, including military from around the world, had gone through this very sought-after course. I had done my initial ride, training at Niagara on a Bell 47. This was an aircraft with a 'bubble' profile front end and was first introduced in the Korean conflict. It was also used in the TV series, 'Mash.' At Penticton, I was checked out on a Hiller 12E, which was still a piston machine but well adapted to mountain training.

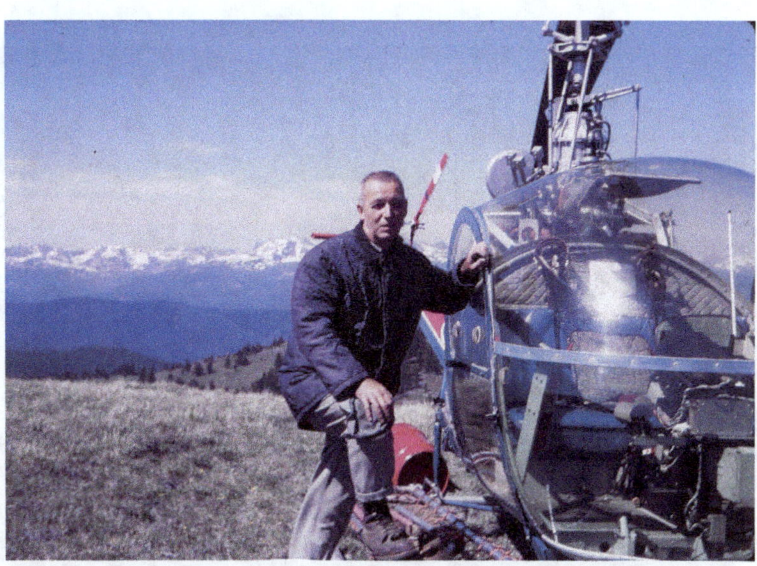

B Tillotson Chief Flying Instructor

Some of the training involved high-altitude reconnaissance and landings. One of the problems with an unboosted, normally aspirated engine is that it loses power with altitude in rarefied air. This has to be compensated for with different techniques than operating at sea level. There are some very high peaks just west of Keremeos. One of the most important things for landing is to determine wind direction and to always land in to the wind. This increases performance and stability, enabling the ability to carry larger loads on taking off and landing. Obviously, there are no wind socks in the mountains or any other places other than airports. You learn how to determine wind direction from smoke, the silver underside of leaves indicating a downwind condition, waves and ripples on a body of water, etc.Above the tree line in the mountains, drifting snow direction, lee side turbulence, and a twitching aircraft tail indicate a downwind condition on the final approach. There are even useful indications from a bald eagle. If they are circling in close proximity to the side of a mountain, this generally indicates the upwind side and smoother air. This greatly helps in the climb of a helicopter to climb faster with a heavy load, e.g. a bucket of concrete or water.

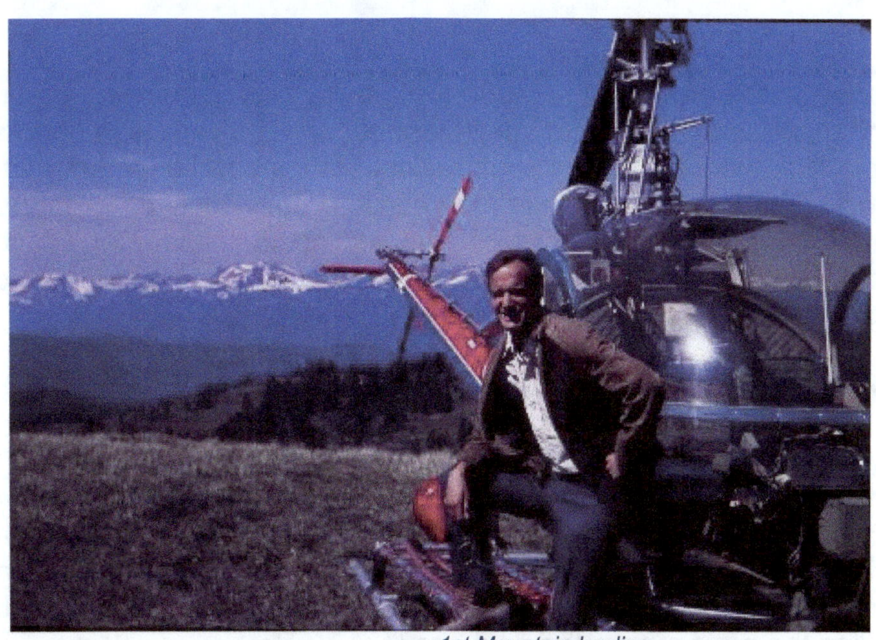

1st Mountain landing

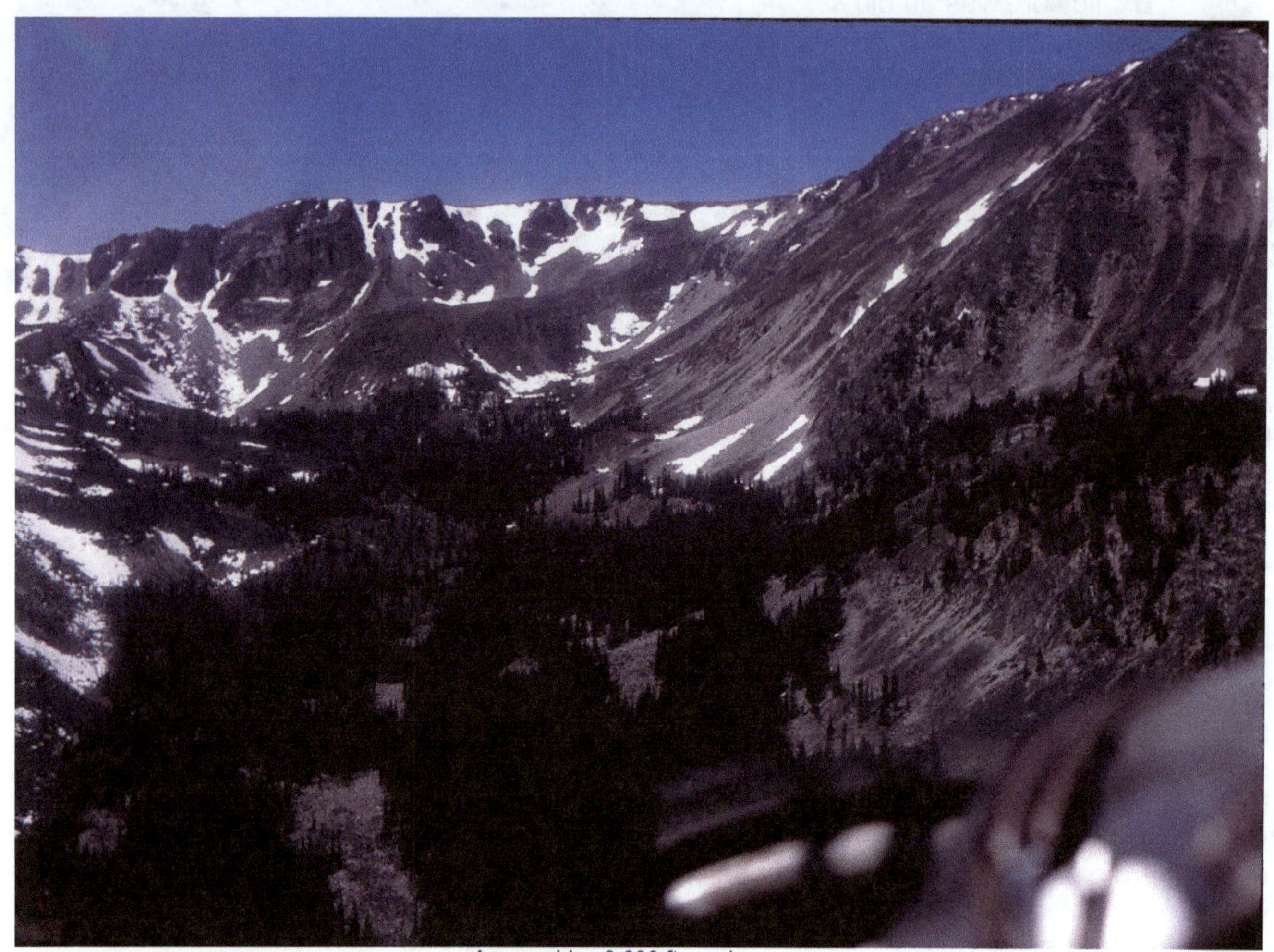

Approaching 9,000 ft. peaks

So we chose one of those 9,000-foot peaks near Keremeos, determining wind direction and assessing the landing spot. I landed, and the view was panoramic. I thought we would immediately take off, but the instructor leaned over, grinned and said, "Coffee time!" This was a great place for a coffee break! I'll never forget Bud on his haunches with a thermos of coffee leaning back against the helicopter. I flashed back to when my dad used to stop for a coffee break on the field, leaning back in exactly the same way against the tractor wheel. They even looked similar!

One day we were doing circuits and various maneuvers at the Penticton airport. He related a humorous story about a training student. Apparently, even before starting flying lessons, he had been obsessed with learning how to hover. Bud's training procedure for that was to ease into it since this is one of the most difficult things to learn. A helicopter is the most unstable in a hover since it can go in any direction. His procedure was to do regular circuits with a 'touch and go' at the end. At the end of each circuit, he would have the student slow up a little more each time before rolling the nose over to the next circuit.

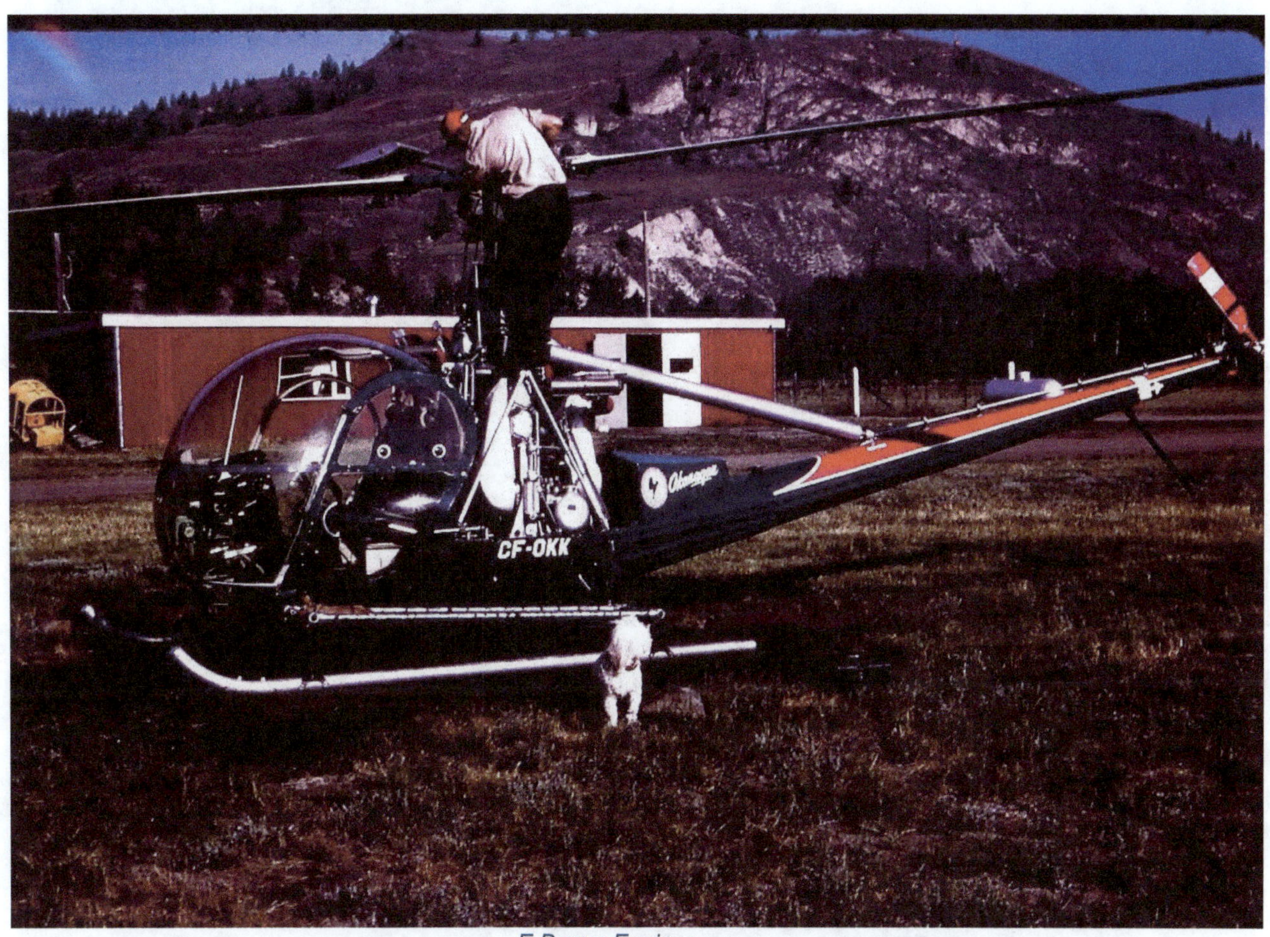

E Brown Engineer

Finally, he did a circuit and came to a complete stop. It suddenly dawned on him, and he just about blew Bud's eardrums out in his headset when he hollered, "I'M HOVERING!"

Another large challenge concerning landing in the mountains when you're learning is the many optical illusions. Because the surrounding terrain is at many different angles, it's difficult to know whether your landing area is level or not. A helicopter has some latitude for landing on the sloping ground but only to a point. Beyond just a few degrees, the 'cyclic' (the stick in the middle held by the right hand) runs out of travel, and the helicopter can roll over. So with experience and a 'figure 8' reconnaissance, you can determine whether the proposed landing spot is suitable or not. So one day, the instructor took me to obviously one of his favourite 'optical illusion' training hills. This was a little mountain near Okanagan Falls in the Okanagan Valley south of Penticton. It was extremely difficult to find a level spot suitable for landing. I finally did, and it turned out to be one of the most valuable training sessions I would ever have. (An interesting note here was that I came back 50 years later, and I climbed that same little mountain on foot. Friends lived nearby, and my wife and I climbed it with them. What a flood of memories!)

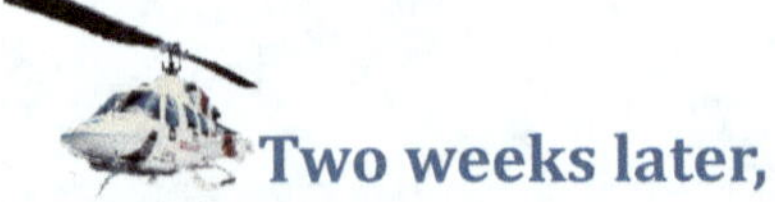

Two weeks later,

and after 25 hours of mountain flying, we were on our way back to Montreal. I would be starting my first job as a commercial helicopter pilot and was 'pumped'! I was very fortunate to have a job the day after my flight test in Niagara Falls. Some of the guys I trained with didn't get jobs for 2 years, and some of them did not at all.

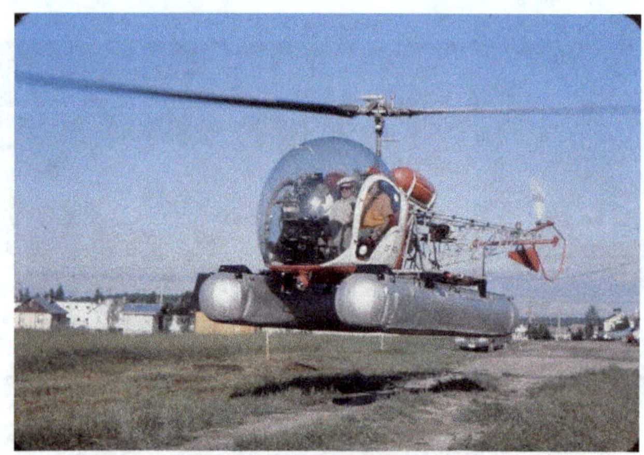

Starting Lands & Forest contract

Back then, rotary jobs were just as scarce as they are now for inexperienced new pilots. One of the things my boss asked in my initial interview was if things were a bit quiet, would I be willing to wash aircraft or even his own car. Of course, I would do anything to start building hours in my logbook. I think it was just an attitude check because he never asked me to wash his car. I ended up rarely getting out of the aircraft and ended up flying over 200 hundred hours in the last half of 1969. This was also the year of the first lunar landing.

I rushed out to buy a little black and white tv to watch it live. *What a year!*

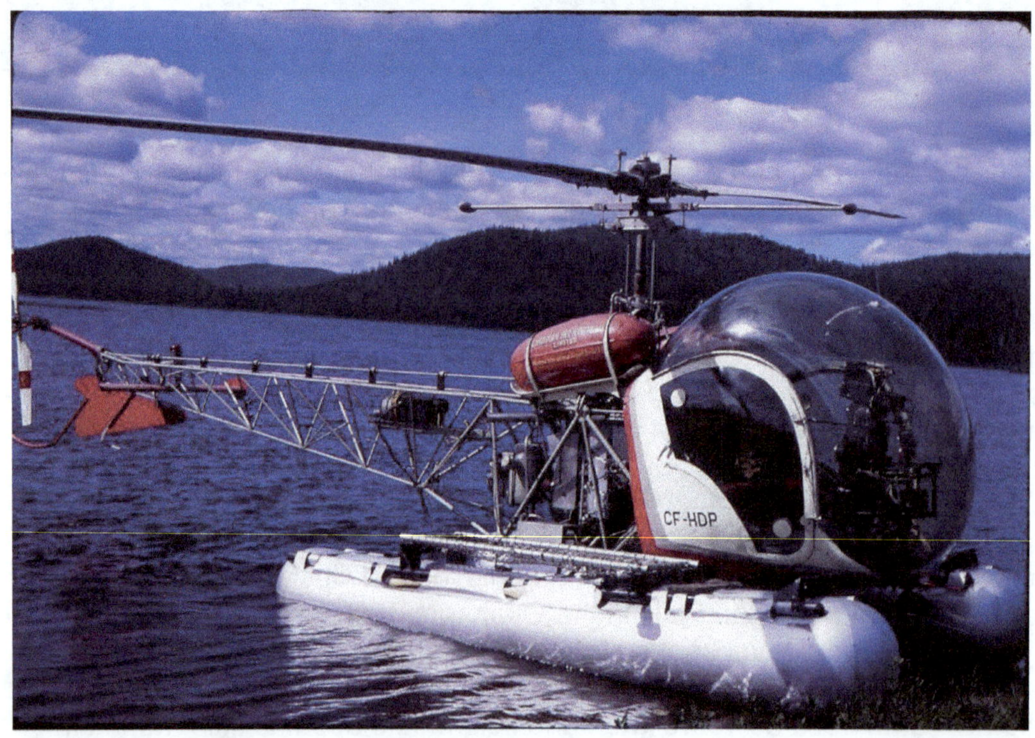

Lake near Maniwaki PQ

One of the first big contracts

I was assigned to was flying a budworm survey between Ottawa and Maniwaki. I had two surveyors on board from Lands & Forests. We flew lines from Ottawa to Maniwaki 135 km north. The damage done by the budworm manifestation was devastation to the pine forests.

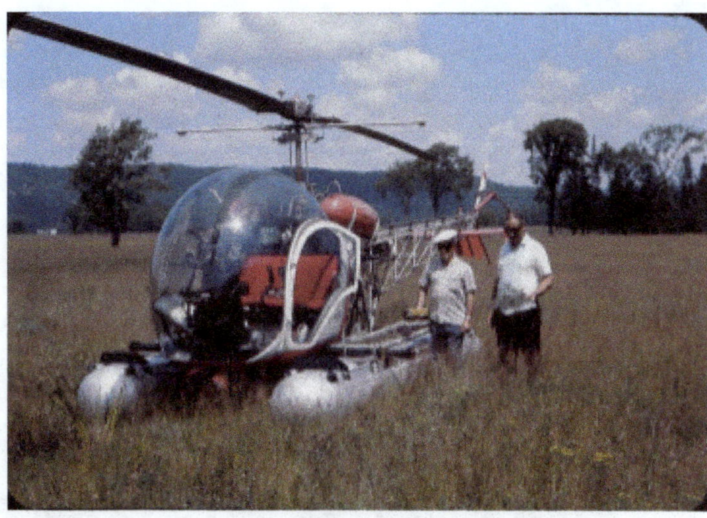

Checking Equipment

These lines were drawn on a map running parallel to each other, about 100 miles long and 2 miles apart. These imaginary lines started in the area of Maniwaki, Quebec and ran down to Ottawa, Ontario. I flew these lines through Gatineau Park to assess the extent of the budworm damage to the forests. The areas of infestation were then mapped and would consequently be sprayed by airplanes with large tanks, effectively killing the parasites. The damage done by the budworm manifestation was devastation to the pine forests.

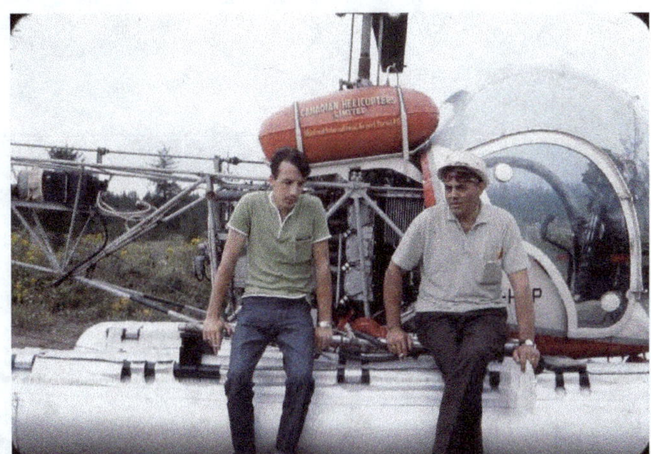

Lands & Forests

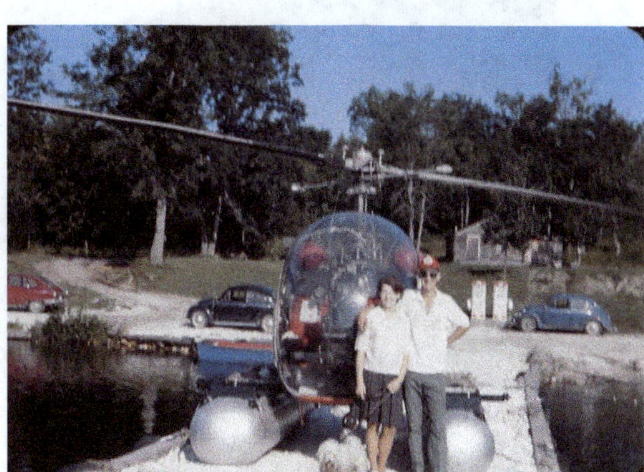

Wife Connie weekend getaway

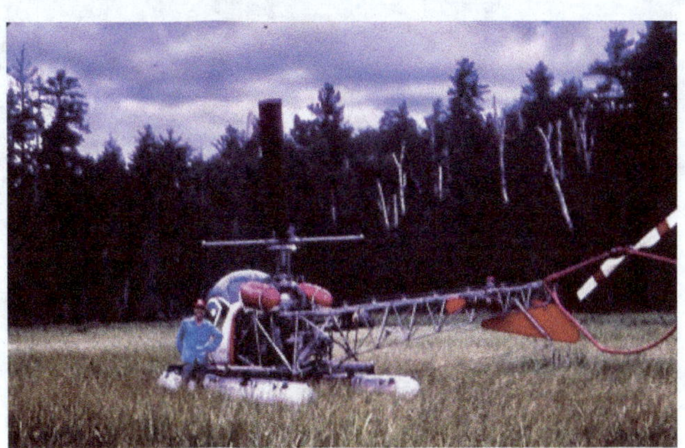

Jerry can fuel stop

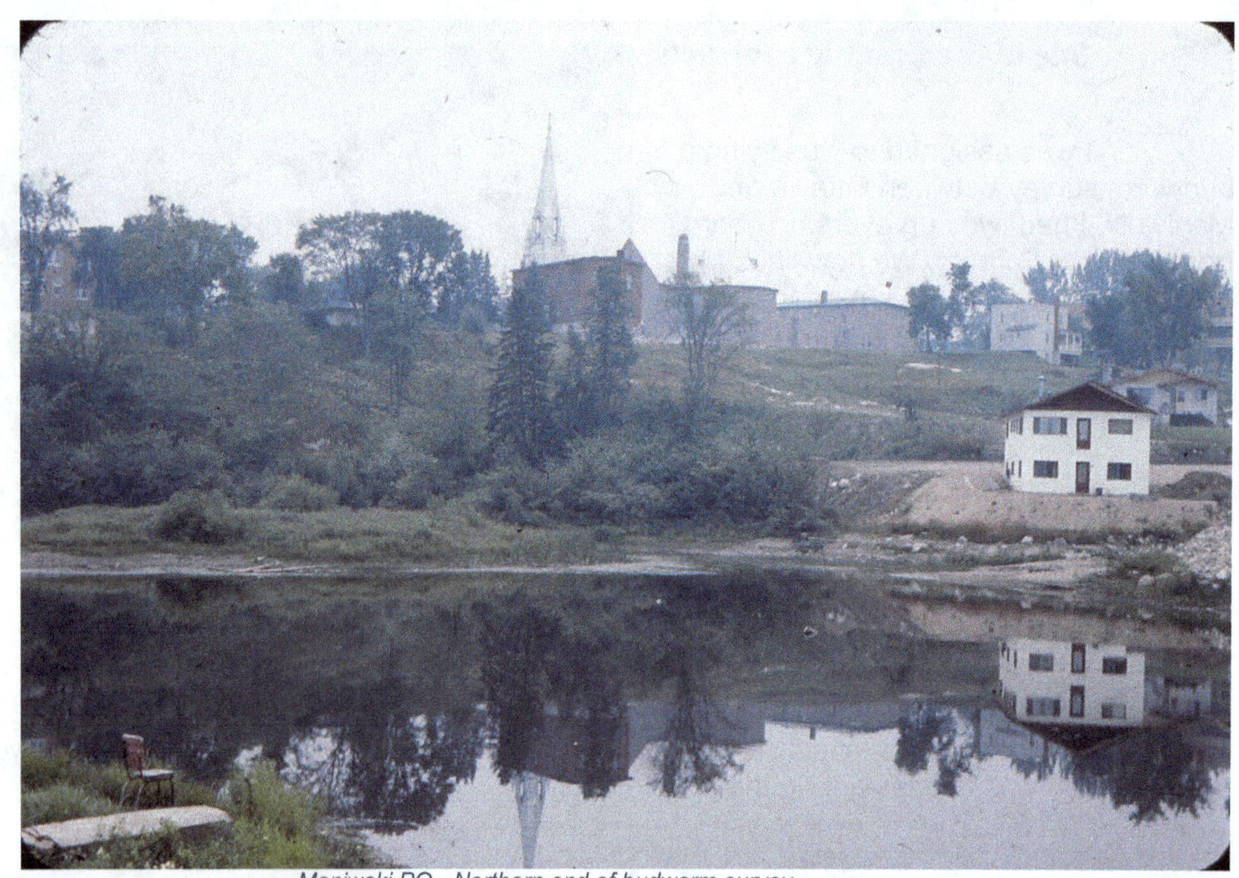

Maniwaki PQ - Northern end of budworm survey

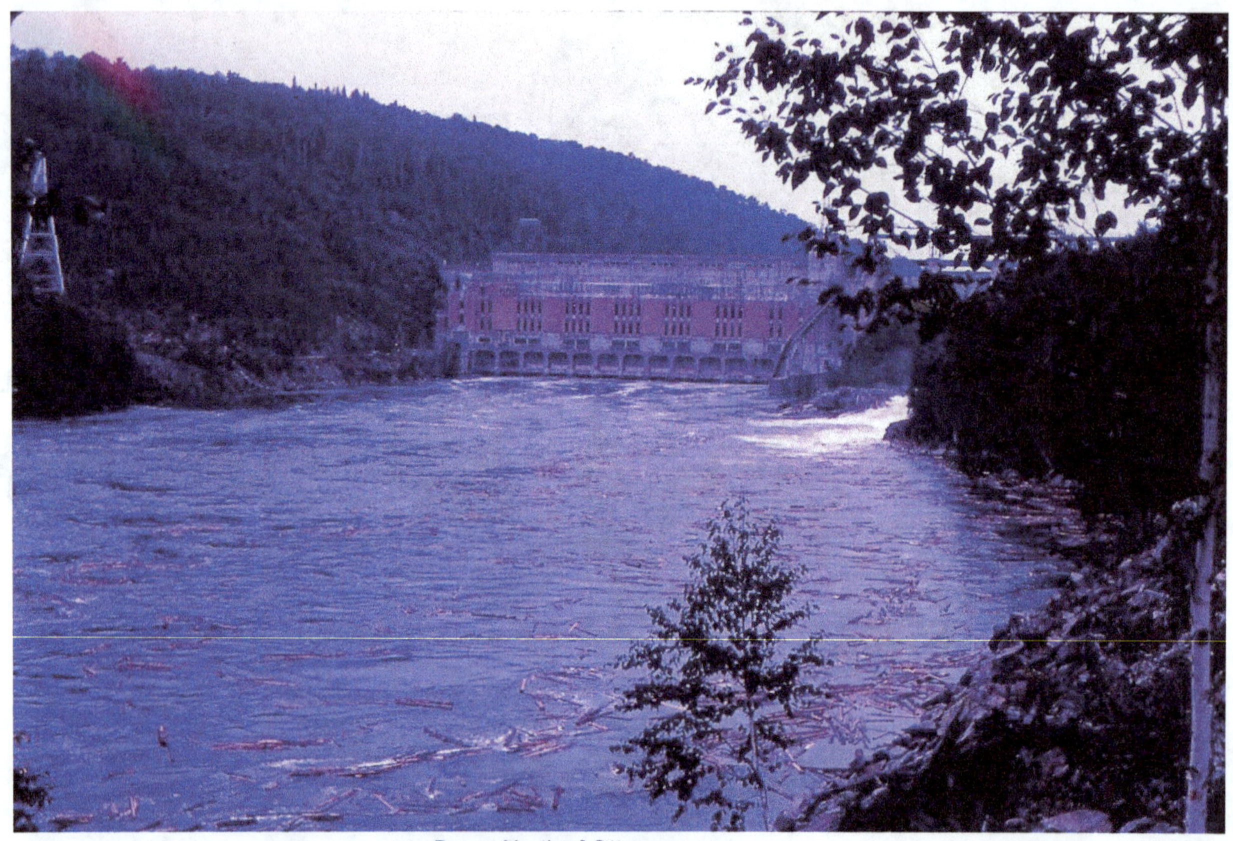

Dam - North of Ottawa

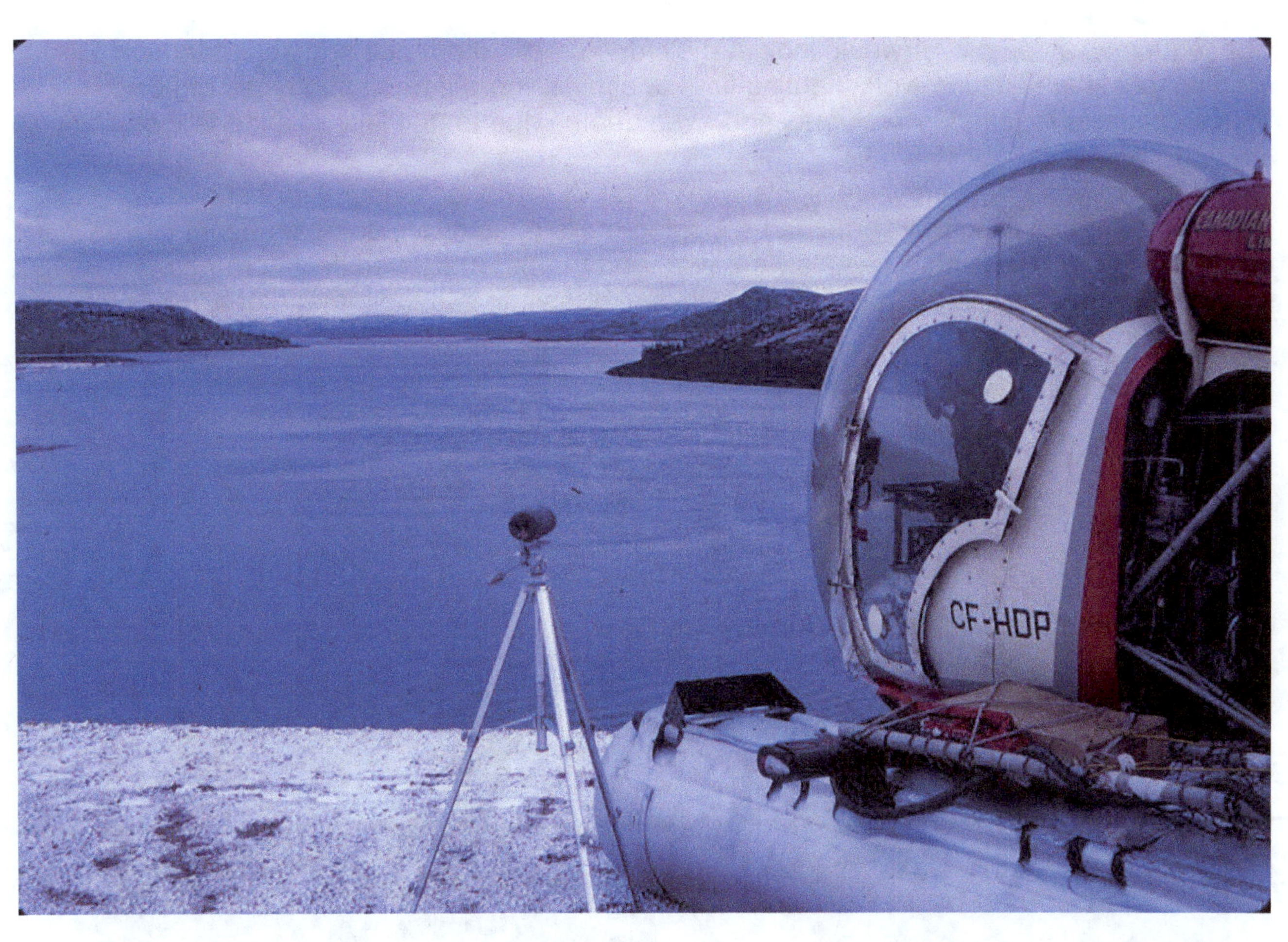

Land & Forest Survey

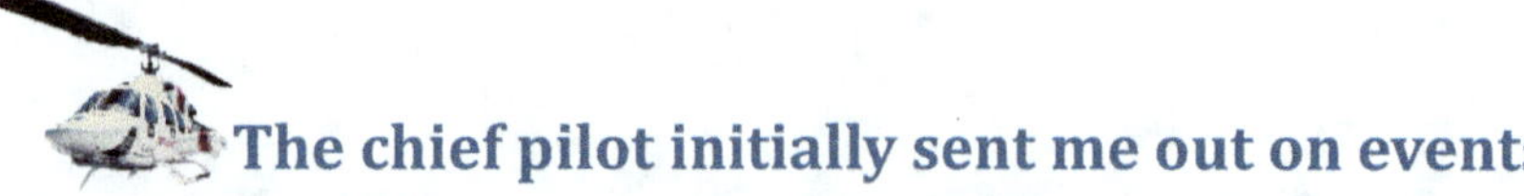

The chief pilot initially sent me out on events

like flying Santa Claus, traffic reporting around Montreal, photography flights, wild game counts, etc. The operations manager and the chief pilot assigned flights to their pilots according to their level of experience. I heard about some pilots around the country who would pad their logbooks to give them an edge in getting that first job.

Consequently, an employer would look at their 'doctored' experience and send them on slinging jobs, high altitude work, fighting fires or similar, more demanding types of flying. This sometimes resulted in accidents and even deaths due to that lack of experience.

Nearing Christmas would involve flights with Santa Claus to local and neighbouring cities. I would land in school yards and shopping malls quite often, doing an aerial candy drop before landing. The kids went wild, and the parents loved it! Unfortunately, some of the Santas were a bit inebriated, which, I guess, fit into their image of a 'jolly' demeanour!

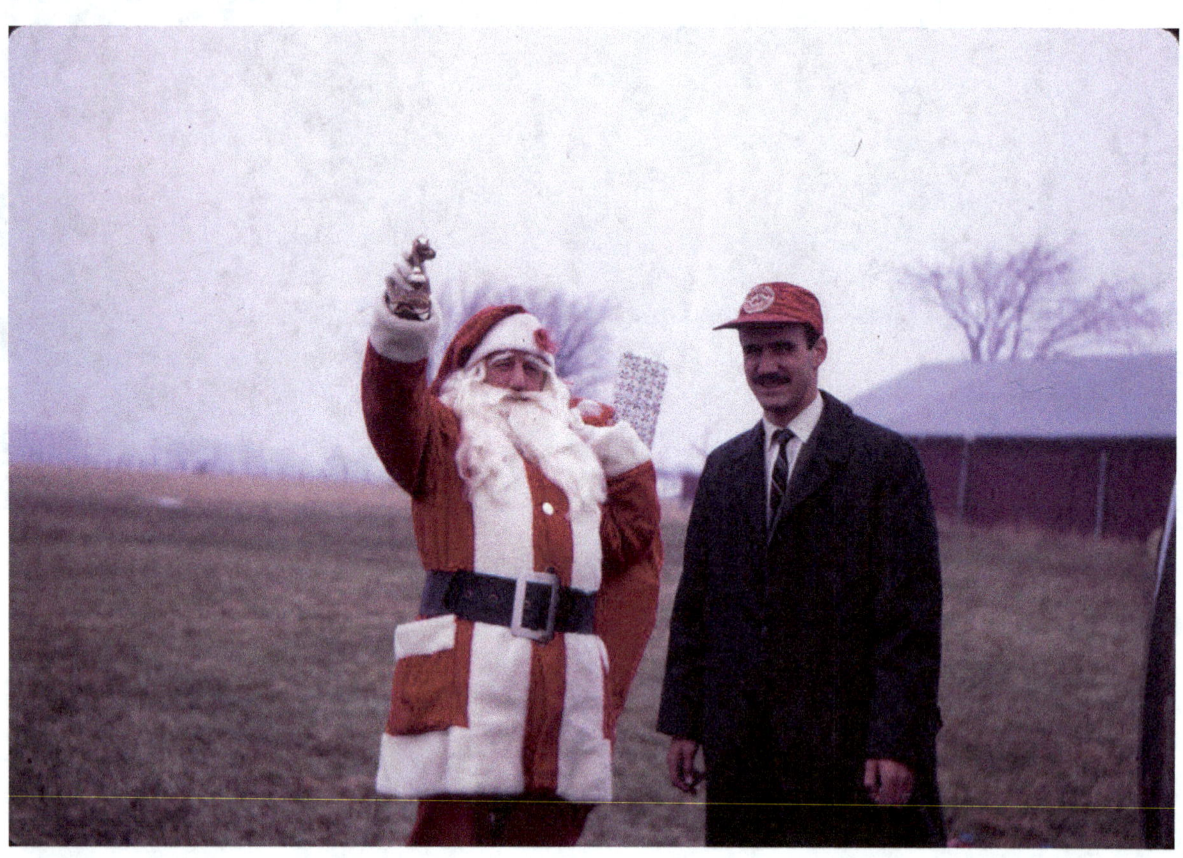

Flying Santa to Cornwall Ontario school ground

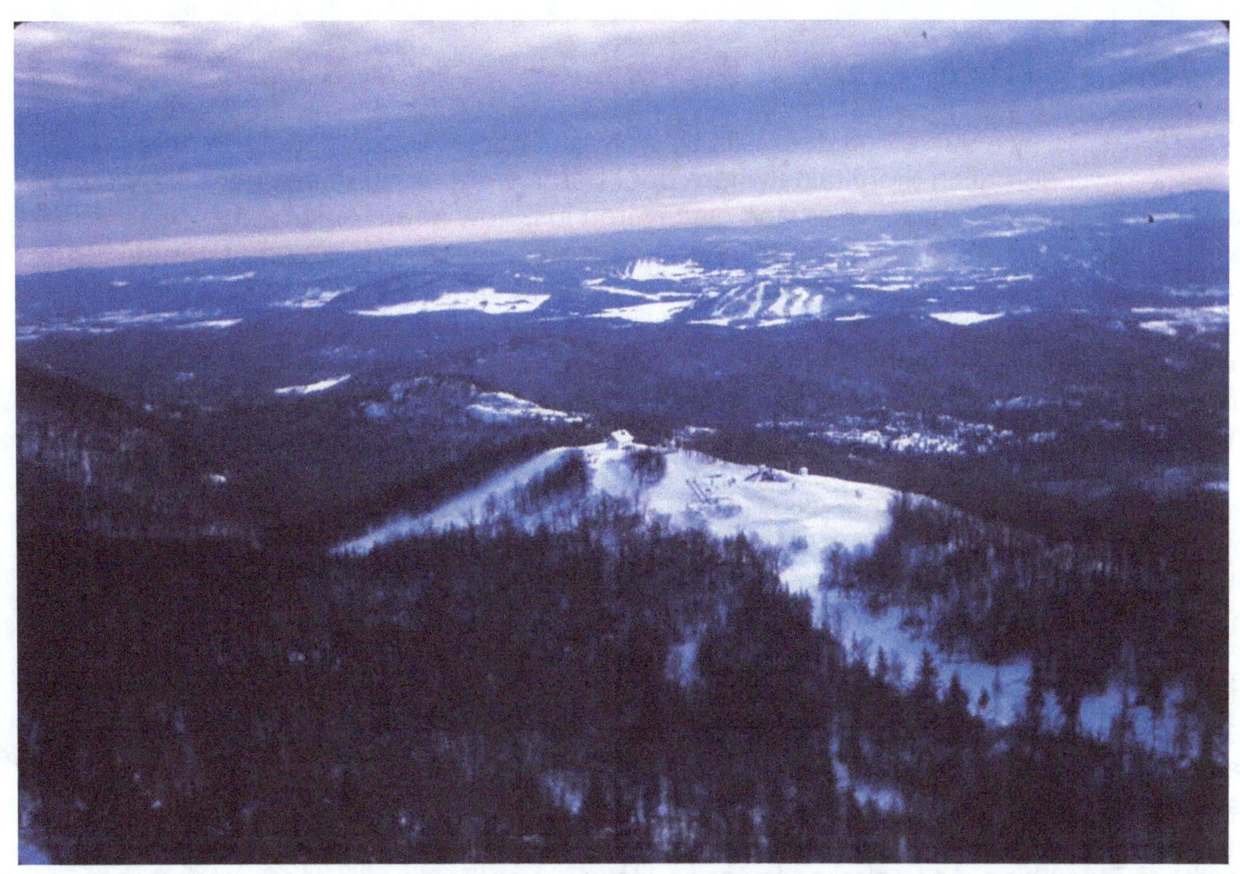

St. Jovite ski hill - Lunch break

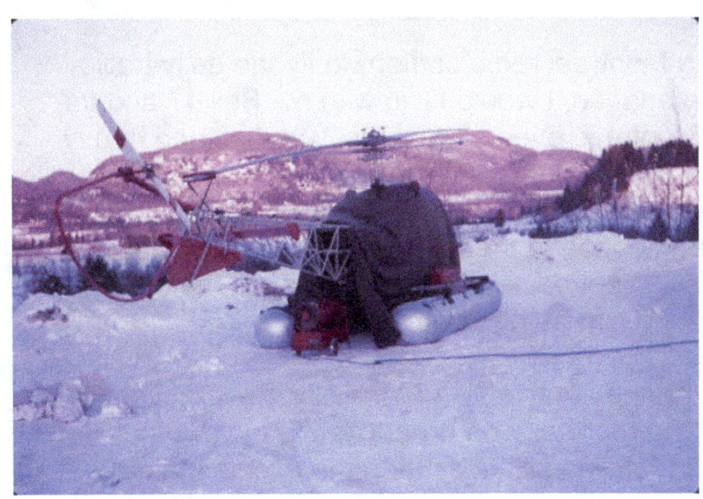

40 below & covered up

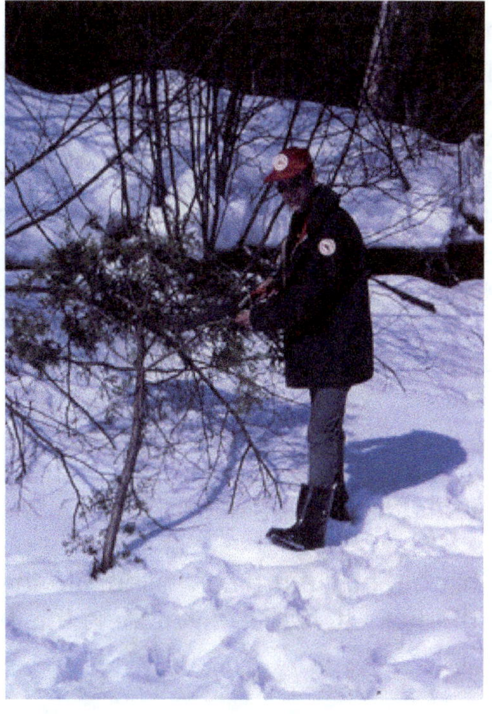

Lunch Time Sawing on a tree for kindling

In February 1970, we were contacted by Fish & Game

to fly a survey on deer kills by wolves. There was an area north of Montreal in the Laurentian Mountains where deer herds were being decimated. So, we tracked wolf pack movements from the air and discovered just how adept these packs were in developed hunting skillsThey generally hunted together in large packs and targeted old, weaker and more vulnerable animals in a deer herd. In an area north of St. Jovite, we tracked a particularly large pack of wolves. They displayed their strategy and hunting skills by splitting up at one end of a lake. They then circled it and attacked a deer from two sides at the other end. The result was the picture to the right.

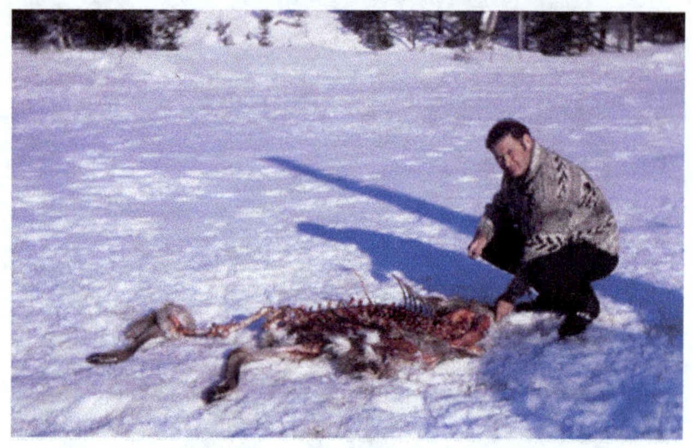

Wolf Kill

Photography flights were generally pretty straightforward, but some were memorable. Because of the maneuverability of a helicopter, you could get some interesting effects. One such flight stood out in the middle of January with the passenger door removed. The photographer wanted a tight spiral downward on a large Catholic church in the centre of a small town. It was basically an inward zoom. This was the final clip of a documentary on this town in the Southern Townships. As I spiralled lower and lower over the church, the photographer exclaimed, "Hold it, keep going a little longer." He then promptly threw up all over the cockpit! But he got the shot he wanted!

The company had a contract with CJAD, a Montreal radio station, to fly the daily traffic report. If our Jetranger was down for maintenance, I would fill in with my Bell 47 and the radio station reporter on board. Traffic in Montreal, even in the '70s, was fast and heavy. You would see some crazy things, all kinds of accidents and traffic jams. One morning during rush hour, we were covering a major artery. There were 5 lanes of traffic moving smoothly and fast. Suddenly we saw a car stopped in the far right lane and backing up! He had missed an off ramp, so he reversed to get back to it! Meanwhile, all the through flow lanes of traffic were maneuvering around him at 120 km/h.

Another day there was heavy ground fog on the south shore of the city. Several vehicles ended up colliding for lack of visibility. As the reporter was broadcasting this, we could see more traffic approaching this fog bank that was still obscuring the accident ahead. Of course, we were helpless to warn them. You have to know a little bit about Montreal drivers; they don't slow up for anything.

Consequently, more cars piled into the existing crashed vehicles, including a couple of semi-trucks. It was like watching this huge pile-up of vehicles in slow motion with no audio!

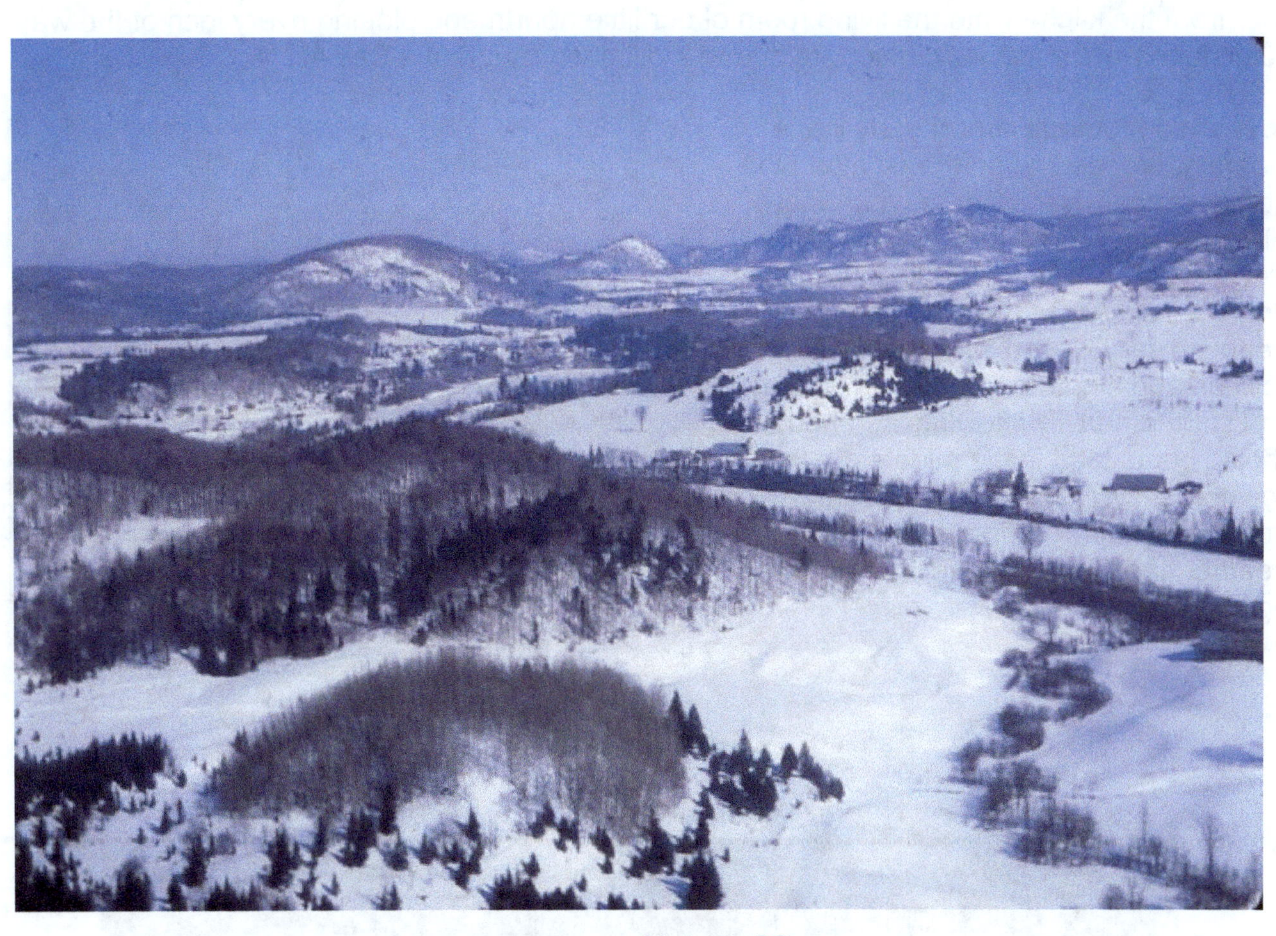

Deer survey area - St. Jovite PQ

The boss called me

The boss called me into his office one day and told me about a very interesting job he was about to send me on. It was to provide aerial support to a movie crew way up in Ungava Bay, east of Hudson Bay. At the time,there was a popular TV show called 'The American Sportsman.' This episode was to feature a famous jockey of the time called B Hartack. They were going to film him on an adventure hunting trip in northern Quebec. He would be featured as the great American hunter going after a trophy caribou. I was excited about this trip, the longest I had ever taken, about 1800 kilometres. I had maps spread on the floor from the kitchen into the living room of our little apartment, plotting every inch of the way! Fuel stops were especially important due to the limited range of a Bell 47.

I departed Montreal airport early in the morning, proceeding northeast along the St. Lawrence River. After leaving Sept Isles and Shefferville airports, my last fuel stops, I continued heading north for Ungava Bay. About halfway there, the weather really closed in with 100-foot ceilings and eighth-of-a- mile visibility. It had started heavily snowing, so I had no choice but to land in the middle of nowhere. I slept in the helicopter and was able to lift off at first light. The weather had lifted, and the rest of the flight was uneventful.

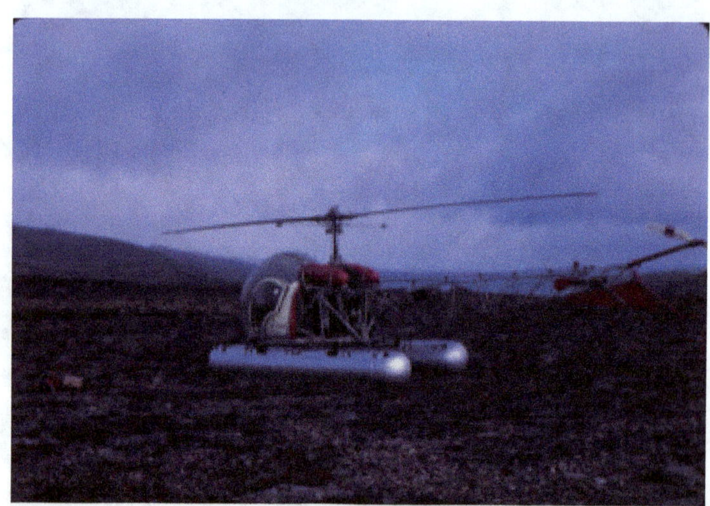

Outfitters camp near Ungava Bay

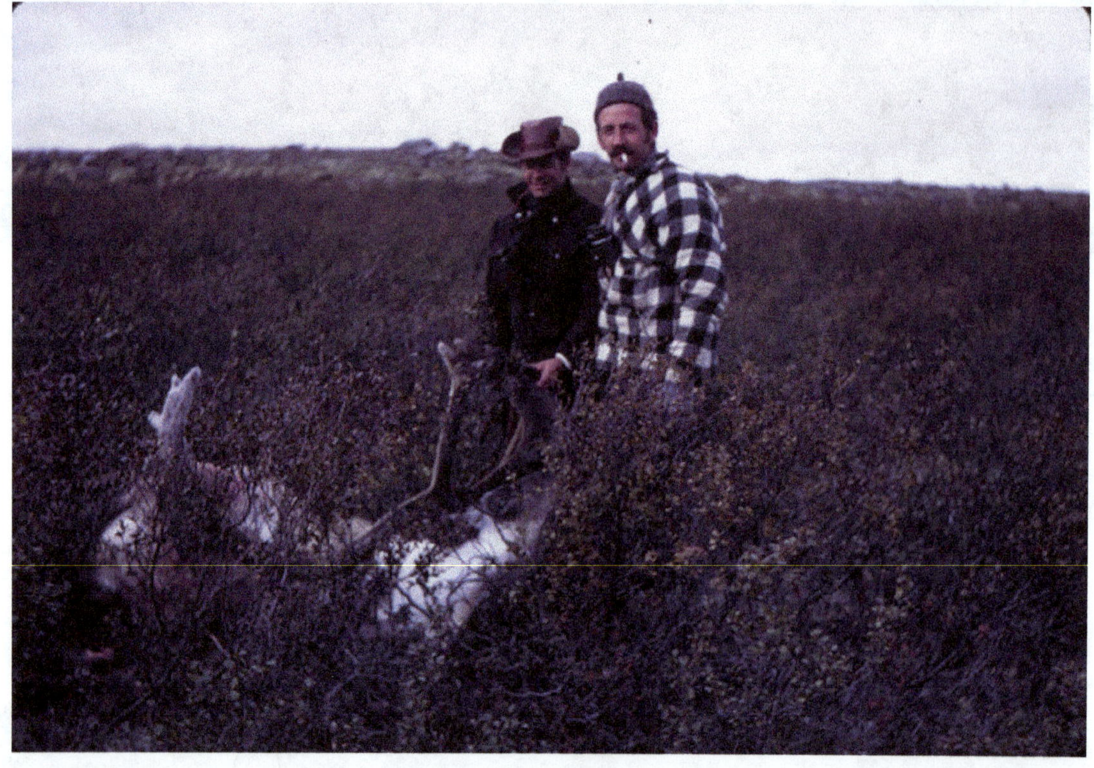

Caribou kill by B Hartack

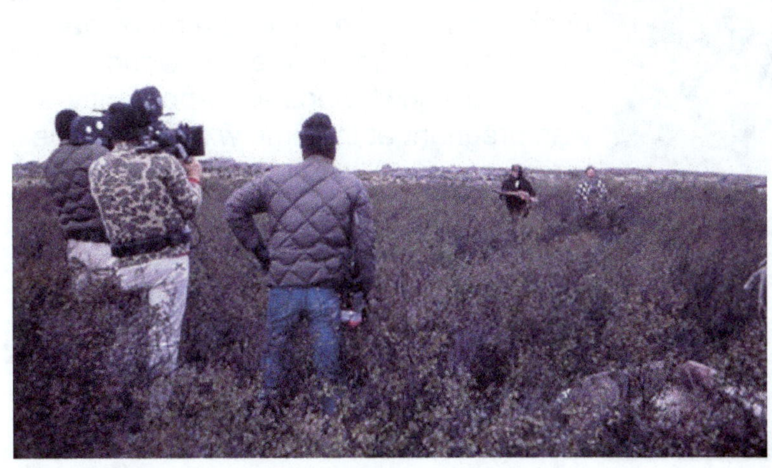

Film crew

I landed at the Twin River lodge, where the filming would take place. B Hartack, the featured hunter, had flown in from Pennsylvania the day before. It was interesting how these hunting films were choreographed. They basically shot the whole thing backwards, and the first thing they had to be sure of was the kill. So we went out with the helicopter to find a herd of Caribou. We found a herd not too far away, and I culled out a large bull with the helicopter and started herding it toward the hunter and filming crew. As soon as I got it near Hartack, I flew away, and he shot it from close range.

Several months later, I saw the whole show on TV, and it was amazing how they put it all together to look so authentic. It showed Hartack landing by seaplane in front of the lodge. Then the tracking scene where the guide 'discovered' the tracks of a large bull Caribou. He stated to Hartack that this was a trophy animal, probably weighing at least 800 pounds! (Of course, they knew that from weighing the dead animal after it had been shot.) After the bull that I had herded with the helicopter was shot, the hunter was told to approach with caution. The guide was heard saying, "Sometimes an animal is only wounded and can still be very dangerous!" Actually, the animal had already been dead for 2 hours!

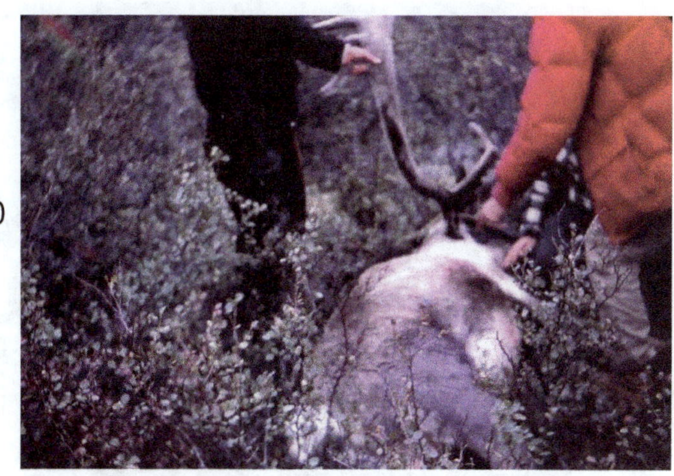

Commentary on the kill for the TV cameras

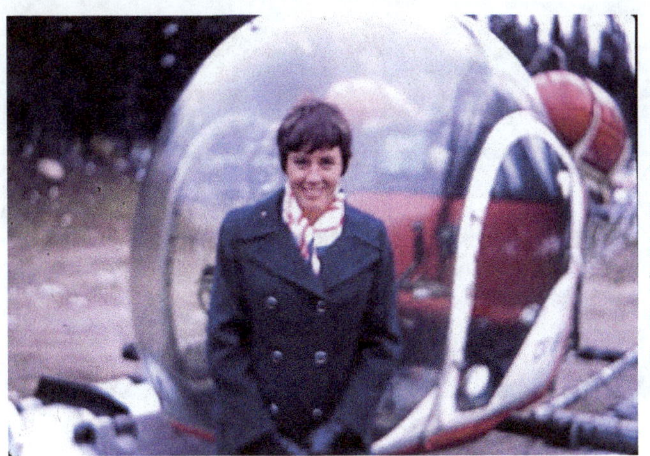

N. Greene/Raine

So after a week, the filming was complete, and B Hartack, including the camera crews, returned to the States. I was headed back to Montreal with an interesting interruption. As I flew within radio range of Sept Isles tower, there was a message from my company to call. N. Greene needed a helicopter so she could scout out a new proposed ski hill in the Laurentian Mountains.

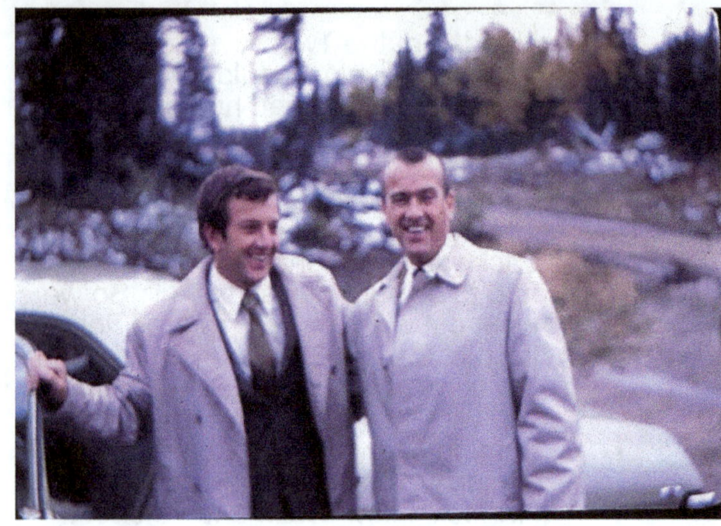

A Raine - husband/coach

It was an honour to meet her and her husband, A. Raine. N. was a renowned skier and had won numerous world titles. They were newlyweds and apparently, she was pregnant at the time with twins. She was even given two pairs of short skis by a fan for the yet-to-be-born twins.

After winning Olympian ski medals, she later went on to become a Canadian Senator in the British Columbia legislature. I look back at those pictures of her posing in front of the helicopter with fond memories.

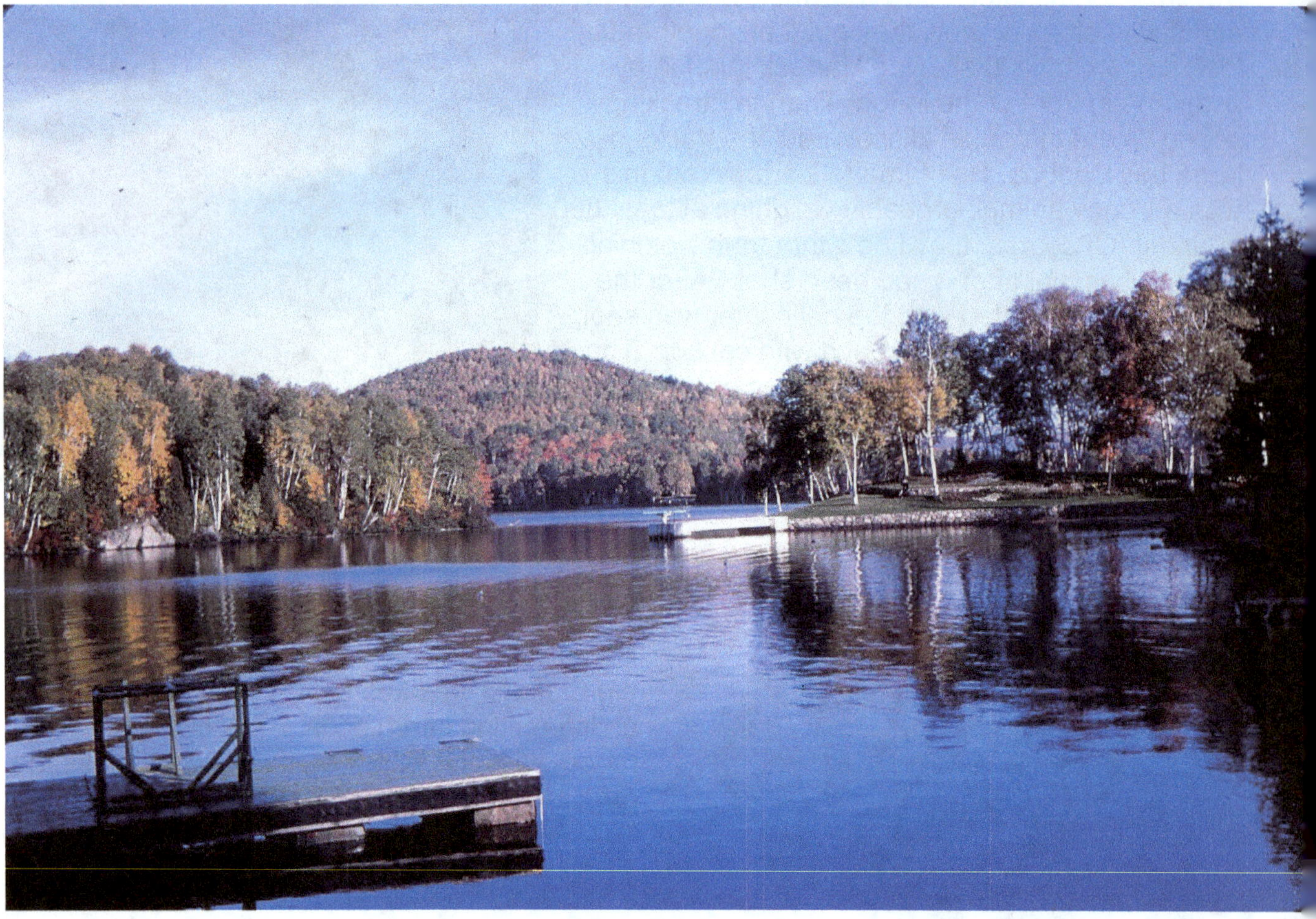

Laurentian Mountain lake

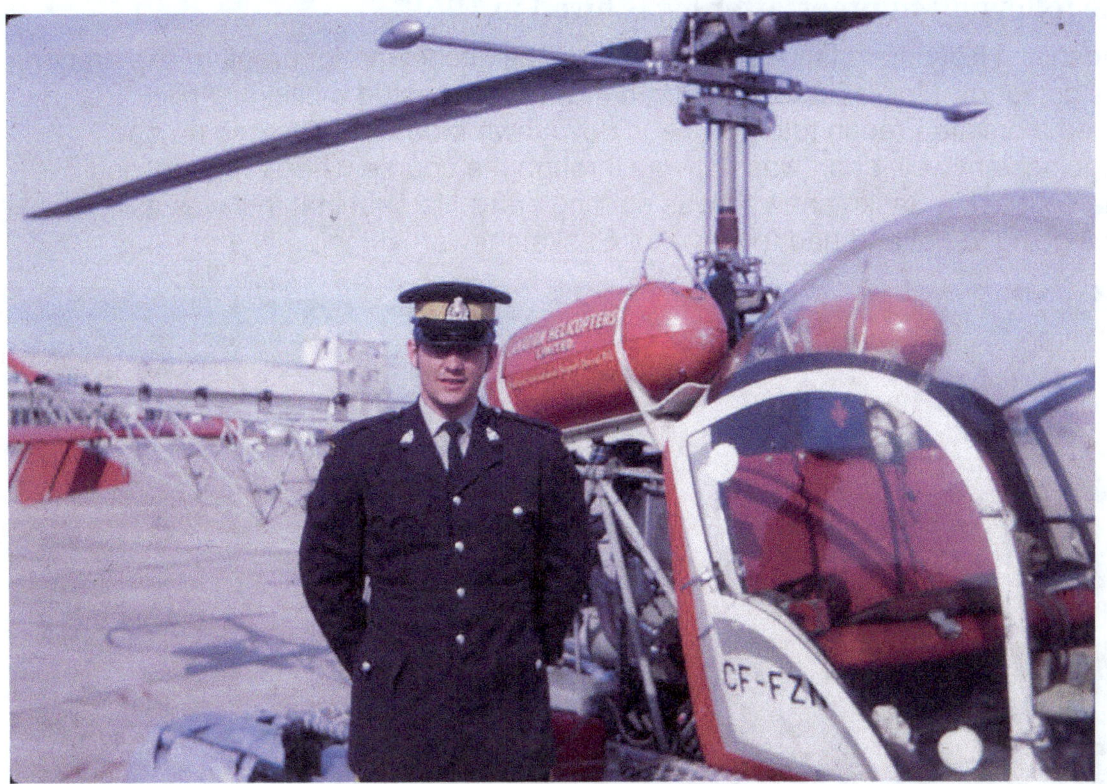

Looking for poachers along the St. Lawrence

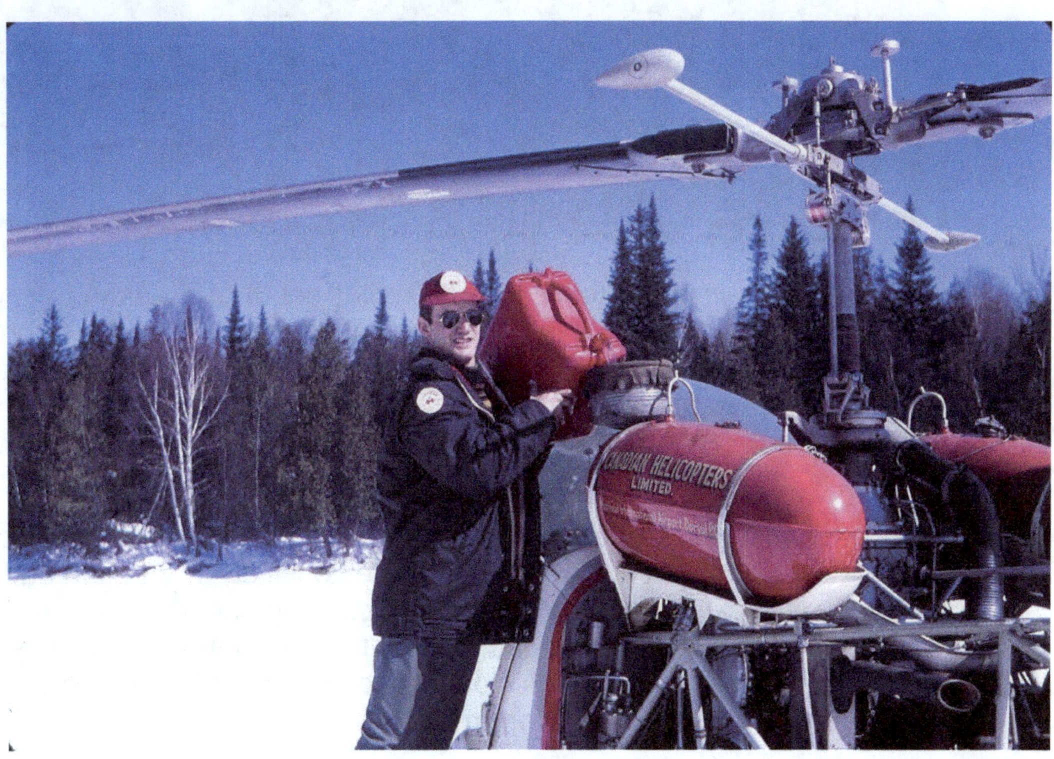

Fuel Stop

The following summer, after I was hired in 1969,

Canadian Helicopters landed a contract in Saskatchewan for uranium exploration. The company, Mokta Exploration from France, requested a bilingual pilot. So, my boss L Ayers hired a private French tutor for me in downtown Montreal. The one on one instruction was going very well, and I was halfway through the course when I was notified by my boss that the contract in Saskatchewan was starting early. He said that this was as bilingual as I was going to get and had to leave for Saskatchewan immediately!

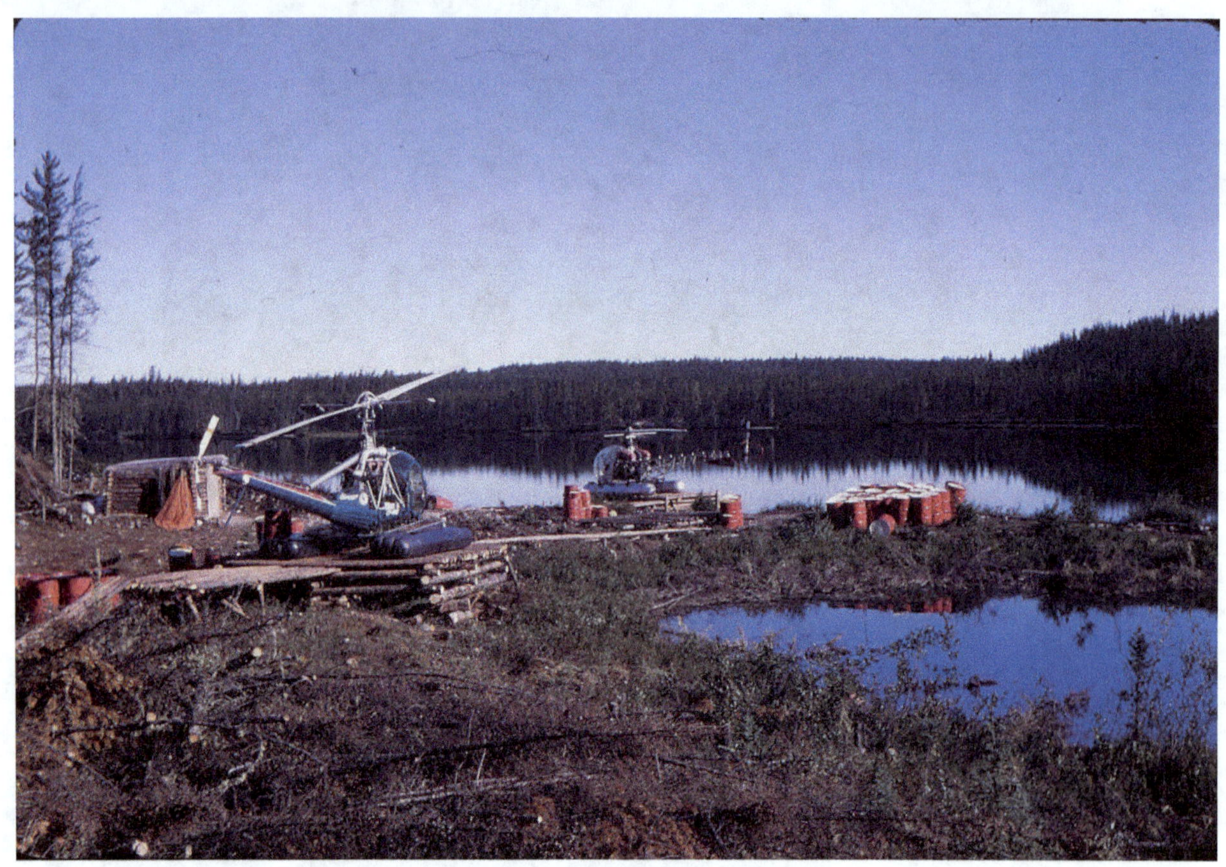

Cluff Lake - Saskatchewan

I arrived at the newly installed tent camp 100 miles south of Uranium City, where they installed the uranium detection equipment inside of the helicopter. With an operator on board, we started a grid exploration to detect & locate uranium deposits. Within a week, there were substantial finds & it was quickly decided that a uranium mine was going to happen. We immediately did an aerial search for a location for the construction of a new airport.

There was another support helicopter from Okanagan Helicopters in Vancouver. This was piloted by a very interesting guy who had flown extensively in Vietnam and had a lot of stories. At first, I was a little skeptical of his adventures of being shot down twice. One of the times was over enemy territory where he was captured by the Viet Cong, his escape & subsequent rescue. I became a believer in all his stories when he showed me letters of commendation & medals for bravery from the US government.

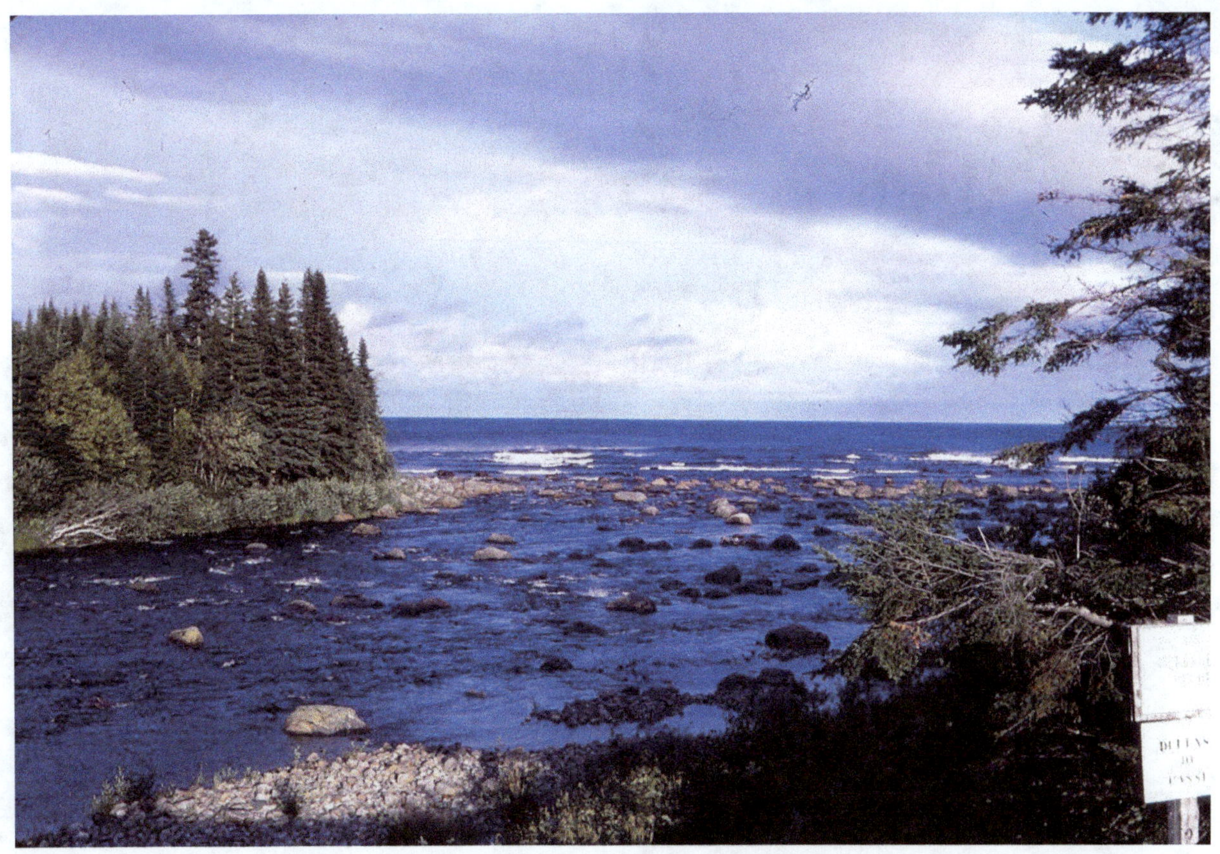

One day he informed me that this commercial flying was boring & that he was going to hire out as a mercenary pilot in Africa. He would go with whichever side paid him the most. So, I had forgotten about him until he showed up on the James Bay Hydroelectric project in the mid-'70s. He had, in fact, hired out as a mercenary pilot in Africa & participated in the conflicts unscathed.

Many years later, I received word Roy had been killed as a passenger in a small helicopter off the coast of BC. How ironic that he had seen so much combative action from Vietnam to Africa & tragically met his end as a passenger in a helicopter piloted by a novice pilot.

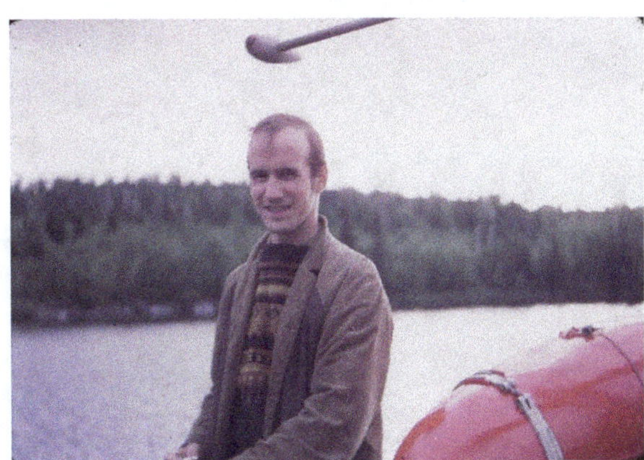

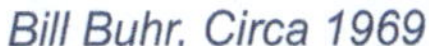

Bill Buhr, Circa 1969

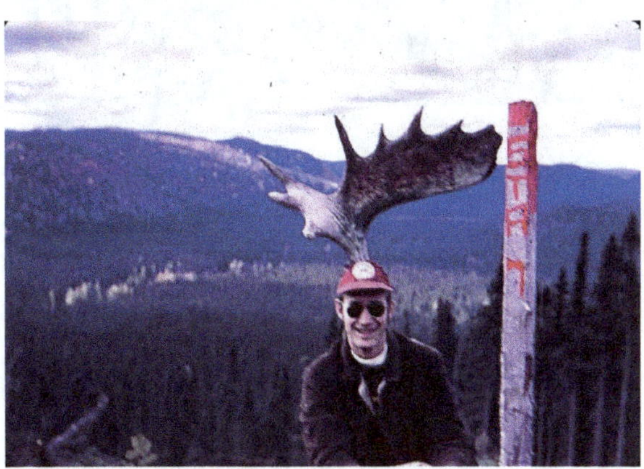

Sanmaur area

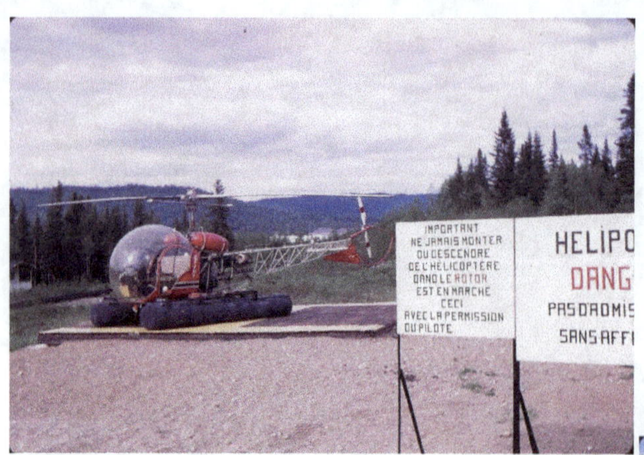

Sanmaur PQ Fire patrol

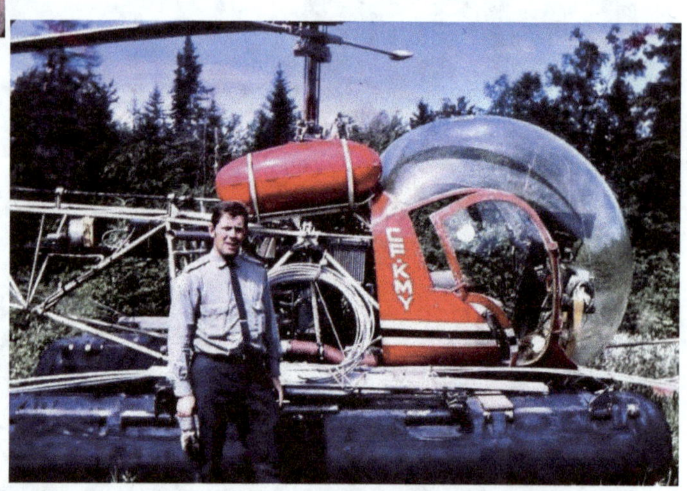

Forestry officer - Directing fire patrol

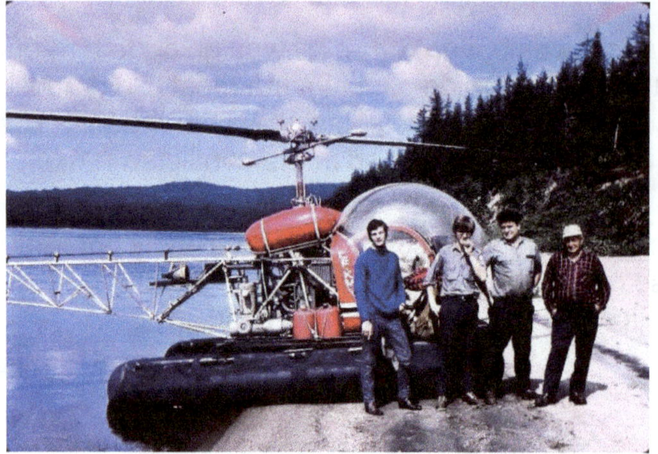

G Vaillancourt float pilot - with forestry personnel

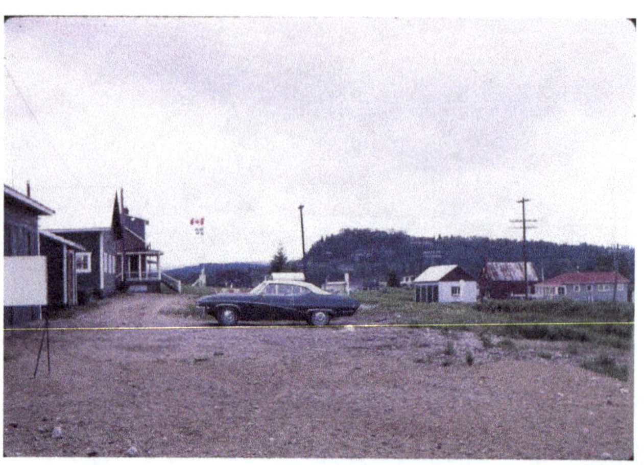

Sanmaur Forestry & helipad

In the New Year of 1970

and Connie was pregnant with our now 50-year-old daughter. Leading up to our first child's birth, Connie was 2 weeks overdue, so the boss kept sending me out on day jobs. He called me into his office one day and said a 3-month contract was imminent, and he wanted me on it. Fortunately, our daughter was born that night, and I flew out of Montreal the next morning with my helicopter and a suitcase.

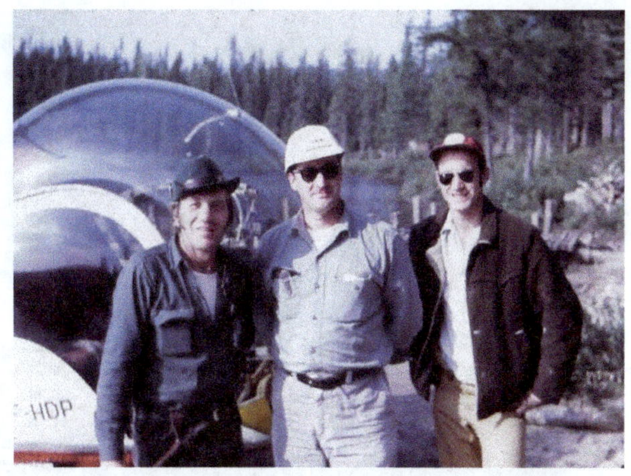

Project manager - Center Janin Construction

This was an interesting and high-flying contract cutting power line right of way to Churchill Falls, Labrador. It was to be a main line for 735 kva transmission towers supplying large amounts of power not only to Quebec and Ontario but to New York State as well. This job would generate a lot of experience and quickly build hours in my logbook. My main focus was flying a lot of lumberjacks daily out to where they were cutting lines and clearing right of way. This also involved setting up line camps with men and equipment, slinging barrels of fuel and transporting many loads of groceries.Slinging was a new experience which in itself required a new learning curve.

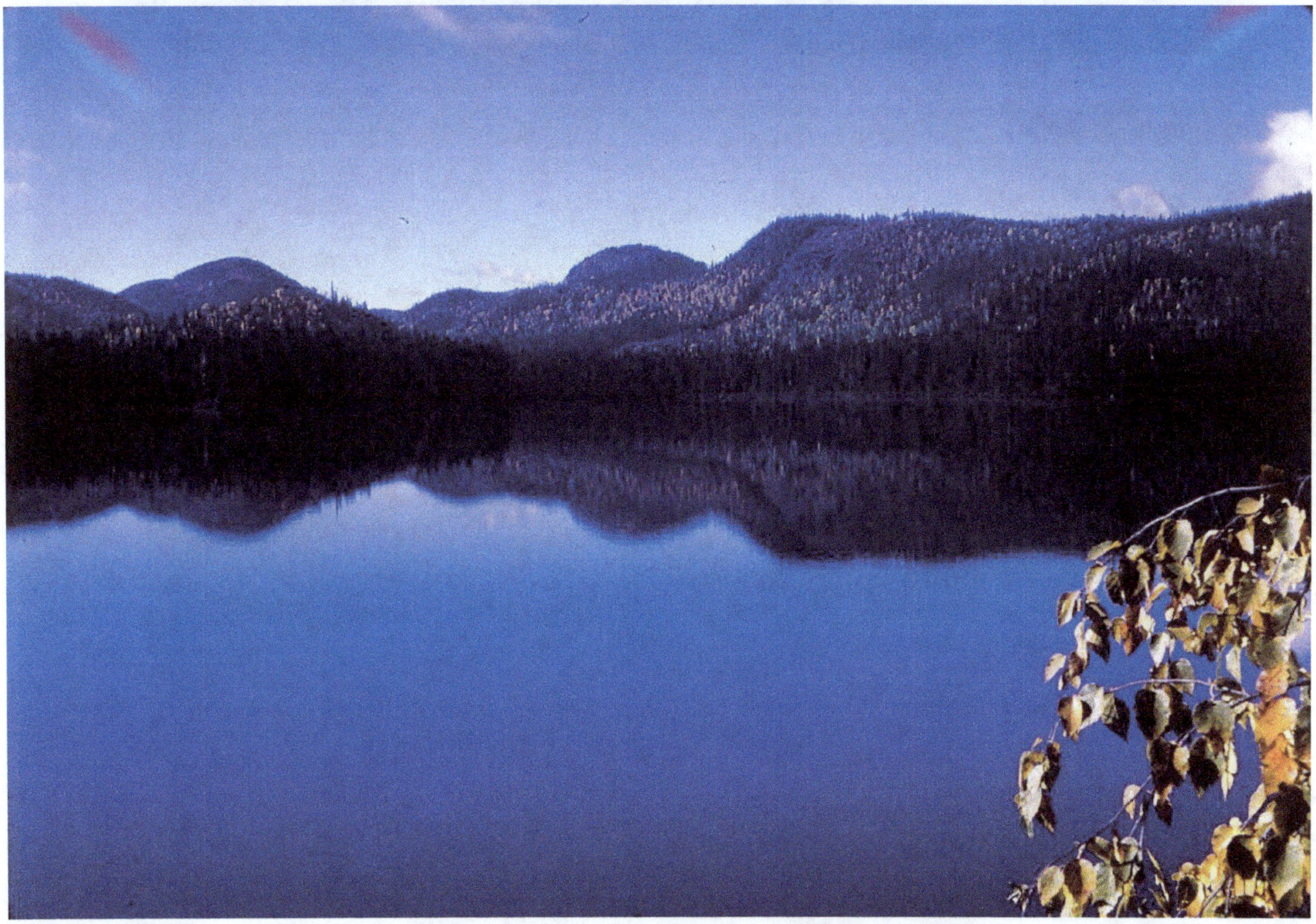

Laurentian mountains picturesque lake

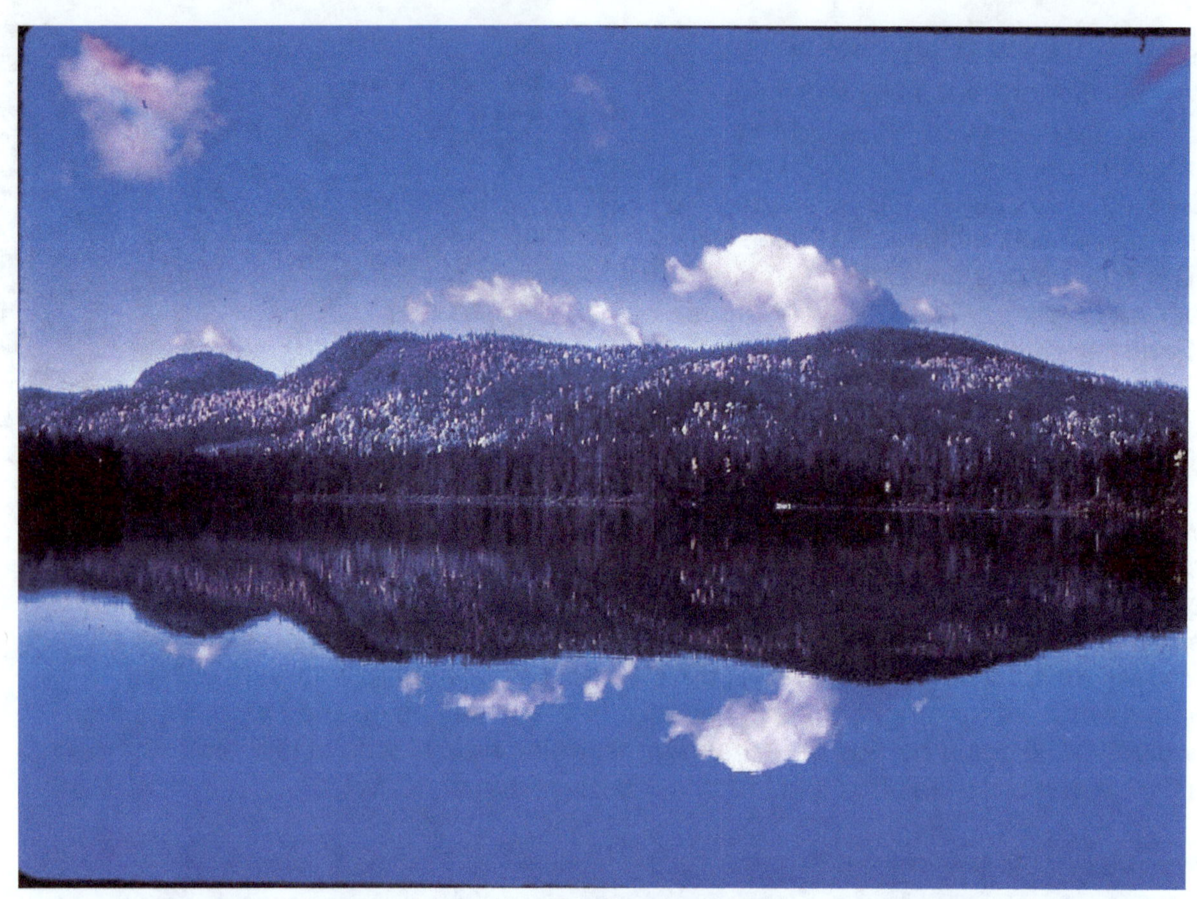

Near Baie Comeau PQ

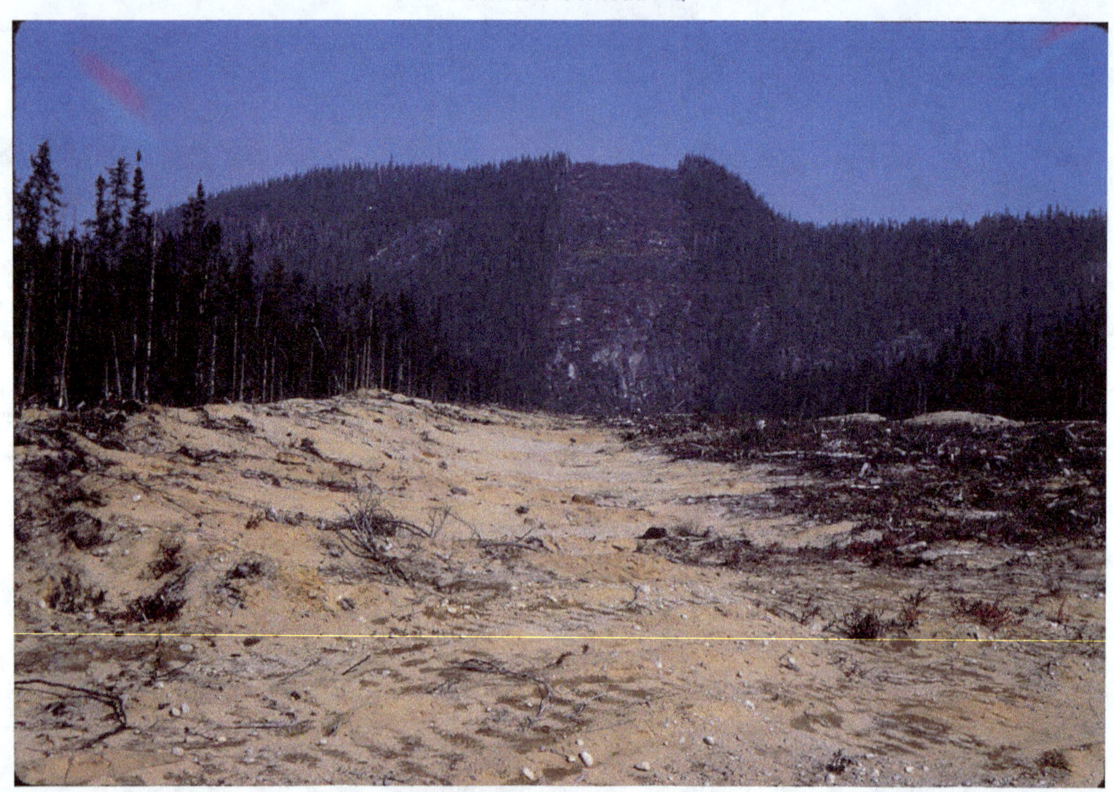

Baie Comeau to Churchill

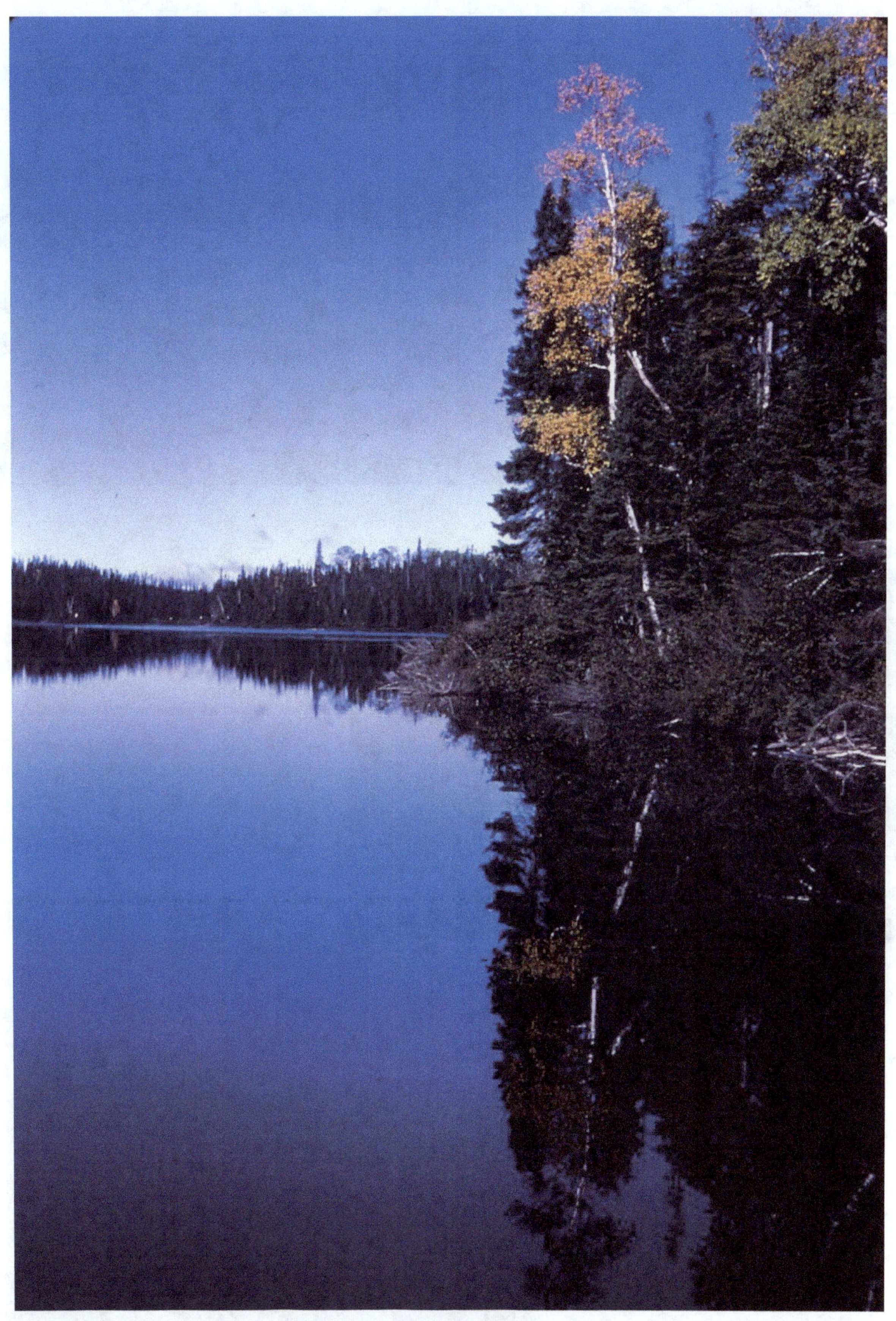

Fall Colours reflected in a serene lake

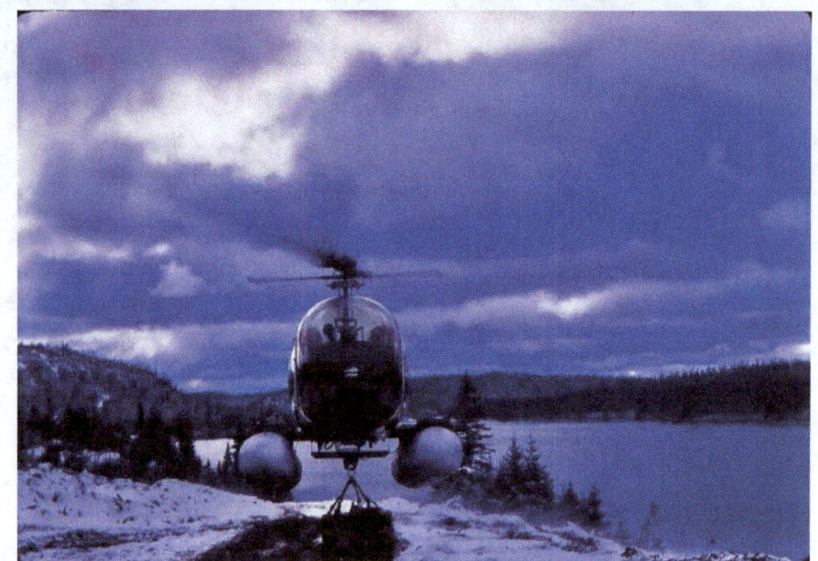

Last load before dark

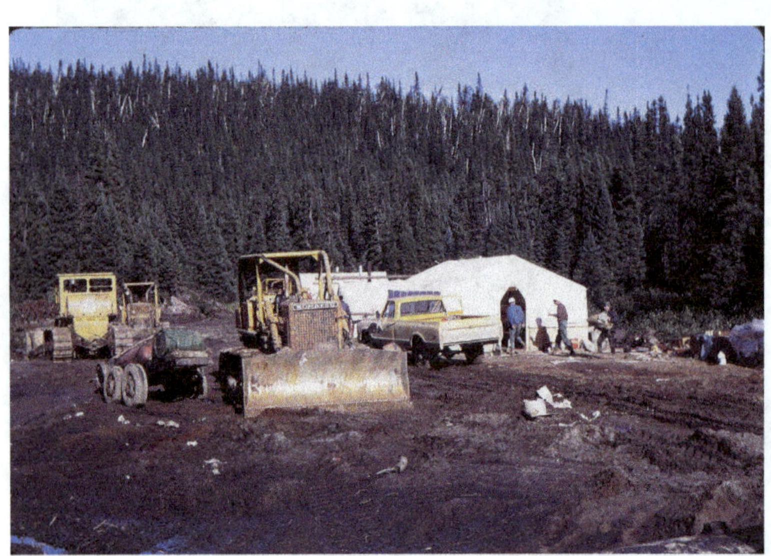

Tent camp - Clearing construction line

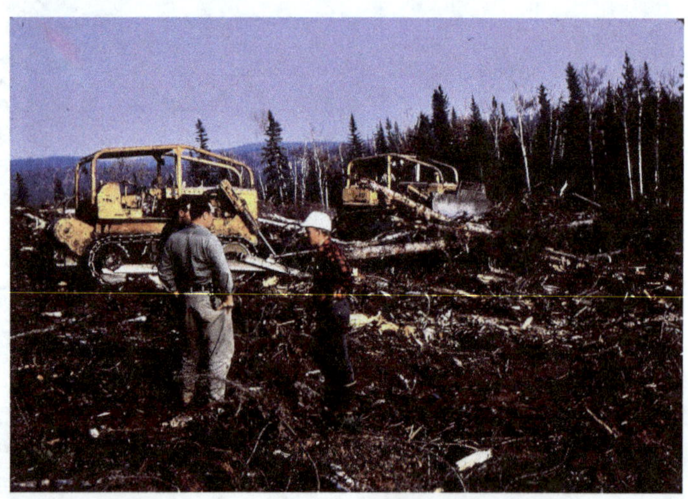

Cat 'skinner' consultation

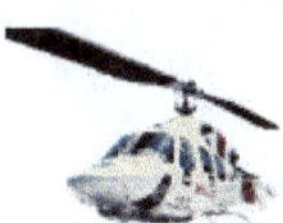

One night the crew boss woke me up in my tent just after midnight.

He had received an emergency call that a caterpillar operator down the line had been seriously injured. He wanted me to fly 10 miles down the line, pick up this operator and fly him to the hospital. The hospital was about an hour's flight away in Baie Comeau on the St. Lawrence River. My first reaction was to say 'no' because a Bell 47 helicopter is not really equipped instrument-wise for night flights. However, apparently, it was a life-or-death situation, according to the camp supervisor. I looked up and saw a full moon and made a decision that I could do this safely. I had only flown a helicopter at night once before in the Montreal area. There were no lights in this mountainous area of the Laurentians, with the exception of a full moon. So I took off and followed the cut line to the camp where the injured operator was located. They loaded him on board with my help as I kept the machine running. Unfortunately, because of the small cockpit and straight-across bench seating, this man had to sit upright. He was in a lot of pain and literally holding his entrails in with both arms. Apparently, a tree had come right through the cab and punctured his stomach area. So we took off, and that full moon was my only reference to stay upright and maintain the right heading to Baie Comeau. I eventually established radio communications with Baie Comeau and Sept Isles air traffic advisories. They advised me that fog was rolling in, and of course, this would make the flight challenges more critical. As I neared Baie Comeau airport, they were calling a quarter mile in fog. I landed in great relief. We loaded the patient into a waiting ambulance. The fog rolled in 15 minutes later, the visibility went to zero, and the airport was closed down.

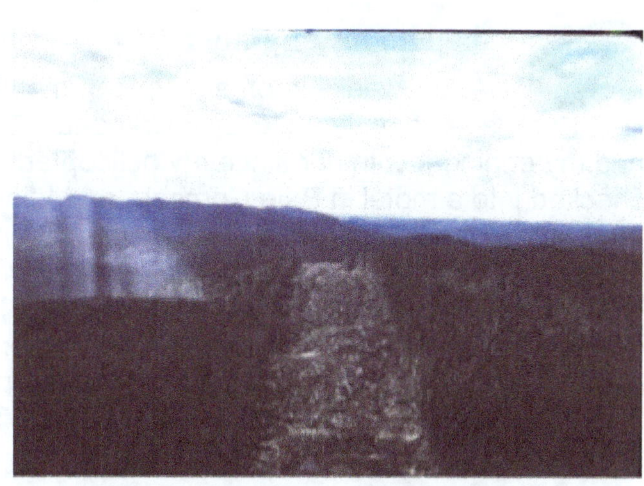

Transmission line under construction

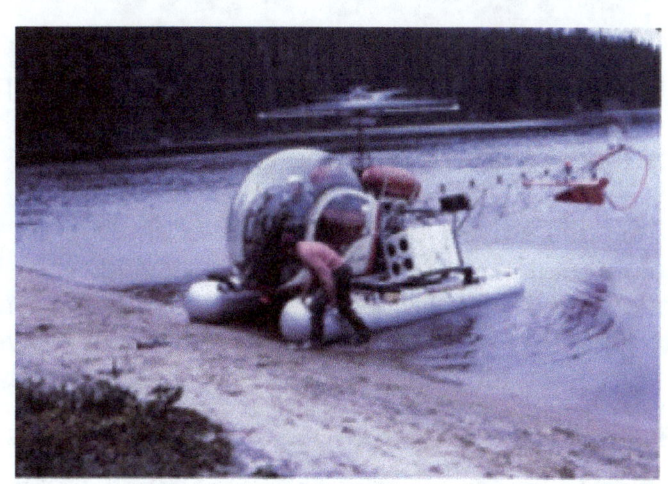

Moving materials for lodge

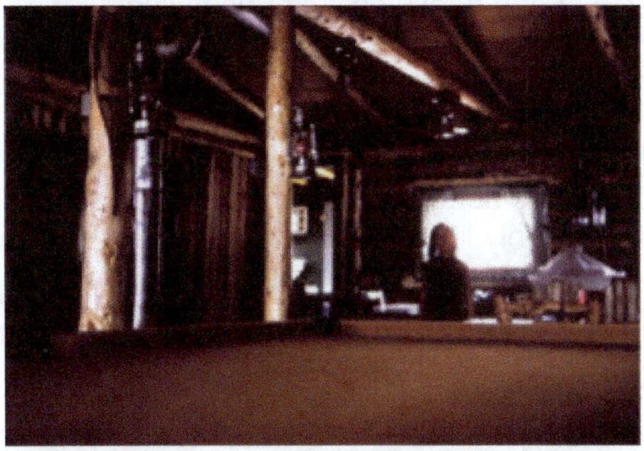

The next morning I went to the hospital and checked on my 'passenger.' The operation had been successful, and he was awake and smiling. Needless to say, he was very thankful and expressed his gratitude. When my engineer from Montreal landed at the airport to do an inspection on my helicopter, he was told I had landed there at 2:00 am. He immediately replied, " It couldn't have been my helicopter; it can't fly at night!" I had to explain.

Gabou fishing lodge near proposed transmission line

She had my engineer

-A few weeks later, a couple of months after I had left Montreal, my wife was able to drive up to Baie Comeau with my baby daughter Michelle. She also had my engineer with her since my helicopter was due for a major inspection. She checked into a motel in Baie Comeau, and I flew down from camp to see my 2-month-old baby daughter. This was the second time I'd be seeing her since the brief glimpse at the Montreal hospital the day she was born. So Connie had checked into a horseshoe-shaped motel on the edge of town. In those days, the laws against landing off-airport were not that restrictive for helicopters. So I landed right in the centre of the complex with my smiling wife standing in the open doorway of her room, holding Michelle. How exciting to see my wife and our firstborn baby daughter.

One final note on that inspection the next day. The engineer signed off the logbook, I said goodbye to Connie and Michelle and took off for my camp an hour away, When I landed, the aircraft was covered in oil. The engineer had not properly secured the engine oil plug. *Luckily the flight wasn't longer, or it would have been a forced landing.*

The progression of the line cutting and clearing was moving rapidly as early winter set in. However, disaster was about to strike. A group of men had requested some time off to go into Baie Comeau for a well-deserved break. They ordered 3 taxis to pick them up on the far side of a lake where the road ended.

The cabs arrived, but the men never showed up. It was discovered that all 12 men piled into a relatively small boat for the crossing. They had no life jackets, and the boat soon overturned. They all drowned. There were 5 members from one family among the victims. So I was tasked to fly the bodies out. Divers had brought them up and lined them up on the beach. These were men I had flown to their work site daily. Now I was flying them out for the last time.

I was on the job for another month when a traumatic event happened to me. Our chief pilot arrived from Montreal with a larger Sikorsky. There were more men to be moved back and forth in an effort to complete a section of the line before winter arrived in earnest. I needed help, and the second aircraft would solve those logistics. A snowstorm was moving in, and we needed to bring all the workers back to camp. We were both running and ready to take off. I realized the sleet was wet and heavy as it started falling. During training, I had been warned that any freezing precipitation could accumulate on the exposed servos and freeze your controls in flight. Remembering this, I hopped out with the machine running to check. Sure enough, the wet snow was accumulating on the tops of both servos. I cleaned off the one servo and was reaching for the second one. This one was only a few inches in front of the shrouded 13-bladed cooling fan. I didn't realize how much suction was generated by the fan. Suddenly I heard a loud 'twang.' I jerked back, thinking something had entered the cooling fan area from the other side. In shock, I looked down and noticed my little finger. It was gone!

The other pilot rushed over and quickly realized what had happened. He was going to fly me to the hospital in Baie Comeau, but the snowstorm hit in earnest, making further flight impossible. So they loaded me in a truck. Instead of a 45-minute flight, it turned into a 2-hour drive along a rough logging road. Just as we were leaving, Tony handed me my glove with my little finger still in it. With a concerned expression, he said, "Here, you might need this!"

So the doctor completed the surgery closing off the stub with cauterization and stitches. He was unable to reattach the finger because it had frozen. That was to be the end of my flying while I was recuperating. It took a lot longer than anticipated and just wouldn't heal properly. After almost 3 months, I was fit to fly again. I called the boss, and he said, "Oh, didn't you get my letter?" "I said, what letter?" He informed me that he had to lay me off because the contract pilot/engineer who had taken my place crashed my helicopter. This time, he had taken off and forgotten to check carb heat, so consequently, the engine failed. (* I refer back to the incident I had in the Cessna right after my training). Back when I was training for my private pilot's licence, I had an engine failure at 10,000 feet from not applying carburetor heat. This exact thing happened to this engineer but at a very low altitude after take-off. Consequently, he had no chance to recover after the engine quit. The company said they couldn't have more pilots than helicopters, so being lowest in seniority, I was gone. Actually, this was the engineer who had earlier caused me to lose all my engine oil with an improperly installed drain plug.

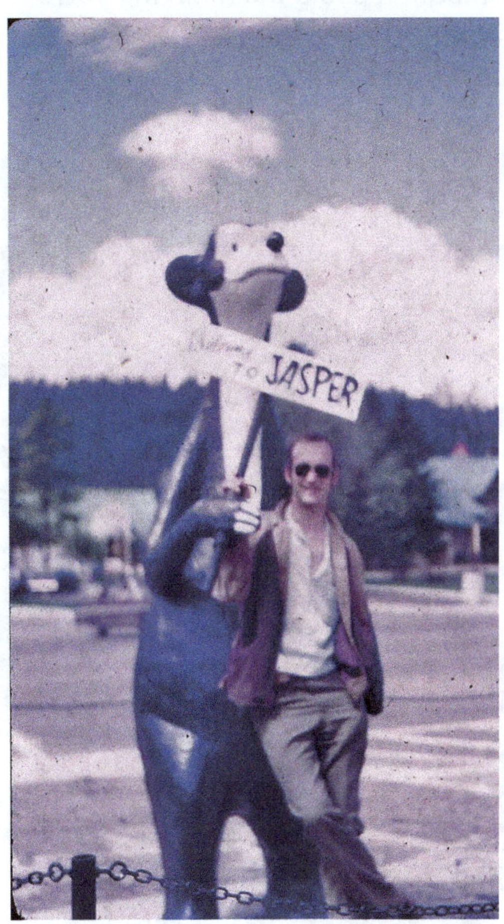

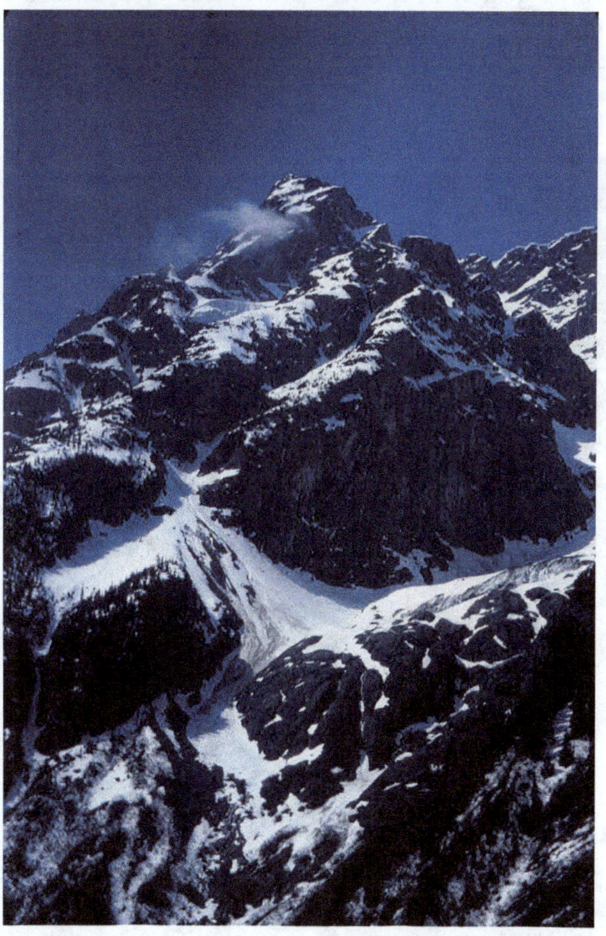

Enroute to Alberta fires

Jasper

The company felt bad and said they'd hire me back as soon as they expanded the fleet. That seemed very vague, so I immediately started sending out applications. Prospective employers were much more receptive now because I had quite a bit of experience and a thousand hours in my logbook. I received a quick response and actual job offers from 3 of the applications in one day. I decided to check out Haida Helicopters in Pitt Meadows in the Lower Mainland. The operations manager was very friendly and had me start immediately. It was the beginning of fire season, and they needed to be ready with helicopters and personnel. So I was checked out in an aircraft a bit larger than the Bell 47 I had been operating. It was a Hiller SL4 turbocharged with a 315 hp engine. The turbocharger meant it could maintain full power to altitudes of 9,000 ft., a huge advantage in the Canadian Rockies.

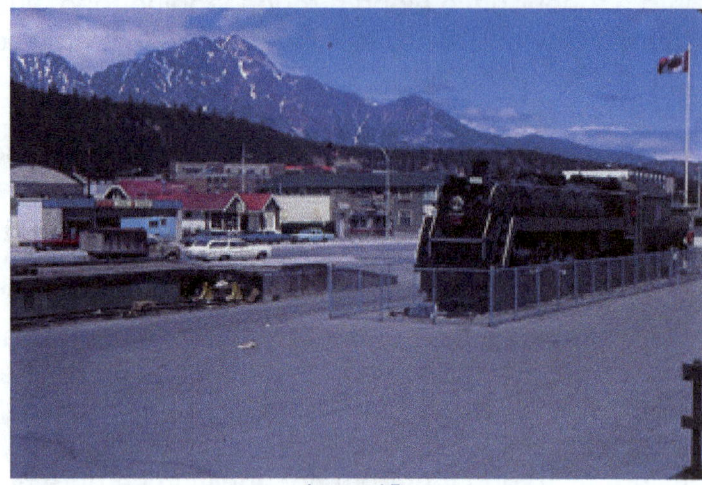

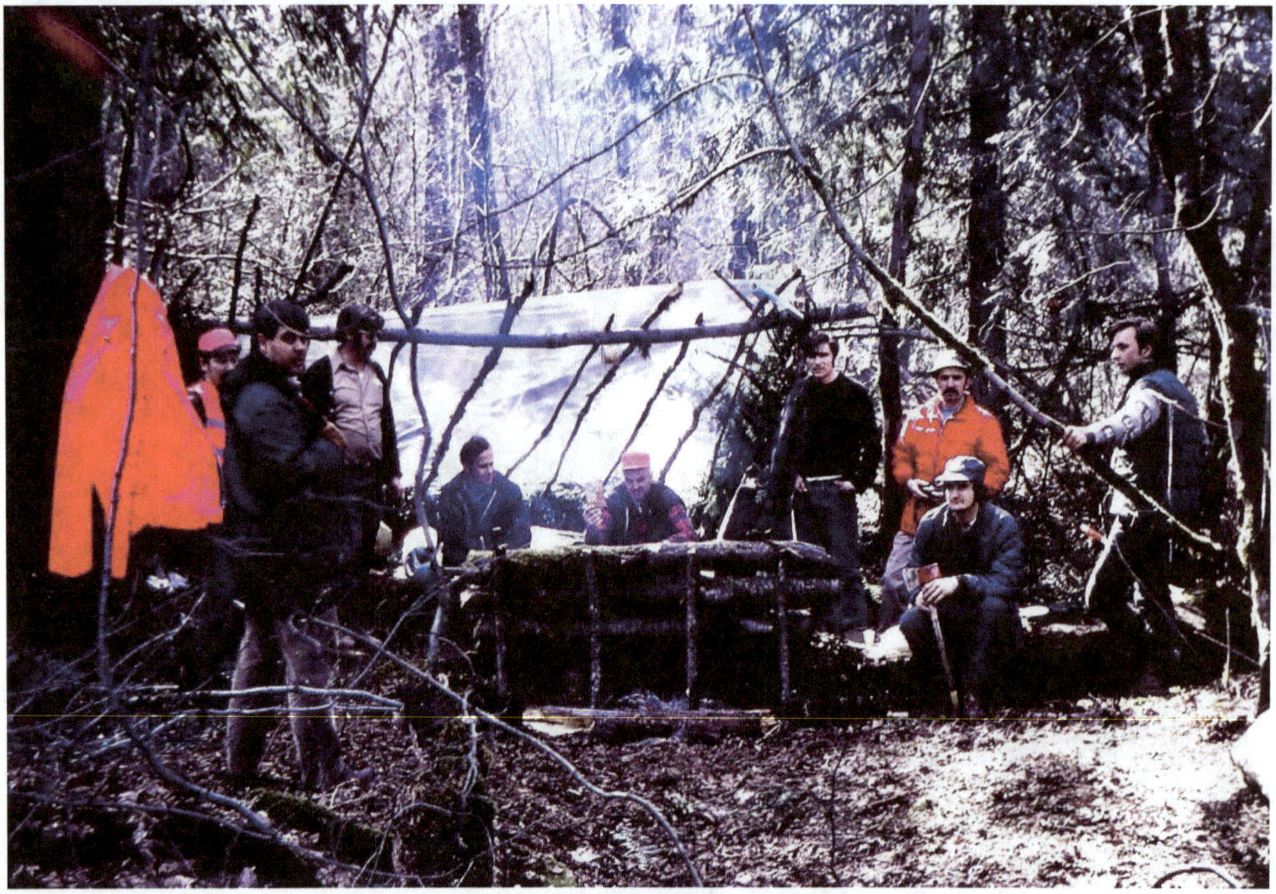

Jasper AB

Pitt Meadows BC Survival Training

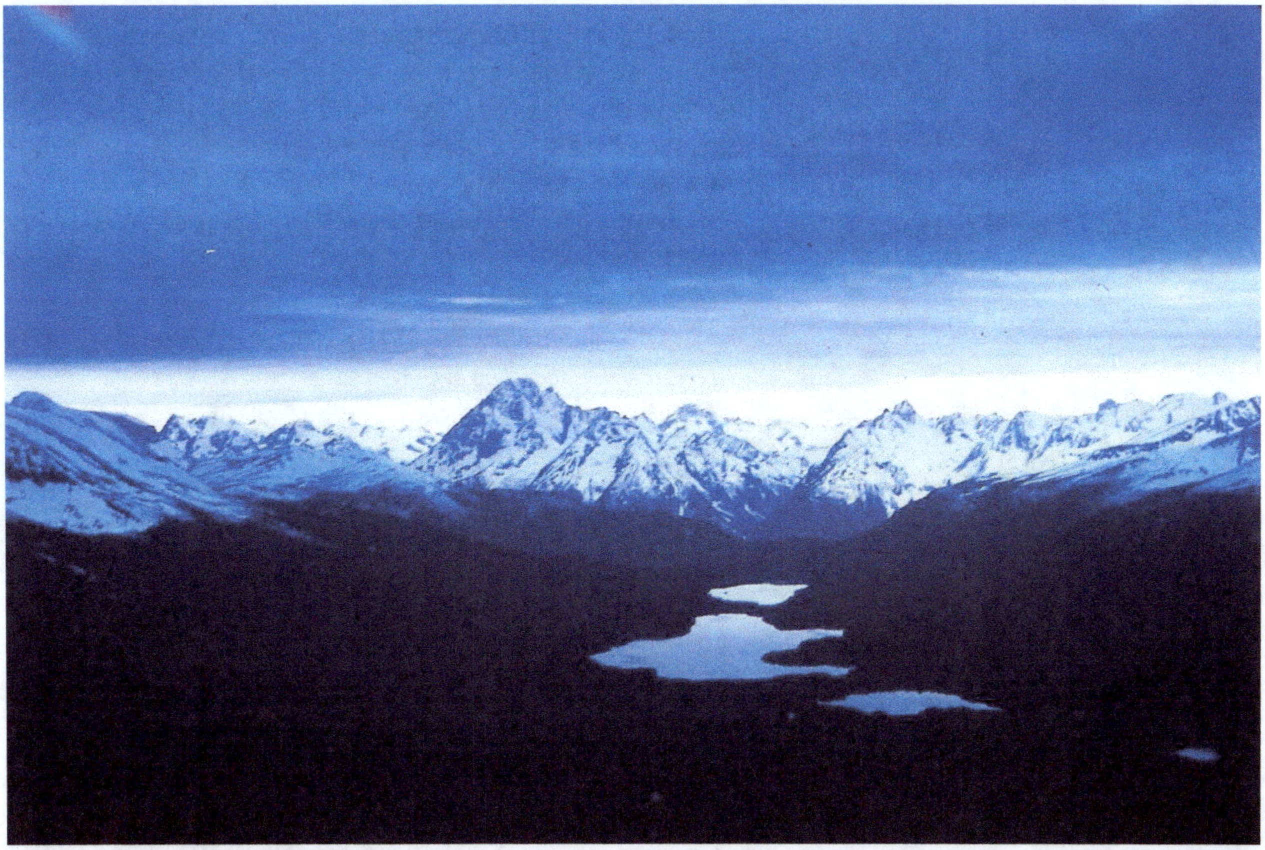

Rocky Mountains

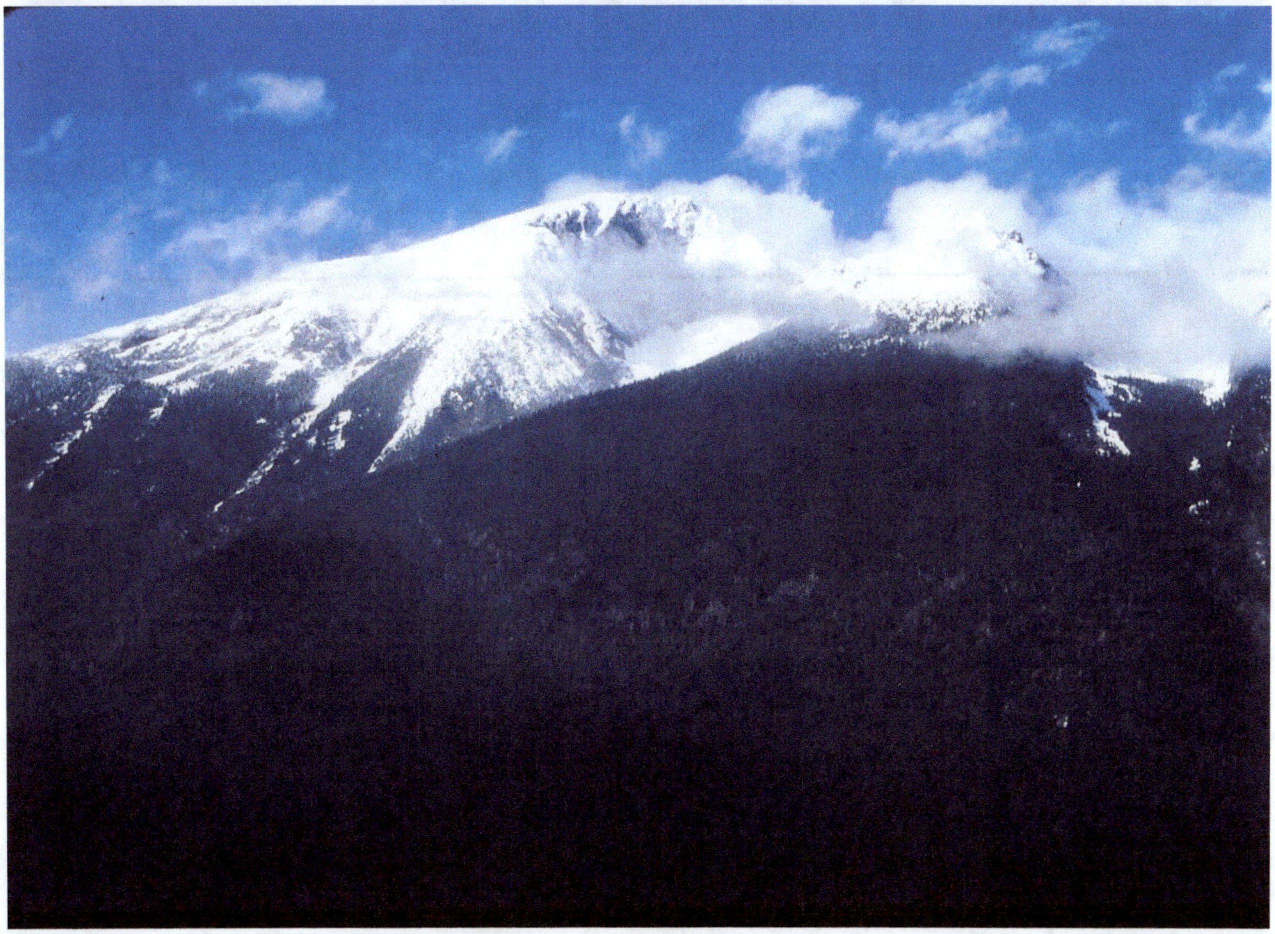

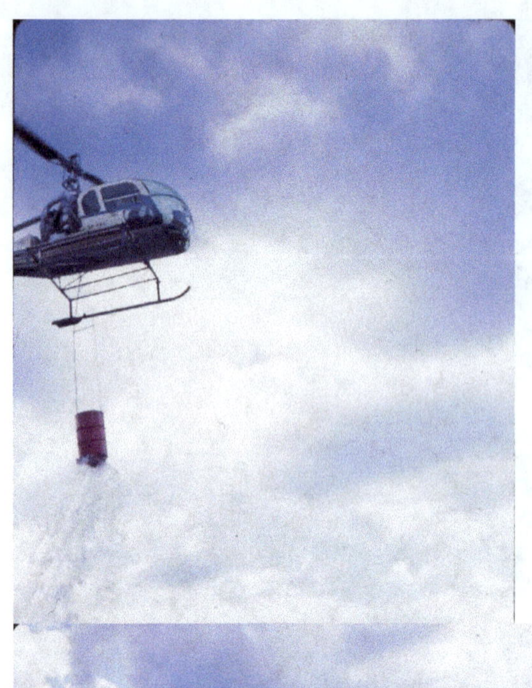

Soon I was headed north to the BC interior. On board were my engineer, a water bucket, a cargo net and other fire-fighting equipment. I practiced and basically self-taught the procedure of bucketing out of a lake near Williams Lake. Fighting fires was going to be a great new experience bombing them out of rivers and lakes!

I practise bucketing at D. Lieb's lake near Williams Lake

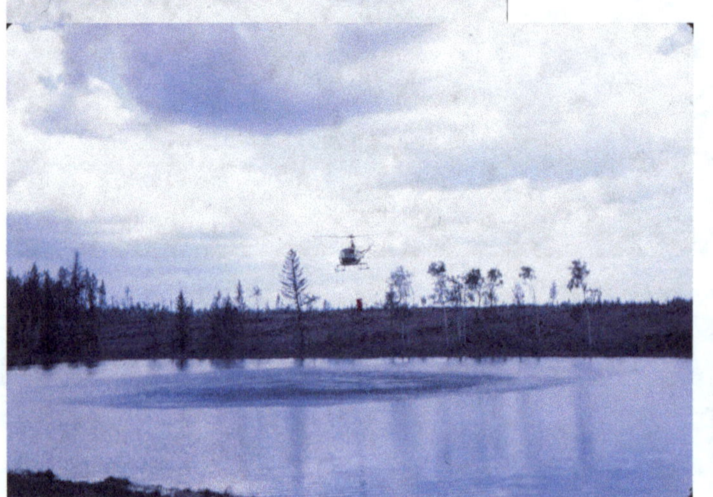

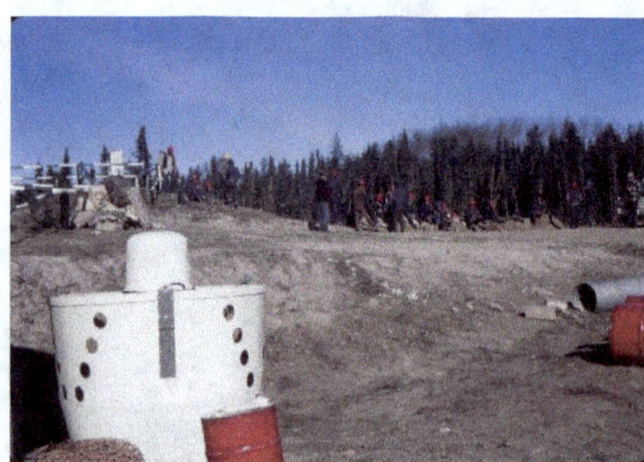

Water bucket ready

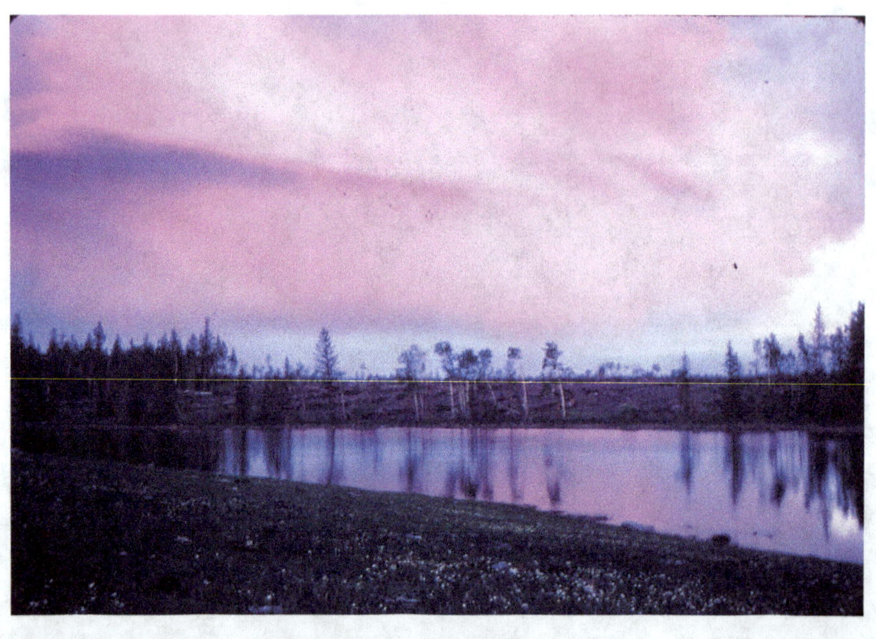

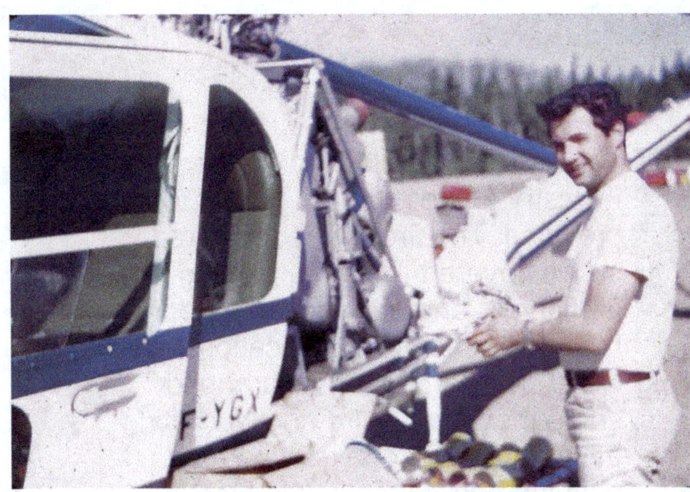

D Lieb- my engine

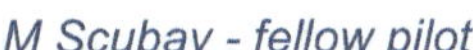

M Scubay - fellow pilot

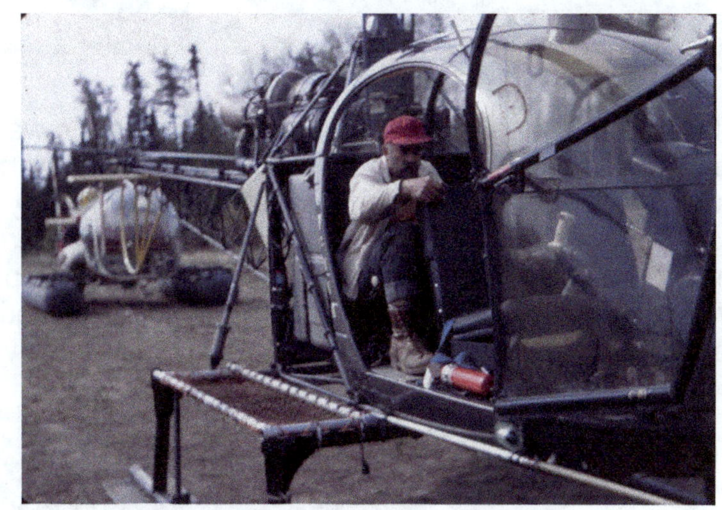

The Fire Crew in North Alberta

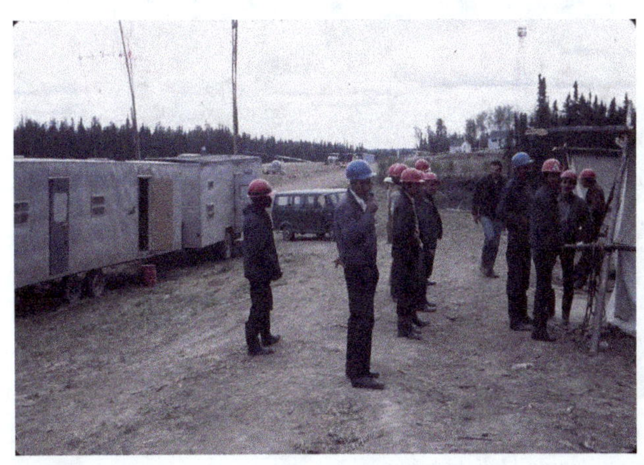

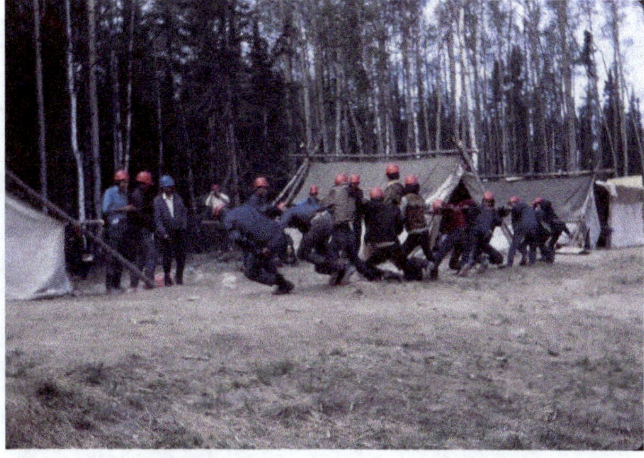

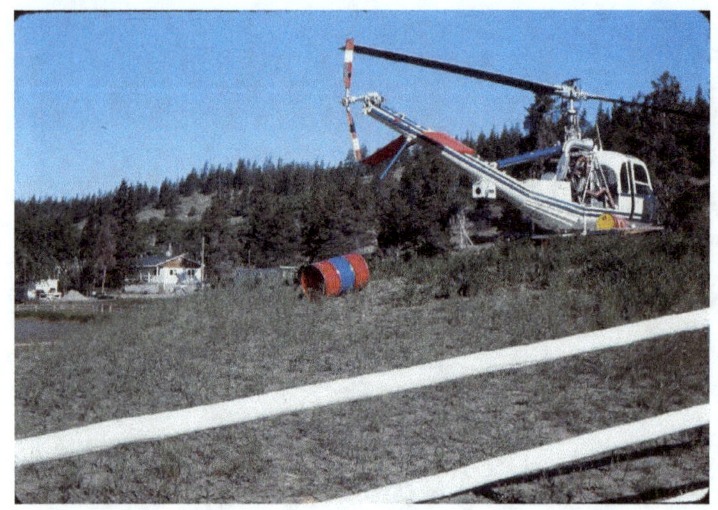

We were then called in by Alberta Forestry to the northern part of the province. The fires were scattered, so we covered the area, moving firefighters and equipment. A near miss happened at one location with a water bomber. I had just dropped some men near a fire and was lifting off vertically out of a confined area. I glanced backwards just in time to stop my ascent as a CL-215 water bomber was on final for a drop. He had not made the standard radio call which resulted in a very near miss.

This was to continue to be an eventful day. On the way back to the forestry strip for refuelling, I suddenly lost hydraulics. This aircraft, without hydraulics, is very heavy on the controls. It's sort of like losing power steering on your car. It's almost impossible to hover and requires a run-on landing with some forward speed. So I set up the approach and had a successful landing in the middle of the strip. The fire boss was upset that I was tying up the strip for other aircraft until I explained my emergency. So my engineer replaced the failed hydraulic pump, and I was on my way again.

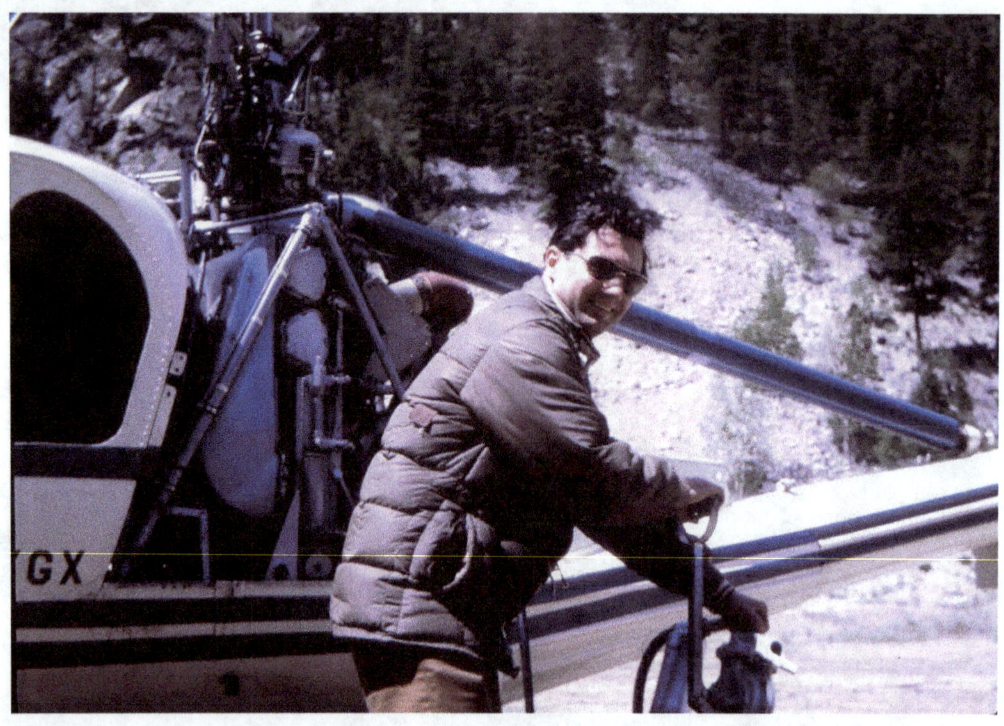

Returning to Pitt Meadows base -Haida Helicopters

This time we were called by BC Forestry

to reposition to Alexis Creek just west of Williams Lake. We refuelled at Williams Lake and took off for the one- hour flight to this small town. I made the standard call to Forestry in Alexis Creek, advising them of my arrival time. It was very hot, and my engineer was very relaxed, sitting in the rear seat with his feet out the window. He was reminiscing about his latest parties and adventures, which had some very colourful parts. When I arrived at the helipad, one of the Rangers was there waiting for me. He advised me that right at the end of my call-in, the frequency was jammed by my stuck transmission switch. This stopped all internal transmissions for the hour. What a way to start a job with a new customer!

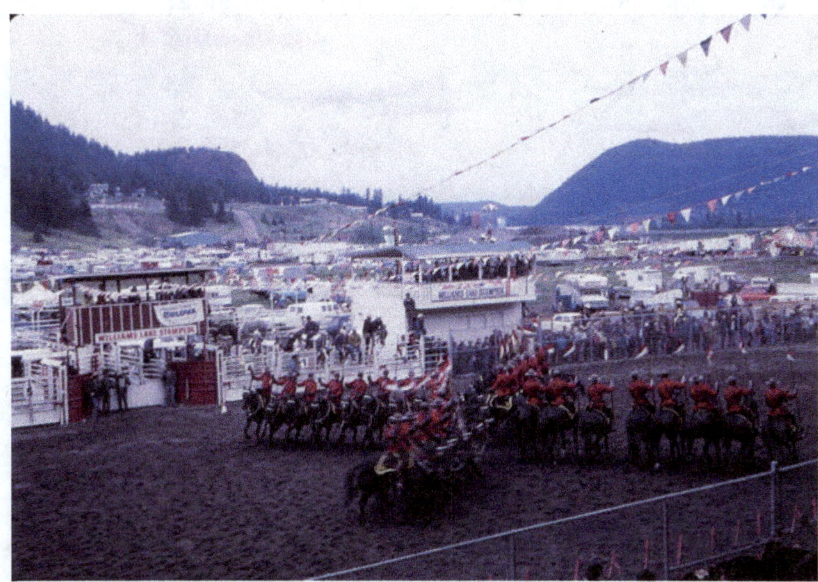

RCMP - Musical ride-Williams Lake BC

They signed a short contract to have an aircraft standing by for fires with some area patrol daily. It's a small Chilcotin town in ranching country with a population of 2,000 people. There's a small detachment with only a few RCMP members stationed there. I got to know one of the constables very well. Over coffee one day, he expressed that he'd never been in a helicopter and was fascinated by them. I asked him if he wanted to go for a ride if I had a break between fires. Of course, he was excited at the prospect and promised to take me fishing as well. The thing I found interesting was that for the days leading up to that flight, his wife was extremely nervous about this. I said, "But your husband faces real- life dangerous situations on a regular basis. She said, but that's different. I understand his job, but flying in a helicopter scares me." I tried to assure her that, statistically, flying was so much safer than driving the family car (or a patrol car in this instance!). This didn't reassure her that much, and she admitted to feeling quite relieved when her husband was back on the ground after the flight. He absolutely loved the flight but still owes me a fishing trip!

I'd like to add an interesting story about one of our other crews roaming around the Yukon on fires. They had a medium-lift helicopter, a Sikorsky S-58T, with a lifting capacity of 5,000 lbs. It was well suited for bucketing fires and placing fire crews. They came upon an old abandoned town that came about during the gold rush days. They landed and poked around in one of the old cabins. They found a trapdoor on the floor and pried it open. Inside was a box with a gold scale in perfect condition. It had a little drawer in its base with a list of the current gold prices for 1849.

They wandered around a bit more and came upon an old saloon. Inside was a full-size pool table made completely of marble! Apparently, it was transported from Europe by ship in the 1800s and ended up in this town. Of course, the cloth was rotted away, but the table was in perfect shape. So they spent half a day removing what was left of the old roof. Then they attached sling gear to the table and started lifting it out vertically. Suddenly one of the slings broke, and the table came crashing down! It broke into a thousand pieces and was destroyed. A table like that would have been priceless!

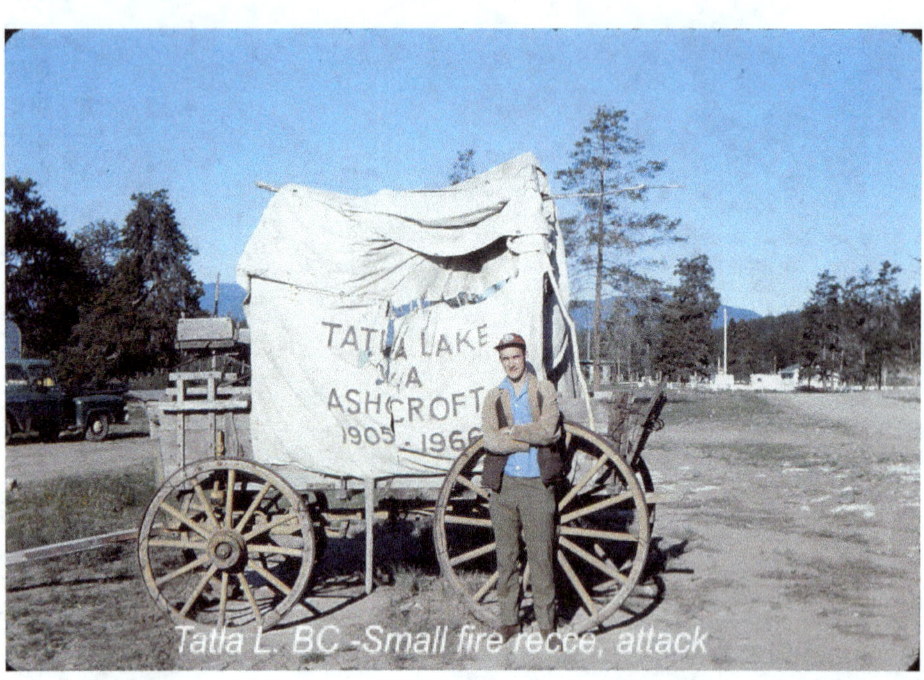

Tatla L. BC -Small fire recce, attack

The contract I was on in Alexis Creek was finished with forestry when I received a call from a BC communications company. They were building a tower further west in the Rockies near the top of a mountain. This mountain, fittingly called Mount Stupendous, is located in the central coastal range near Bella Coola with an elevation of 8763 feet. They needed a concrete base for the tower at the 7700-foot level. Crews had been flown up there and built the base forms. I was tasked with flying buckets of concrete up to their site. The cement buckets were full and heavy. Even with a turbocharger, I still had a piston engine, and this was the highest altitude I had ever worked with the Hiller. The climb up was slow, and I really needed a boost from the uplifting air. The second load up, I spotted a bald eagle just lazily circling around near the same mountain. They always favour the smooth uplifting side of a mountain and are valuable clues. So I continued the climb as I went over to the area of that eagle. I quickly gained clean, uplifting air, and it was like riding a freight elevator! Fully loaded, my rate of climb increased dramatically. Nearing the final trip, I was hovering over the forms expecting the load to be released by one of the ground crew. Suddenly there was a bit of a downdraft, causing a descent, and the bucket got wedged in the form. I used maximum power and wiggled back and forth. Finally, I freed the bucket, and the crew was able to hit the release handle. I love happy endings!

So this job was completed, and it just became a part of a continual stream of calls to take on the vast array of applications suited to helicopters. As a pool pilot, this made my job description very interesting as I never knew what was coming next or where I'd be going.

After fighting a resurgence of fires

in central BC for a month, the helicopter was due for a major inspection. This required us to return to home base in Pitt Meadows. So that day, the engineer and I took off for the Lower Mainland, which turned out to be a very unusual flight. We left Williams Lake for Pitt Meadows via Lillooet and Gold Bridge. Passing Lillooet, we were on course and on our scheduled flight plan. As we proceeded, my engineer commented about a major railroad that used to be in that area. We assumed it must have been lifted and rerouted. This was before GPS days, and as I studied the map, things were not making sense. Also, we were climbing into higher terrain instead of descending. As we were getting right into the glaciers, I knew we were definitely lost, turned around and studied the map. I pinpointed our position, and by this time, fuel had become a consideration. I had slowly been diverging off course and missed the southbound turn to Pitt Meadows. This proved to be a valuable lesson for the future, that being, don't park the maps until you are certain you're on the right track! Besides our remaining fuel being a consideration, it was also getting dark. Now knowing exactly where we were, I landed in the valley below.

Early the next morning, we decided to get as close to a road and civilization as we could, leaving a 10-minute fuel reserve. I told my engineer we would land when the predetermined time was up on our useable fuel. Just as the remaining fuel time was up and I was looking for a place to land, we came up on a forestry station west of Lillooet. I was on final for the forestry helipad when the hydraulics quit. Luckily they came on again just in time because there was no room for a run-on landing. Consequently, I was able to hover and land normally on their pad. Fortunately, they had aviation fuel on their base, so it didn't need to be trucked in. We were able to notify search and rescue before they were about to initiate a search on our overdue ETA. There were a lot of relieved people when we landed at Pitt Meadows after not showing up the day before at the airport.

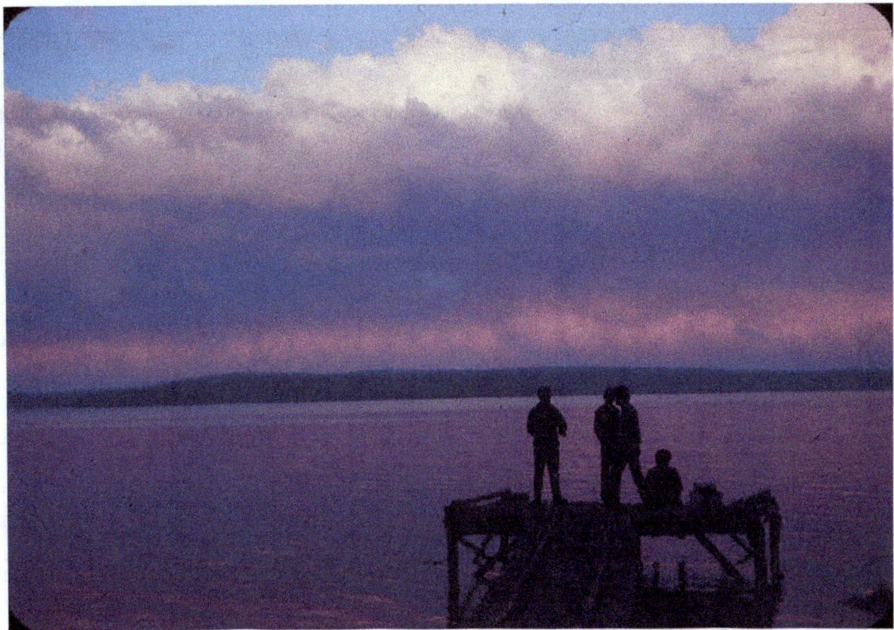

L. Wescapis 100 km north of Matagami PQ

In the early '70s, a large hydroelectric

project kicked off in northern Quebec. This was an ambitious multi-billion dollar endeavour to harness the power of major rivers in the James Bay area. There would be a number of large dams built to generate power for large parts of Quebec, Ontario and the state of New York. This would be a windfall of new work for many companies, not the least being aviation. Fixed-wing and helicopter companies increased their fleets in preparation. The company I flew for, Haida Helicopters, would be in the black after many years of running deficits.The flying hours per aircraft accumulated annually were unprecedented.

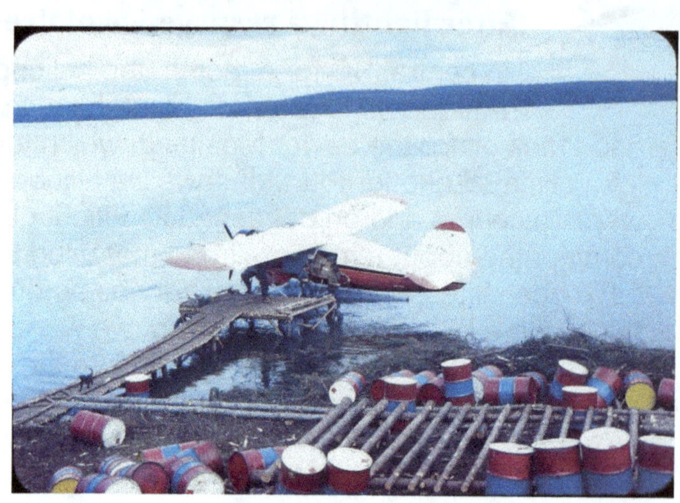

Jet fuel delivery for the 2 helicopters

I was quite excited to leave the world of small piston helicopters and graduate into turbines. These were much faster aircraft and sometimes referred to as jets, e.g. the Bell Jetranger. I received a call from our company operations manager to hop a commercial flight to Montreal and then Matagami up in northern Quebec. He would check me out on an Alouette II, a French aircraft made by Aerospatiale. This is a 5-place turbine helicopter with cruising speeds of approximately 120 mph. Finally, breaking the 100 mph barrier was an exciting step for me; I was used to cruising at only 80 mph in the average piston machine. The checkout was a bit unusual in that the ops manager did it without dual controls. It was only one hour of dual instruction, and he turned me loose on the job.

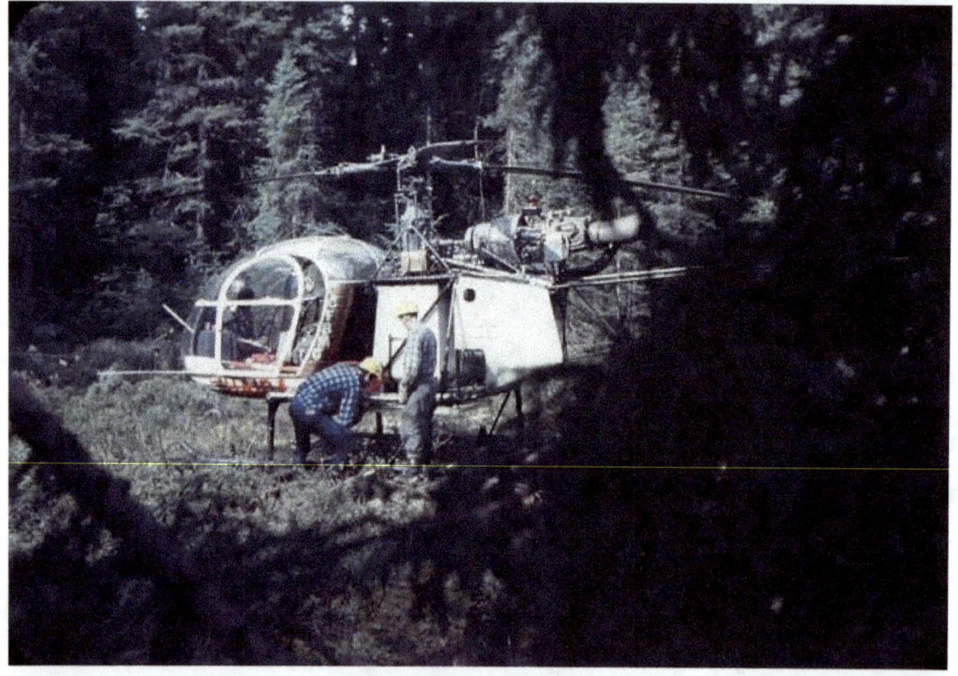

Dropping off lumberjacks with the Alouette II

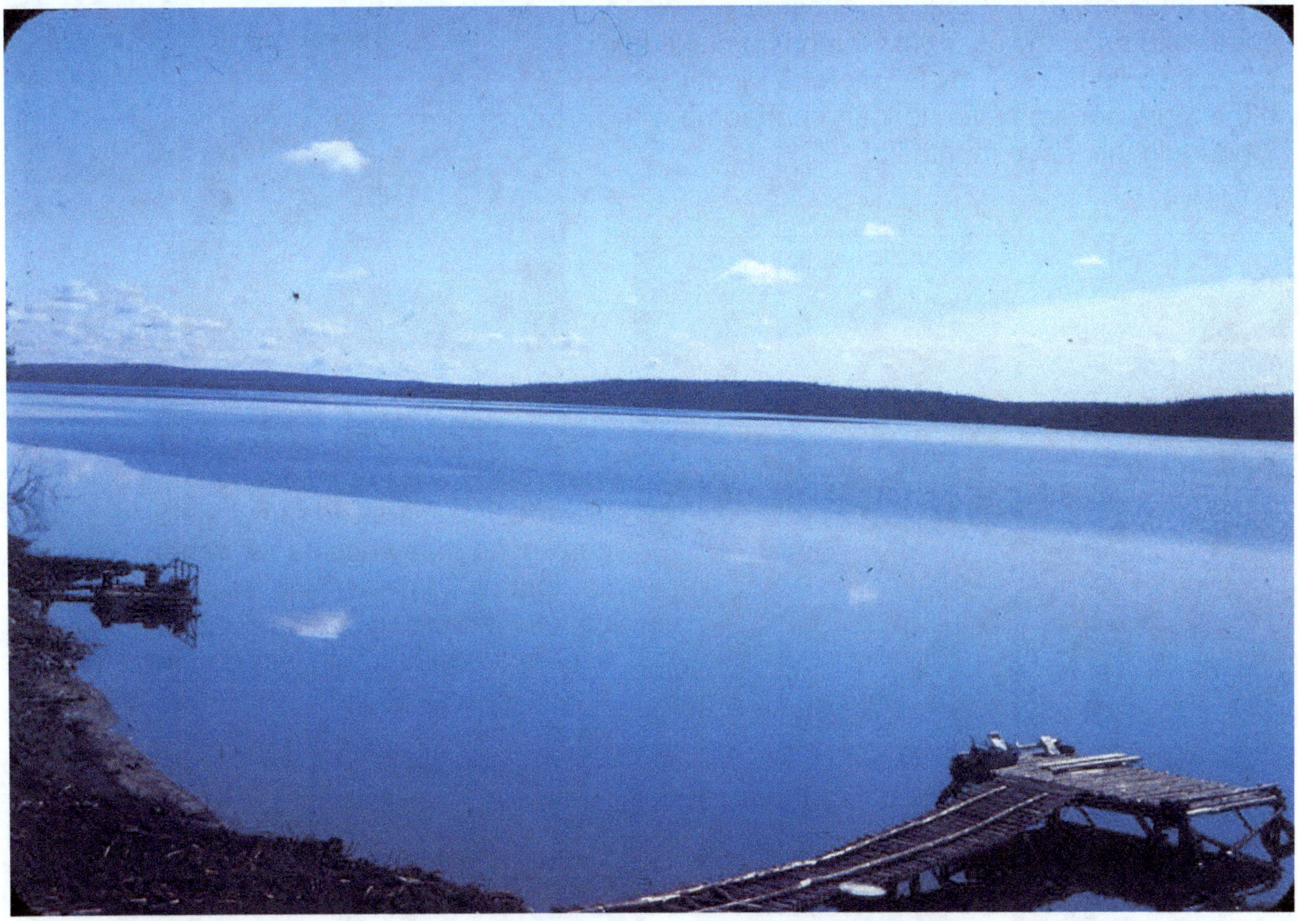

Lake Wescapis - Camp #5 comes with my tent and fantastic pike

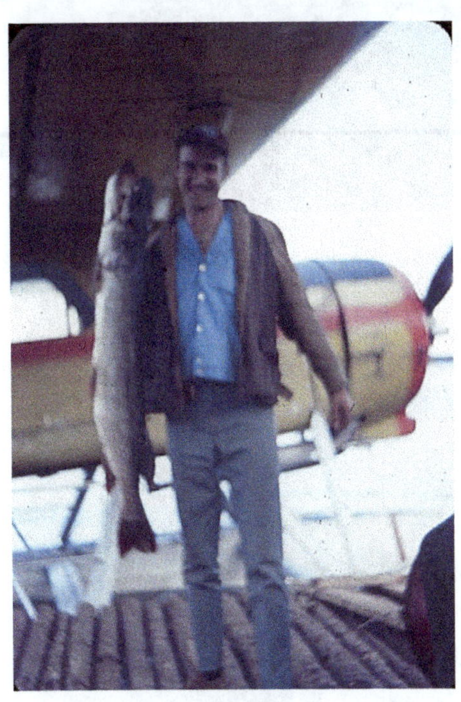

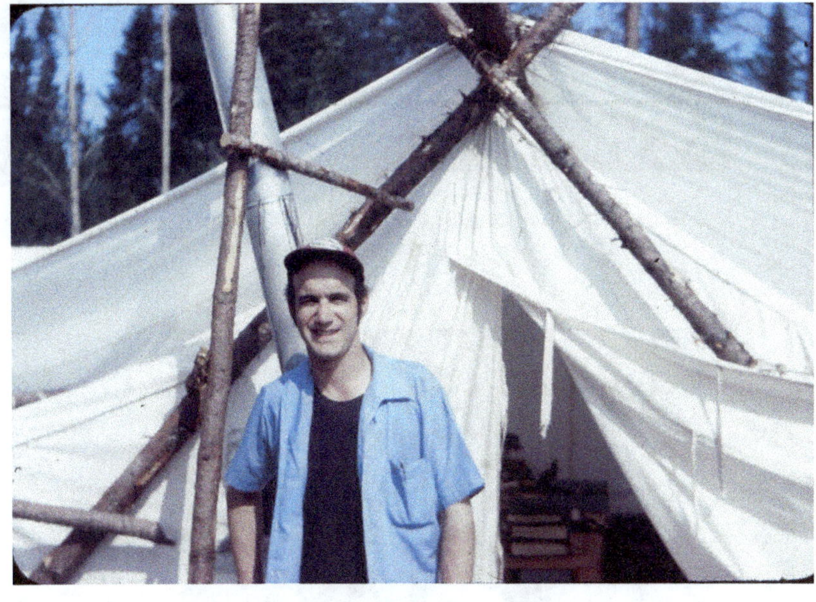

This was the beginning of extensive flying and logging, an average of 7 to 8 hours per day. It was intense, with as many as 50 or 60 landings/take offs per day. I would not see my family for 3 months, and the tours became even longer. I ended up with 477 hours in the last 6 months of 1971.

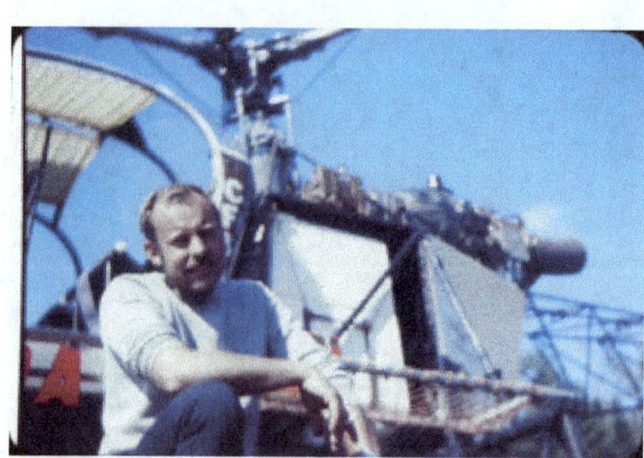

R Peltier - Engineer

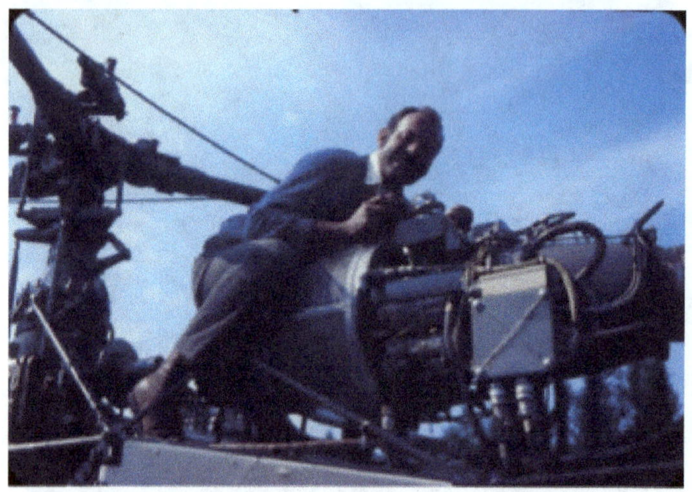

Turbine inspection

I wanted turbine time, and I got it! Back then, there were no restrictions on days worked in succession or flying hours. I am convinced many accidents were caused by straight pilot fatigue. You had to really fight complacency and cutting corners. I was very fortunate in that I was accident-free for my entire career of 44 years, but some of my colleagues were not as fortunate.

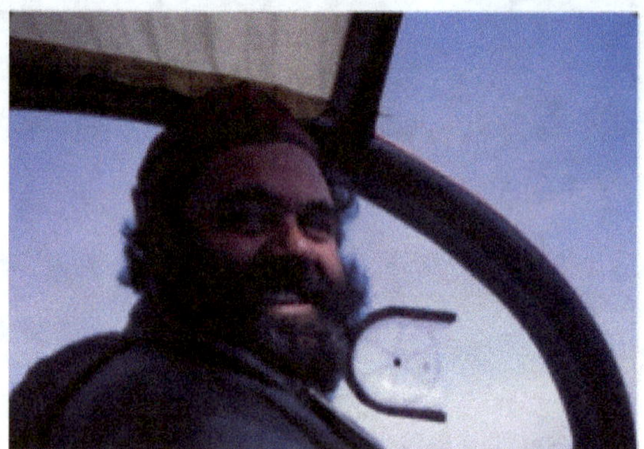

Built helipad on line for pickl practise bucketing at D. Lieb's lake near Williams Lakeup back to camp

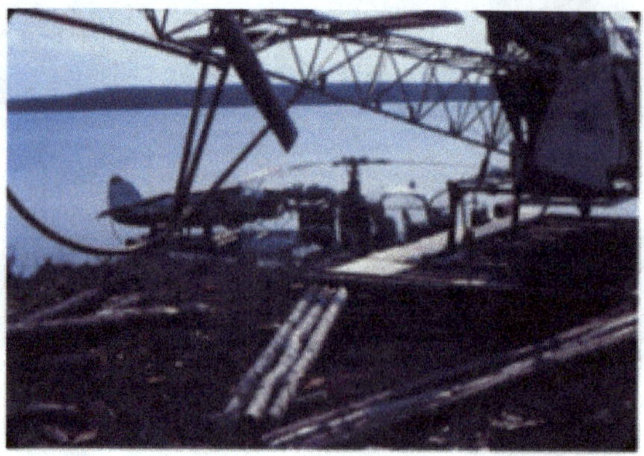

Helicopter pads overlooking the lake & seaplane dock

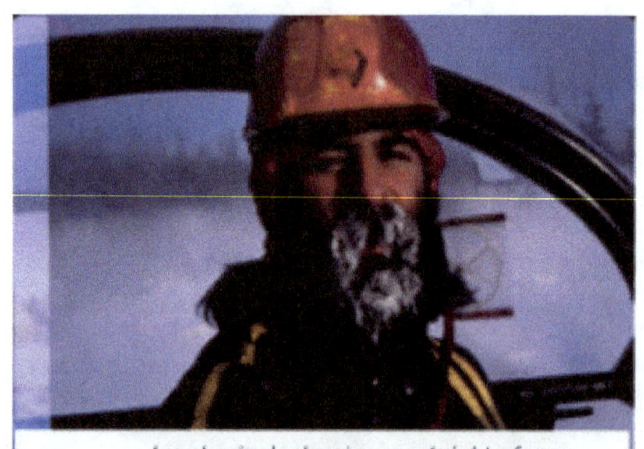

Lumberjack clearing road right-of-way

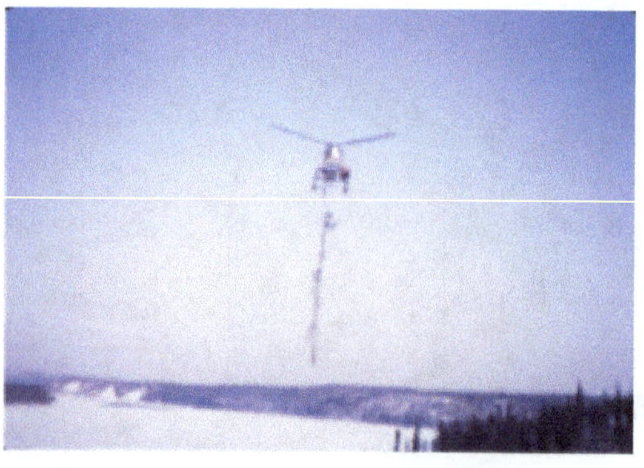

Slinging firewood for camp stoves

Flying on the James Bay

project gave me a tremendous amount of new experience. So the initial flying was to establish tent camps and fly men out from them to start cutting lines. These slash lines would eventually be turned into highways and transmission right of ways all the way to James Bay. These roads were generally established near picturesque rivers and lakes. We usually had great camp cooks and excellent food. There were good caretakers who kept the camp organized and the half-canvas, half-plywood tents clean. In the wintertime, they kept the pot-bellied stoves stoked with wood keeping the tents warm even at 30 below. Usually, there were anywhere from one to six helicopters based at each camp. We all felt we were pioneering a new area of Canada and helping to make a giant project possible.

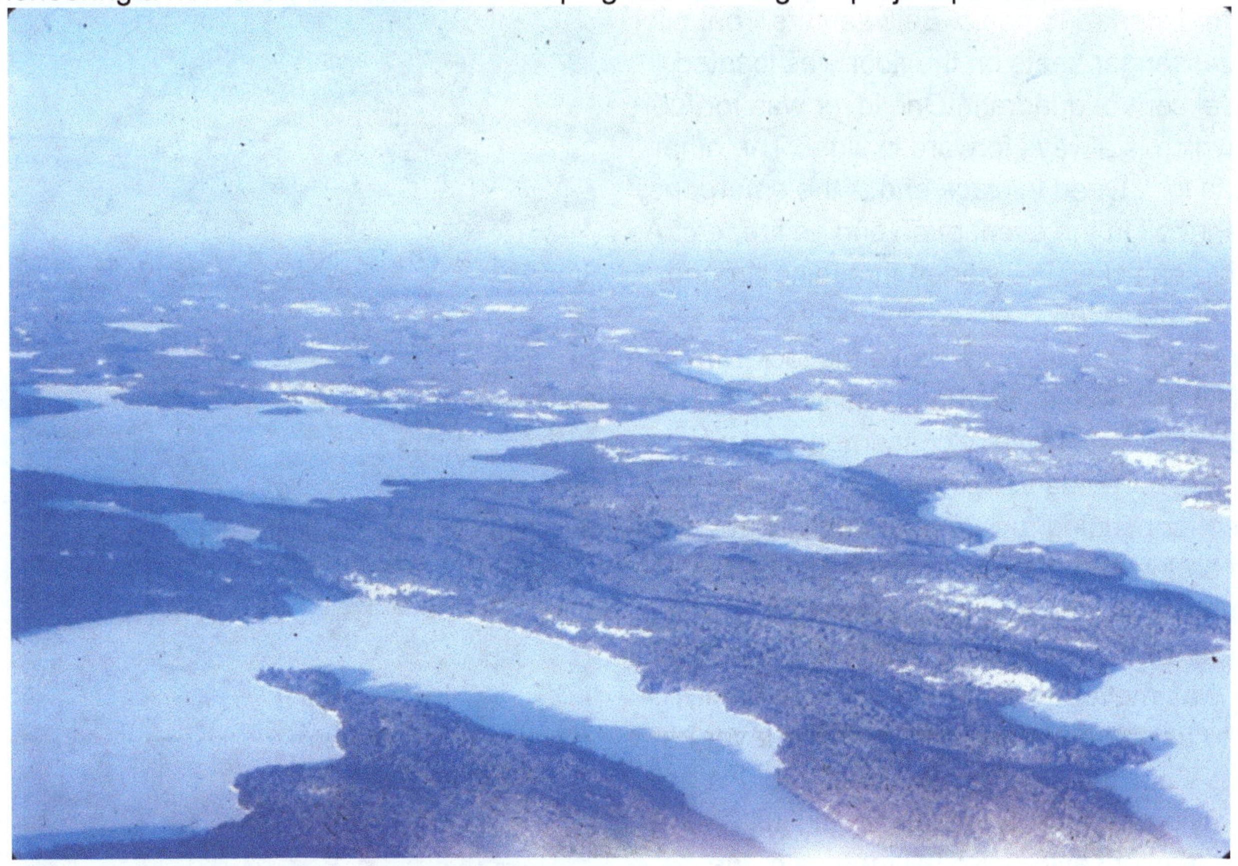

James Bay area

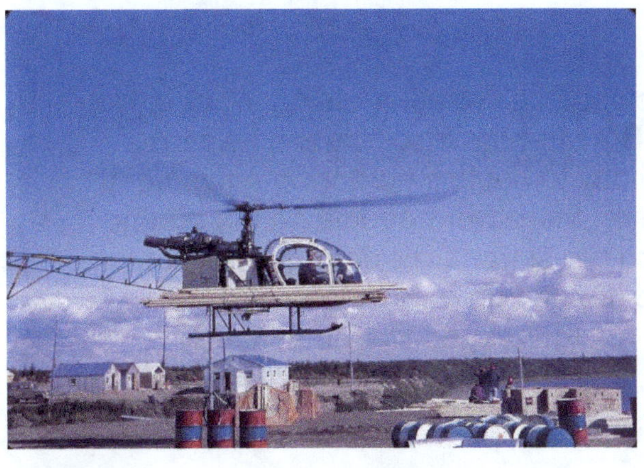

We moved a lot of men and equipment around each day as the development progressed further north. Every once in a while, there would be an event worth mentioning that was out of the ordinary. There was no radio contact with the men we flew out every day cutting line. They'd usually be within 20 to 30 miles, so twice a day, I'd fly out to check on them. There could have been a falling tree, a chain saw or some other accident that happened.

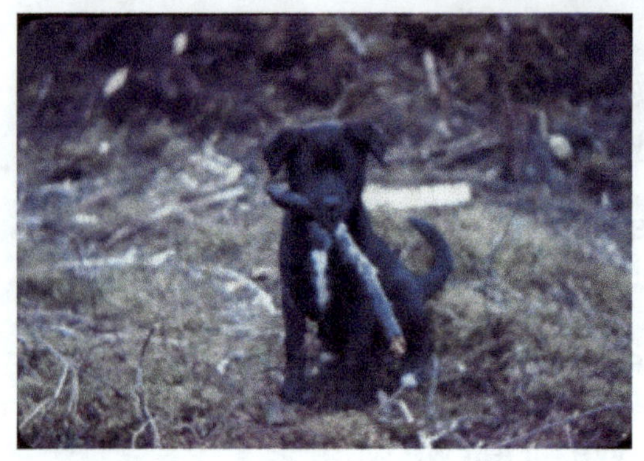

The local natives had a lot of dogs, and they would give us one as a kind of mascot while in their area. I was given a beautiful black Labrador Retriever. I would take him along whenever I was alone. He loved to fly, and as soon as the helicopter started, he would come running. I was only a few miles out of camp on a line check, and the dog seemed to be restless. Normally he just sat quietly in the back seat looking out the window, but all of a sudden, he was trying to come up to the front seat. This was a fairly large dog, and he got stuck under that seat and started to panic. Between the front pilot and passenger seats on the floor was located the fuel control quadrant. One lever was for fuel flow which is always forward in flight. The other lever is lock wired in place and is the emergency fuel shut off in the event of an engine fire, etc. As the dog panicked, he started thrashing around, and one of his legs hooked around the emergency shut off lever, broke the lock wire and actually moved the lever out of its slot. So, needless to say, I'm very concerned as I'm leaning over trying to free the dog and, of course, continuing to fly the aircraft with my right hand on the cyclic. I was over the solid forest and unable to land and especially in an emergency if the engine quit. The fuel shut off lever was moved even further as I was finally able to extricate the dog and push the lever back into its slot. Needless to say, that dog didn't get to go flying with me anymore! I could just hear the chief pilot saying, "So tell me again, the helicopter crashed because of a-what...?!"

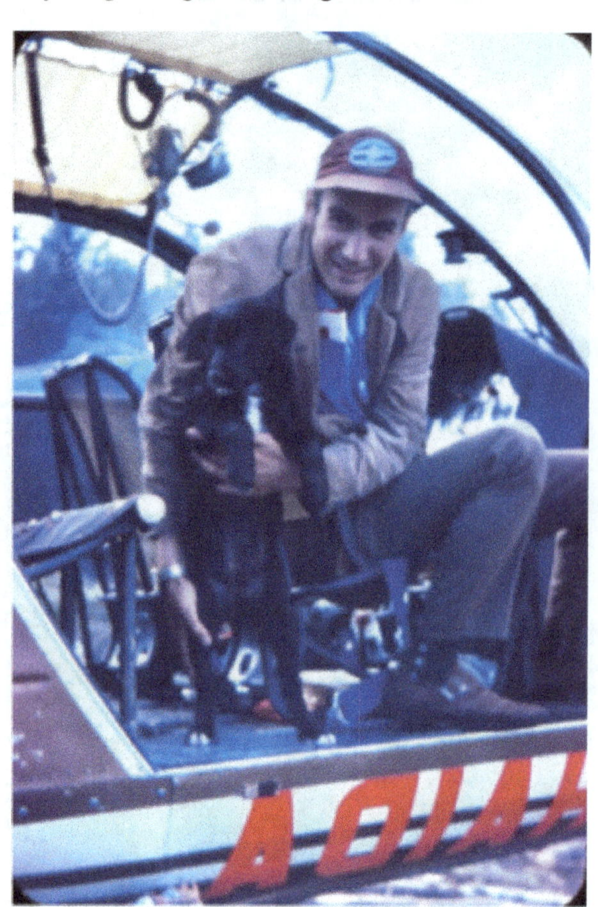

My lab BimGee - loved flying

I actually had another interesting incident with a dog. At another camp that winter, I became really close to a beautiful 'Heinz 57' dog. He was extremely loyal and followed me everywhere. But after the last incident, I wasn't going to have this dog flying with me. I took off one day to haul some drilling equipment. As I circled back over the camp to proceed on course, there were people on the ground waving frantically. I looked back at my cargo rack on the starboard side of the helicopter, and there was the dog happily riding along. He had hopped up onto the rack just as I was lifting off. I was afraid he might jump or fall off, but I managed to land as eager hands took him off safely.

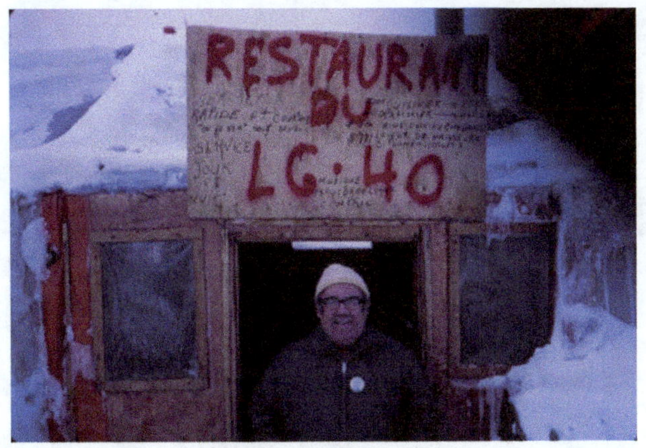

LG-40 tent camp

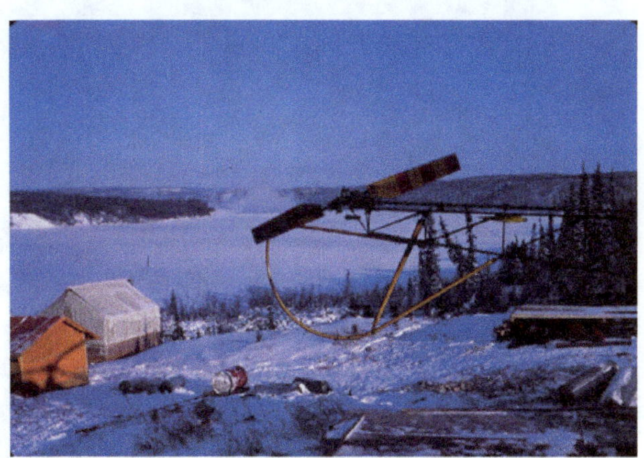
Cook shack at our camp on La Grande River PQ

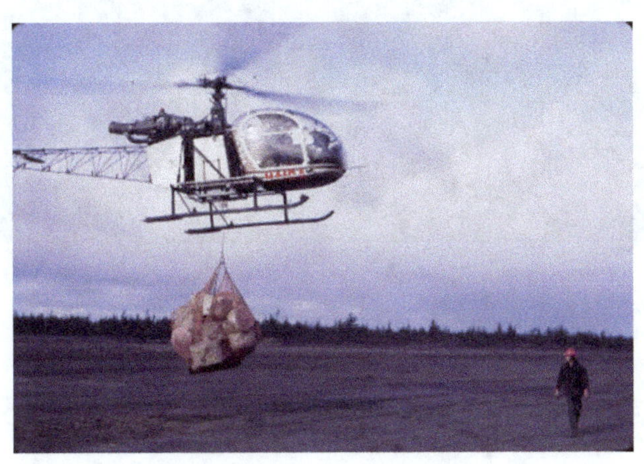
Camp supplies

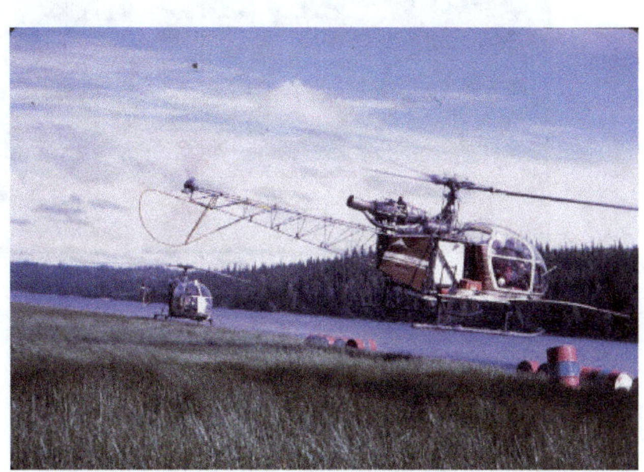
Fuel stop

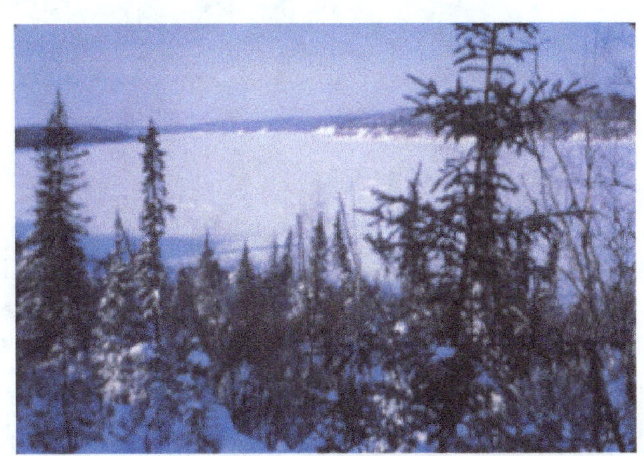
LG-40 - new day

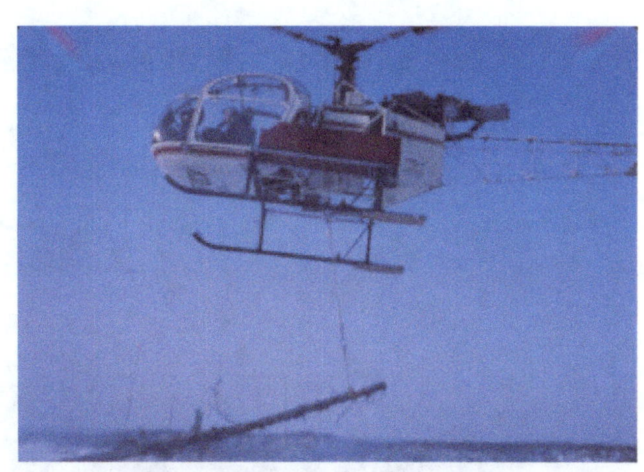
Slinging trees needed at camp for firewood

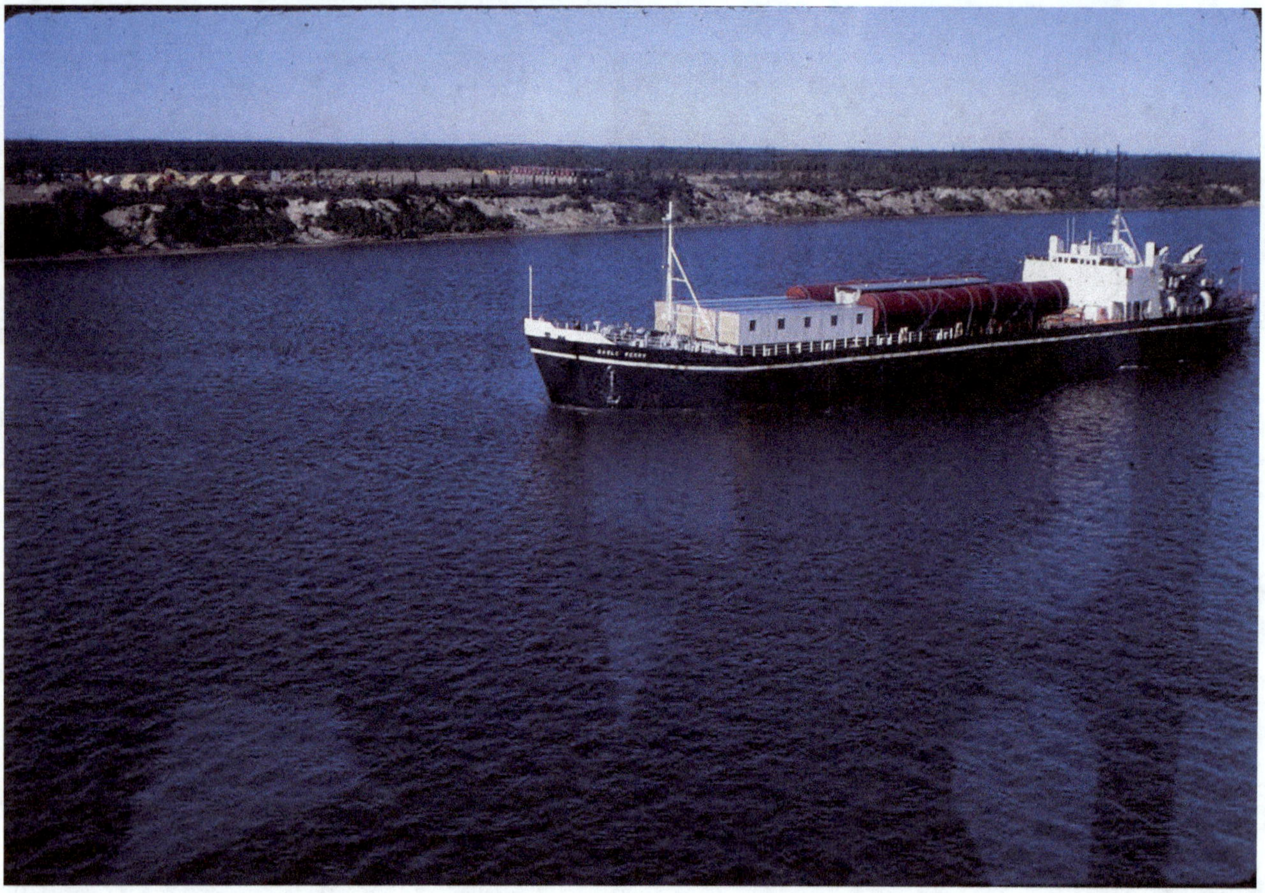

Cargo ship coming into Fort George

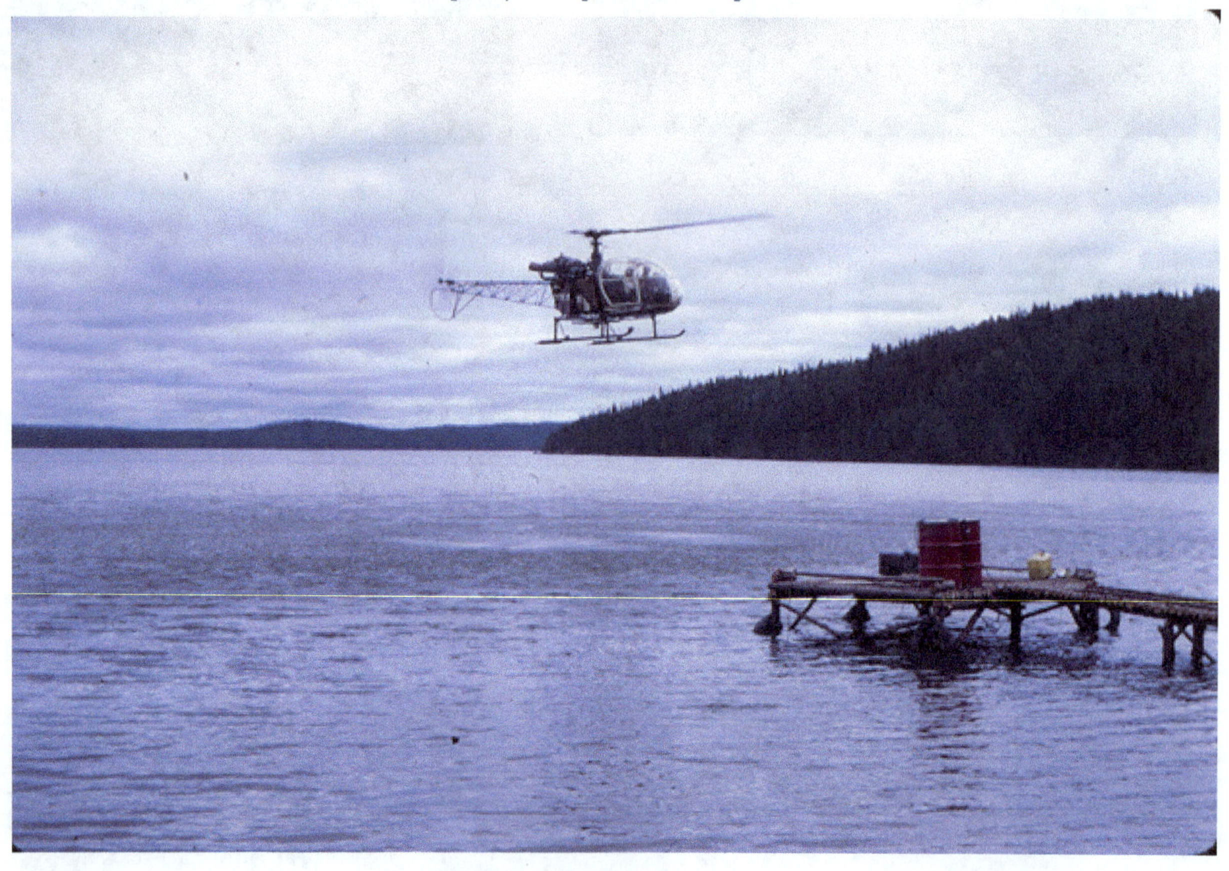

Towards the end of December 1971,

one of our helicopters was needed back at Pitt Meadows. I volunteered for the ferry flight to get off the beaten track and see some new countryside. Also, it was Christmas and time to go home and celebrate with the family. I was tired after all the intense flying and welcomed some time off. The engineer and I got an early start and got as far as Kenora that evening. We did a quick flight around town, checking for motels. We spotted a great looking 30 story, round hotel right in the centre of town on the bank of Kenora Bay. It had a large parking lot, perfect for landing right beside the hotel. It was a beautiful new hotel, and we had rooms on the tenth floor overlooking the lake.The next morning we checked out, and as we reached the parking lot, we were met with cars totally surrounding the helicopter! We were parked next to 4-foot retaining walls on 2 sides, but there were cars on our port side and fairly close to the tail rotor. However, it had gone down to minus 30 degrees C. during the night, and we needed heat. Not required for a turbine engine but for the transmission and tail rotor gearbox. We rented one from an operator at the nearby airport who brought it over. After an hour of heat, it was sufficient to thaw things out and start the helicopter. We were loaded and ready for take off, but there was a very strong crosswind. I had to lift off very carefully because of the concrete retaining walls on 2 sides and the proximity of the cars to the tail rotor.

That night we landed at my parent's farm en route to Vancouver. I was relieved by one of our company pilots in Calgary, and I had a quick return to my home in Pitt Meadows via Air Canada. So after a great Christmas and time with the family, I was back up to northern Quebec in the dead of winter. The camps had moved further east from James Bay. There was visible construction on the first large dam harnessing the La Grande River. There were 6 helicopters and landing pads in my camp on the banks of this major river. Some days we'd all be flying various directions for various jobs. Everything from drill moves, staging line lumberjacks, terrain reconnaissance for onward developments, grocery runs to supply thousands of personnel, etc. Because the contractors on this massive project worked on a cost-plus basis, some of the helicopters were really misused. I remember one day, a camp boss had me fly 120 miles away to pick up a carton of cigarettes for him. Even back then, a helicopter went for $600hour. So that carton of cigarettes costs over a thousand dollars. I guess smoking is expensive!

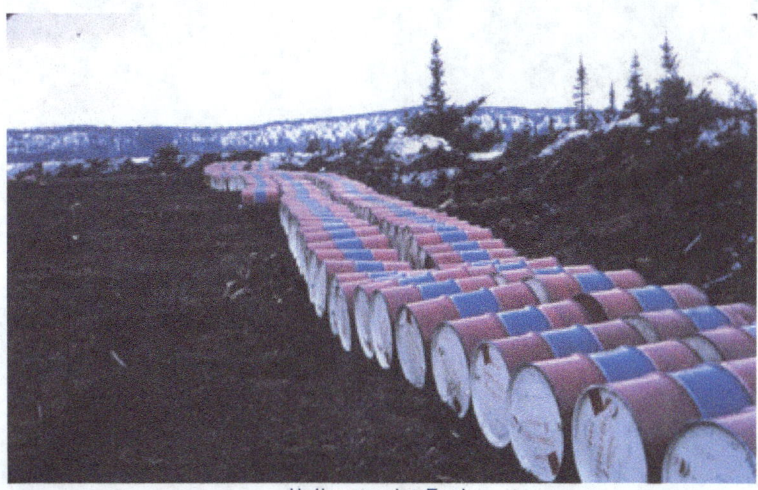

Helicopter Jet Fuel

Occasionally there would

be a requirement for only one helicopter on a particular day. Then that duty pilot would first fly the rest of us out to a nearby trout lake before his scheduled flying. There was an interesting but typical lake in the James Bay Area. Most of the lakes were full of trophy fish because of their inaccessibility.

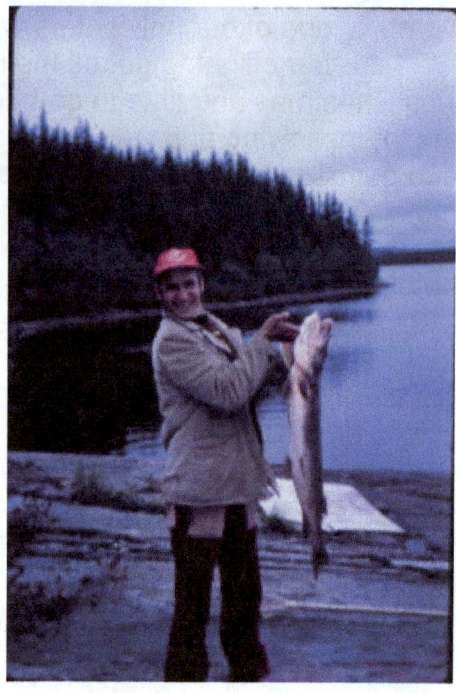
Abundant pike in virgin lakes

We had fished this tiny little lake in the summertime as well with great success. Casting from shore, it actually became a challenge to see if you could get your hook back without a fish! These beautiful rainbow trout were so delicious coming out of ice-cold water in the winter. Fried up in pan-fried butter was a nice change from camp food.

There was the odd day when I was free to relax, so I would take the helicopter in search of a good fishing lake. This was not a problem in James Bay since there was almost as much water as there was land. Most of the lakes in this remote part of Quebec were inaccessible since there were no roads. Perhaps the odd First Nations person had fished them if there was a village in the area, but generally, there was an abundance of fish. So when I had a helicopter on floats, I would randomly pick a lake and land in the middle of it. Sometimes, as I casted out, the wind would catch my line and wind it around the main rotor. It would be a bit of a trick to climb up and unwind it so I could take off again, but it had to be done. If the fishing was poor, I'd just take off and try a different lake till I found a good one.

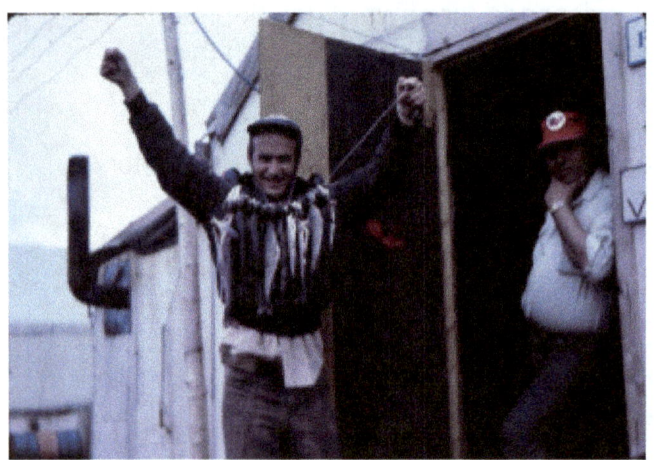
Fresh Rainbow trout for supper

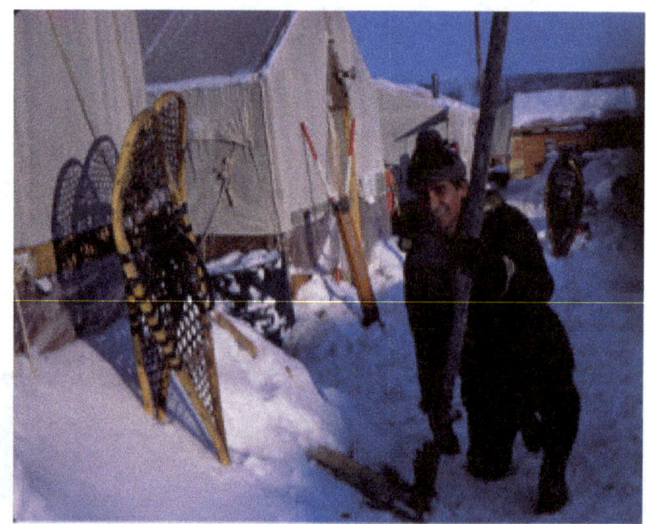
Cutting firewood for tent stoves

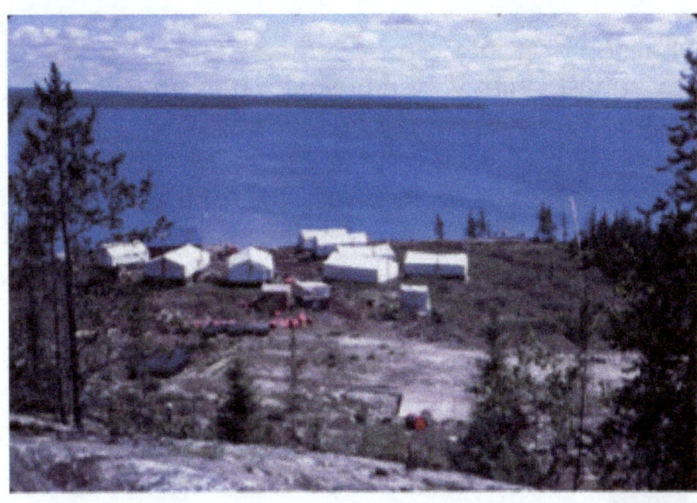

Camp #5 north of Matagami

One beautiful summer day, I was returning to camp, and there were sharply defined cumulus clouds at 3,000 ft. I was missing flying in the B.C. mountains, so for the fun and practice of it, I set up an approach to the top of one of the clouds. As I reached a hover over the 'landing spot,' I rolled the helicopter forward and dove out the bottom of the cloud. Years later, when I told my grandsons that I had landed on a cloud, I had to be very careful to explain that it was only a 'pretend' landing.

One day they needed a bunch of empty fuel drums moved to a pickup area near Fort George. I had dog number three in the back seat, but this time there was no worry about him interfering with the fuel quadrant. It was a slow flight because of the enormous drag on all those drums in a couple of cargo nets and unusually turbulent. Normally a helicopter can absorb a lot of turbulence in its rotor system but not this time. All of a sudden, I noticed a bunch of liquid moving to the front of the cockpit and covering the floor. Icouldn't believe my four- legged passenger had thrown up and was 'sicker than a dog'! When I returned to camp, I opened the door, and my engineer and I were contemplating how we would clean up this mess. It was 30 below outside, so this pool covering the cabin floor froze instantly. My engineer hit it with a bung wrench, and it all cracked up. We just threw it out like pieces of pizza, and the floor had never been so clean!

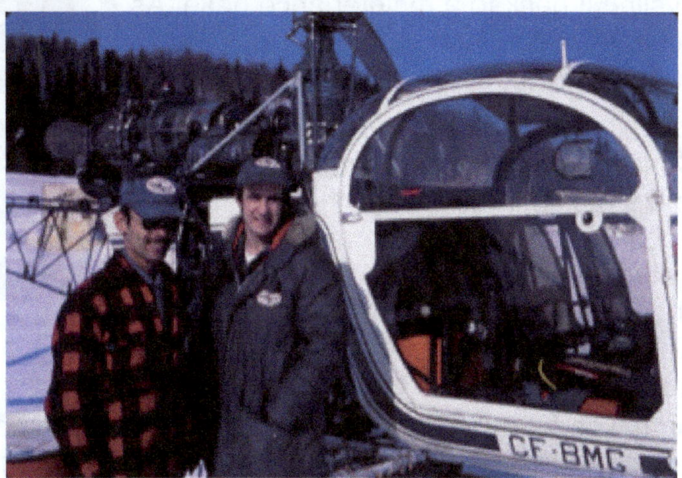

B Fidelity - engineer

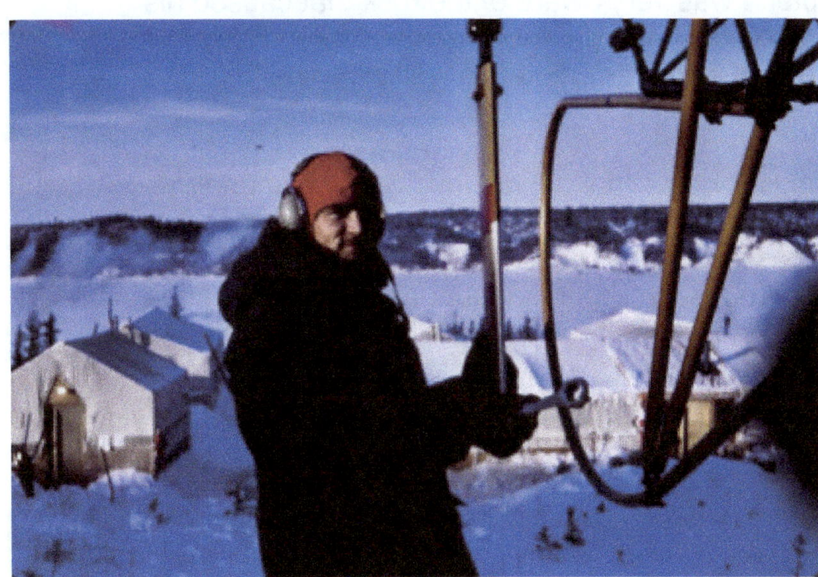

Daily tail rotor inspection by J Broadbent - engineer

As the year and the project progressed, the flying activity increased even more. There were additional helicopter and fixed- wing companies becoming involved.

One day Bow Helicopters sent one Alouette II helicopter from Calgary armed with a contract and a Japanese pilot. Kobayashi was a gentle, quiet young guy who had newly immigrated. Unfortunately, in a rush to get the aircraft on the job, they only gave him limited equipment, no Herman Nelson and no extra slinging gear. Out in such a remote area, we were not concerned about office politics or competition. We were operating under harsh conditions and crossed company colours to help each other. It was still 30 degrees below zero, so we loaned him a Herman Nelson and extra cargo nets when he had a big slinging job. Later on, after his accident, we were glad we had been helpful to him.

Later that summer, a small Cessna lost an engine and 'dead sticked' into a small river. The aircraft was intact, and Koby was sent to sling it back to a maintenance base. As he was picking it up vertically, he wasn't quite centred over the load.

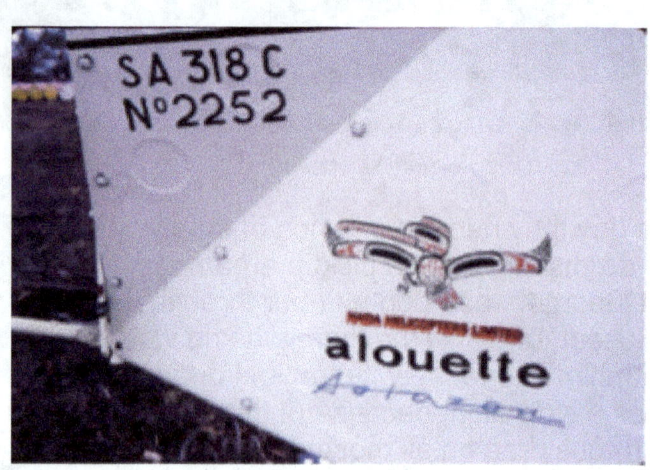

Haida Helicopters logo

Consequently, the load swung sideways and struck a large rock in the river, causing Kobi to lose control and crash into the water. Observers on shore were obviously shocked and about to dive in to rescue Koby from the submerged helicopter. Suddenly he popped to the surface but what was funny was he had the logbook in his hand! Fully submerged, he had the presence of mind to grab the aircraft document. Now that's dedication or, more likely, just a knee- jerk reaction.

So the next day, I slung out his helicopter. I was very aware of the rock that caused his crash as I lifted his helicopter clear. My company bought the wreck and hired Koby. That was another reason why we were glad we had treated him well when he first arrived. We were now all flying for the same company.

There were another couple of interesting incidents that did not involve my company. A pilot with the competition was bothering a moose one day. He was reportedly hovering over the swimming animal, bouncing his skids on the back of the terrified moose. Suddenly the moose got a solid footing on a submerged sandbar and reared his huge set of antlers. It caught the skids, and the helicopter crashed into the lake. The aircraft was a write off, and the pilot was fired! Justice!

Another pilot with the same company thought he'd pick up a little extra cash. Without the company's knowledge, he picked up a moose that had been illegally tracked and shot from the air. He slung it right into Matagami, and his picture was on the front page of the Montreal Gazette. Everything was illegal about his activities concerning the wild game. He, too, was fired!

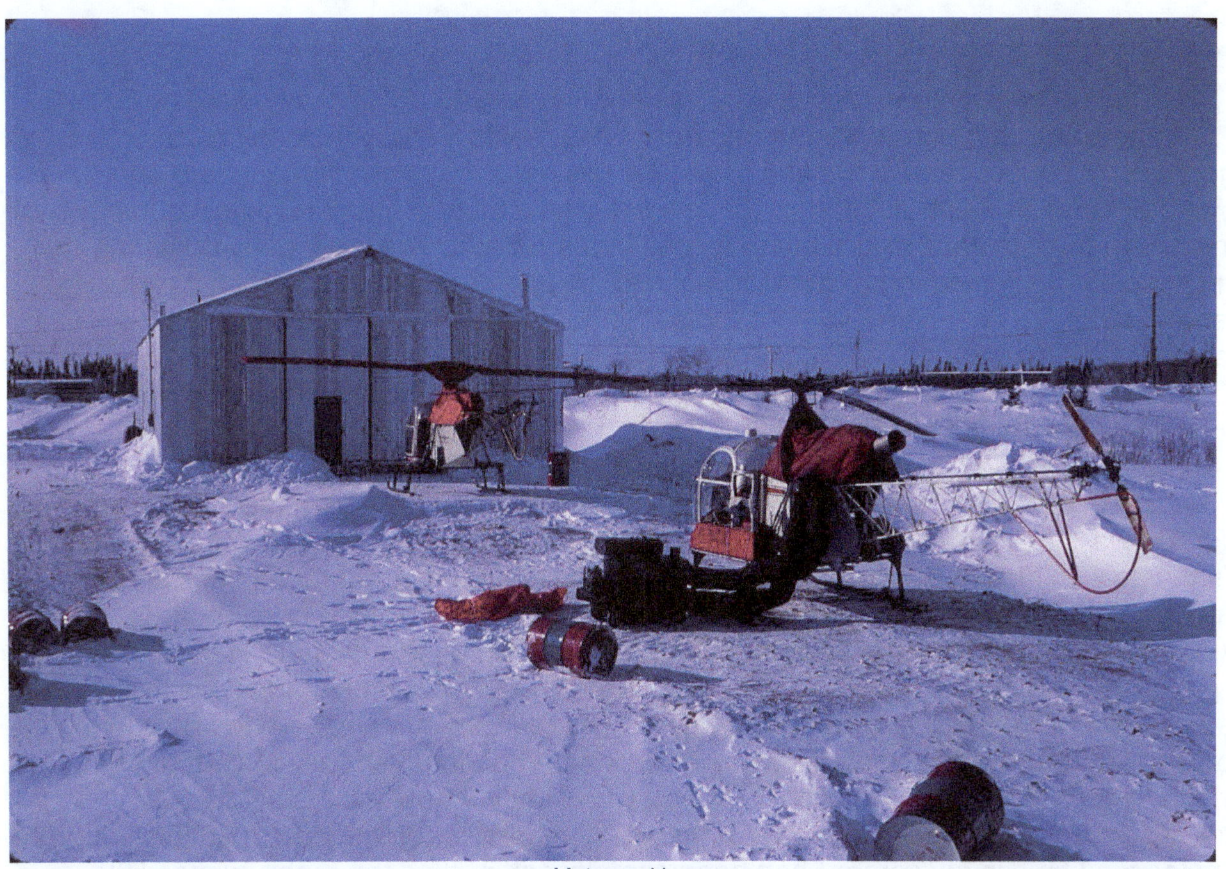
Matagami hangar

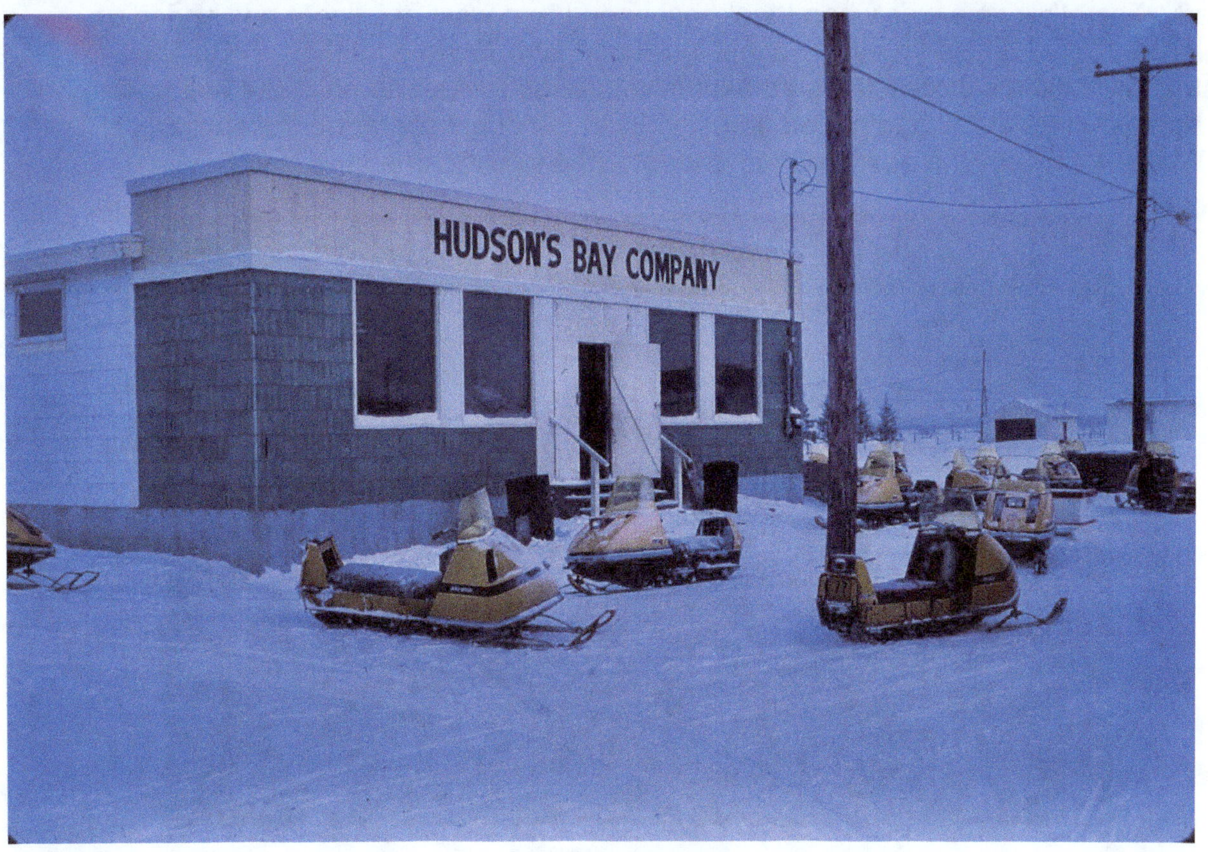

Fort George PQ

In the middle of the forest fire

season, my company received a call from Ontario Forestry. They were not familiar with Alouette II's but had heard they could lift heavy loads for their category and might be ideal for fighting fires. They asked if we might demonstrate one down at their base in Sault Ste. Marie. Since there was a bit of a break in my schedule in James Bay, my company asked me to fly down to the Sault. This sounded interesting and a chance to do something a little different. So my engineer and I loaded up a water bucket and other fire fighting equipment for the demo and took off for the Sault. As we flew over the last range of the Laurentians right on course, Sault Ste. Marie came into view. I stowed the map under the seat as the airport was straight ahead. I landed, and my engineer and I started off loading our gear. Just about then, a forestry official came over, and I said, "Hi, you must be the gentleman who ordered up the helicopter." He said, "No, it wasn't me, but when I need one, I generally get an American machine." He wandered away, looking a little puzzled. So, I'm thinking, well, he's pretty unpatriotic; what's wrong with him?! I'm looking around and notice quite a few American flags and aircraft. I'm starting to think it's some kind of holiday Canada is celebrating, honouring our American neighbours. Then a customs officer wandered over and said, "Hey, you boys probably want to clear customs?" I said, "Oh no, we're Canadians, and so is this aircraft." He started smiling and said, "Son, do you all realize you're in the good ol' U.S.of A. ?!" Embarrassed, I realized what I had done; I had inadvertently landed at an American airport! He said, still smiling, "Tell you what, I never saw you. Just take off, and you'll see Ontario Forestry's heliport right on the other side of the locks." So this was the second time in my career I had been complacent, putting the maps away a little too early. The other time was when I took that wrong turn west of Lillooet and ended up at a glacier. So we hopped over the canal locks and introduced ourselves to Ontario Forestry. The next day I gave them an extensive ground and air demo of the helicopter. They liked what they saw and ended up using this type of helicopter on their provincial fires. We took off early the next morning and returned to our camp in James Bay.

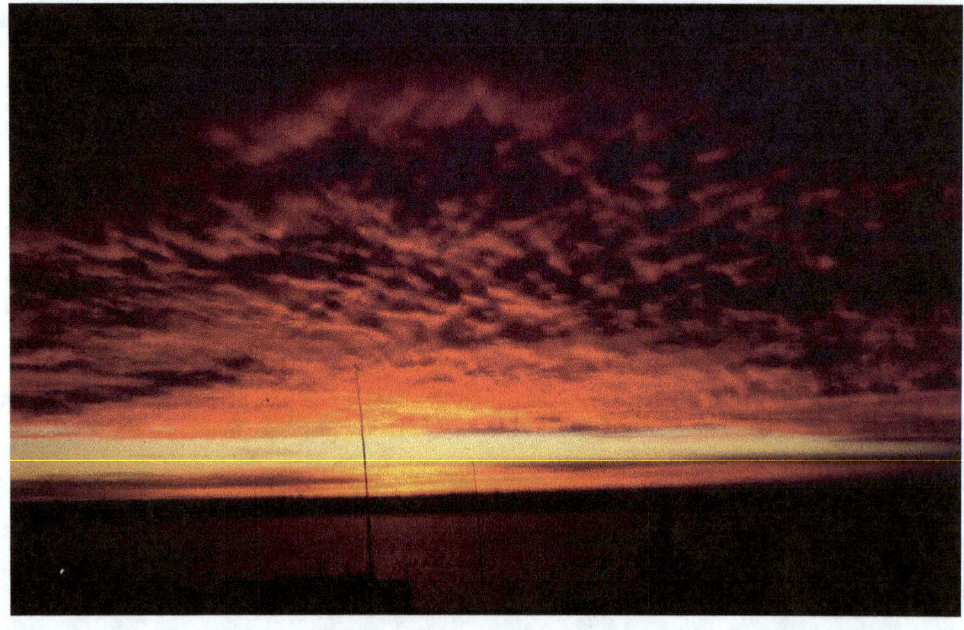

Sunset - Baie Comeau PQ

I resumed flying crews

out each morning to the respective lines they were cutting through the forest. I had just taken off with the last 5 man crew and was at a 1000-foot altitude crossing a section of our lake. One of the men said, "Oh no, there go my new gloves!" He had left them on the cargo rack, and they flew off into the lake. Just for the fun of it, when I got back to our camp, I started doing some mental calculations as to where the gloves might have ended up. I assumed the gloves would float or this would be a wasted exercise. So I was doing 120 mph when the gloves flipped off, and I was halfway between a peninsula and the far shoreline. When they dropped, I assumed they landed in the water behind me. The surface winds were 20 mph from the northwest. There was also a small river running into this part of the lake, causing an east-west current. So I added in all the vectors for likely drift direction. As I said, this was just a fun exercise with no great expectations.

When I picked the crew up that night, I told this guy to hop back in, and we'd go get his gloves. He said, "It's a waste of time; they're gone." He & I took off, and I pulled into a hover at the far side of the lake. I hovered along the shoreline about 20 feet, and there were his gloves bobbing up and down! I think I was as shocked as he was, but I kept a straight face. I think it was more luck than anything else, but obviously, the calculations didn't hurt. Needless to say, this lumberjack thought I was the greatest pilot in the world!

Towards the end of one day, there was quite a traumatic weather incident that bears mentioning. I was returning to our camp 30 miles away when the weather took an unexpected turn for the worse. I could see rolling black clouds approaching like a wall at a very high speed. There was no place to land, so it turned into a race to try to reach the camp before the storm hit me. I managed to reach a road running past our camp when it struck. The hurricane-force winds and turbulence were incredible, and visibility dropped to near zero. It was also full of sleet which quickly started covering my windscreen. For the last few miles, I was slowed up to about 40 knots. The only visibility I had was where the aircraft heater kept a small area clear between my feet.

As the camp came into view, my engineer was waiting beside my pad. He was relieved to see me, as was I to finally land. As the summer wore on, winter set in early, and soon it was December. The company again needed a helicopter back in Pitt Meadows for a local contract. So I again volunteered for the ferry flight. We had actually increased our helicopters on contract in James Bay to seven Alouettes and a Bell 205. The 205 was a 15-place medium-size helicopter which I hoped to be checked out on eventually. This had left our home base in BC very short of helicopters.

So my engineer and I took off

on a bright clear morning and headed west. Besides seeing a lot of scenery across Canada, it was always a perk to land at the farm and see my parents. On the final leg, I happened to fly right over the University of Saskatchewan in Saskatoon. I shuddered to think I almost became a dentist instead of what I was doing now! Then as I cleared the zone, I notified Saskatoon Tower I was on final for Dalmeny. It was a thrill for me to land in the playground of my old high school. My company didn't mind, so I ordered a couple of drums of aviation fuel to be delivered to the school grounds. It was a small token of appreciation on my management's part for all the weeks and months I'd worked in James Bay.

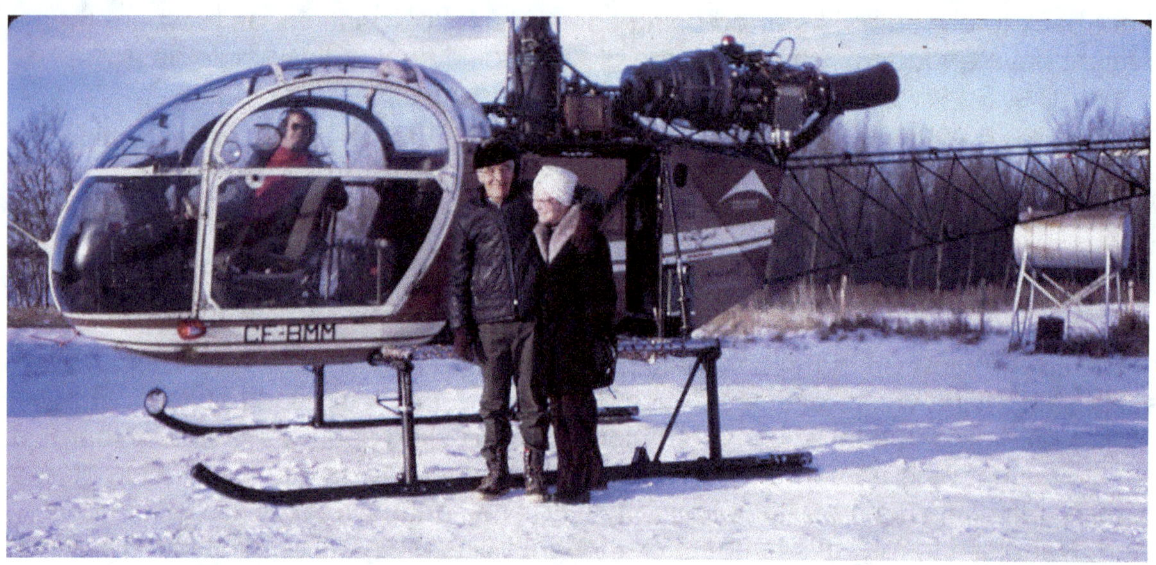

1972 Stop at Mom & Dad's farm - ferry flight from Quebec to Vancouver

So the next day, I gave rides to old classmates who happened to be around, including a senior classmate, R Schultz, who was the first one who arrives on a Skidoo. Then I landed at various neighbours' farms and other locations in the area. Some of the surprised people I took for short rides included S Doerkson, L Baerg, Uncle Ed and Aunt Bertha Buhr and our family garageman, A Fehr. When you're flying a helicopter daily, you take it somewhat for granted. You forget that people outside the industry still get quite excited to be able to go for a helicopter ride. Especially when the pilot turned out to be 'little Billy' from Mennon! Their excitement was, in turn, very fulfilling for me.

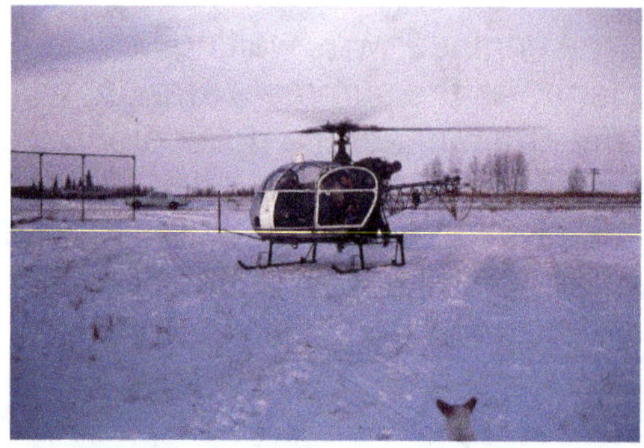

Landing at my old school in Dalmeny

In January of 1973

,there was an opening for a Hydro Quebec base pilot in Baie Comeau, Quebec. I was tired of being away from home for months at a time, so I thought this would be an excellent opportunity to take a base and be home with my family. We moved within 2 weeks and rented an apartment in Hauterive, a small village on the outskirts of Baie Comeau. I was fairly conversant in French, but my wife and little girl were not. So this was a challenge for them living in a mainly French-speaking town for shopping and daily activities. I came home one day, and Michelle, who was 2 1/2 years old at the time, was playing with a little French neighbour girl. I quickly picked up on some very picturesque language.

Michelle was using French swear words with a perfect accent. I said to my wife, "Did you hear what she just said?!" Connie said, "Not really; I thought it was just baby talk." I assured her it wasn't baby talk! It's interesting that kids learning a new language always pick up swear words first, not really knowing what they're saying.

Flying for Hydro was an interesting and very challenging time. Sometimes it was quite routine, flying line patrol inspection for hours at a time. These were the main lines going to Churchill Falls. It was a challenge to maintain a 50-knot ground speed at all times, whether up wind or downwind. You had to remain vigilant because you were right on the wires to enable a close inspection of the towers. One Hydro inspector sat in the front seat, and his partner in the back. Interestingly, these were the same lines that were constructed after I had originally flown the crews that cleared them years ago.

At times you had to fly maintenance or repair crews to the base of the towers. These were the very high voltage 750 KVA lines that sometimes ran in parallel. So again, you had to be in close proximity to the live wires because of the near separation from surrounding trees to the towers. Taking off, you only had about a hundred feet of clearance from your rotor blades to the parallel wires. One day after a big snowstorm, I was in a vertical descent from near the top of the tower to its base. As I got closer to the ground, the downwash from the helicopter caused the usual whiteout like the inside of a milk bottle. So to maintain visual reference, you could not lose sight of the tower structure. All of a sudden, one of the Hydro guys opened the door and was about to get out. He thought we were on the ground but were actually still 50 feet in the air! He just assumed I had landed on the soft powdery snow at the base.

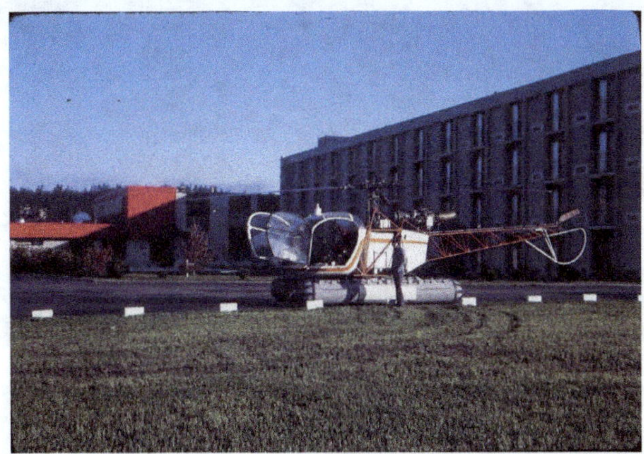

Return to Quebec for fuel

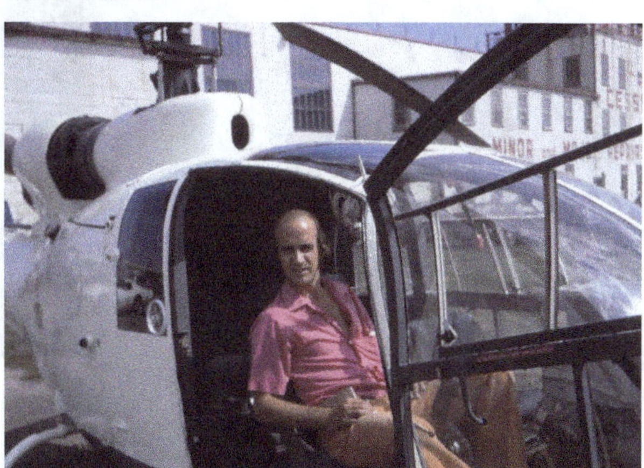

On spec in Quebec City

In late March, I got a call from Hydro

that there seemed to be some kind of problem on one of the main lines. As soon as it was light enough, we flew out of Baie Comeau about 50 miles to the trouble spot. There was a problem, all right; there had been a freak freezing rain storm through the night that collapsed 34 towers. The ice was so heavy it didn't just knock over these huge towers but collapsed them straight down. The wires themselves between the remaining towers in the area had a 2-inch circumference of clear ice. This was the worst freezing ice storm that had been seen in many years. They asked me to hover along the remaining lines to see if the rotor downwash would break the ice off, but it had no effect. So the collapsed towers were on a main section of the line that supplied power to large parts of Montreal and New York City. There was a real urgency to get them rebuilt and power restored. They brought in a total of 34 heavy lift helicopters plus a lot of men and equipment to get the line up and running in record time.

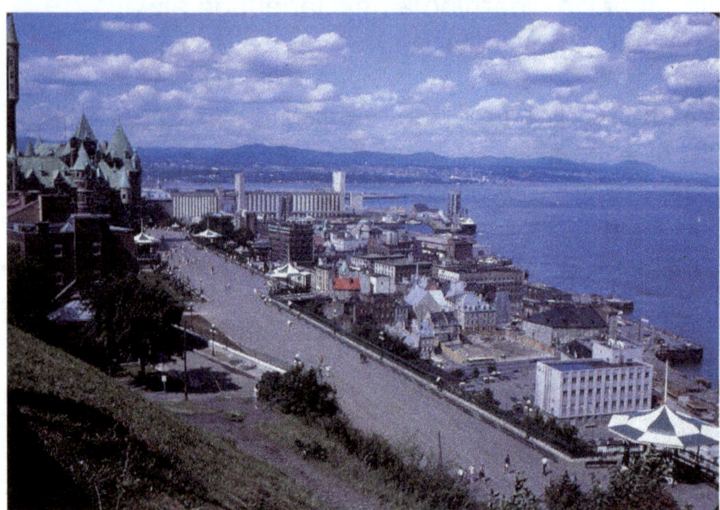

Old Quebec City Plains of Abraham

Later that year, Haida Helicopters bought a Quebec company called Lac Ste. Jean Aviation. This could have meant having to stay in Quebec permanently, so we decided to move back to Nanaimo, BC. My wife was very understanding about moving from one end of the country and back again within a 6 month period!

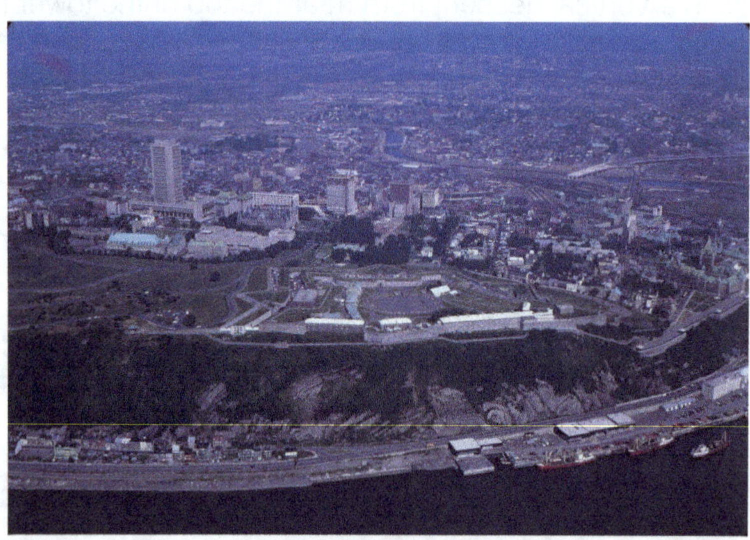

Quebec on the St. Lawrence

So I again became a pool pilot

out of Pitt Meadows and went straight back to Quebec for various jobs. We had a short contract out of Montreal to fly a river pollution job along the St. Lawrence River. They removed the skids and put the Alouette on float gear. This would enable me to land on the water with the river pollution crew to take water samples. They largely concentrated on the shipping lanes between Quebec and Montreal. We'd land every few miles on these lanes as well as the mouths of creeks flowing into the St. Lawrence. Sometimes the pollution was very severe coming from large factories on the banks. Apparently, the fines from Environment Canada were not very severe, and they just kept on polluting. Some of the freighters going along the river were massive. On one of the landings, I realized just how big they really were from close up. The hydrologist was out on the float getting a sample which took about 5 minutes. Since we were right in the middle of a shipping lane, I could see a large freighter approaching. I wanted to leave, and he said, "Just a little longer." Looking up at the bow and the wall of water he was pushing gave you a true perspective of their enormity. I was quite happy to get the signal and take off!

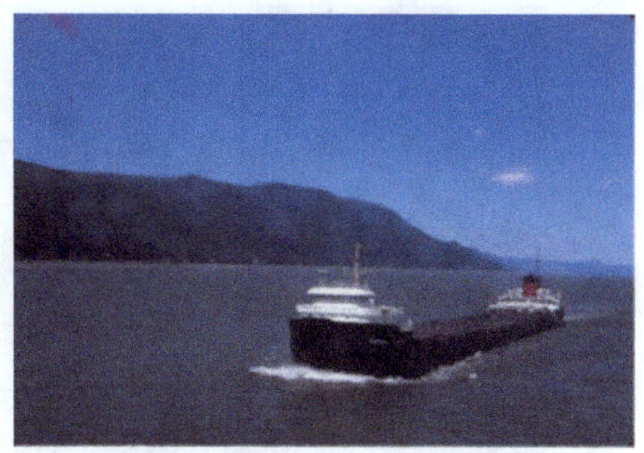

Landed on shipping lanes for samples

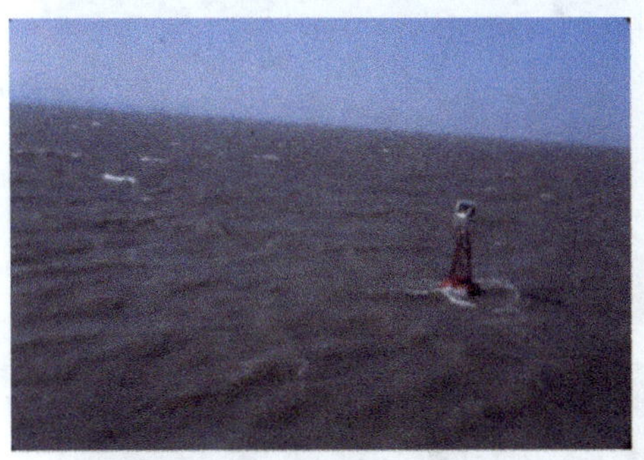

Landing beside shipping lane buoy

River pollution survey on the St. Lawrence River

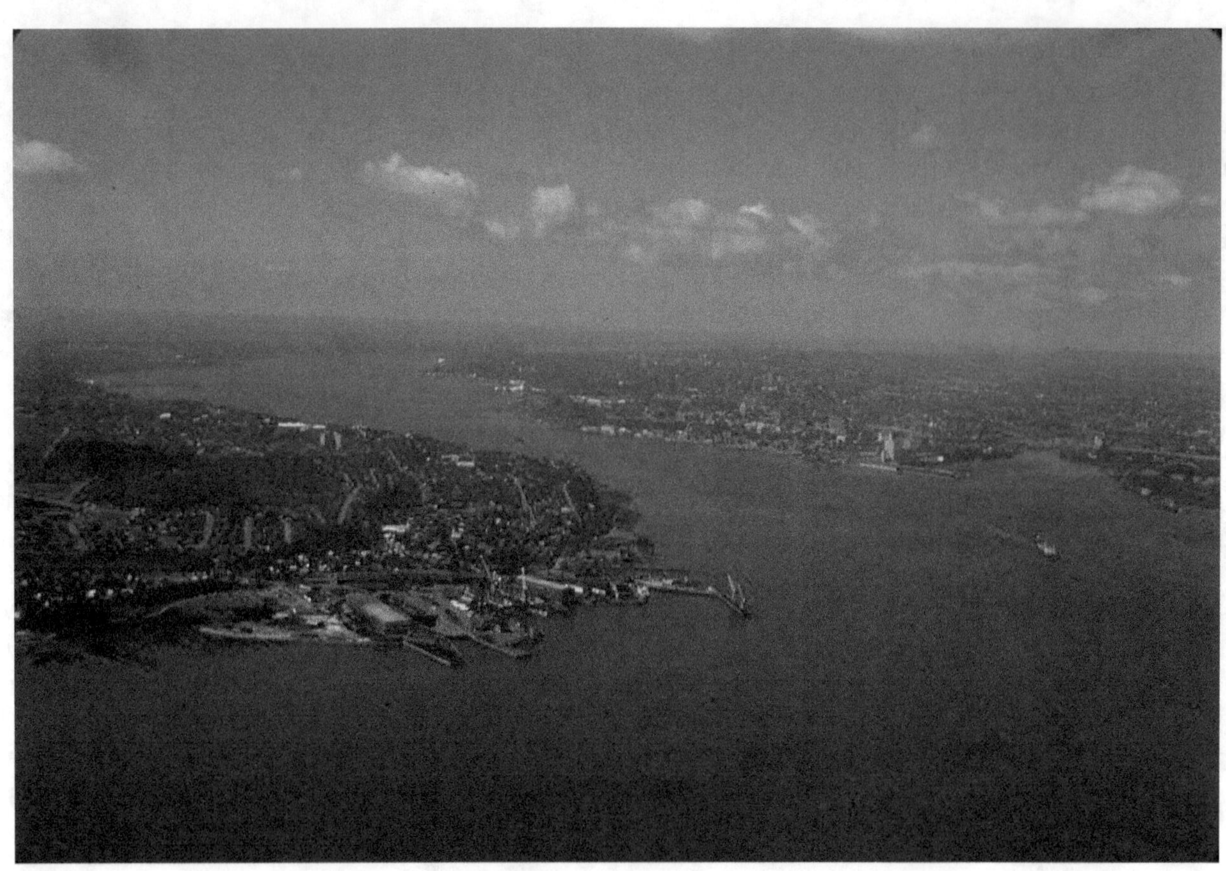

Beautiful day for landing on the shipping lanes

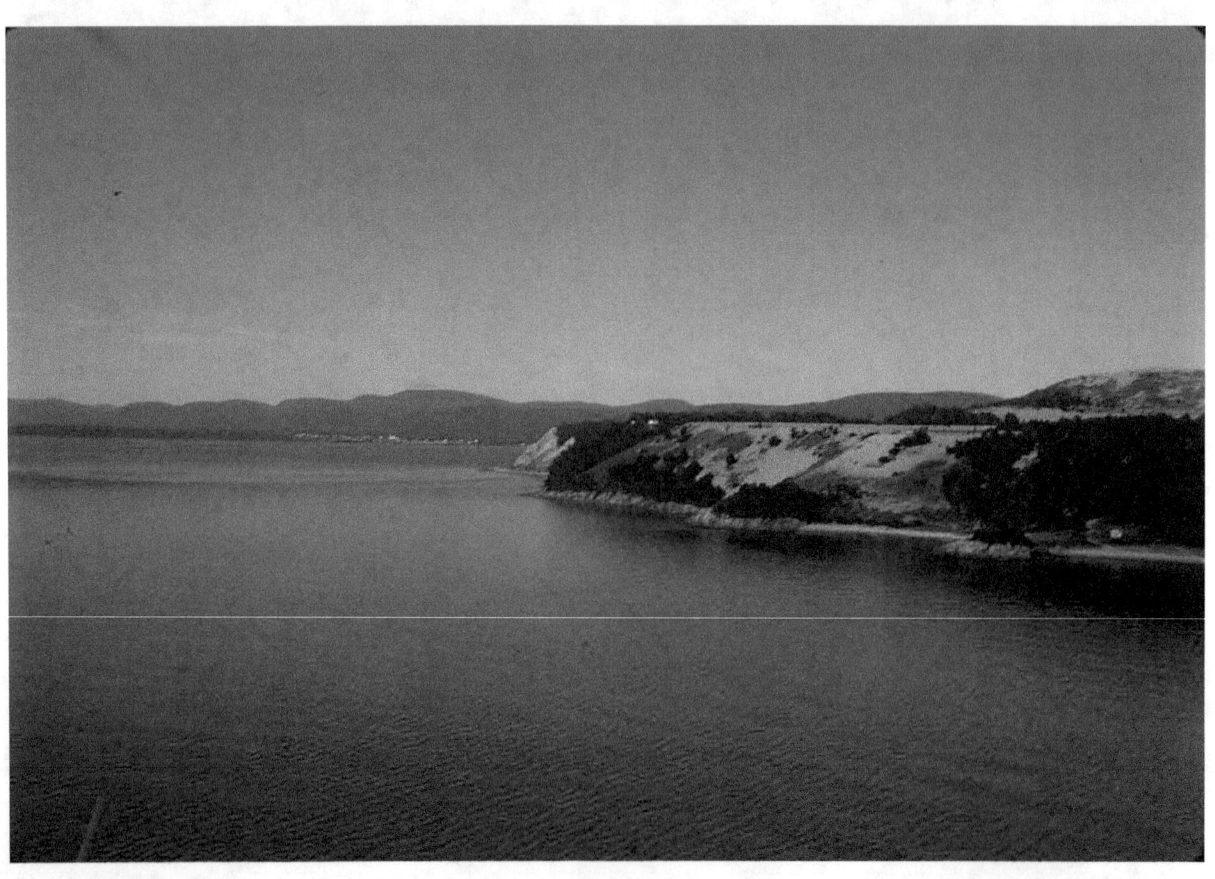

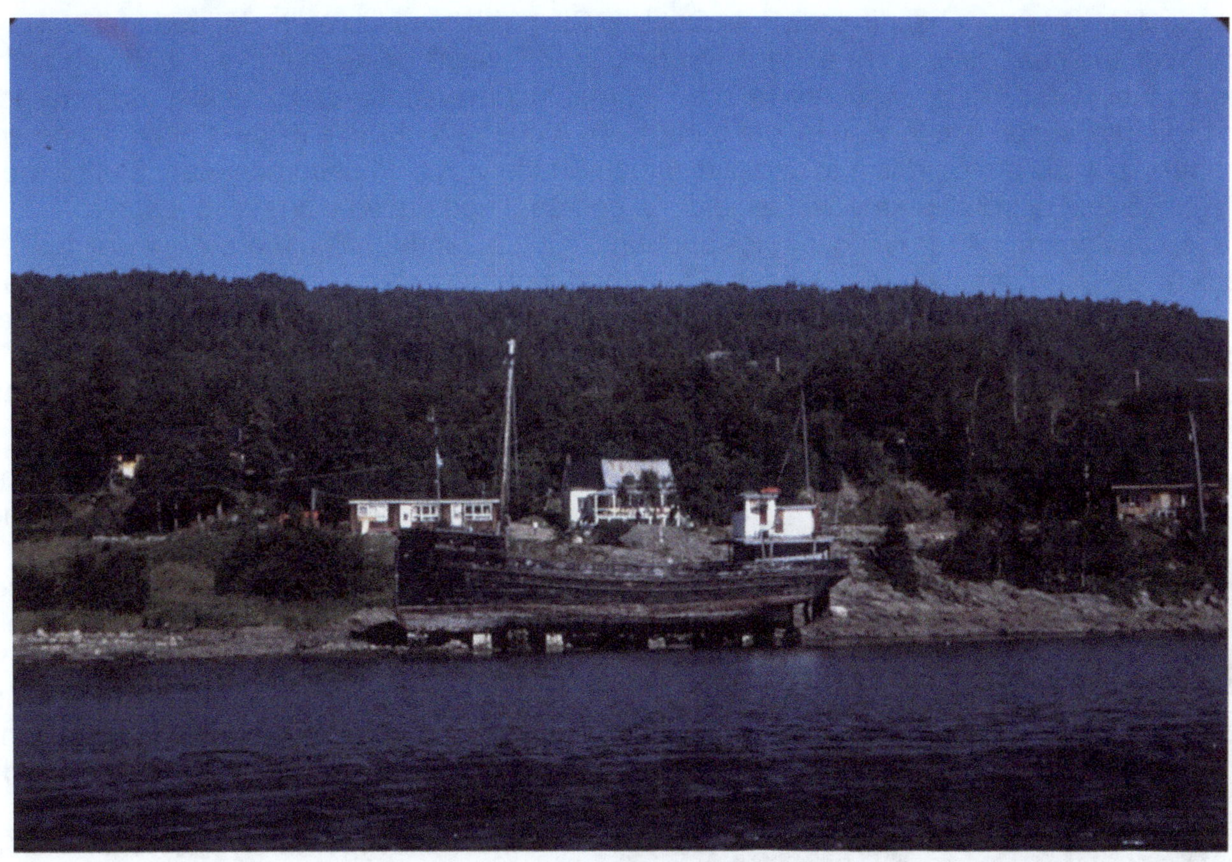

Progressing towards the mouth of the St.Lawrence

Each evening we would pick a nice motel along the shoreline to land and stay for the night. One evening it was getting dark as we were approaching the town where we'd be staying. I spotted a drive-in theatre and thought we'd have a little fun, so I came into a high hover over the parked cars. We watched the cartoon from 100 feet above but of course, no sound!

This drew a lot of attention as people flashed their car lights, waving and laughing! I then rolled my nose forward, and we landed at the hotel a short distance away.

The next day we were heading towards Quebec City, which was to be a planned fuel stop. However, the headwinds were extremely strong, and I wasn't going to make it. Landing and having fuel trucked to me would have been a great inconvenience and time lost. So I picked an isolated gas station and landed by the pumps. An Alouette II burns a mixture of kerosene and naphtha, but it is also certified to use diesel fuel. So the very surprised attendant fuelled me up with diesel but didn't clean my 'windshield'! Of course, I had drawn a crowd, but again Transport Canada had very loose rules about helicopters landing off airport. We were soon back on the river and near the Quebec City Airport, right on schedule. The following day we were nearing Montreal and nearing the end of the contract. We had had another good day and covered large portions of the river. We spotted another nice-looking motel with a swimming pool right on the banks of the St. Lawrence. The motel owner was very excited to have us stay there. A helicopter is an attraction and is good for business.

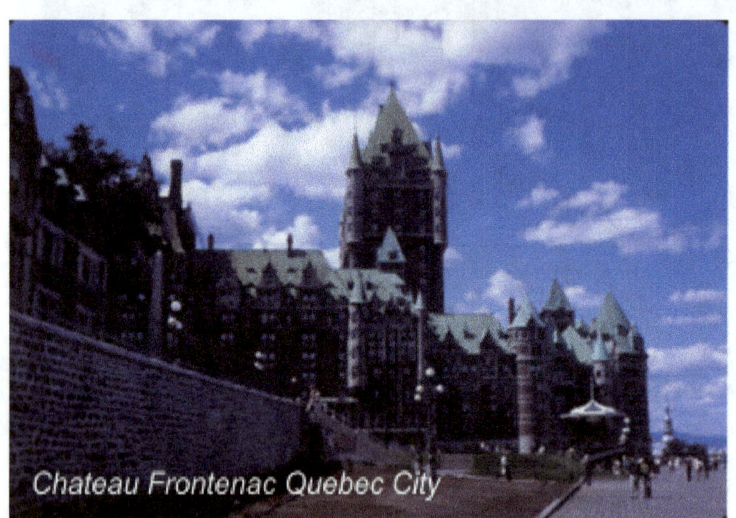

Chateau Frontenac Quebec City

Tourists will often stop to look or even end up checking in for the night. So he had us reposition and land inside the fenced off pool area for security. Since he didn't have a restaurant, I asked him if there was a good steakhouse nearby. He described one, and I asked him if he minded calling us a cab. He said, "Oh no, just take my car." (he had a brand new Riviera!) I said, "Thank you very much, but you hardly know me." He said with a grin in a heavy French accent, "You have a beautiful helicopter; you're not going to hurt my car!" So we had an excellent dinner, and the next day I asked about laundry. Of course, he quickly had his wife do all of our laundry for free! I felt like I would really like to pay back all his hospitality. I noticed he had no aerial shots of his motel in his postcard rack. He said he just couldn't afford to do that. So I asked him if he knew of a good photographer. "Oh, but of course, mon ami, my brother is a police sergeant in Montreal and an excellent photographer." So the sergeant came out the next day, and I took the passenger door off the helicopter. We got some great aerial shots that could be turned into postcards. As we checked out, he and his wife were so appreciative, and it was hard to say goodbye.

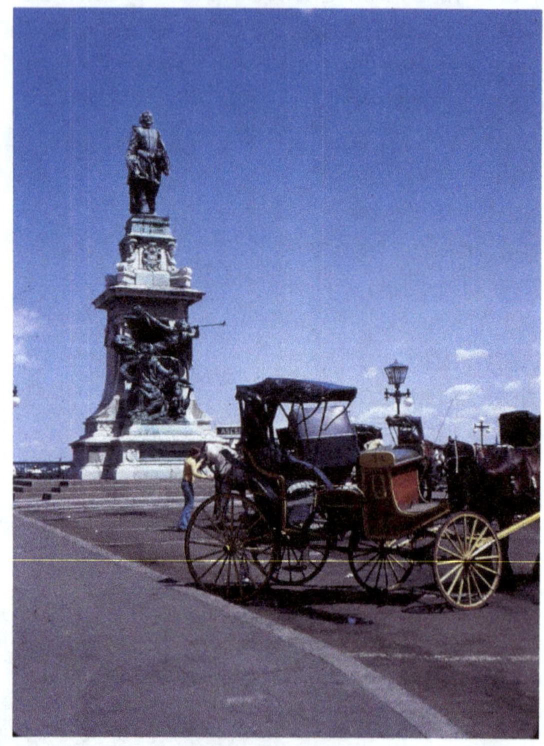

Carriage rides downtown

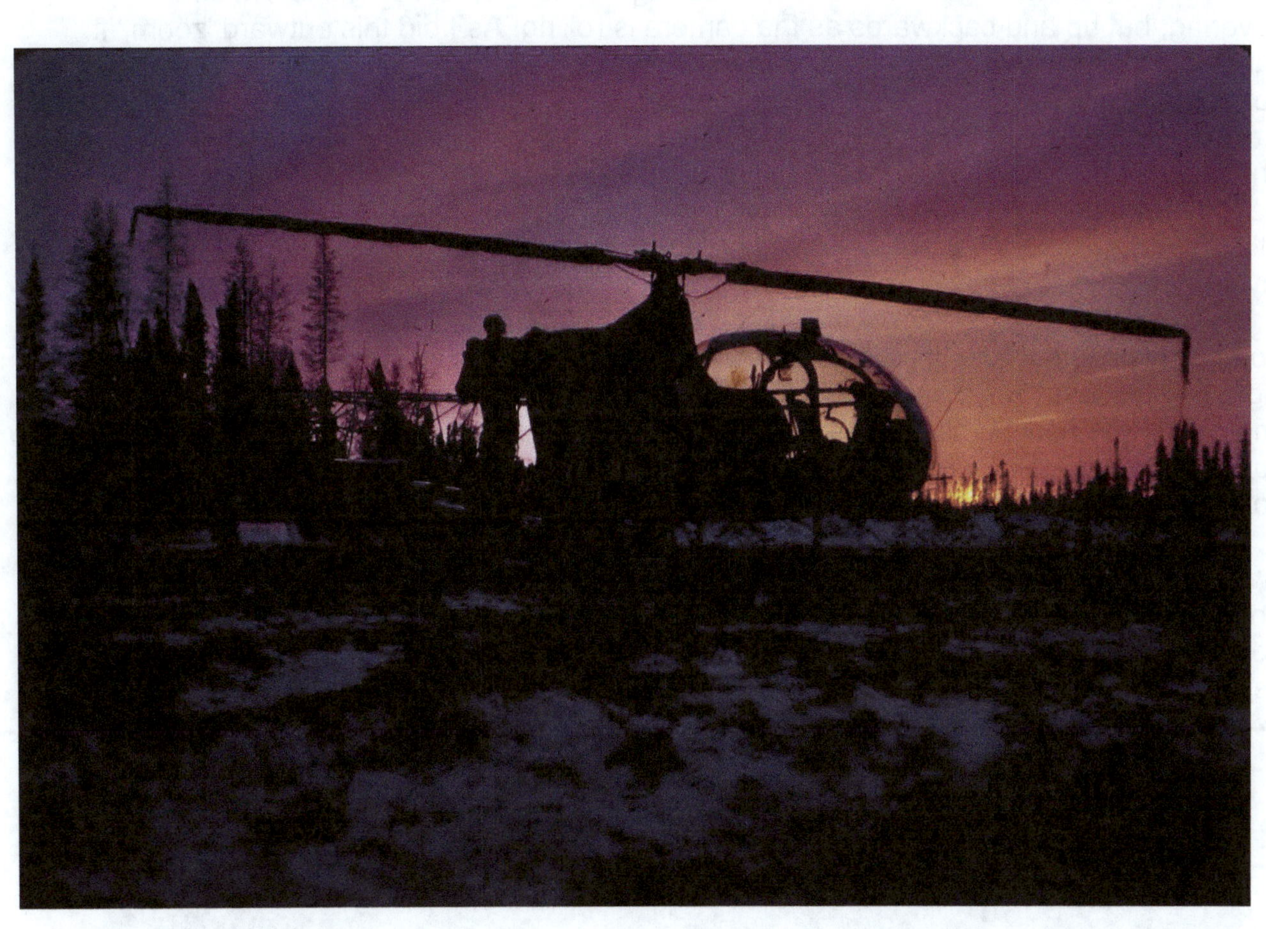

As I've said before

, it's so interesting flying in the pool, and you never know what's coming next. I finished up in the Montreal area, and it just so happened Canada Immigration needed a helicopter to shoot a promotion.

They were advocating easier immigration restrictions for a certain limited time period. The location for the government shoot was to take place in the centre of Montreal on top of Mount Royal. The producers put this together in a very clever way. Quite a number of actors representing immigrants carrying suitcases started emerging out of the park forest. As I'm hovering nearby with the cameraman on board, about 30 'immigrants' laid their suitcases down together in a large clearing. While they're doing this, I'm still hovering, but up and backwards as the camera is rolling. As I did this outward 'zoom,' it came into focus that all the suitcases together formed a large Canadian flag. It was well done and very effective.

There was a bit of a negative to the day. During a break in the shoot, I flew back to Dorval airport for fuel. I had time for a little snooze in the pilots' executive lounge at Atlantic Aviation's hangar. It was fun going full circle and coming back to the location of my first flying job 3 years ago.

So I had a beautiful little 35-millimetre camera with a retractable lens. It took great pictures and nicely fit in my jean pocket. Haida Helicopters had given all the pilots and engineers who had worked at James Bay these cameras as part of a cash Christmas bonus. Unfortunately, somebody lifted it from the side table as I was sleeping. I guess not all visiting executive pilots are trustworthy!

I was still speculating and did a few more odd flights around Quebec City. One day the Snowbirds showed up for an airshow over the city. I took off from the airport and had a front-seat view of the whole show. Quebec Tower gave me an authorized clearance to be at their altitude but to remain clear of the area they'd be performing. Quite an experience with such a great view of the Snowbirds and Quebec City in the background!

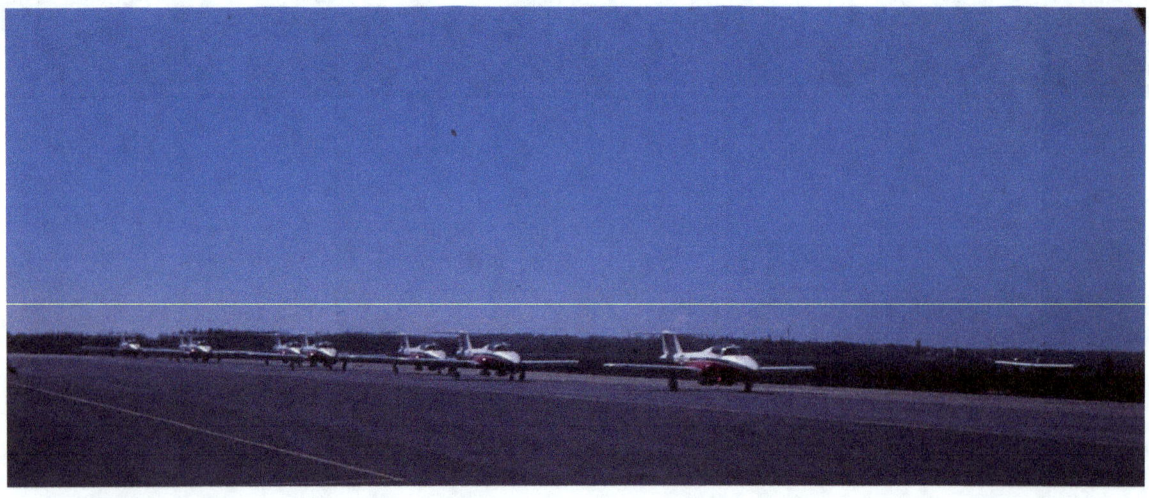

Then it was back to BC to

fly a magnetometer survey on Vancouver Island. This was an extensive survey looking for iron ore deposits in the top three- quarters of the Island. The area would be from the northern tip of the Cape Scott area down to Lake Cowichan south of Nanaimo. The aircraft would be based out of Tahsis, being fairly central.

The survey lines were 2 miles apart, traversing the island from east to west. This was still before GPS, but we had precise aerial photos of the terrain, which made navigation relatively easy. The magnetometer was suspended on a 300-foot line beneath the helicopter. As we followed the lines, the technician wanted me to maintain a height of 350 feet above the terrain on the radar altimeter. This would put the magnetometer 50 feet above the ground and would supply the most accurate readings to the monitors carried inside the helicopter.

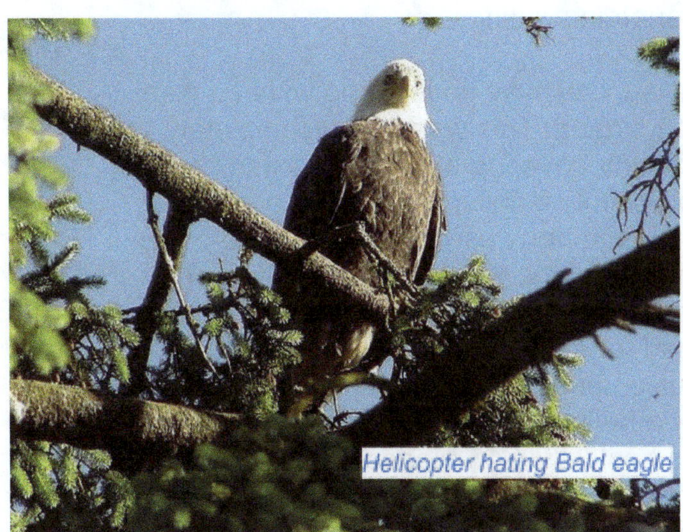
Helicopter hating Bald eagle

We covered the entire survey area in 3 weeks. There was one problem with Bald eagles in certain areas. It was nesting season, and they were very protective of their nests. As you follow certain lines, you are, at times, doing a vertical climb at a lower airspeed. We were halfway up a mountain when suddenly I saw an eagle diving straight for us with its wings folded. So I broke line and circled back to start it again. At the same location, there was another attack, this time by 2 Bald eagles. Obviously, the 2 of them were a pair protecting their nest. So we finally had to abandon that line and do the next one 2 miles over. An adult eagle weighs about 14 pounds. The tips of the main rotor are travelling at close to 400 mph. If an eagle hits the rotor at those speeds, it will do a tremendous amount of damage (especially to the eagle!).

One day back in Tahsis, the technicians wanted to double-check the length of the 300 ft sling to the magnetometer. So as I hovered up, they marked it off in 100-foot increments. They marked off the first 100 feet and then signalled me to continue the vertical climb. But he had actually got his signals confused and was just motioning frantically. Suddenly the helicopter started vibrating badly, and the controls were 'frozen.' I managed to get the aircraft on the ground in one piece, and obviously, something had gone very wrong. As I was going up, the nylon line had blown over in a big bow and snagged on a nearby backhoe. Since the signalman seemed to want me going up instead of down, the line stretched till it snapped. The severed end went up into the main rotor, which caused it to wrap around the main control rods. These pitch rods froze my controls instantly. I was very fortunate that the aircraft didn't crash, and it just proved how quickly a simple exercise can go wrong.

In 1974 we had a sudden news flash

that we'd be merging with our competition, Okanagan Helicopters, based out of Vancouver. After going head to head with them for years for a lot of the work, we were now one big happy family. Many of us found it hard to switch loyalties overnight; however, the opportunities became evident. We now had access to a huge fleet and a worldwide market. At this time, Okanagan was the third-largest company in the world and would eventually become the largest.

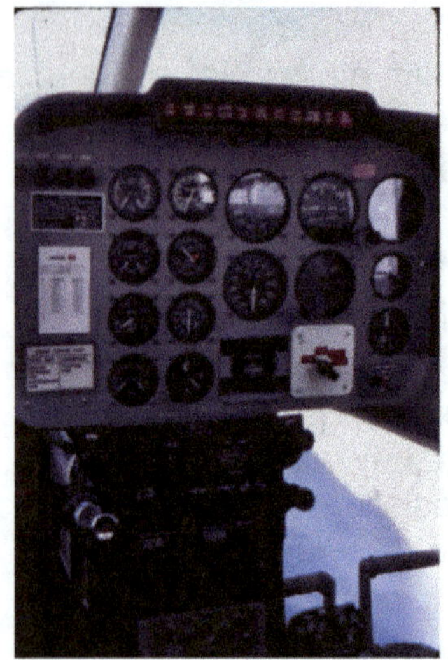

Bell 206 cockpit

With the new company colours came a complete indoctrination to a new aircraft checkout, a Bell 206. This is a 5 place turbine helicopter I was interested in flying for some years, and widely used in the industry. Also, a refresher in a mountain course out of Penticton. This was a bit of déjà vu from when Canadian Helicopters had sent me here 5 years ago for my initial mountain training.

So this contract was successfully ended, and within a week, another contract was signed. This was with a completely different mining company covering exactly the same area. Since I was now completely familiar with the area and the scope of the work, my company used me again. The only difference in the flying this time was a change of aircraft. Instead of an Alouette, I would be flying a Gazelle, another French helicopter. I had recently checked out on this aircraft, and it was exciting to fly. It was fast, with a cruise speed of 163 mph and a top speed of just under 200 mph. This was phenomenal for a helicopter and partly due to a redesigned tail rotor called a fenestron. This is basically a 13-bladed fan located at the normal tail rotor location at the rear of the aircraft. Because of its speed, the whole area was covered in an even quicker time. Climbing the mountainsides at a vertical speed of 2400 ft/min was extraordinary as well. It was literally like driving a sports car!

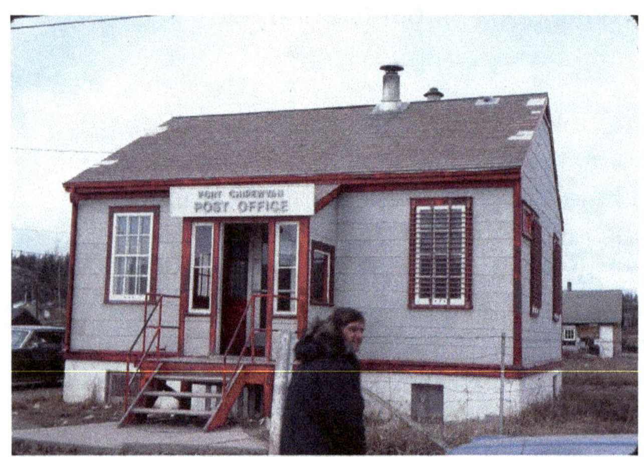

Fort Chip post office

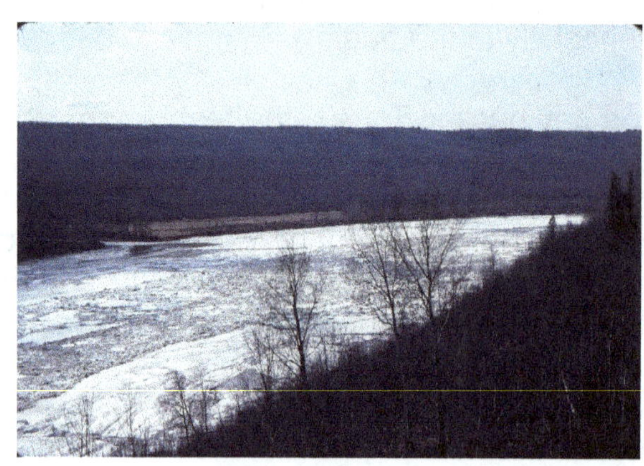

Ice breakup survey- Peace River

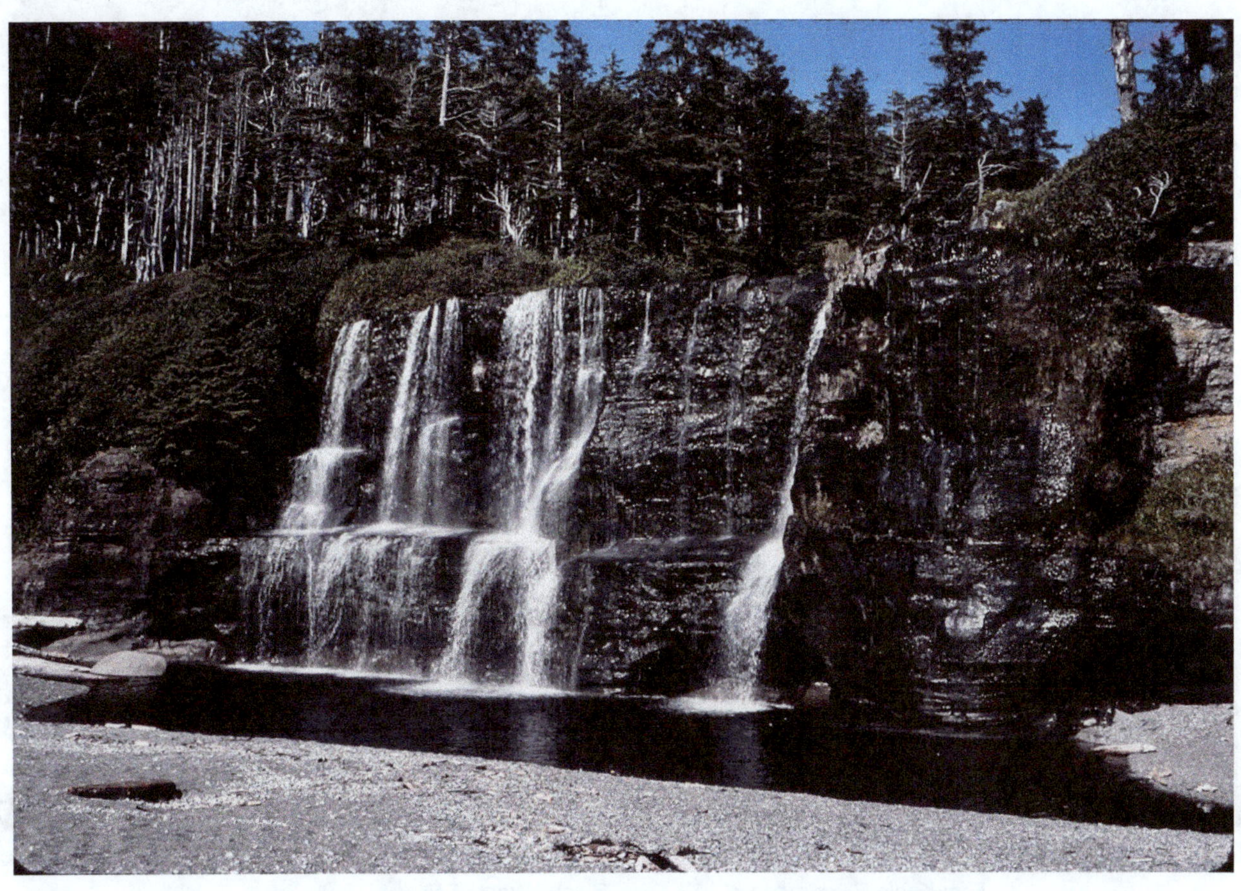

Falls west of Lake Cowichan - Pacific Ocean

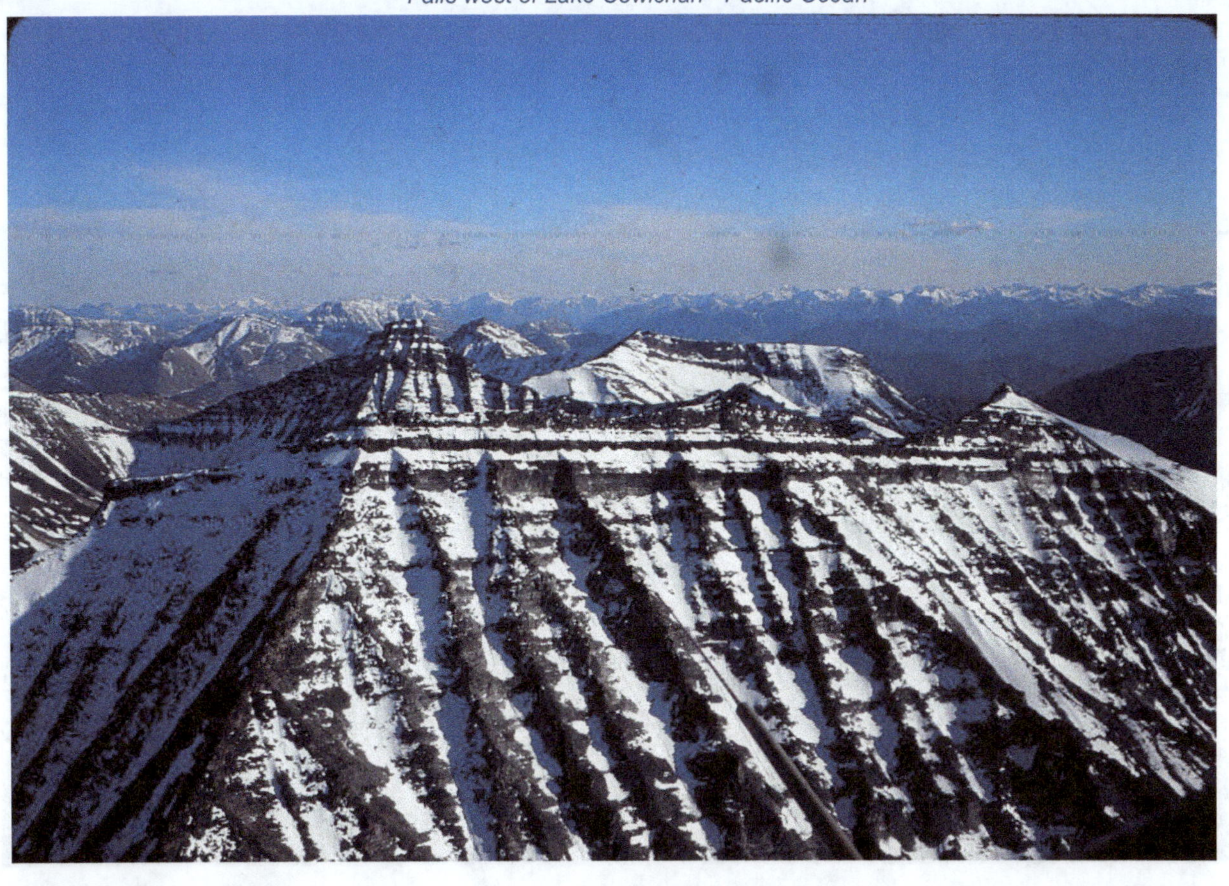

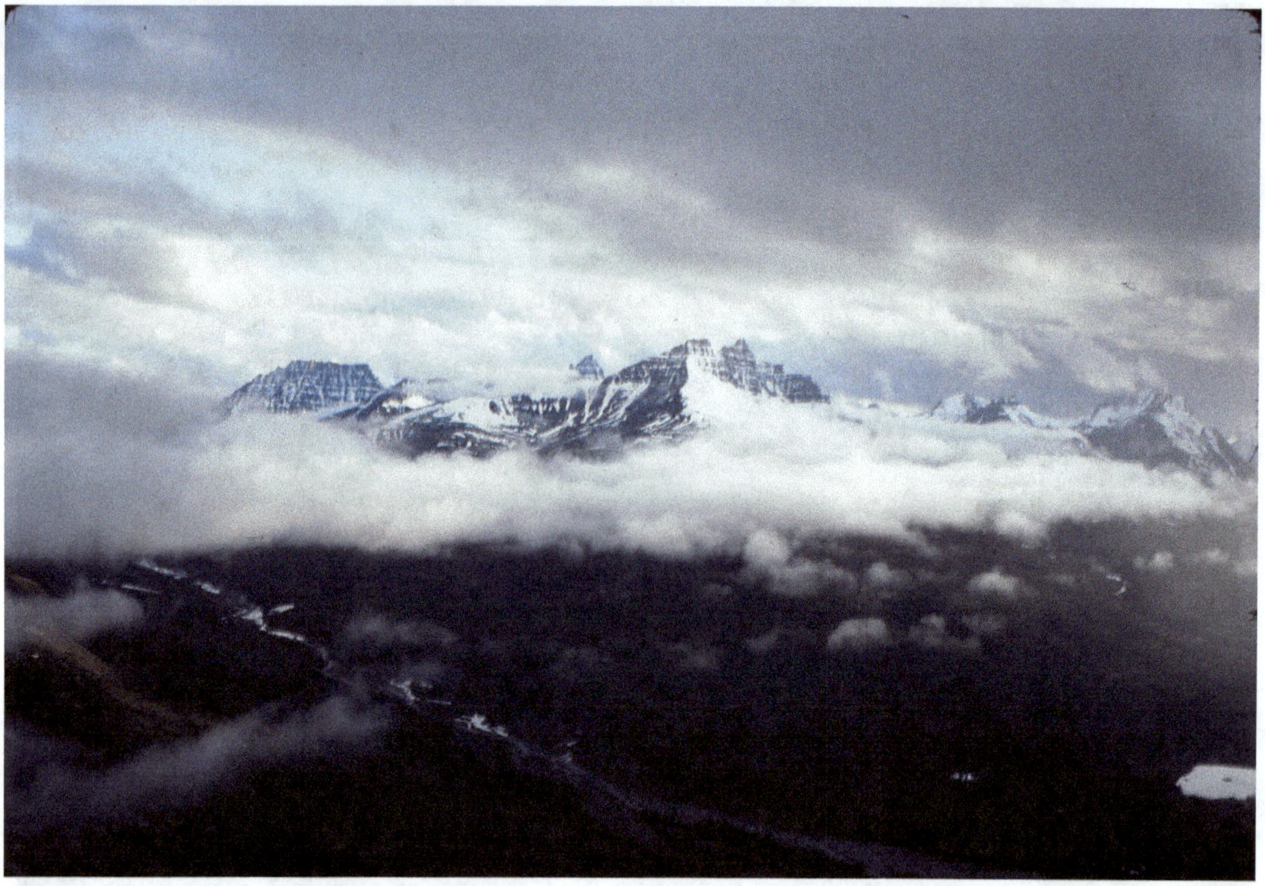

Top: Keele River range Below: West of Normal Wells

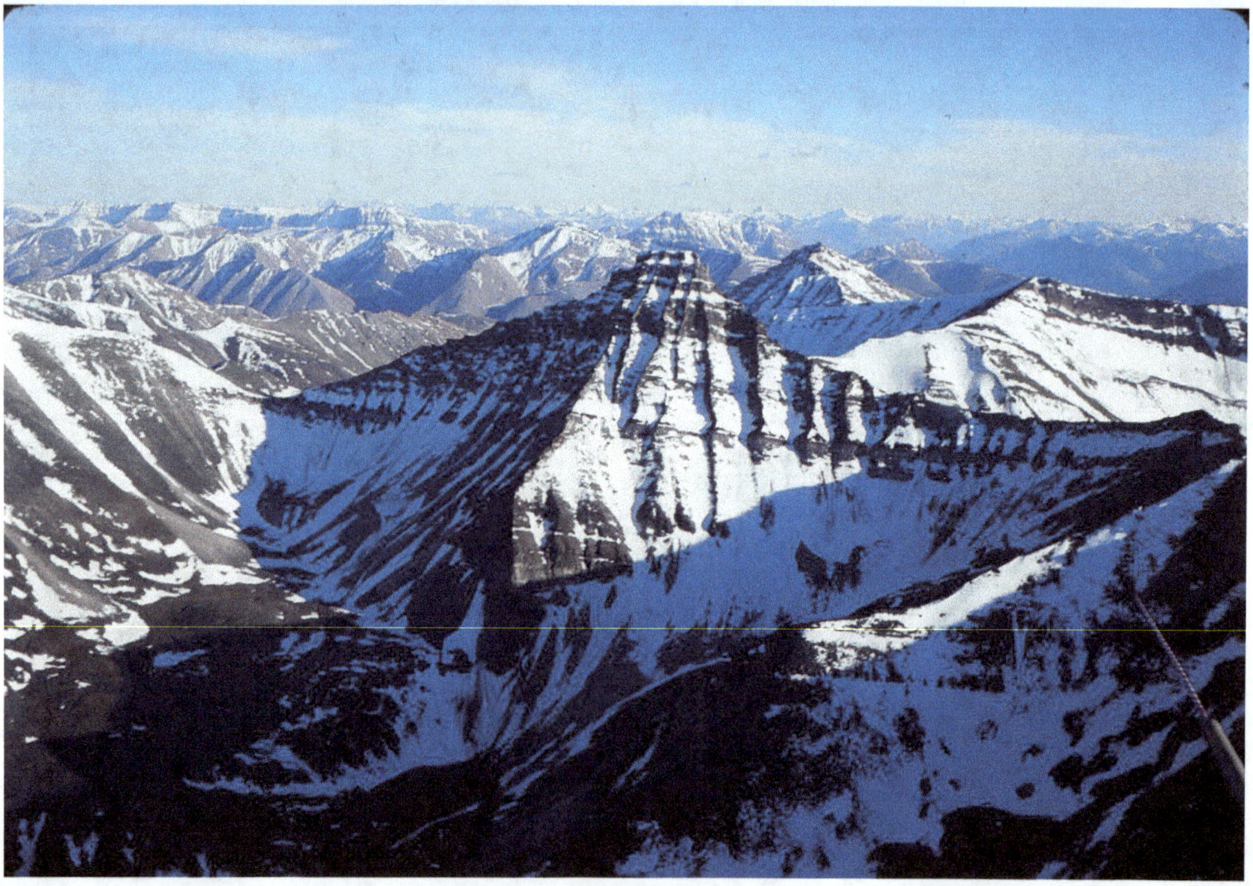

I was soon out on new jobs

I'd never experienced before with this aircraft. An interesting job involved snow surveys just north of Revelstoke. Towards each Spring, avalanche experts check the depths and stability of snow in avalanche areas. This involved landing at high altitudes on the mountainsides and ravines, especially near major highways. At one landing in a pass of 8000 feet ASL, they invited me to leave the helicopter and break trail for them to the sample spot. We're all on snowshoes, and I realized I'd been set up! It was extremely hard work in 20 feet of powder, and at that altitude, I wasn't in nearly the shape or condition they were in. For future landings, I chose to remain behind at the helicopter!

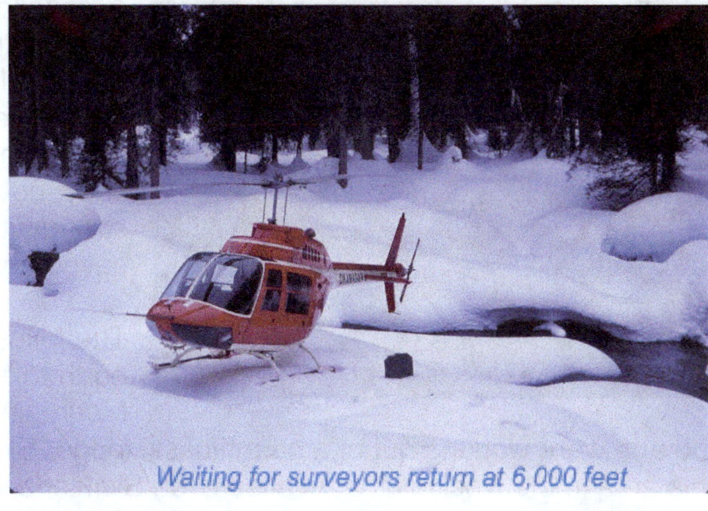

Waiting for surveyors return at 6,000 feet

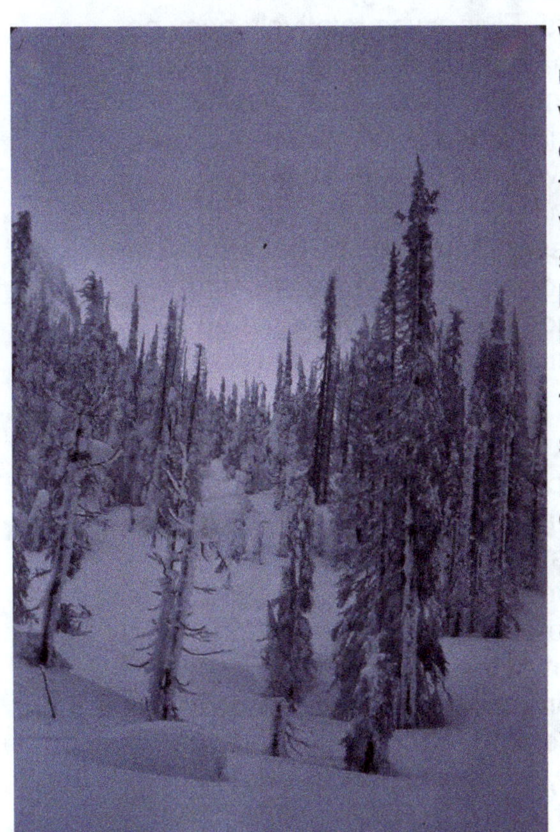

Whenever they found certain areas to be unstable and potential avalanche dangers, they would use dynamite. The area would be overflown, and dynamite sticks would be thrown from the helicopter. One of my colleagues had a very close call. The crew member in the back seat threw out the bundle of dynamite, but it landed in the cargo rack on the side of the helicopter.

There was about a 20-second delay on the fuse, so there was not enough time to land. The guy panicked with good reason and quickly crawled out on the rack and hucked the dynamite away. It had no sooner cleared the aircraft when it blew up. Needless to say, no cargo racks were allowed for future flights!

One day I had a very close call myself. I had taken off from our base at Revelstoke with a 4 man snow survey crew. They had picked a cirque at about the 6,000-foot level. A cirque is a deep depression on the side of a mountain, open on one side to the valley below. Since the winds are unpredictable, it's always a challenge to land into the wind. Once I had determined the wind direction, I set up for final approach to be into the wind. There was one dwarf pine in the landing area I wanted to keep in sight to avoid a whiteout when the downwash hit the powder. I was about 300 feet back at about 100 feet above ground. Suddenly I hit something, I was thrown up against the belts, and the helicopter went into an extreme attitude. The powder blew up, and visibility immediately went to zero.

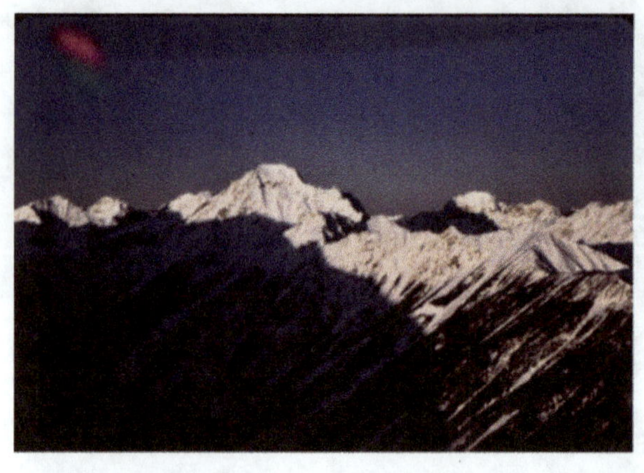

Adrenaline rushing, I went on instruments, levelled the aircraft, pulled full power and flew out of it! I circled back to see what in the world had happened. There were my skid marks on top of a 100-foot totally obscured snow-covered rock mound. I feel very strongly that God guided me out of that and saved a very bad accident!

The following week I was sent a little farther north to Mica Creek to fly skiers for Canadian Mountain Holidays. We had 2 aircraft on that job and were working out of a beautiful ski lodge. Skiers came from all over the world to this area in the Rockies that rivalled even Switzerland. They were promised 3,000 vertical feet of skiing each day. On the first flight of the day, the guides would go out with us to pick the peaks. They would generally be at the 6,000 to 8,000-foot levels. The view up there was incredible, looking out at all the surrounding peaks. Flying was relatively easy on clear days, and in the cold, the air is generally very stable and smooth. It was more of a challenge when visibility was obscured and you were landing above the tree line. The snow-covered mountain tops blended with cloud cover at the drop off sites. Along with powder snow from the downwash, it could be a complete loss of visibility when landing. So you avoided a hover and forced a landing quickly before you lost your horizon.

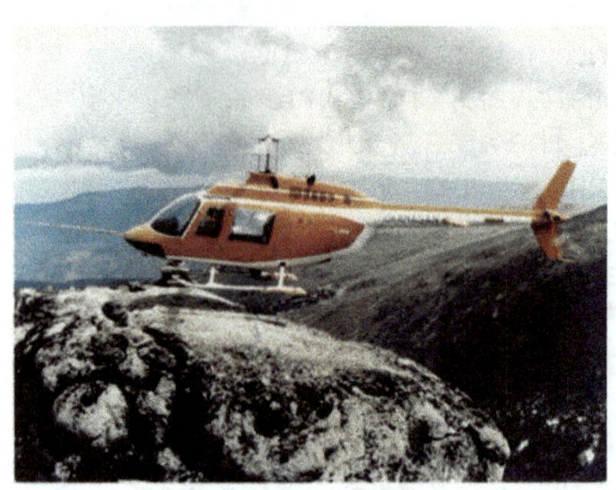

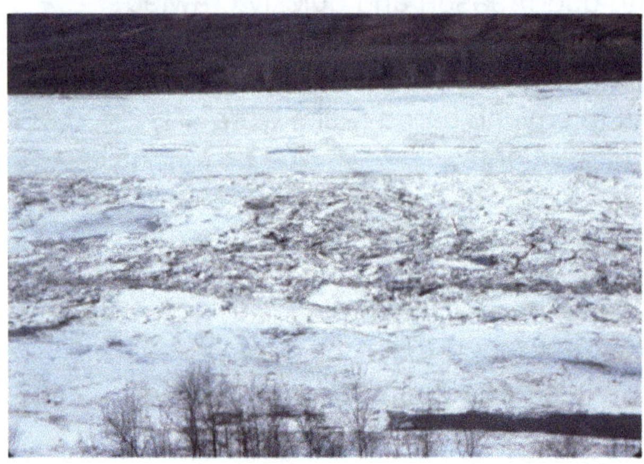

One particular skier was a character and a bit of a party animal. We would fly him to the slopes all day, and they were pretty long runs down. It was strenuous, but he seemed to be in pretty good shape. After his last run of the day, he would head straight for the bar and stay till closing time at midnight. Then he'd usually find a room party and probably didn't go to bed till at least 2:00 am. One night he had been in the lounge for hours and decided it was too dark in there. So apparently, he came back with a chainsaw and cut a huge hole in one of the walls. I'm not sure how he didn't get arrested or kicked out of the hotel. But the hotel management must have thought it was needed because they put in a nice big-picture window the next day! He would be up early regardless of the night before and put in another full day of skiing. I inquired about who this guy was and where he was from.

Ironically, it turned out he was a brain surgeon from Los Angeles! I guess this was his way of releasing stress!

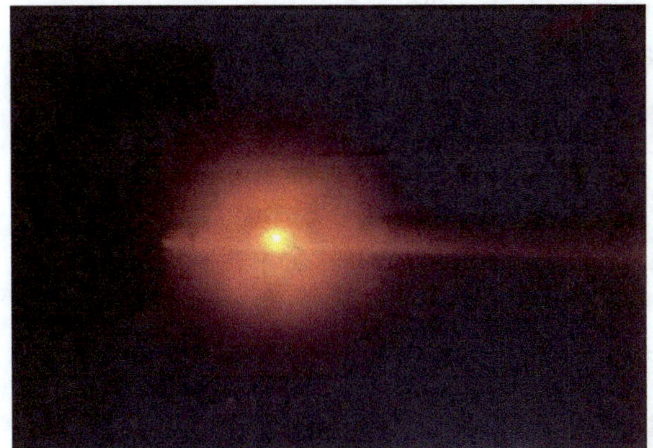

One day the National Film Board contracted us to film some downhill skiers for a short film. So I took the rear door off for the cameraman, who had the camera fixed to a special Tyler mount. I hovered beside 2 skiers launching from a 6,000 ft peak. I followed them down, hovering sideways, and we were getting some great footage. Halfway down the mountain, we saw them heading for a 70 ft. cliff, and there was no way we could warn them. The first skier went airborne, and when he disappeared, the second skier had enough warning to take a wide turn & avoid the drop off. The fallen skier was like the cartoon where he's upside with crossed skis on the surface of the snow. The second skier stopped beside him and quickly dug him out. Fortunately, he had landed upside down in about 14 ft of powder and was completely unhurt. They carried on down the rest of the way, and the Film Board had a great clip of skiing in the Canadian Rockies.

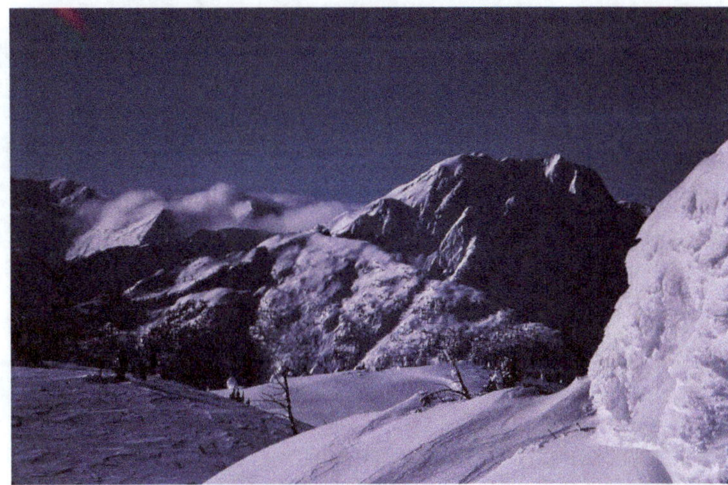

Last Landing of the day at Altitude

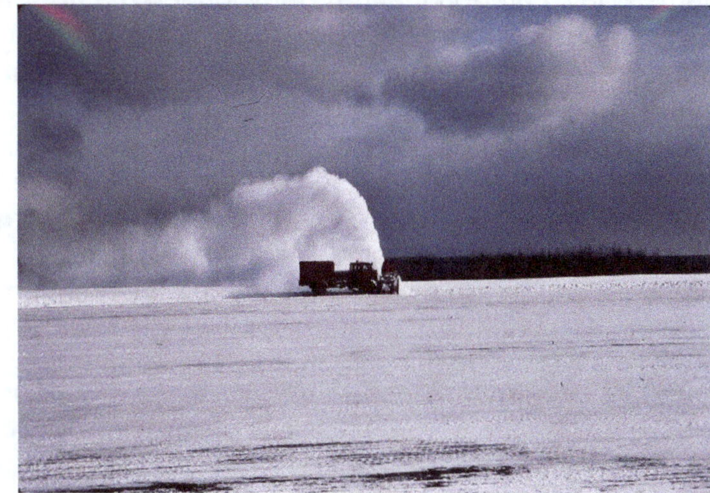

Revelstoke Airport- Clearing Run ways

In spring 1974, I was needed

for another tour in James Bay, this time under the colours of newly adopted Okanagan Helicopters. I'd be flying a Bell 206 on which I had been recently endorsed, and not the Alouette II that I'd flown there previously. I still preferred the Alouette because of its lifting capability, but the Bell was faster, with a 125 mph cruising speed.

When I was asked to do a ferry flight from Vancouver to Montreal, I had the pleasure of flying the Gazelle again. The morning I took off from Vancouver airport, the weather was absolutely beautiful CAVU (ceiling and visibility unlimited). This enabled me to fly Calgary direct over the mountains for my first fuel stop. I climbed to 14,000 feet which is about the human limit without oxygen. I landed in Calgary in record time, and as I was heading into the terminal for a coffee, I was met by an engineer for Aerospatiale. He was one of the company's design engineers who manufactured the Gazelle. He asked if I minded if he checked over the aircraft. I said, "Sure, I'm not an engineer; it's always good to have professional eyes on an aircraft before the next flight." I came back after the aircraft had been refuelled, and I had my coffee to go. He said, "Come over here; I want to show you something." It was one of the steel pit pins that held the cowling together over the engine. It had worked its way loose and had been literally hanging by a nylon thread directly in the intake of the turbine engine! The short nylon retaining cord had almost been rubbed right through. If that had severed completely, the steel pit pin would have gone directly into the compressor blades and caused the turbine to disintegrate. This easily could have happened when I was at altitude, blissfully unaware and taking in the spectacular view! It would have been a forced landing somewhere in treacherous terrain near the Columbia ice fields.

So, needless to say, I took off from Calgary feeling extremely grateful to that engineer! Because of prevailing westerly winds and the speeds of this aircraft, I got to Montreal in record time. Ground speeds averaged over 200 mph and a top speed of 240 mph at altitudes between 6,000 to 8,000 ft. Of course, I had to stop at the farm again. I only had time for a few rides this time which included my uncle Ken Opheim and our old neighbour across the road, J Baerg.

I dropped the aircraft in Montreal and then flew commercial to Matagami up in James Bay. I crew changed with another company pilot and carried on to a tent camp east of James Bay. Later on that day, they loaded me up with groceries to restock another camp 100 miles further east. Halfway there, I noticed a slow reduction in my engine oil pressure. As it approached zero, I was set up for an emergency landing in a clear area in the bush. Because I was relatively new to this aircraft type, I quickly shut down as a precautionary measure. I got out and checked the oil level expecting to see it very low. It was completely full and had no leakage anywhere, so I assumed the gauge had failed. When I went for a restart, the battery was completely dead. What had happened was the generator had failed, causing the battery to die and, consequently, the oil pressure gauge. So my two passengers and I set up camp just as it was getting dark. We had 400 pounds of groceries, so we ate like kings! The next morning at first light, my camp boss sent out a search helicopter. I had been right on course, but I still had the biggest smokiest fire going. It's a strange feeling when you don't make your destination, and it certainly causes concern to the ones expecting your arrival.

As a continuing phase of the hydro development in James Bay, I became involved in a whole new challenge of flying. This was incorporating helicopters, because of their stability, to pioneer a new method of conducting a geodetic survey. The idea was to hover vertically over a transit emitting a laser beam vertically. This beam was displayed on a 2-foot square screen mounted on the front of the helicopter in full view of the pilot. The helicopter would rise to ever-increasing heights until it became visible to a surveyor positioned several miles away, and he could take a reading on his transit. This was extremely accurate, resulting in large areas being mapped in one day. This proved to be extremely challenging for a pilot learning this for the first time. The training usually took several days of practice. Basically, you had to keep the vertically projected beam on the 2-foot screen mounted on the front of the helicopter. So you hovered over the transit, and as you increased height, the pencil-sized blue dot would get larger and larger. If it slipped off the screen, you had to go back down and 'capture' it again. We were in radio contact, so as soon as the distant surveyor got a reading on you, that part of the triangulation was complete. This required a lot of skill and precision because, basically, you were hovering over a 2-foot square on the ground. As the days went by, moving from area to area, you became more and more skilful. It was like learning how to hover all over again, except this time, your only reference was that little blue dot, and you never took your eyes off it. One day turned into a humorous incident. Usually, the distant surveyor caught you at about 1,000 feet above the ground, depending on terrain and line of sight. This time I was going up and up, and no call, so I thought it was extra mountainous, and there was no line of sight. The blue dot had faded and had grown to the size of the screen as I was just going through 3,000 feet above the ground! Just then, he called and said he must have missed me. So basically, I was 3,000 feet above a 2-foot square on the ground! Humming birds must have been envious!

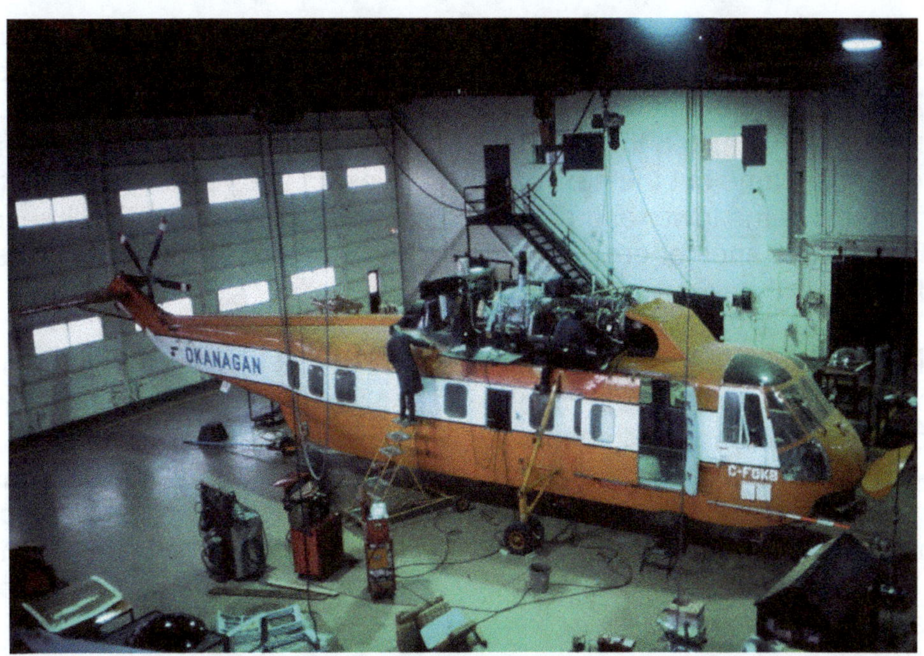

S 61 - major maintenance Vancouver base - Okanagan Helicopters

1975 continued to be a revelation

of new experiences as a Vancouver pool pilot. Okanagan held a base managers' meeting annually, and sometimes you got to cover the bases. This included Cranbrook, Revelstoke and Campbell River for me that year. I had just arrived at Campbell River and received a call from BC Tel to meet them in Port McNeil the next morning. They needed a small 150- foot tower to be attached to an existing 300-foot tower. This would give the local residents an extra TV channel. I gave the tower crew a briefing, and they hooked me up

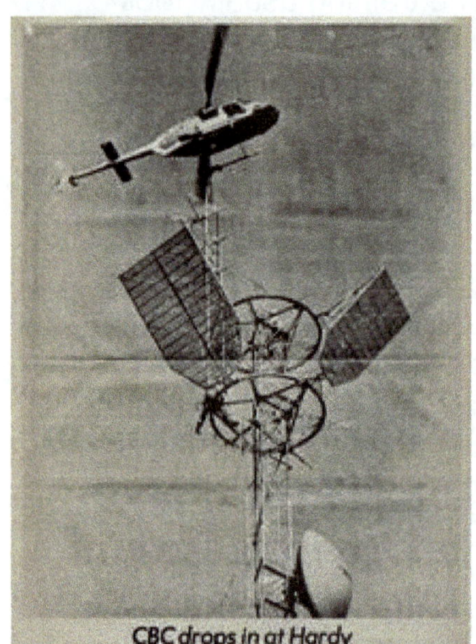
CBC drops in at Hardy

to the small tower. I would hover it up to position on top of the main tower as the crew would secure it with a 'Come-a-Long.' I took the door off so I could set it using vertical reference. This was a method used to look straight down at the load, and it allowed for more precision than using radios. As I hovered above the two towers, the crew below seemed to be taking a long time to secure the shorter tower. I gave them a 'cut' sign and went back down with the load. I asked them what the problem was, and they said they were trying to attach it with a 'U-Clamp.' I told them, "No, just get it secured, and you can clamp it later." So we went back up, and they had it secured in less than a minute. So back on the ground, I said, "Now, wasn't that a lot quicker?" It turned out they got the clamp to work after all. This, under a helicopter hovering 250 feet above them!

Just a couple of addendums. This crew had never worked under a helicopter before on a tower. They didn't advise me of that when I gave them the standard safety briefing. One of the crew, not used to the down wash, had actually slipped off the tower and was hanging by his belt. They admitted they didn't usually use belts but did this time. The local Port McNeil paper came out the next day, and I was on the front cover. A picture of the helicopter high above the tower and crew. The caption read, "A new TV channel added, and Bill HILL does another great job!" (Bill Hill was the base manager I was filling in for! I never did correct them.)

I was just ferrying the aircraft back to Vancouver when I got an emergency call. The Squamish River was raging with Spring runoff, and two kayakers were stranded on a log jamb. They had lost their kayaks and apparently were in danger of hypothermia. Normally we didn't get involved with search & rescue, and usually, they called Search & Rescue in Comox. But I was close, so I flew over and found them quickly. I was able to place a skid on a log in the river. I did a 'hover balance' on a log as they crawled in from either side. As I said, sometimes you never knew what the next call was going to be, which made life interesting.

I had been looking very forward

to getting a checkout in a medium-sized helicopter. This was a 15-place aircraft called a Bell 205. I finally had enough hours and experience to qualify, so I received the call to our Penticton base. All helicopters fly pretty much the same, so the checkout is fairly straightforward. In fact, the bigger they are, the more stable they generally are. You can also lift a lot more. This size of the helicopter could lift about 5,000 pounds of water in a fire bucket, a sling load or internal cargo.

Part of the checkout included practicing using a much larger water bucket. The instructor was a seasoned senior pilot with a real sense of humour. We were doing circuits, picking up water out of Skaha Lake just south of Penticton. There were quite a few tourists watching us from a viewpoint on the side of the highway. Fred said, "Hey, let's go and bomb them! I said we can't do that. We'll flatten them with 5,000 pounds of water! No, no, no, just drop it down the centre of the highway, and the spray will get 'em!" So I came in low and fast and released on the highway centreline. The spray definitely got them as they waved and ran for cover. Then Fred said, "Oh right, Okanagan is on the tail. Quick, dodge around that next ridge!"

Next was some slinging practice with another heavy load, this time an old wrecked car. Fred had a friend with a junk yard full of cars and had his permission to pick one up. He hooked me up to an old Buick, which probably weighed about 4,000 pounds. So I set it all over the place, including confined areas in the bush, without releasing it. Finally, we were done with it, so I was going to set it down back at the scrapyard. Fred had a better idea, just fly over the yard and let it go. So at 1000 feet and about 80 knots, I punched it off, and we had a good laugh wondering if it could be repaired! Worked great, and we headed back to the airport for fuel. The next slinging exercise was to take a load to altitude and set it on a mountaintop. The base engineer hooked us up to a large commercial welding machine. Fred picked a 6,000-foot peak a little west of Penticton to set it on. After figuring out the winds and doing a reconnaissance of the landing area, I set it gently down without releasing it. While I was hovering, Fred got out of his seat and said he'd be right back. He walked back into the cabin, opened the large sliding door and jumped out! I was surprised, to say the least, and when he climbed back up, I asked him what that was all about?! He said, "Had to get rid of some coffee." Away we went, and I relate this story to this day. Just a note about F. Baird. As I mentioned previously, he was an excellent pilot with a lot of experience and a great sense of humour. A couple of years later, he was flying a pipeline job in Peru. He lost an engine over a three-canopied jungle and dropped the last 300 feet to the ground below.

Unfortunately, he was crippled and permanently confined to a wheelchair, but he never lost his sense of humour.

So my checkout was complete on the 205, and fortunately, there was some work for it around Grand Forks and Osoyoos. We had a contract to fly tree planters up to the mountains at logged-out areas. This was a great experience and relatively easy flying on this aircraft that was new to me. However, it was fairly hard to get airborne. This shouldn't have been a problem since the 205 should easily handle the weight of 14 passengers. So I flew back to Penticton to have it checked out. It turned out that the compressor blades in the engine had FOD (foreign obstacle damage). This required that the engine had to be removed for overhaul and a new one installed.

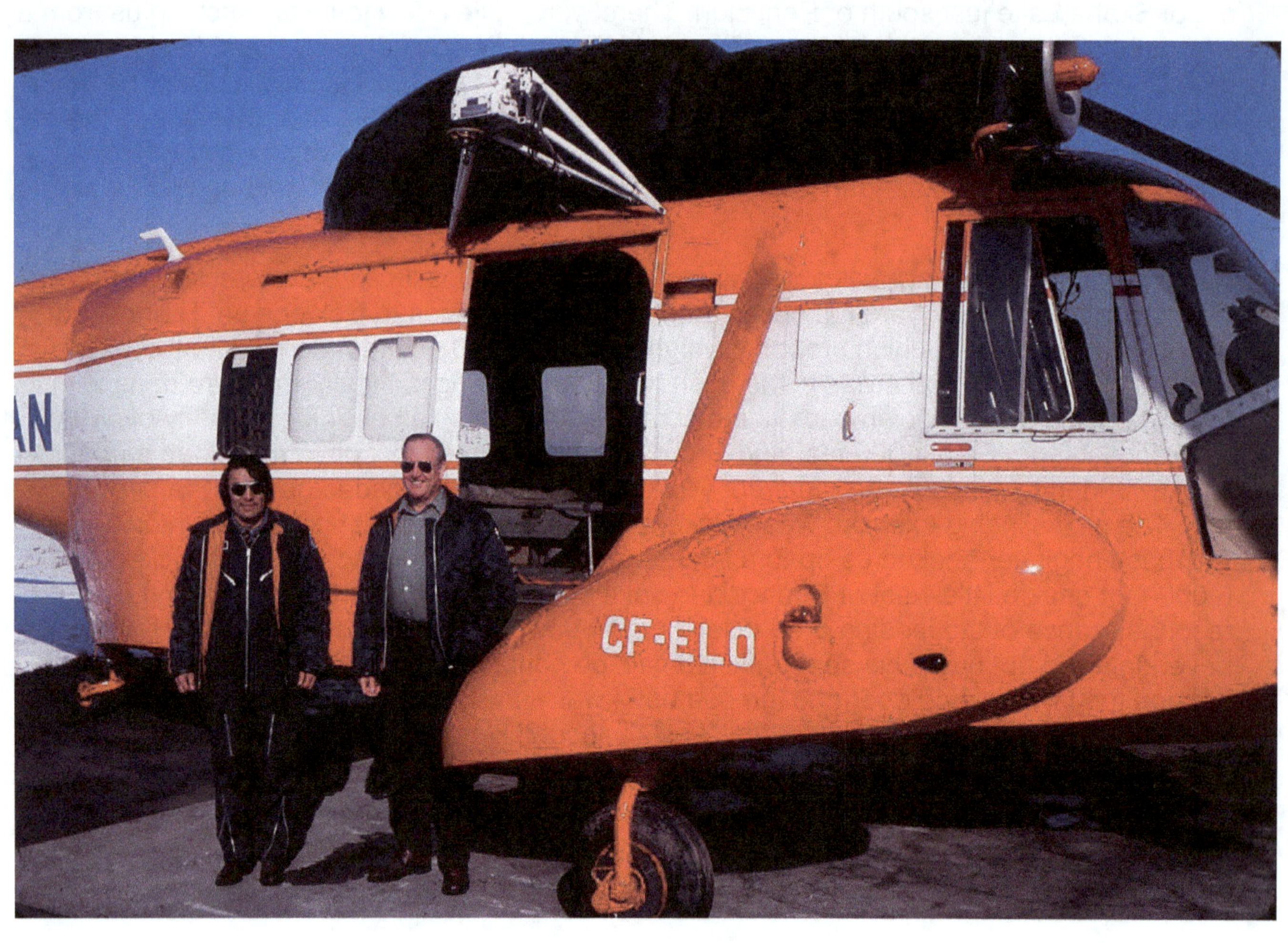

M Mcdonagh - (Rt) Instrument instructor

The next job would take me

up to the high Arctic, a first for me. We had a contract with Panarctic Oils supporting their search for new oil fields in the Arctic Islands. I was based out of Cameron Island, a drill site looking for oil. This was near the magnetic North Pole, so the aircraft compass just spun in circles and was completely unreliable. I had a short course in Edmonton on operating a GNS (Global Navigation System) installed in the helicopter. Navigation was predicated on triangulation with a minimum of 2 satellites and was very accurate.

The terrain in that area was flat and featureless, but flying in the Arctic was interesting. Mid summer was the land of the 'midnight sun' because it never set. New crews on 12-hour shifts would come on at midnight and needed something moved. So after a full day's flying, you had to just grab 'catnaps' when you could. My engineer would do his daily inspections and maintenance, usually late at night. A large Arctic wolf usually watched from a nearby distance, so we kept a wary eye on him. I had related this to my wife in Nanaimo, and then she overheard our daughter one day playing outside. She said to a neighbour kid, "You know where my daddy works? There's a big wolf by his helicopter. I sure hope he doesn't eat him because I love him, and he's the only daddy I've got!" There was a lot of interesting wildlife in the Arctic that was fascinating to see up close. There were seals on the ice that never strayed far from their holes. If I came in fast downwind, sometimes I could block the hole with one float on the helicopter. This gave me a chance for some great closeup pictures of a frustrated seal. I would immediately fly away so as not to be a threat to the seal. Occasionally I would see some huge spectacular polar bears. More incredible pictures from the helicopter as a bear would jump off an ice floe into the water and swim to the next one. One day I came upon a huge herd of musk oxen. As I approached, they formed a text book circle with the cows and calves in the centre and males with horns pointed outward. As soon as I got closer, the helicopter's downwash would cause them to scatter and reform farther away again. Again, not to bother them too much, I would take pictures and quickly fly away. The arctic foxes were amazing and pure white. The camp cook often threw scraps of food out to them. They got to be quite tame, and one of the crew used to take one of them along in his tundra ATV. It playfully bit him one day, and unfortunately, he contracted rabies. He was flown south to Edmonton for some painful inoculations in his stomach. Apparently, a large population of animals in the Arctic are carriers of rabies without showing any signs of the disease.

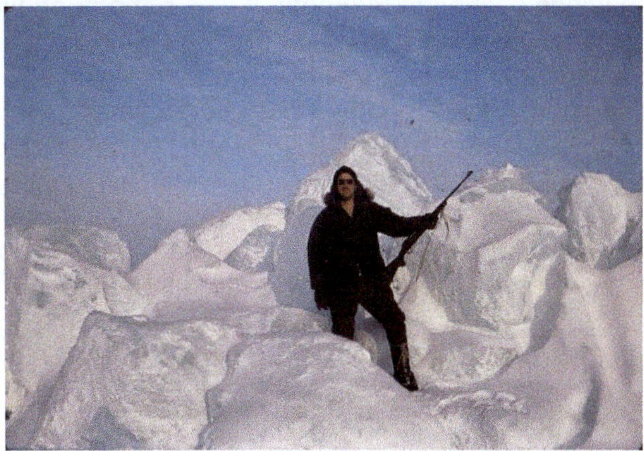

I was the designated camp guard for Polar bears

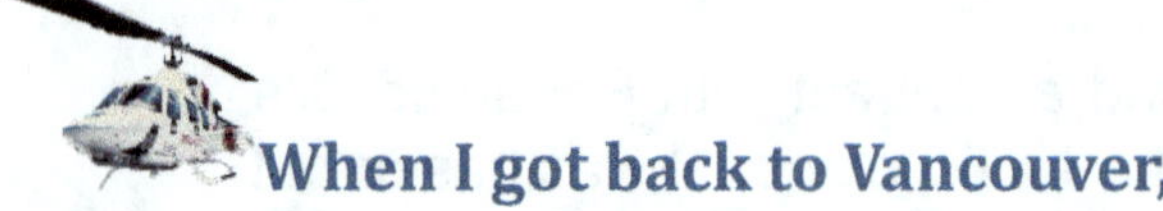

When I got back to Vancouver,

I was asked to pick up a Bell 205 in Toronto. It was needed for power line construction in the Fraser Canyon. I was more than happy to build time in mediums, and I always enjoyed the cross-Canada ferry flights. I had an interesting engineer whom I had worked with in James Bay. He liked to fly, as most engineers do, as these aircraft always had dual controls, so I would give him the controls in flight. He was a bit argumentative, and if he strayed off course, I would correct him, but he would insist he wasn't. I let it go to a point, but it's always a good idea to be on your flight-planned track. In the event you had some kind of emergency, it made it much easier for Search & Rescue to locate you.

We were about half way between Dryden and Winnipeg, and Joe was describing some parties he had been to in a lot of detail. He was always an incessant talker and especially so right then. Joe was a bit rough around the edges and had formerly been a heavy-duty mechanic. He was being very descriptive, with a lot of colourful language thrown in. In the 205, you can talk to each other through your headsets on the intercom. I had switched to the Winnipeg tower frequency, but we were still talking to each other on the intercom. However, he's using a foot- activated transmit button on the floor. I was still new to this aircraft, so I said, "Joe, are you sure you're not transmitting on frequency? He said, oh no, this button on the floor is intercom only." Just then, Winnipeg tower said with a lot of tone, "Air Canada 587, you're transmitting on frequency!" The captain responded, "No, it's not us, but it sure is one interesting conversation!" Joe shut up for the rest of the day.

Continuing en route after a fuel stop in Winnipeg, I landed at our farm north of Saskatoon. This was about the fourth time I had stopped to see mom & dad, but the first time with a large helicopter. The 205 has a tremendous, hurricane-like downwash. 'Sparky,' the collie came out to bark at me. He went rolling, along with the picnic bench! Mom & dad scooted around the corner of the house and found shelter. My Uncle Ken Opheim quickly drove out from Saskatoon to take pictures. He was fascinated by the length of the main rotor blades, which are 48 feet in diameter. He actually measured the distance between the blades and the corner of the house.
Of course, I had to take mom and dad for a ride before we continued on to BC.

The day after dropping the aircraft off to the crew at Yale, I was sent up to Tuktoyaktuk in the Northwest Territories. Sun Oil had some drilling operations out in the Beaufort Sea. They needed a medium-sized helicopter for moving some heavy casings, pipe and other materials from rig to rig. One day we were moving a lot of pipes, and weather conditions were severe. It was minus 35 degrees, with winds gusting to 30 knots. It was not a good time for the heater to quit, but it was imperative for the pipe to be moved, or that rig would be shut down. With my door removed to set the pipe by vertical reference, it was extremely cold. Even our mikes froze up, so I couldn't talk to my engineer. However, the job was completed, and we were able to return to the base camp to have the heater repaired. I parked beside the shack, housing a generator and steam plant.

Through the night, the wind shifted, and steam had poured over the helicopter all night. We came out in the morning to see that the helicopter had turned into a huge Popsicle. Luckily the weather was out that day and we couldn't fly because it took hours with a Herman Nelson heater to melt all the ice off of the blades and airframe. The joys of Arctic operations!

I felt that I had gained quite a variety of experiences in the VFR (Visual Flight Rules) 'bush' world. So I really wanted to get an IFR (Instrument Flight Rules) rating which would open the door to large, heavy-lift helicopters. If flying IFR, there is generally a 2 man crew in Canada. I thought another pilot in the cockpit would be great! Somebody to discuss the operation with and decision making. In the following years, I found this to be true, but you had to guard against the odd personality conflict. Many older pilots had been flying solo for many years and were used to making their own decisions. Usually, they adapted to a two-man crew quite quickly, and others, not so much. To avoid conflict and 'independent' practices, Transport Canada came out with a standard called CRM (Cockpit Resource Management). This had worked well with airline crews for years, and because helicopters had entered that world, it was a logical step. This all boiled down to safety. Sometimes it became a dangerous situation in the past where a new copilot had to conform to incorrect procedures because "This is what the captain wanted!" So CRM solved this problem in that, with checklists, the exact same procedural steps for that aircraft were always followed. You could mix/ match crews so that pilots may have never flown together before, but it still resulted in a complete standard of conformity.

It's hard for the company to pull a duty pilot from the field because they rarely have extra pilots. However, I was diplomatically insistent, and they finally brought me in and even paid for the IFR training. This could be done in an airplane because instrument flying is basically the same in fixed wing as rotary and a much cheaper route. So I was signed up with the Victoria Flying Club for a 40-hour course on an instrumented Cessna. It seemed very strange to get back in an airplane after flying helicopters for the last 7 years. But it's like the old adage of 'it's just like riding a bicycle !"

The training was fun and challenging, and then it was time for a ride with Transport Canada. I flew over to Vancouver International to pick up the TC Inspector. Back then, they had two standards for an instrument rating. If you did a really good ride, you qualified for a Class I rating. This allowed you to fly down to the same minimum ceilings and visibility on an instrument approach as the airlines. If you passed the ride but hadn't flown it with a certain precision, you only received a Class II rating. I had been warned by my instructor that they rarely gave out a Class I on an abinitio (initial) ride. I wanted to prove him wrong! I had studied very hard for ground school, and the flight exercises had gone well.

So we got an IFR clearance from Air Traffic Control and took off from YVR. The clearance was a bit complex, changing altitudes, intercepts to navigational aids and tracks, holds on nav aids and procedure in the event of a communication failure. I took off from runway 26L and attempted to contact Air Traffic Control. The inspector was simulating Air Traffic Control and didn't respond. There was my communication failure! That made me follow a new clearance adhering to 'in the event of a communication failure.' When that exercise was over, I carried on with a new clearance. This involved changing altitudes, hold and an approach to the Boundary Bay Airport near YVR. After only about 40 minutes in the air, I was shocked to hear the inspector requesting a return to the Vancouver airport. An initial ride traditionally is supposed to take about an hour and a half. He didn't say a word, and I was trying to figure out what I had done to fail. As we cleared the runway and were taxiing in, I asked him when I could do another ride. He said, "You're done. That was a perfect ride. I'm giving you a Class I ." Needless to say, I was ecstatic!

So all that was left was to get the rotary endorsement which I did the following week with a company check pilot. This was done in a much larger instrumented helicopter in Vancouver. I was on my way to twin-engine IFR-certified helicopters and a whole new world!

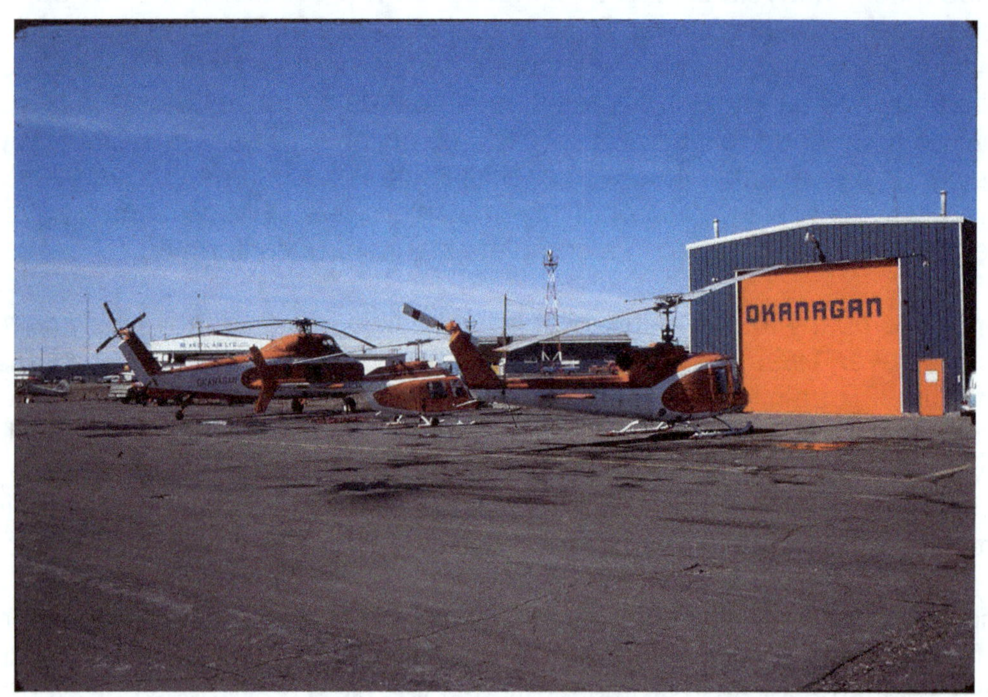

Return to base - Fort St. John

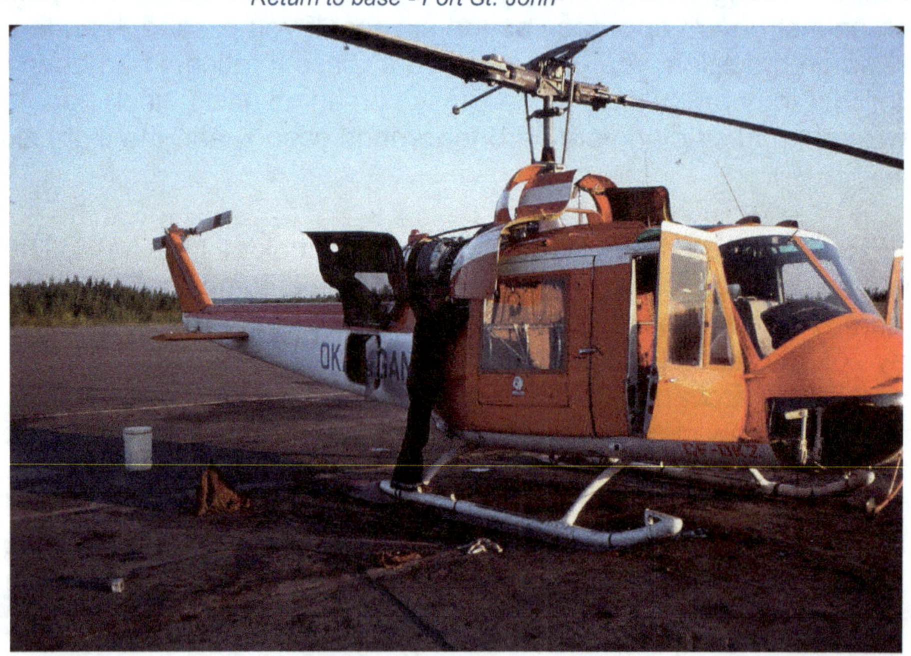

Routine check

After a bit of time off,

I was sent back to the high Arctic. This proved to be another interesting job and a new experience. It was a contract with a research company flying hydrologists out from a base camp. This consisted of a couple of Parkall tents out on the ice of the Beaufort Sea 100 miles north of Tuktoyaktuk. The hydrologists were studying ice movement resulting from tides and winds. My job was to move them around on the ice within a 50-mile radius of the camp. There were a lot of polar bears in the area, and we had to be vigilant. The pilot I replaced had an experience with a large polar bear that came within inches of him. He had been on his back working on the cargo hook beneath the helicopter. When he came out, his interest was immediately captivated. There was a bear up on a pressure ridge about 100 yards away ripping at the camp flag. What really startled him were the bear tracks right beside him as he lay on his back. They weren't there when he crawled underneath the helicopter half an hour ago!

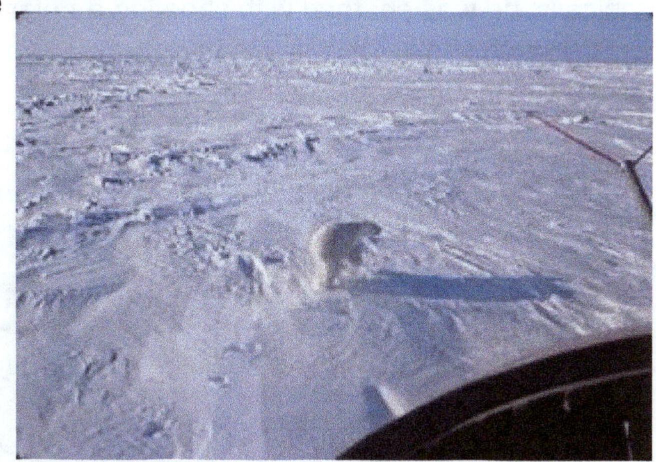

So when I arrived in the camp, I was handed a 303 calibre rifle.

The Inuit guide had to leave on a family emergency, so I was the new polar bear watchman! I knew this rifle because my dad had taught me how to use it, but I wasn't real comfortable taking on that responsibility. The camp boss had cleverly set up a bear 'alarm' around the camp perimeter as a warning. This was a wire about a foot in height off the ice and connected to an alarm. During the day, if any bears got too close, I would chase them away with the helicopter, usually for a couple of miles. At night we would fire off flares over them. They generally wouldn't be back; however, there was one bear that did. He was quite slender and seemed to be suffering from malnutrition which made him especially dangerous. As I hovered over him and the downwash hit, he suddenly reared up on his hind legs. As I quickly increased my height, his front paws just missed my skids. If there had been contact, the helicopter would have rolled and crashed. If I survived the crash, I would have had to deal with one angry bear!

There went another guardian angel!

One night the bear alarm went off about 3:00 am. I quickly grabbed the rifle and went outside. The whole area was floodlit, and I thought I spotted him about 50 yards away. As I took aim over his head, I realized it was just a large white packing crate! I also quickly realized I didn't know where he was and needed to take cover. As I rushed back into the Parkall, the bear had been right there in the shadows and swatted the porch as I dove through it!

A few days later, I dropped the 2 hydrologists about 40 miles out from the camp. The camp dog was with them to act as an alarm for any bears in the area. Sure enough, a large bear gave chase to the dog, which promptly ran away. The bear simply altered his course of attack a couple of degrees and pounded straight toward one of the hydrologists. A polar bear doesn't care if it has 4 legs, flippers or 2 legs. It's meat. So the guy dropped the bear as it was about to lunge.

Ironically, he was charged with shooting a polar bear without a license and fined $3,000, even though it was in self-defence. That bear is probably now hanging in some MP's office in Ottawa!

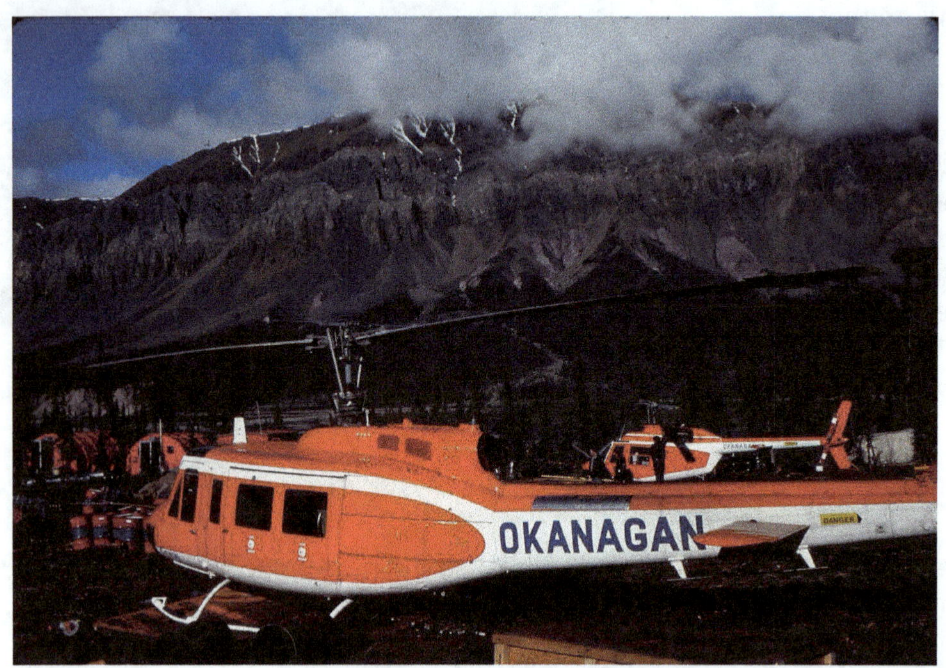

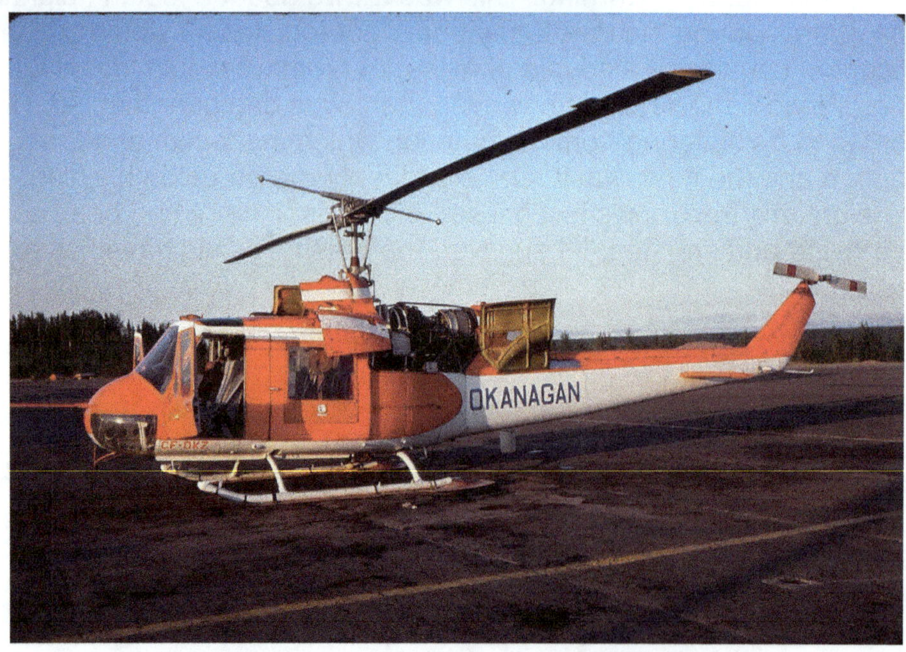

Preparing to depart for another fire near Fort St John

1976 and the start

of another fire season in BC. I was working fires in the Interior around Chetwynd. Mid day I received a call from another company aircraft. It was the base manager from Fort St. John saying he needed a bigger helicopter on a fire southeast of the city. He described the location of the fire and some local landmarks. He did not give me the lat & long coordinates, which, as it turned out, would have been more helpful. However, I found the fire, and it was in a perfect location for utilizing my 400-gallon bucket. There was a lake right beside the raging fire, which was perfect for a bucketing operation. I was able to do 4-minute turnarounds, and the fire was totally extinguished about the time I needed to refuel. When I landed in Fort St. John, the base manager, M. Berg asked, "WHERE were you?! " I described the location and told him I was surprised he wasn't there as he said he would be. The more I described the precise location, the more he laughed. He said I was close but not on the right fire. He said, "Forestry just paid us $20,000 to back burn that area!" (A back burn is accomplished by using a tiger torch slung beneath the helicopter.) This initiates a controlled burn which acts as a fire guard to stop the main fire.

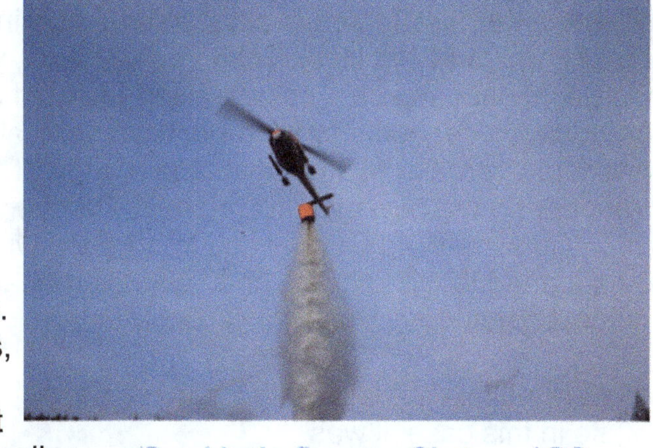

'Bombing' a fire near Chetwynd BC

The next day in areas west of Ft. St. John, due to hot, dry conditions and lightning strikes, there was an increasing number of fires. I had just dropped 16 firefighters at one fire and got an emergency call to extricate 6 guys I had dropped off earlier. I had advised their crew chief that this area was potentially dangerous. If the wind shifted, the fire up on the ridge could come down and trap them where they were. That is exactly what happened. When I arrived on the scene, they were totally surrounded.
Large fires, like this one, often generate their own winds, and I estimated gusts up to 100 mph. Visibility was down to about an eighth of a mile as they quickly went to work with chainsaws to clear a small area. This allowed me to get into a low hover as the crews opened the sliding doors and piled in from both sides. Needless to say, they were quite relieved, and I was glad to fly out of the area!

A few weeks later, we had a number of helicopters on fires near Pemberton, just north of Vancouver. Fires can be intense, obviously, but it is satisfying to be able to control and eventually extinguish them. Usually, the fire boss would go out with you on the first flight of the day. He would outline the areas that should be fire guarded with dropped retardant or hit directly. So basically, you were your own boss for the rest of the day, hitting areas that were spreading. It was not uncommon to have 30 aircraft, water bombers and helicopters of various sizes on a fire. Winds can reach speeds of 200 kmh, and visibility is reduced to an eighth of a mile in smoke. It's extremely important to maintain traffic separation when you're all in close proximity. This generally works well as long as everybody gives constant position reports. If one or two do not do this, it can jeopardize the whole operation.

Fighting fires at Pemberton involved a different technique because of the steep mountainous terrain. To be effective on fires burning at the base of the pines, you had to approach the fire at eye level. Then very close in, you flared the helicopter so the bucket went straight out ahead of you, releasing the load at the same time. This was an effective way to get at the base rather than vertically overhead. However, it was important to approach at a bit of an angle and not 90 degrees to the mountain in case the trapdoor on the bucket didn't release. The inertia of 4,000 pounds of water moving forward was something you needed to be gone when you hit the trigger. That's exactly what happened to me later on, and I was glad I had the angle to easily fly out and avoid the mountainside!

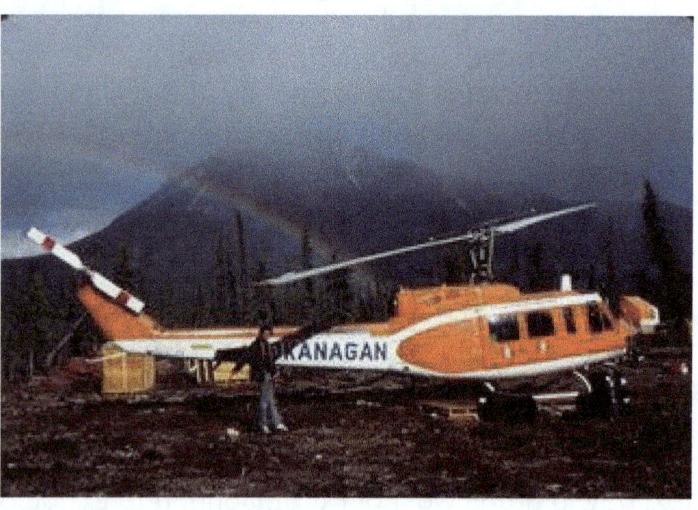

There were no lakes nearby to bucket out of, so in this case, it was necessary for forestry to build a 'mud' tank. This was a large container they built in the valley, which was constantly filled with retardant. It's an orange-coloured retardant which helps outline a fire guard and is also very effective on fires. At vertical altitude drops, water tends to evaporate, but retardant adheres to the trees. So we would simply hover over the mud tank and fill our buckets. As I moved down the valley, I did have a lake to bucket out of later on. I noticed a large group of people on the beach, but with each pick-up, I was able to remain a good distance from them. They seemed to be upset that I was disturbing them, which of course, was unavoidable. At the end of the day, my engineer called me over to the helicopter. There was a bullet hole in the door post just above my head! On one of my pick-ups near that crowd, I heard something like a pop can falling inside the cabin.

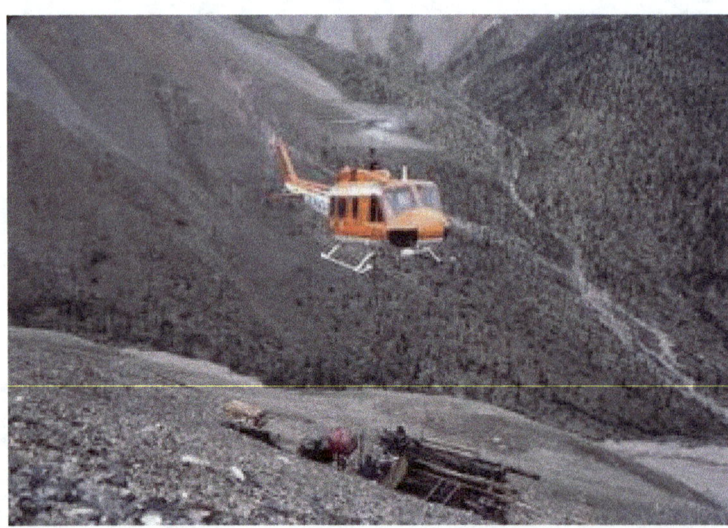

Setting up a drill base

This didn't make sense at the time, but we could only conclude someone had taken a shot at me. There were obviously more risks on that fire than I thought!

Like I say, as a Vancouver pool pilot,

there was always a lot of variety of assignments. Okanagan added a brand new Bell 205 to the fleet, and it was badly needed up in Inuvik. So I was airborne bright and early out of our main base in Vancouver. This is a relatively quick flight in a fixed-wing but not so much in a helicopter. Because of the need, I ferried right through before the days of mandatory duty time restrictions. I always enjoyed ferry flights and appreciated the changes in scenery and geography. After several fuel stops, I was on the last leg about 100 miles south of Inuvik. It was midnight, and the sun was low on the horizon. It had been a full day, and I was starting to feel a bit dozy. Suddenly I had an engine fire light! If the sun is at just the right angle, it can shine through the cowling on an engine fire probe. I banked slightly away, and the light went out, but it certainly caused me to be wide awake till I landed!

A week later, I received a call from our operations manager. He asked me to replace one of our guys who apparently was jeopardizing an important contract. For some reason, this pilot was being belligerent and not getting along with the job manager and his crews. This was a 4-month contract with Shell Mineral, and our company obviously wanted to retain it. So the ops manager flattered me by saying how diplomatic I was with customers and sent me in.

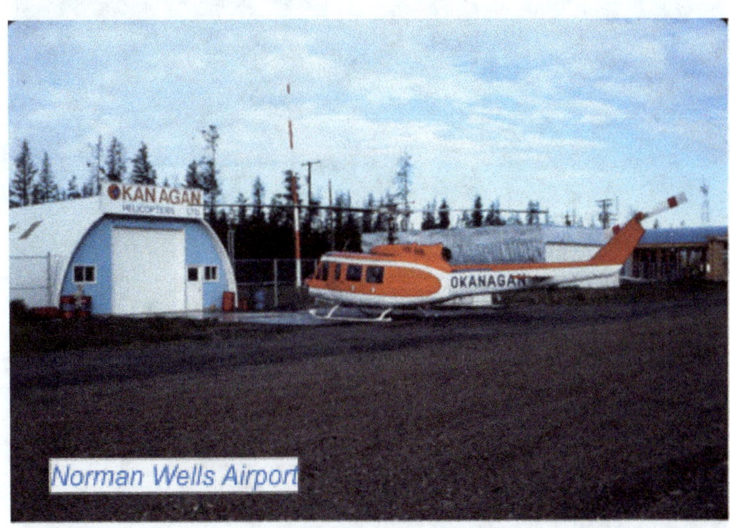

Norman Wells Airport

This was a well-set-up camp located about 100 miles west of Norman Wells. It was a beautiful spot on the banks of the Keele River, surrounded by the Mackenzie Mountains. Living in this camp in the middle of summer was like a paid vacation, complete with your own helicopter! The main objective of the Shell mineral division was to find large copper deposits. We had two helicopters in camp, a 5 place Bell 206 and mine, with a 4,000-pound lift, a Bell 205. The 206 spotted out geologists in the surrounding area to gather samples (we called them 'rock doctors!). One day a third- year geology student was cutting a rock sample in half. He was using a portable saw with a masonry-looking blade. It cut through the 8-inch rock like butter. I remarked that it looked pretty impressive.

Then he said, "Just put your thumb on the wheel." I politely declined because I saw what it had just done to the rock! So he actually did it first without any harm. He explained that flesh is just too soft, and this type of blade will only cut into something hard like a rock.

I was primarily involved with moving drillers and their drill equipment. Occasionally I would supply the camp with a grocery run to the Wells. I would sling their drills, platforms, pumps and equipment to various locations, including mountainsides. One day I had a particularly heavy load of steel well pipes to be placed at a site half way up a mountain. I radioed ahead to the crew and told them to make sure the area was clear because this would be a 'no hover' sling load. As I was on a short final, I could see one of the drillers had left something in the middle of the area. It was his lunch bucket that ended up being flat as a pancake! Later that day, I had to place a long line of water hoses up the side of the mountain to another drill site. I hooked on to the end of a 600-foot length of hose and threaded it through the trees to the ridge above. As I was hovering up with it, I could see a large black wolf in the trees heading towards my engineer, who had hooked me up. Luckily we were in radio contact, and I was able to warn him.

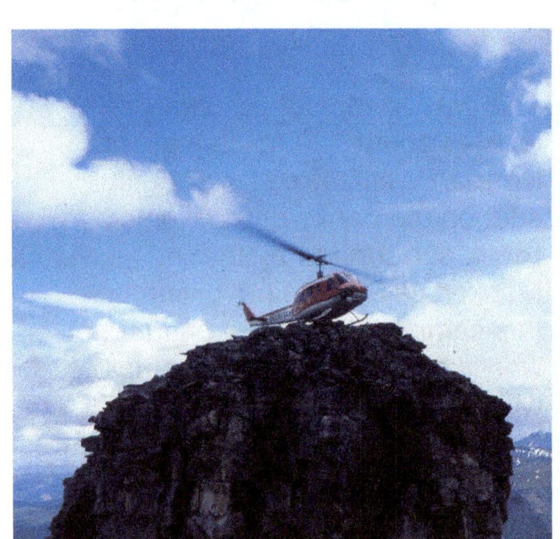

Keele River mountain pinnacle

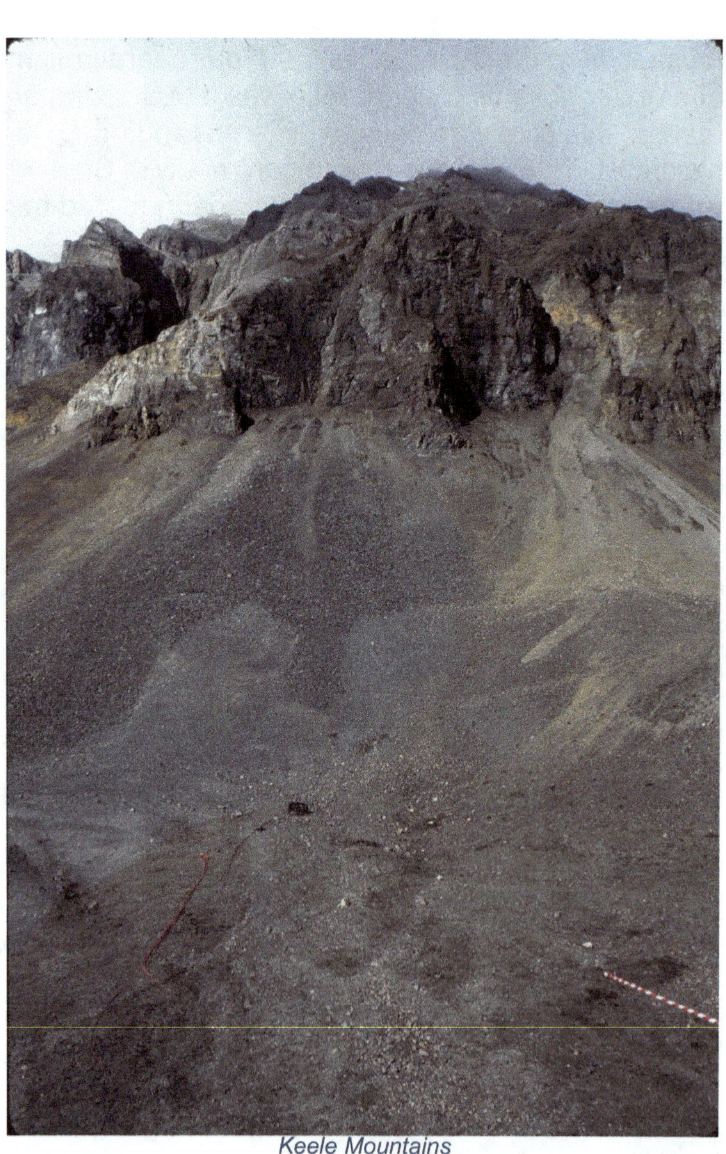

Keele Mountains

There were some interesting breaks in the daily routine.

Nahanni Air had called our office wondering if we had a medium-lift helicopter in the area. One of their pilots had lost an engine on a Beaver with floats and had successfully deadsticked it on to the Keele River. This was only a 15-minute flight downstream from our camp, and we reached it quickly. My engineer and I landed on the sandbar where it was beached. We rigged it up quickly for slinging and spread a large cargo net over the wings. This would keep the plane from 'flying' up while slinging it to Norman Wells. So I hovered over the plane, and he hooked me up. I used full power, and it wouldn't even budge. This didn't make sense as the weight (4500 lbs) of this aircraft, even with floats, should have been manageable. Suddenly we thought of the floats and that they might have water in them. Sure enough,they were full of water, and at 10 pounds per gallon, that was a lot of weight! So we pumped out the water, and I was again hooked up. I moved slowly forward, skidding the Beaver along the sandbar, and I was airborne. The airplane flew beautifully, but because of the drag, I was only able to make about 60 knots airspeed. Our 'bird dog' company Bell 206, had picked up my engineer off the sandbar and was accompanying me back to the Wells and keeping an eye on my load. The thing that was hilarious was that pilot had a terrific sense of humour. I had flown alongside E Cameron for years, and he was the company comedian. Because of my reduced speed, he was able to literally fly circles around me. He would be ahead, on either side or above me, cracking jokes the whole time! I had never laughed so hard in my life, and it made the one-hour flight to the Wells very entertaining! A week later, I got another call to pick up another Beaver.

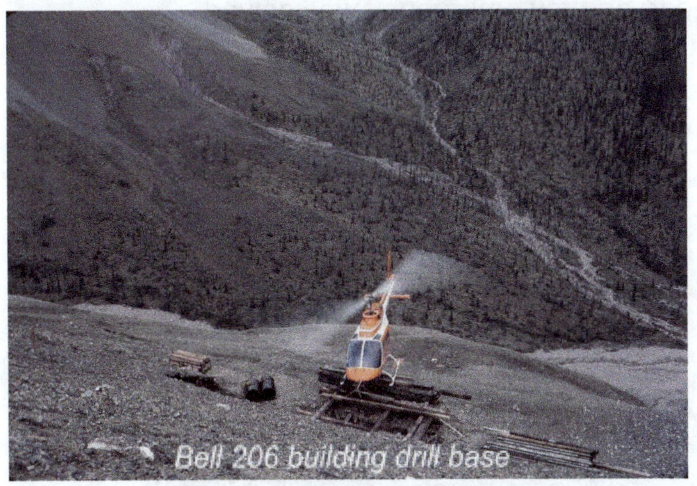
Bell 206 building drill base

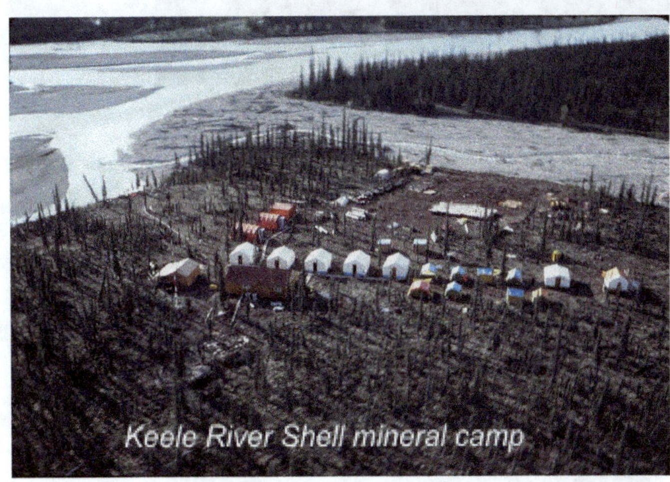
Keele River Shell mineral camp

It had crashed right after takeoff from the Fort Good Hope airport. It wasn't in as good a shape as the previous one but was still repairable. It was also much lighter than the earlier Beaver because it had wheels instead of floats. The owner of Nahanni Air was again very grateful to get his second aircraft back.

Back to the Keele River camp, as they had more work for me moving a fly camp near our main camp. I was deadheading back after the move and had only one passenger in the front seat. I started a descent into our camp, and as I eased the cyclic back (the main directional control), I suddenly felt a restriction. I moved it slightly forward and had even less travel trying to move it aft. Any kind of control failure can be extremely serious. It's like losing your steering wheel in a car. The only way to land with a jammed cyclic is to do a very fast running landing, as you can no longer hover. I had a sandbar picked out in the Keele River and was setting up an approach. The passenger must have felt something because he said, "Oh, is my lunch pail bothering you?" It was in his lap and right behind the cyclic on his side. He removed it, and my emergency was solved. From then on, the only passenger allowed in the front seat was my engineer!

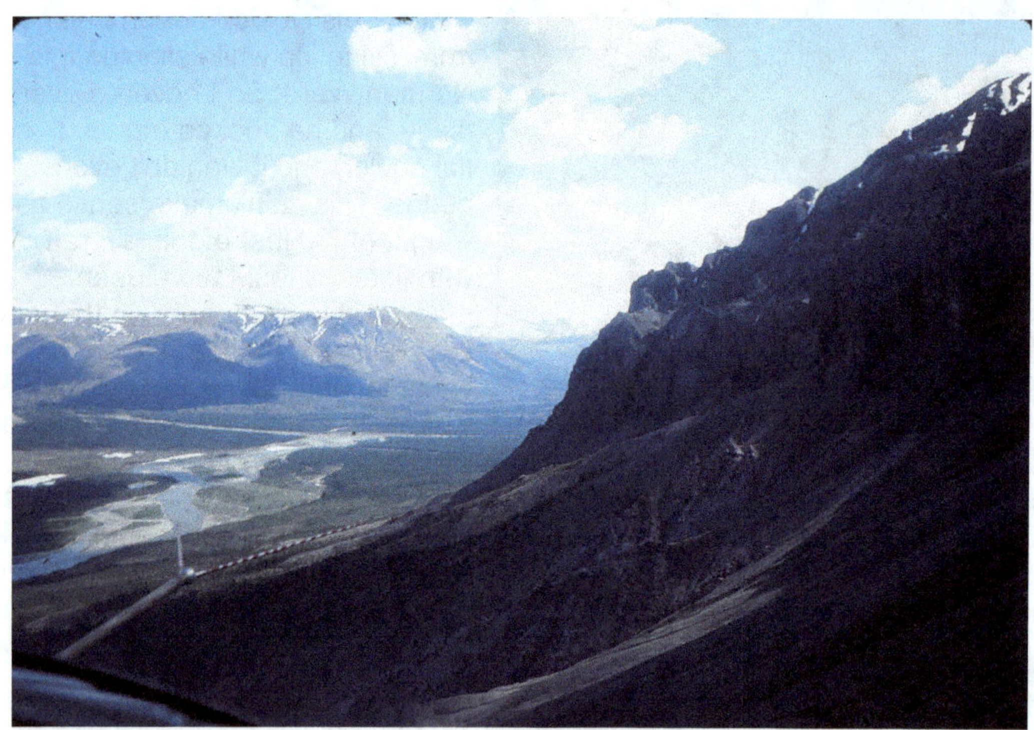

Keele River & mountains

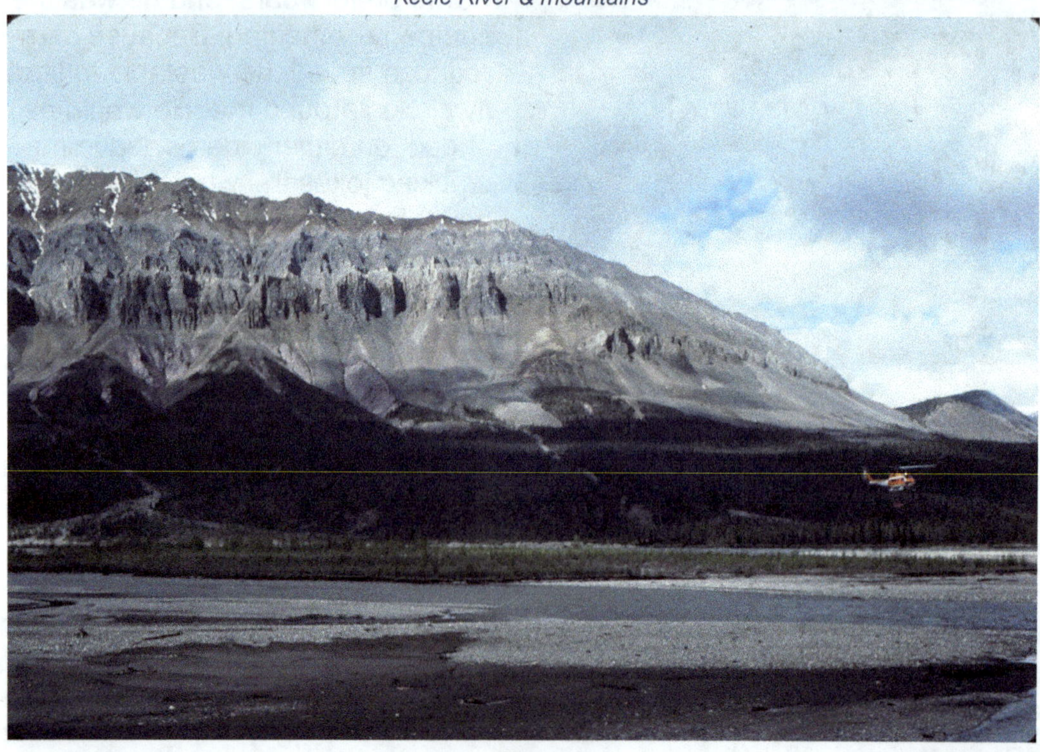

After another month

my tour was done, and the aircraft was due for some extensive maintenance at our base in Revelstoke. On the way south, I had the privilege of stopping in to see an old school friend, Reuben Loewen.

Reuben & I had gone to grade school and all the way through high school together in Saskatchewan. He, friends and family had been developing raw land 80 miles north of Fort St. John. So on July 7th, 1977, I landed on his land for the first time. It was amazing to see how many acres they had cleared and had successfully raised crops. There were professional land and agricultural advisers that warned them that this land was unsustainable. Reuben and his relatives proved them wrong and even won awards for their bumper crops. So, not having a lot of time, I was able to give Reuben a quick aerial view of their place, and I was off again.

The next tour was back up to Fort Nelson. An interesting call came in the next day to search for a missing private American aircraft. As I related earlier, we generally don't get involved with search and rescue; however, all their aircraft were tied up on other calls. With a couple of local officials on board, we began a search at the last reported position. We found the downed Cessna 120 miles southwest of Fort Nelson and landed beside it. The CEO and his secretary had spent the night in their tent and were uninjured. He had been lost and ran out of fuel trying to find the Fort Nelson Airport. He had 'deadsticked' into a clear area and did a good landing. We flew them back to Fort Nelson, and the next day I slung the aircraft back to the nearest road. The Cessna was in perfect shape as I placed it on the waiting truck flatbed.

Ironically, I learned later that the driver had done a lot of damage to the fuselage as he secured it. Apparently, he had used a 'Come-a-Long' and destroyed the fuselage by winching it down too tightly.

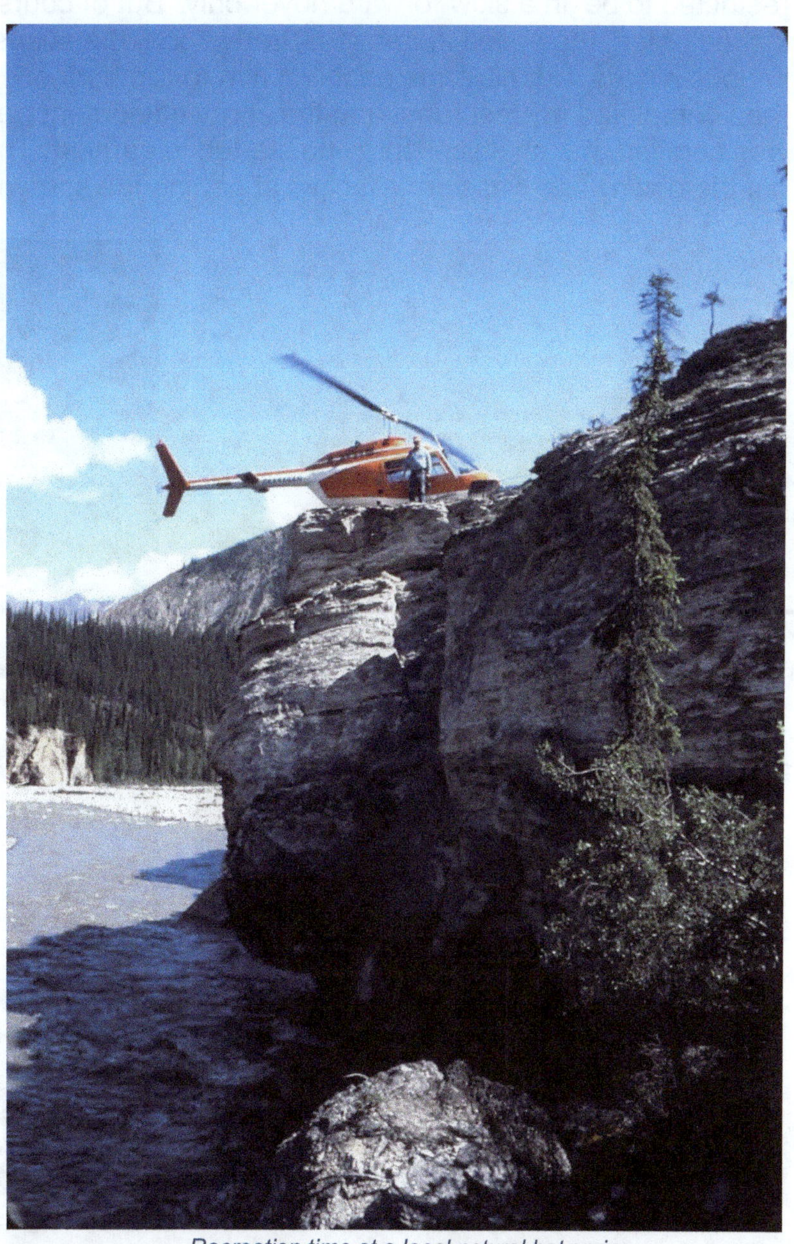

Recreation time at a local natural hot spring

A few days later, my company needed

to certify some new spray equipment for BC Forestry. Twenty-foot booms were installed on either side of the helicopter. Then I had to hover backwards, sideways and forward to establish Vne (never exceed speeds). Then, various speeds in flight to see if there were any adverse effects. Finally, an internal tank was installed and filled with coloured water to test spray patterns. This spray equipment was to be used for budworm control which was devastating to pine trees. Many years later, there would be a worse threat with Pine Beatles. With all the spray equipment and tanks installed, there needed to be some final tests to check spray patterns and coverage. So off to an area in the Fraser Canyon where bud worms had infested the trees. A company helicopter was used to place small white cards in the upper portions of the pines in a test area. This in itself was an interesting (and fun) job for the forestry student and the pilot. He was suspended on a cable below the Bell 206 and would place these cards in the trees as the pilot hovered along. Transport Canada had approved this special operation but was restricted to be 'In a slow forward hover only.' But of course, as soon as the MOT inspector left, the speed increased. Pretty soon, the suspended 'passenger' was creating various airfoils with his arms enabling him to climb, descend and slalom back and forth! I then completed my test runs, and the spray equipment had the desired results. After it was certified, the chemical spraying started in earnest. The spread was not only great, but the downwash was very effective at getting the spray mixture deep into the trees.

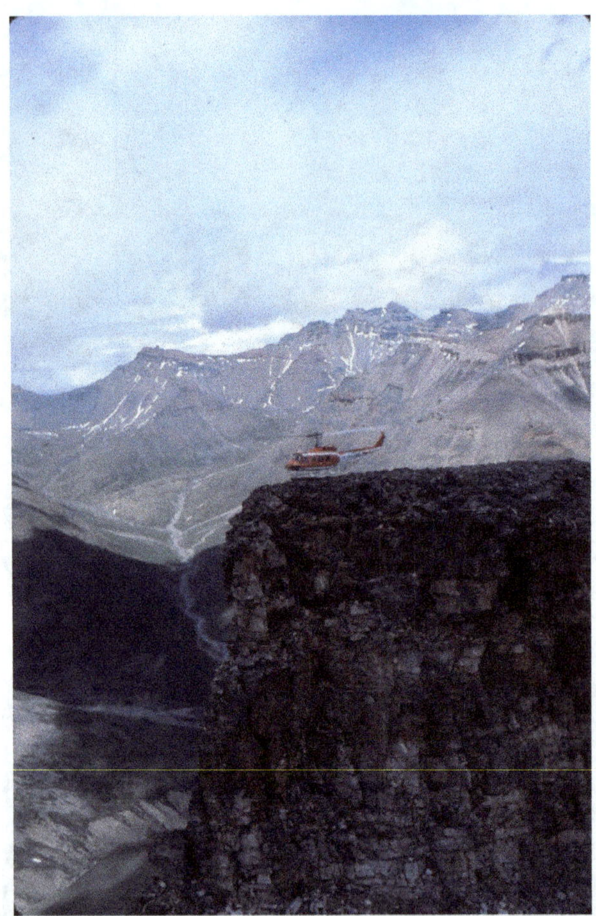

Move complete - coffee break!

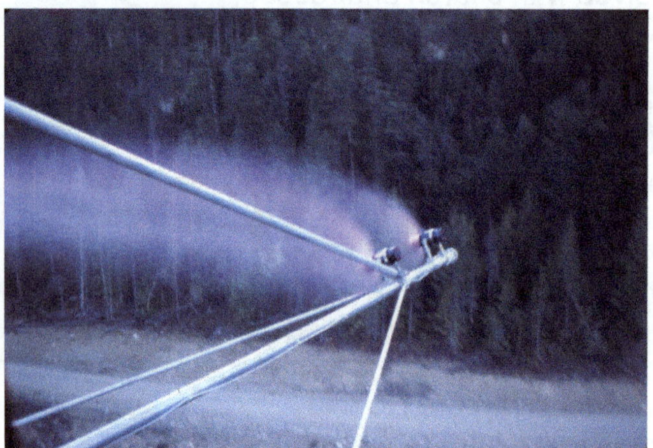

Testing spray equipment for Spruce Budworms

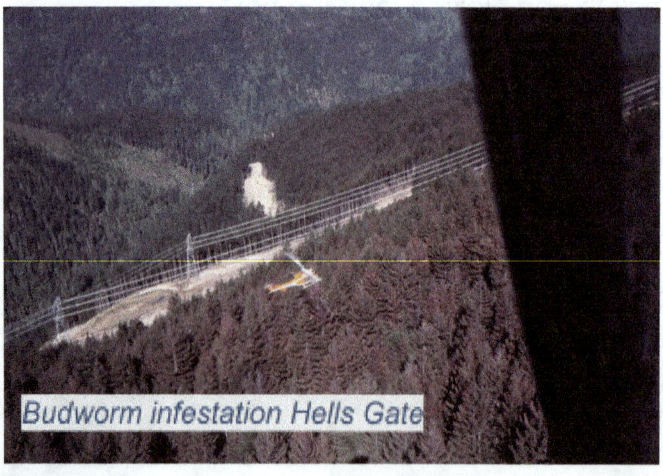

Budworm infestation Hells Gate

Summer of 1977

I was checked out on the company's largest helicopter, a Sikorsky S-61. This was a beautiful, stable aircraft capable of lifting 10,000 lbs. The initial checkout took place in Inuvik, Northwest Territories & I became a certified copilot. I was then involved in various jobs around the Territories & BC. We moved a lot of heavy equipment & supplies off of barges in the Beaufort Sea. The following week, we received a call to move a large beehive burner across town in Prince George. These burners are used at sawmills for incinerating waste wood & sawdust.

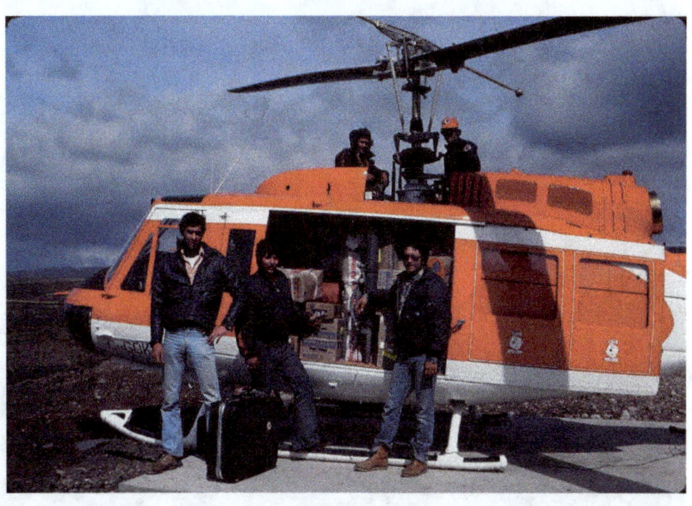

Loading groceries for our camp

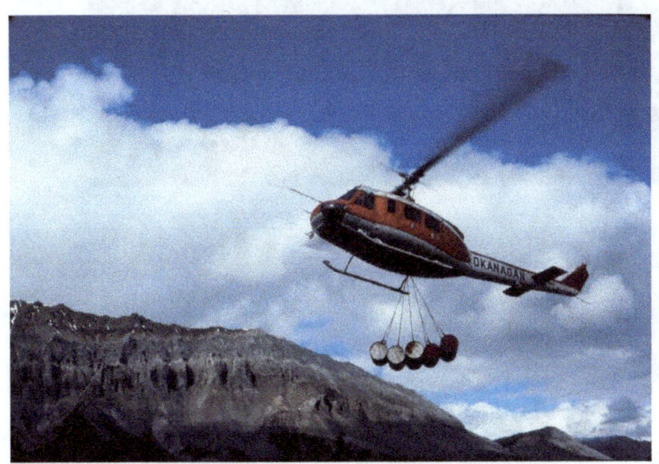

Bringing jet fuel into camp

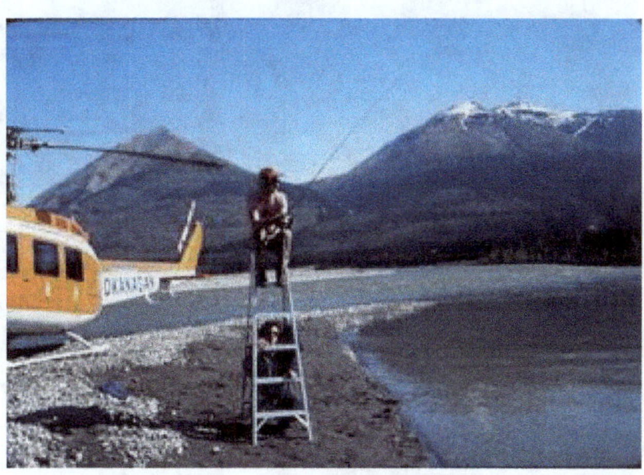

Fishing on the Keele River

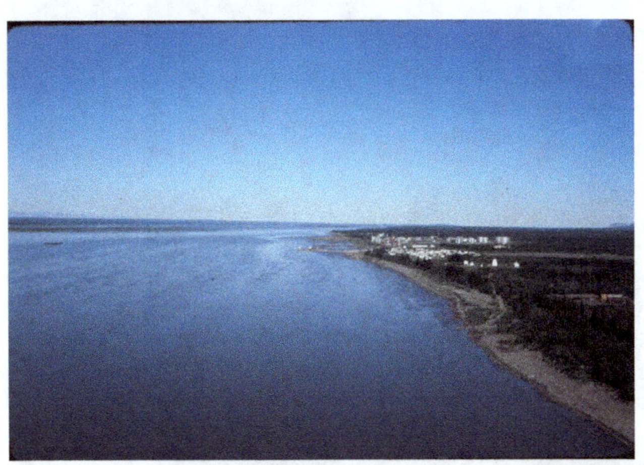

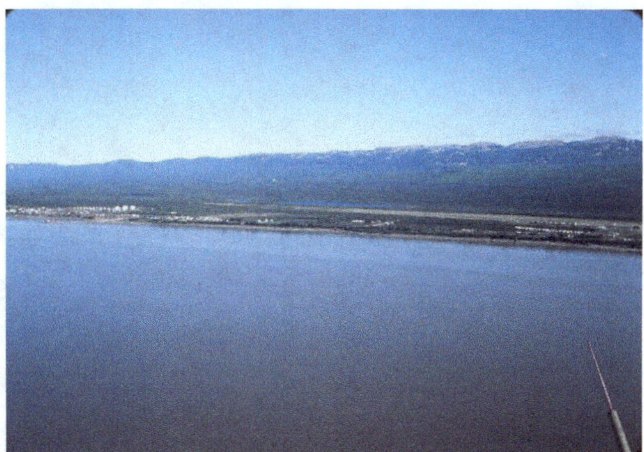

Approaching Norman Wells

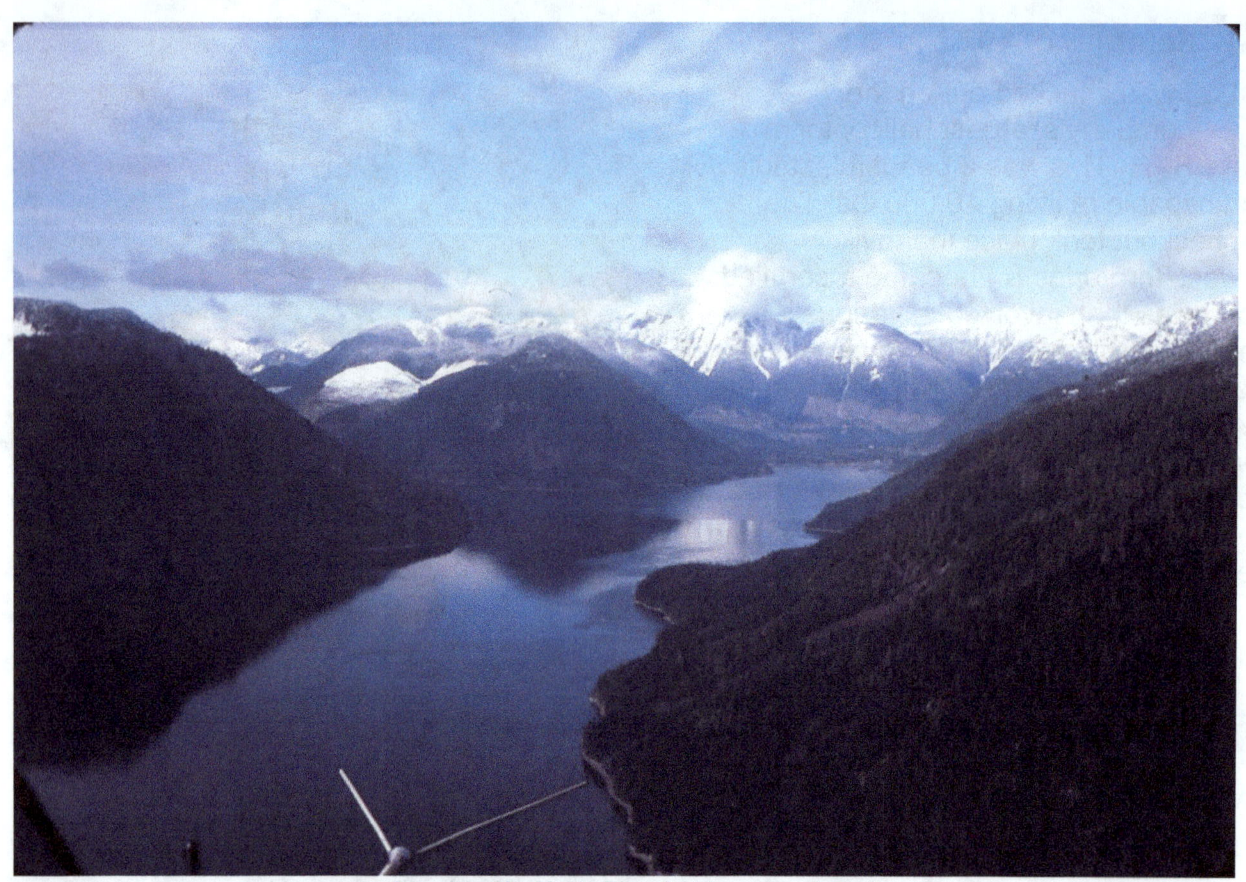

Departing the Keele River for Vancouver Island

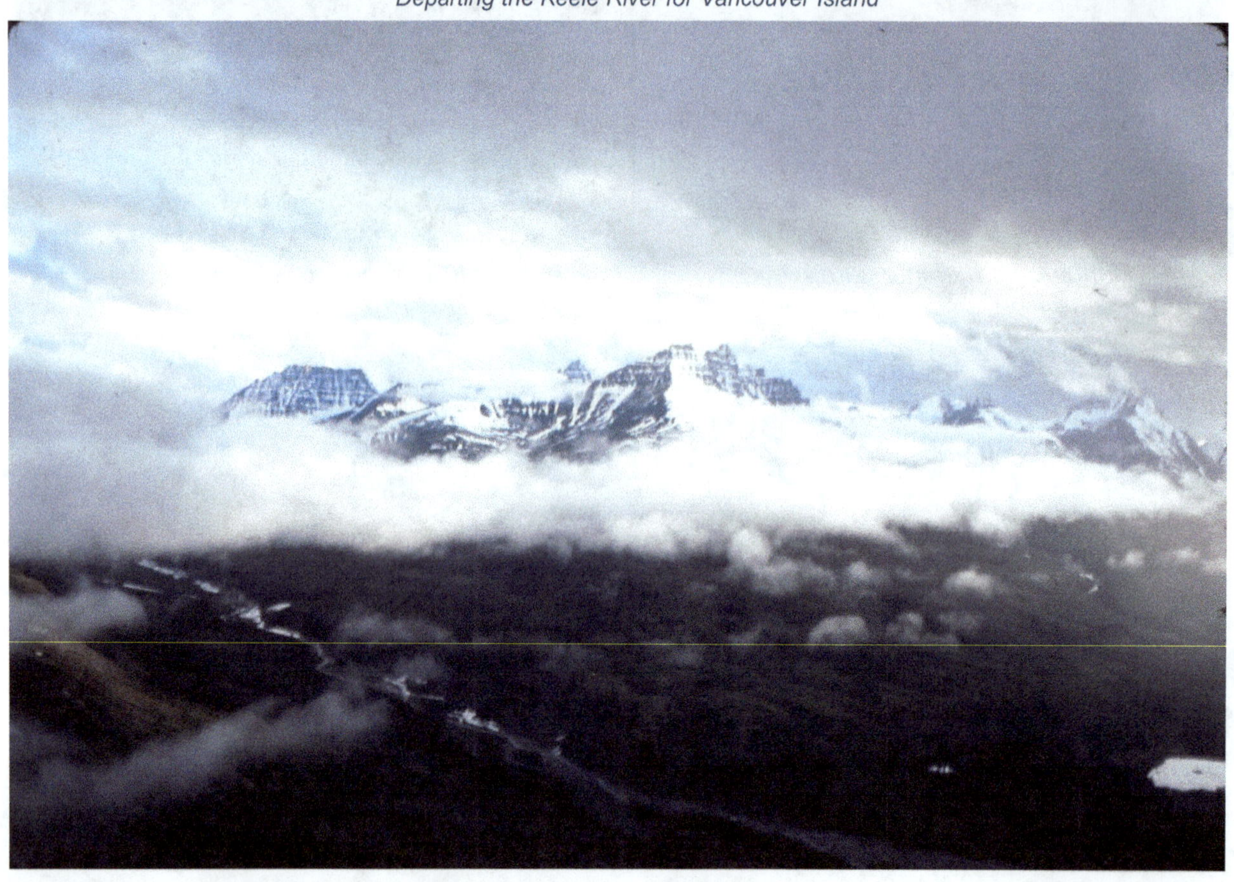

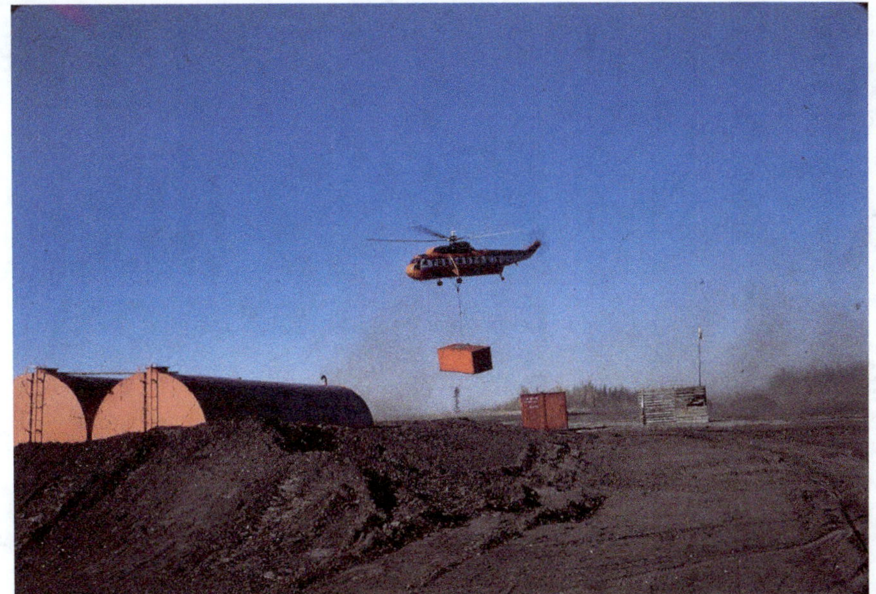

Bringing jet fuel into camp

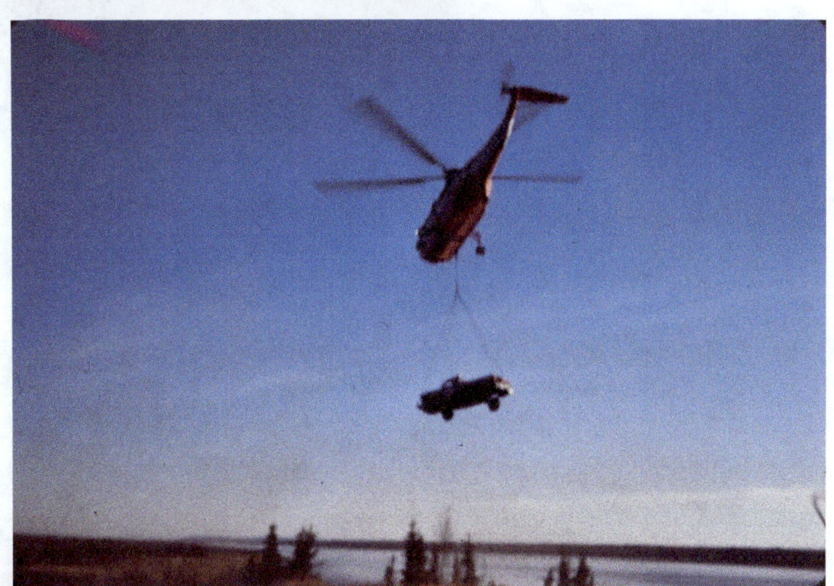

Truck required at construction site

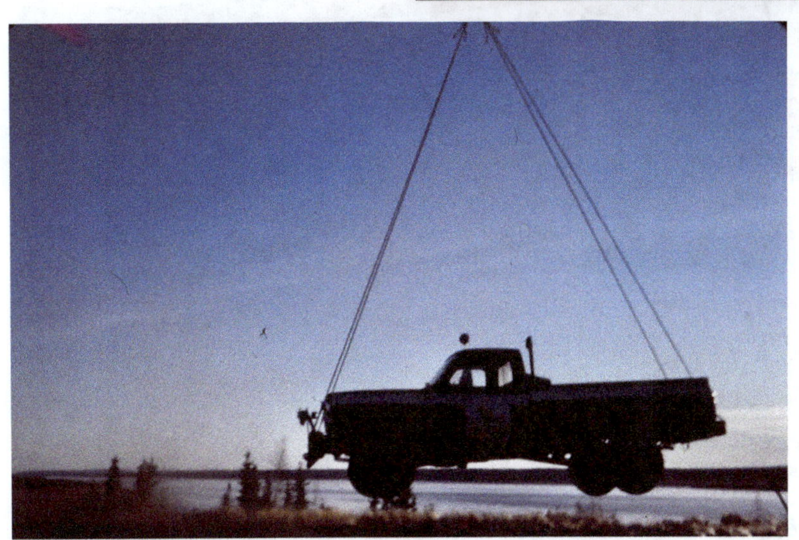

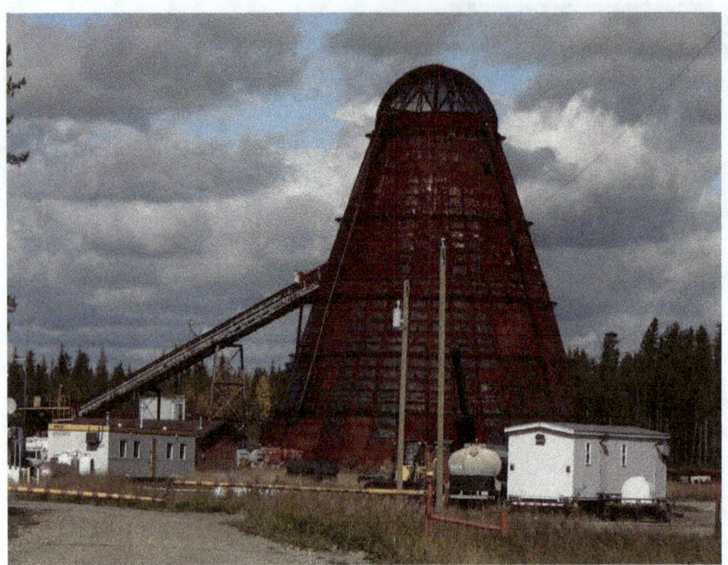

Prince George mill site

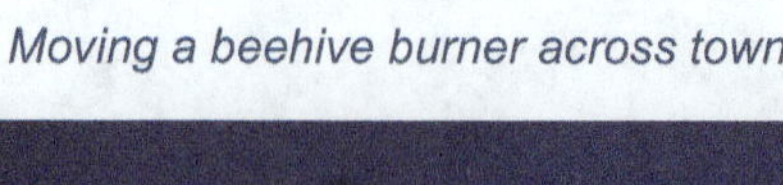

Moving a beehive burner across town

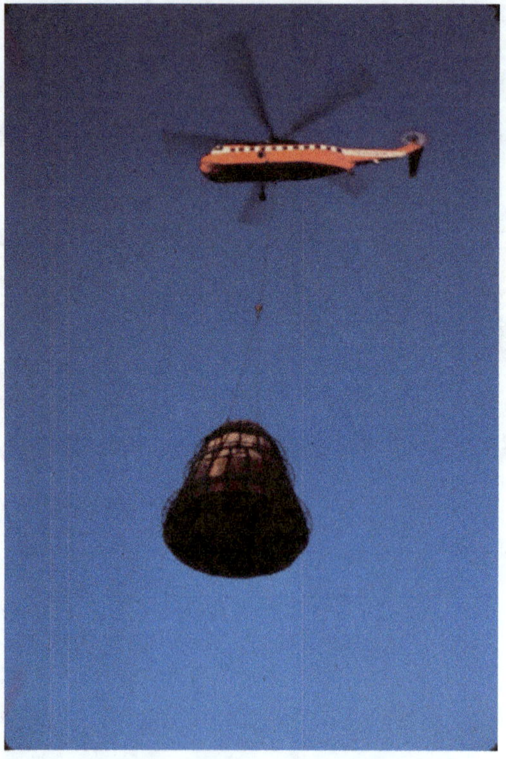

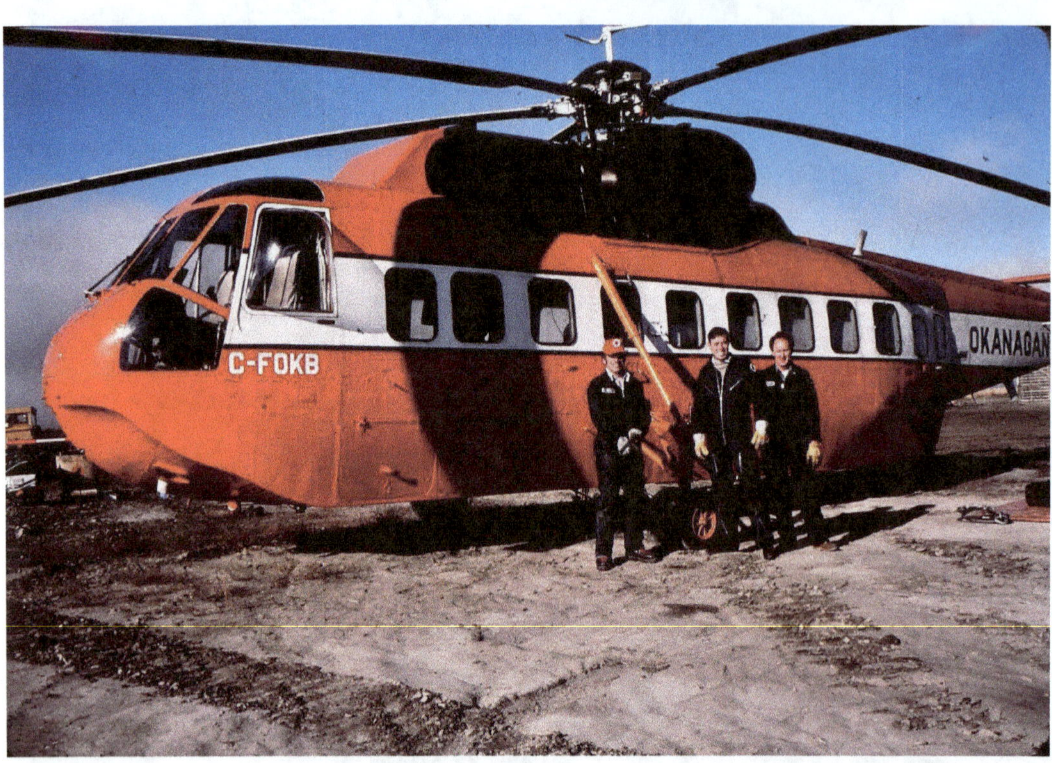

Prince George jobs done - Leaving for Vancouver

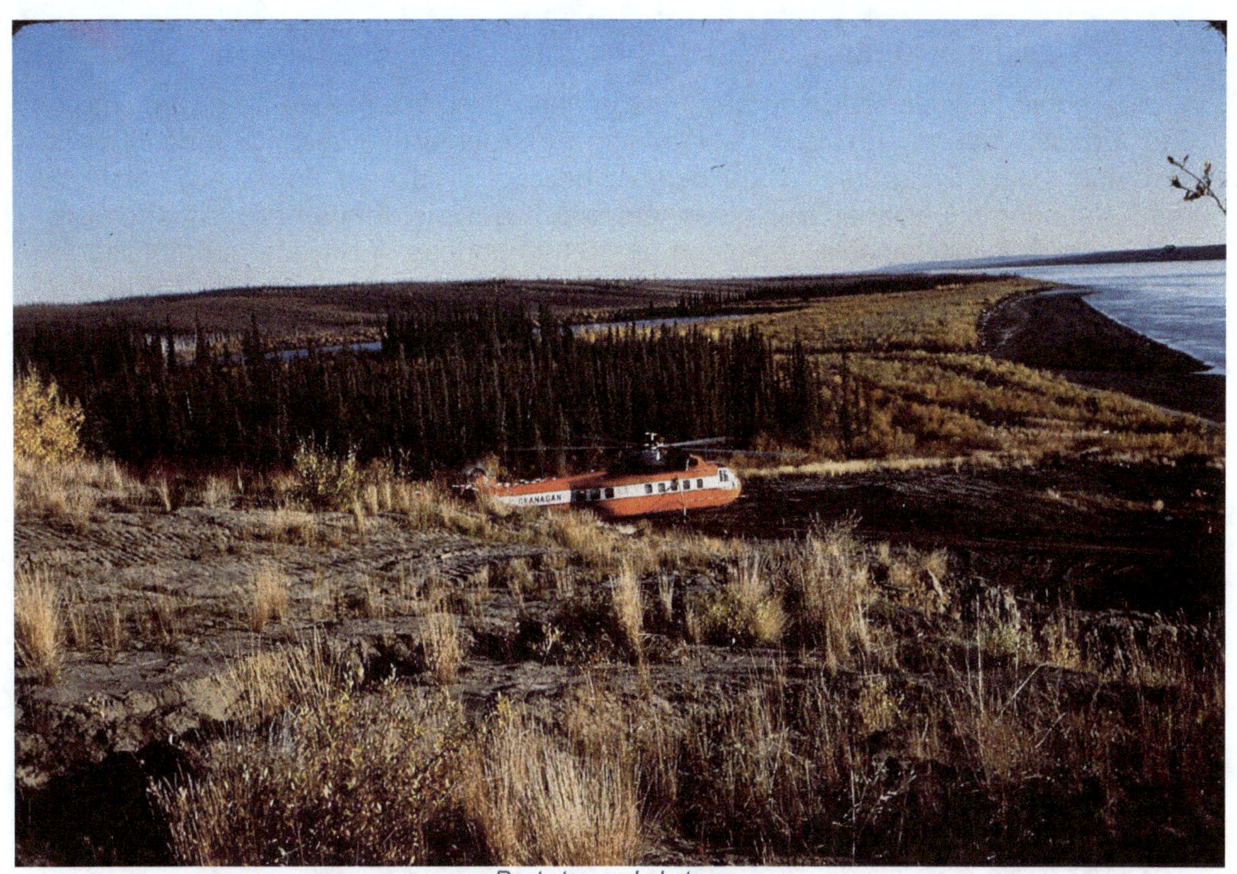

Rest stop and photo op

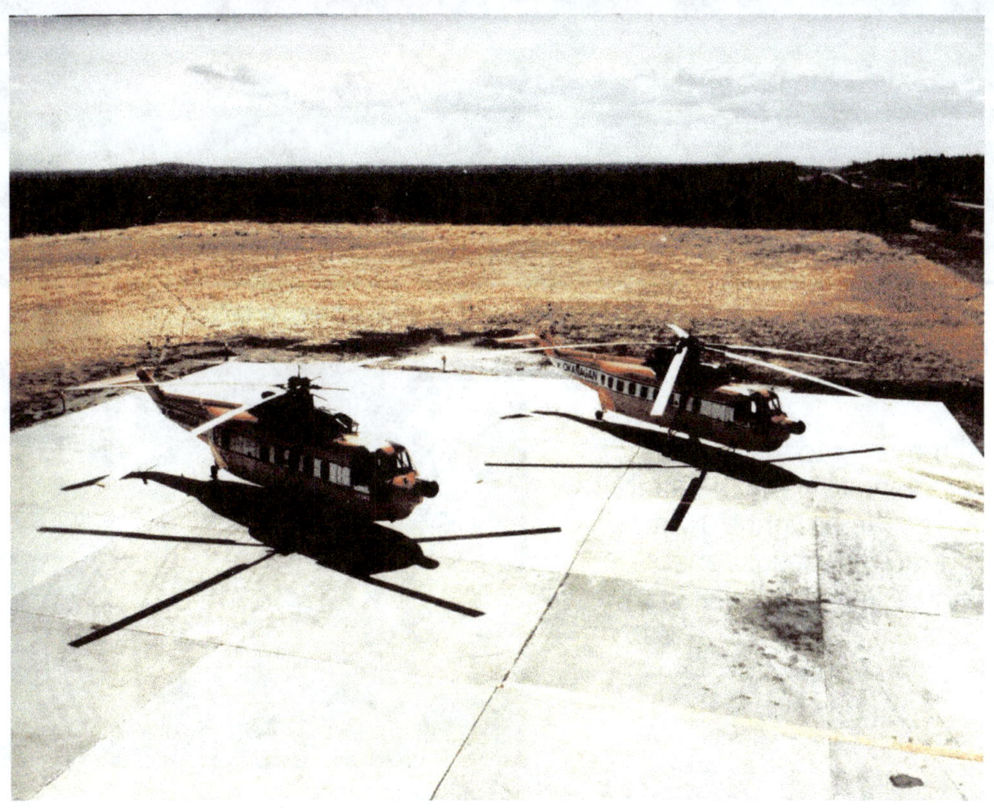

On landing pad in Edson, Alberta

1977 was the beginning

of a whole new life style and progress in my career. We moved from Nanaimo to Edson, Alberta, to fly a coal mining contract with Luscar Sterco. This involved adding to my flying time in the biggest helicopter I'd ever flown, a Sikorsky S-61. It had a seating capacity of 29 passengers and two pilots. It is a heavy lift aircraft with two GE engines and capable of picking up 10,000 pounds. If anyone is unfamiliar with this helicopter, it is the one that is used to land on the Whitehouse lawn. It is also completely IFR certified to fly in cloud and accomplish fully instrumented approaches without any visual reference. This had been my goal for acquiring an instrument rating a year and a half previously.

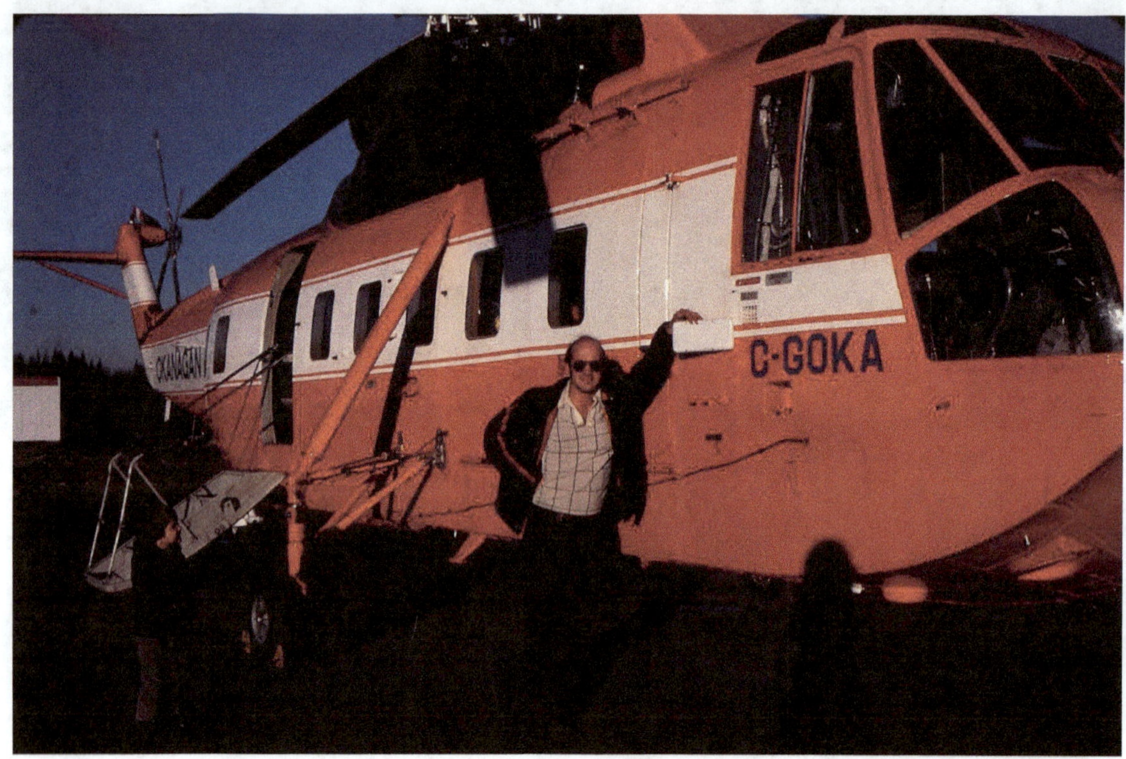

Sikorsky S-61 arrives in Edson AB for Luscar Stereo contract

So not only did I move up to the aircraft I wanted, but I was going to be home every night with the family. We bought a 10-acre parcel with an old farmhouse just east of Edson. We had three kids: Michelle 7,Chad 4 and Dean, 1 year of age. This turned out to be a great place for them growing up.

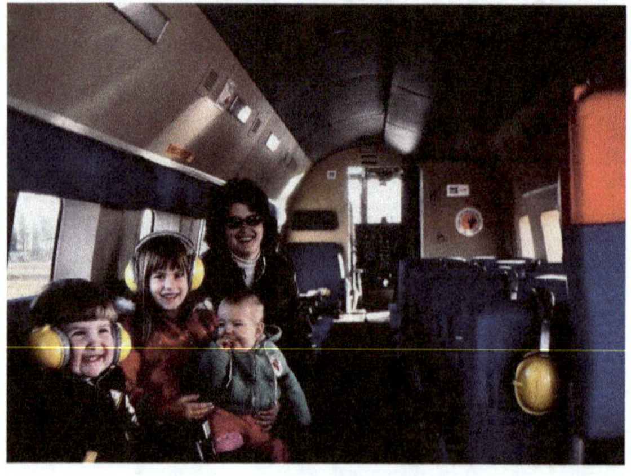

Connie, Chad, Michelle & Dean - Photo op!

I had been raised on a farm in Saskatchewan and always wanted that life for my kids someday. We were just on an acreage but were surrounded by real farmers. They were able to get involved with the neighbours, baling, picking stones, calving and other farm activities. At our own place, we had some animals, horses, calves, dogs and cats. We always knew where the kids were; they were on the school bus, or we were driving them to town 10 miles away for whatever they were involved in. The big thing for me was to finally be at home instead of being away for 8 months of the year.

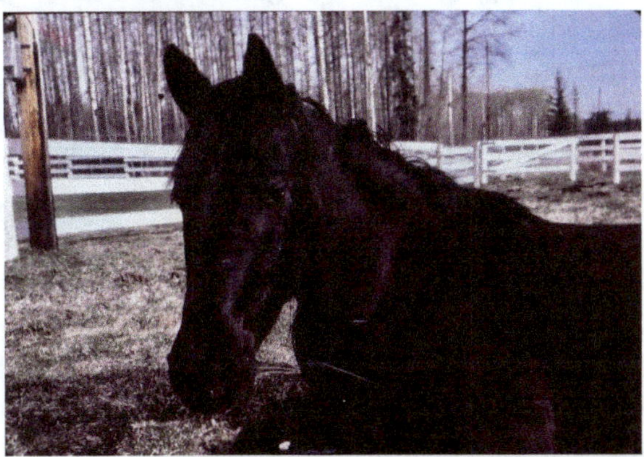

Michelle's horse 'Majesty'

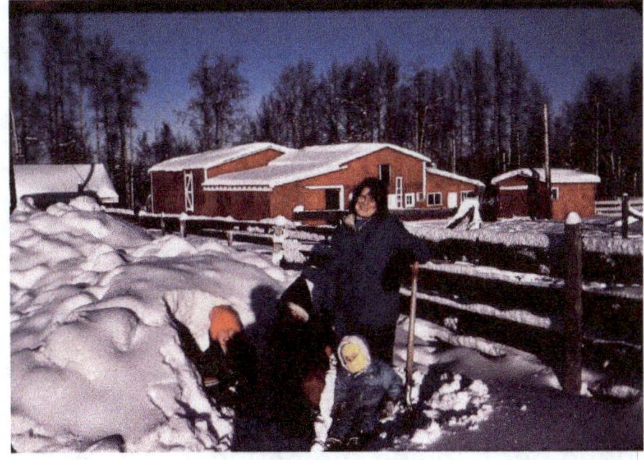

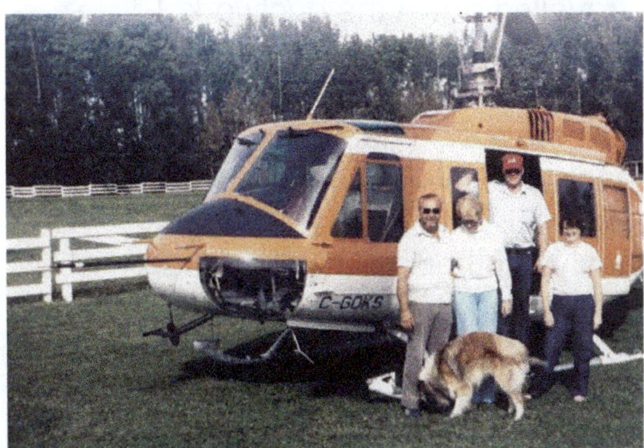

Friends, Neil & Mickey stop by on a ferry flight

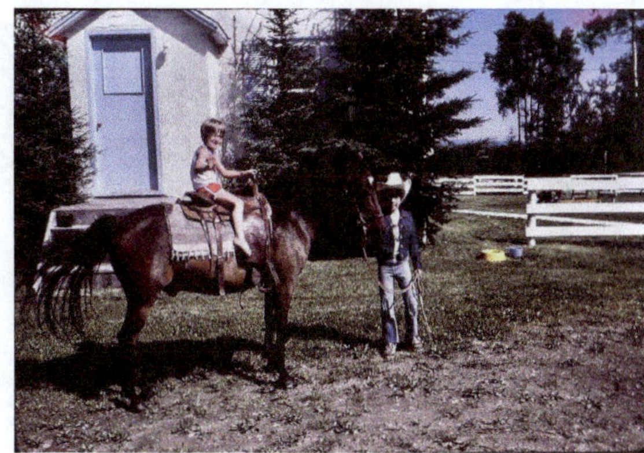

Dean on 'Ringo'

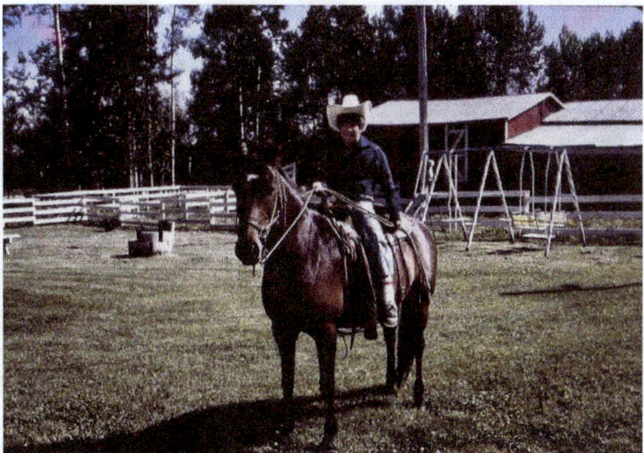

Chad going for a ride on 'Ringo'

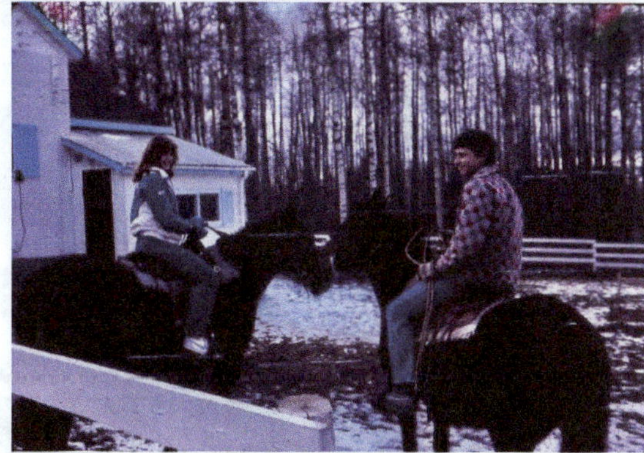

Michelle riding with Tony

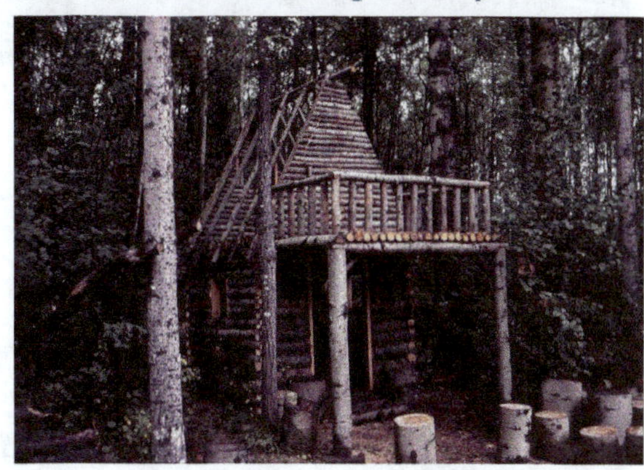

Little fort built for son Dean

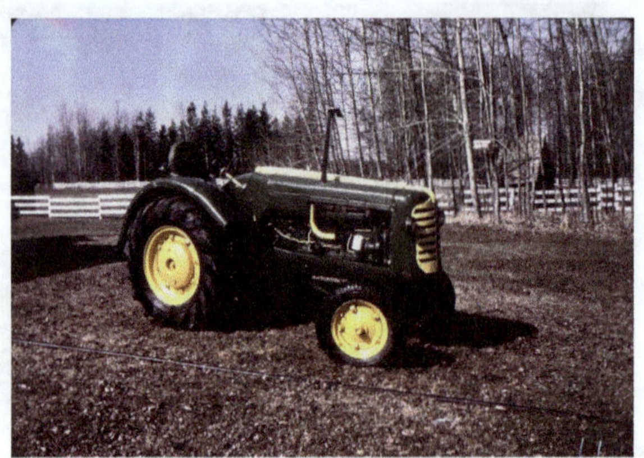

Oliver - rebuilt & restored

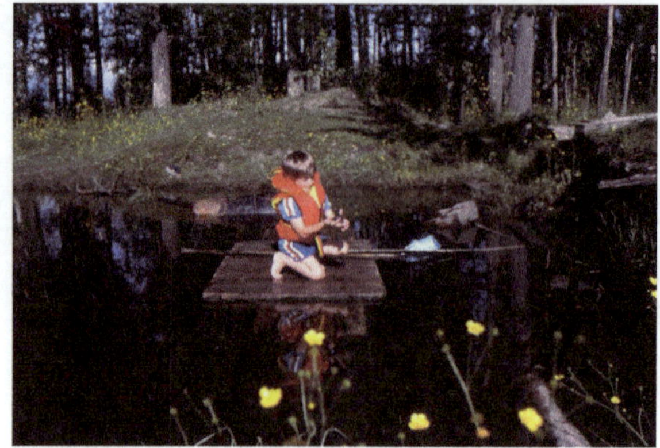

Dean rafting on the pond

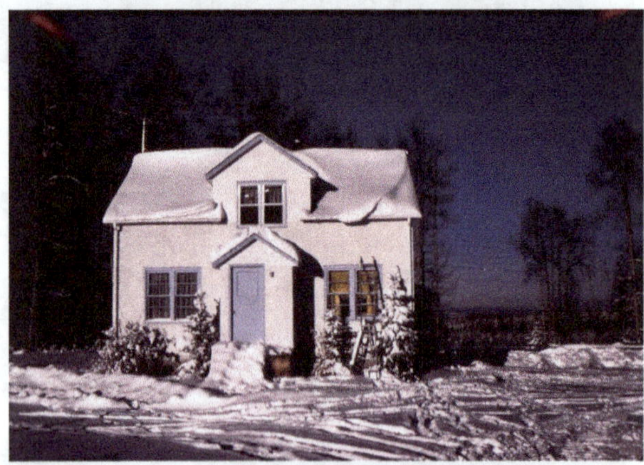

Newly built shutters on house

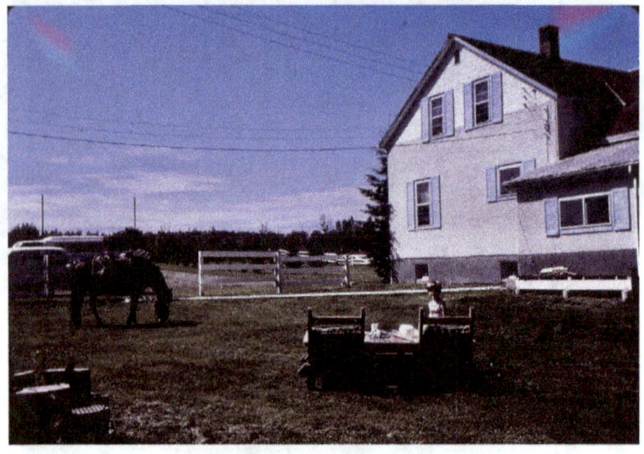

House - extensive renovation

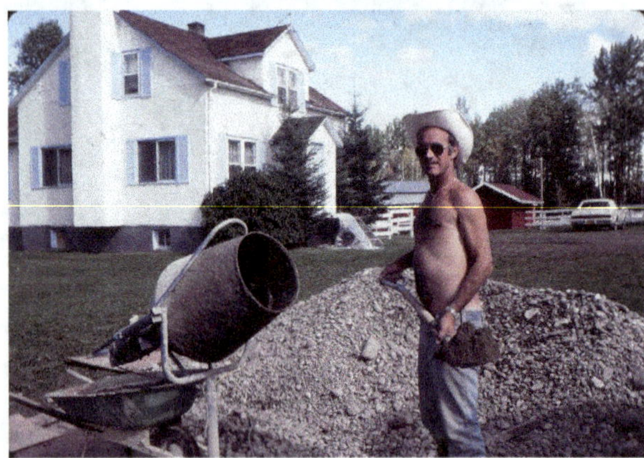

I gained a lot of experience doing major renovations to the house. It was about 50 years old and was very well built by a German journeyman carpenter. Apparently, he had apprenticed for 11 years, and his workmanship showed in this house. In a 30-foot span, the room was only out of square three-eighths of an inch. I removed a bearing wall in this living room area and installed a laminated beam in its place. I think a lot of precision in this house was attributed to dry unplaned lumber. A 2X4 was a full 2 inches by 4 inches.
The renovation was extensive and took several years to complete, but the result was transforming. I have to add one additional humorous note. Over a period of months, a number of my tools were mysteriously missing. They could not be found anywhere. One day I happened to be upstairs and heard a strange rattling sound. In the master bedroom, there was my 4-year-old son Dean, dropping my latest tool down the open heat outlet! He was giggling and must have been loving the sound it made as it travelled down the ductwork. I went down to the basement and disconnected that duct from the furnace. There were all the tools I had been missing! Dean's creative mind showed a lot of promise, and 30 years later he was helping to analyse other creative minds as a licensed psychologist.

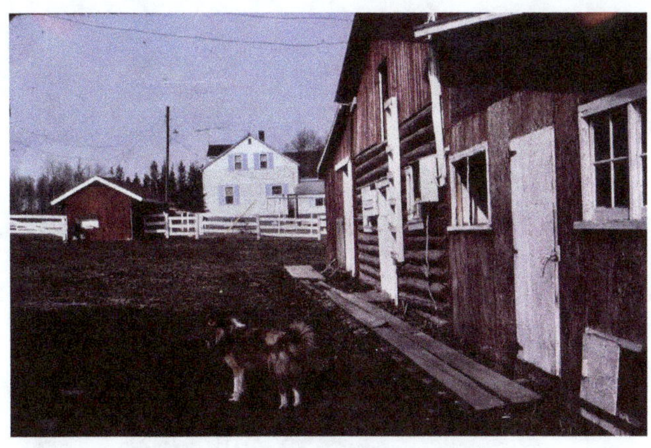

Barn before painting & our Collie

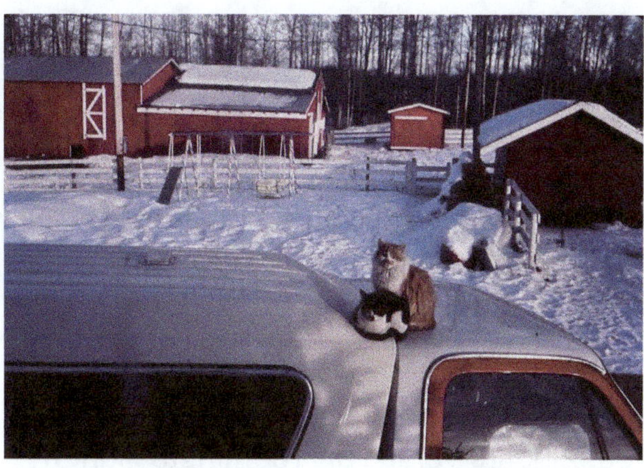

Newly painted barn & cats looking

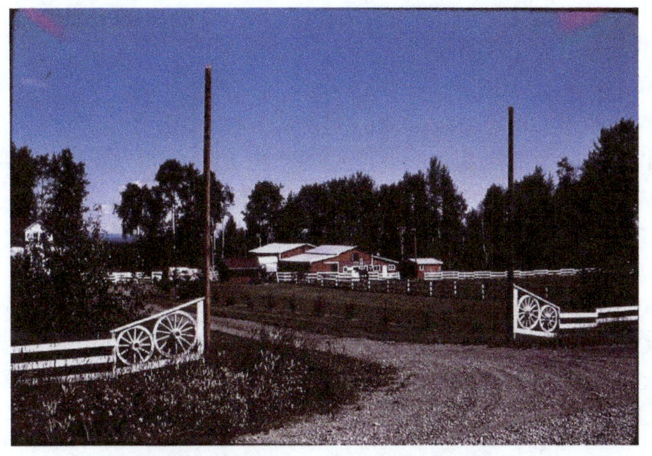

Barn, house & new fence all painted

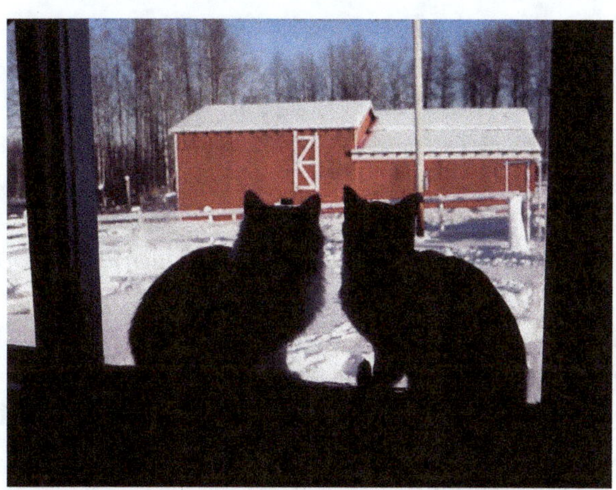

Cats perched on porch

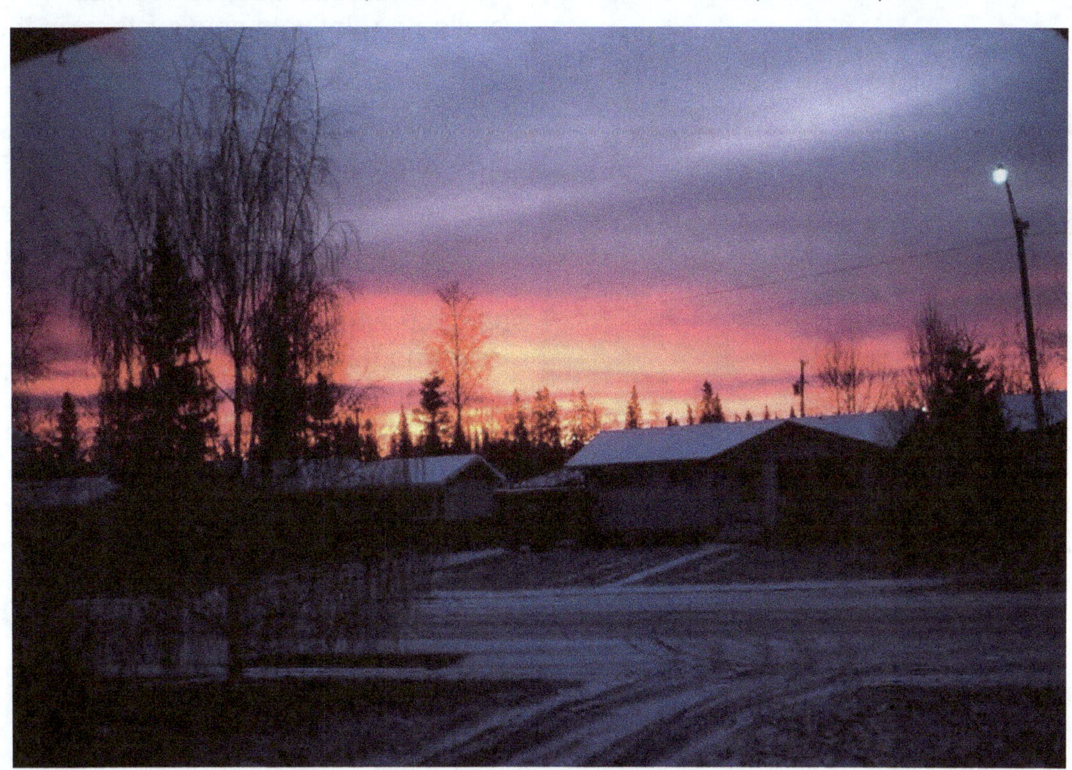

The operation for the large coal stripping mine south of Hinton was dovetailed to move a lot of men efficiently. Enter the two large Sikorsky S-61's. They were configured to carry 29 miners each. Consequently, we could move 600 men over a 24-hour period. This made the helicopters very cost efficient even at the tariff rate of $3,000/hr. If these men had been transported by road, it would have taken a bus almost 2 hours versus an 18- minute flight by helicopter. That translated into a lot of man-hours saved over the year. The only problem was that our marketing people oversold the helicopter as usual. With a twin-engine aircraft, you should still meet certain criteria in the event of an engine failure on takeoff. Going to emergency procedures conforming to certain airspeeds and engine red-lines on the remaining engine, you should be able to fly away at gross loads. However, at increased elevations and temperatures, this was not always possible. But, to fly the contract as signed, we could compromise the flight manual numbers a bit without compromising safety. We may not always be able to fly away with an engine failure, but we always had good reject areas for a forced landing. An additional note to this about helicopter operations in general. Through the years, you couldn't always 'fly by the book' in regard to a lot of flight operations, but you never wanted to compromise flight safety.

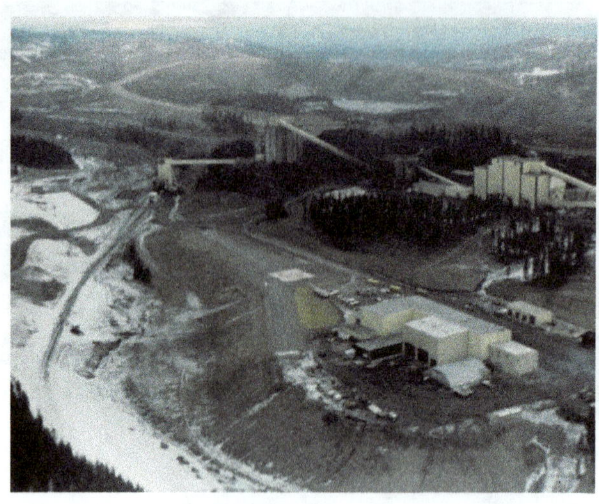

Mine Site

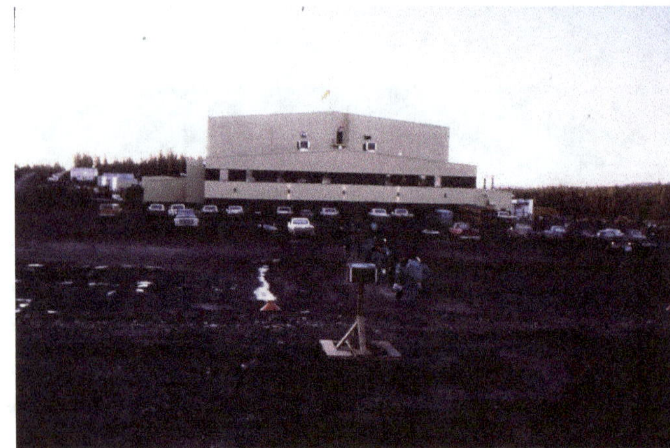

New hangar in Edson

For navigation and complete instrument approach capabilities, our company installed a relatively new system on the ground. It was called an MLS (microwave landing system), which gave you the same instrument approaches that were available at airports. The sensitivity was adjustable on installation, which turned out to have great accuracy. The tracking and approach angle met all the requirements, so Transport Canada gave us limits down to 200 feet above the ground. This meant we could do the instrument approach in solid cloud down to 200 feet on the radar altimeter. If we did not break out and become visual at that point, you then did a 'missed approach.' This doesn't mean you 'missed' your landing area but only means to go around for another approach or return to your departure point.

The S-61 has a flight stabilization system but not a full auto pilot. So for all flights visual and on instruments, you were always 'hand flying' the aircraft. A typical shift was four return flights from Edson to the mine at Coal Valley. If the cloud base was low, you then accomplished the trips on instruments. There were days, especially with a lot of inclement weather on the lee side of the Rockies, where instrument flight was a necessity. So you could end up shooting eight full instrument approaches, four at each end. Hand flying the aircraft at all times required more concentration if on instruments. Consequently, you became mentally fatigued a bit, especially if you had been picking up ice on the blades and/or the fuselage. Ice accumulation is a large factor for helicopters that don't have deicing capabilities on the rotor blades. Depending on the helicopter type, tolerance levels of ice are directly related to flight performance. If conditions are just right, ice can accumulate rapidly on the rotor blades, especially in cloud.
This results in decreased performance to forward airspeed and lift. Depending on the severity, it might be necessary to go to a different altitude or reverse course entirely.

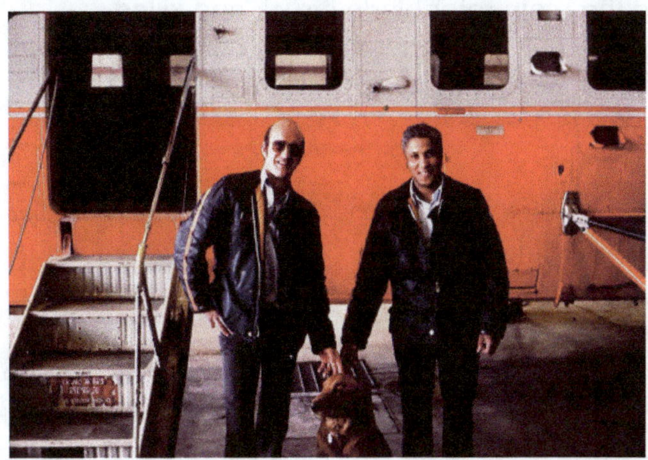
Lead check pilot – W Ramsey

The S-61's main rotor blade profile could handle a fair amount of ice. However, if you had accumulated some ice prior to the approach, you had to decide whether to carry on or not. If you had picked up too much ice and had to do a missed approach, you may not have enough power to climb out again to clear the surrounding mountains. If you committed to the approach, you wanted to be sure you could break out and land.

During mid-summer, we often encountered typical prairie thunderstorms. Cumulonimbus clouds can build up to heights of 40,000 feet, creating heavy rain, lightning and large hailstones. Flying through these storm cells can tear the largest aircraft apart. It's imperative to miss these cells at all costs. A jet aircraft can fly above them, but a helicopter can't reach those heights, so we must get around them. As we were out of controlled airspace, we could not receive radar warnings from air traffic control. But, our S-61's were equipped with onboard radar, enabling us to 'paint' storm cells. We were then able to avoid them by going around or flying in between them. One day we were returning from the mine, keeping an eye on an approaching storm. Our radar was showing an extensive line of storm cells. We were 'scud running,' just above the tree tops and threading our way home. Suddenly, a large pine directly in front of me blew up from a large bolt of lightning! A few miles later, another tree was hit and immediately caught on fire. I had never seen strikes like these in real-time before and was very relieved to land back at our base. The rest of the miners returned home by bus that day!

Two years after my checkout on the S-61, I qualified for a captain's ride. This was the ultimate goal, and I felt ready for it. Unlike airline procedures, twin- engine, 2-pilot helicopter procedures are a little different. To gain experience, as a new copilot, you actually change seats every other leg or trip with the captain. This way, when you have enough time and experience, you're completely familiar with the captain's position. With the airlines, the copilot can fly from their side but generally don't change seats until they are qualified captains. Interestingly, as comfortable as I was on the captain's side, it was a completely different feeling wearing the 4 bars for the first time. You quickly realized that the responsibility and final decision-making all fell on you. I distinctly recall one night early on when we took off from Edson with 29 passengers. The weather was right on limits, and moderate icing was forecast. I had a newly checked-out copilot from the Vancouver pool in the left seat. It was a different demanded feeling of responsibility along with tremendous confidence. I was ready!

Our company made a very interesting purchase, buying another S-61. This aircraft was bought from New York Airways in 1981 after its crash in 1977. That was a tragic accident on top of the Pan Am building in New York City. While loading, the landing gear collapsed on one side, the aircraft rolled over, and the main rotor blade struck and killed 4 passengers. A piece of the blade also killed a pedestrian 80 stories below. The aircraft was repaired and replaced one of our heavier S-61's in Edson. The airframe was quite a bit lighter, enabling us to carry larger payloads.

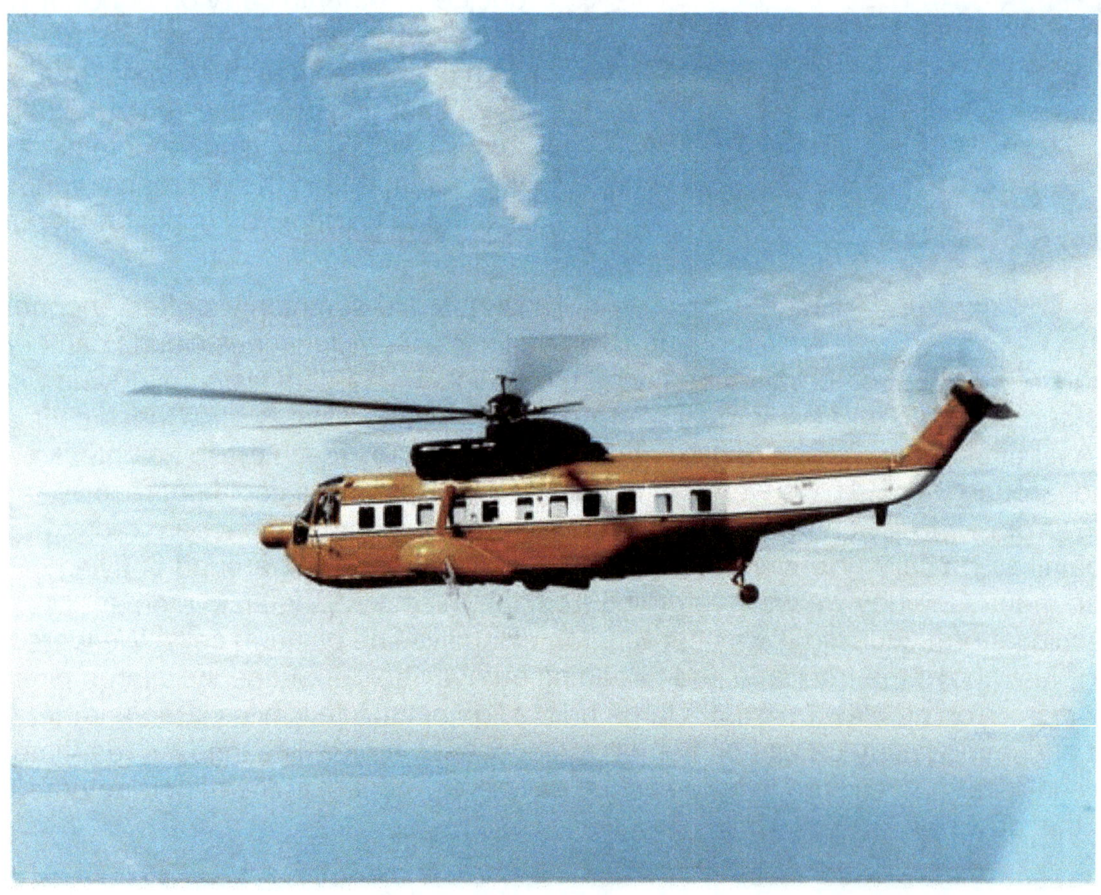

At our Edson base hangar, there was a separate waiting room for the miners. They would be escorted to the helicopter and entered via the air stairs door. Luscar was very strict about on-time take offs. As soon as they were seated and the door closed, we were airborne. There were several shifts of men, and they were generally well-behaved. However, the 'C' watch was not. In flight, they were always 'cutting up,' taking their seat belts off, being loud and even lighting up marijuana at times. One day our chief pilot was filling in from Vancouver. A piece of mud came flying up from the back and hit the windscreen between the two pilots. He was not impressed! So every time this crew acted up, we kicked them off, and they were made to go to the mine by road for 2 weeks. They hated the long drive plus a twelve-hour shift, so they would behave for a while till it was all repeated for some other infraction. One of our engineers was also a skydiver and competed in various competitions. We discussed having him dress up like a new miner, and then he'd purposely act up en route. One of the pilots would get out of his seat, open the sliding door and throw him out! He'd have his parachute on underneath, and this would be a good lesson to this misbehaving crew. However, we decided against it since it might traumatize somebody too much, and we'd be faced with a lot of paperwork!

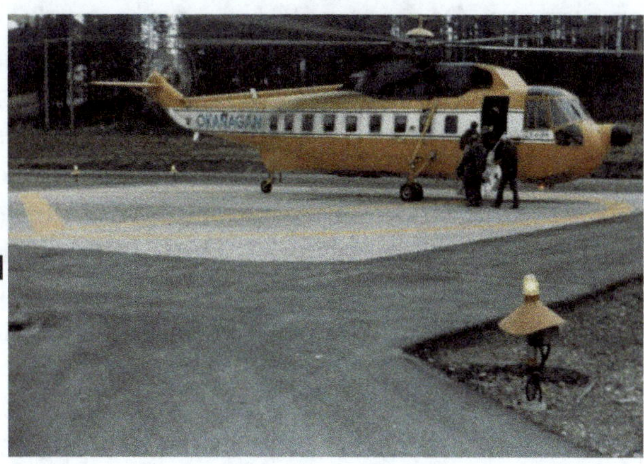

Landing at the coal mine to pick up coal miners

One day this engineer asked me if I would take him up to practice some skydiving. He had a competition coming up in Canmore and wanted to try out some new maneuvers. I had never thrown anybody out of a helicopter before, so I asked him what altitude and airspeed he would like. He said, "Let's try 10,000 feet and zero airspeed." So up we went, and at 10,000 feet, my copilot got out of his seat and opened the large sliding door for him. I slowed up to a hover at zero airspeed (which felt a little strange at that altitude), and out he went. I did a tight descending turn to follow him down. He tumbled for a bit and then, with his arms extended, started various maneuvers. As he went through about 3,000 feet, he seemed to be doing something in his belt area. It just seemed like he was getting much too low, but I assumed this was part of his routine. Suddenly his chute blossomed just before he touched down. I thought he was cutting things a bit close. I landed shortly after, and he was very shaken! He had tried to deploy his main chute at the normal release altitude, and it failed to open! So when I saw him scrambling in his frontal area, he was actually having trouble getting his reserve chute to open as well. His girlfriend had been watching from the ground and knew he was in trouble. He related to me that would be the last time he would have someone else pack his chute!

One of the big things about this job was that you had to guard against complacency. When the weather was a factor and flying by instruments was a necessity, you were very aware. But when the weather was fine, the trips were very routine, and you had be careful to not cut corners. This could be as simple as skipping checklists or general

awareness. One example for me personally was when the Stanley Cup playoffs were going on. The Edmonton Oilers were on their way to winning another Stanley Cup starring Wayne Gretzky. Part of our navigational instrumentation was an NDB (nondirectional beacon). It was a versatile instrument with a couple of functions. If you took it off the navigational mode and selected antenna, we could listen to the Oilers games. One night was a beautiful clear night I was flying and really immersed in the game. I looked up halfway to the mine and didn't see our normal ground references. So I decided I better check and select the NDB back on 'Nav' mode.
The needle pointed to the mine 90 degrees to my right. I was actually on a heading to Calgary! Another instance that took place occasionally was the copilot having a little 'catnap'. This happened in nice weather when he wasn't really needed, and the flying pilot was aware and in control. This happened to me one day after spending some long days renovating our house. The 'built-in' clock always kicked in about the time to descend, and I had a shock when I looked over. The captain flying was slumped in the belts as well! Instead of descending, we were still at 6,000 feet over our landing pad. I reached over and hit the vertical release lever on his seat, which caused the seat to abruptly drop.Needless to say, he woke up in a hurry and was embarrassed. To give the miners a reasonable explanation, I grabbed the intercom and informed them we were giving them a little tour over the town as we started the descent.

So these were a couple of examples regarding complacency, which can affect all the crews. The incidents were not dangerous but a good object lesson to everyone. We had a very professional, safe operation, and sometimes it required a bit of 're-tuning' around the edges. A good solution to giving the crews some variety was to give them tours to other parts of Canada or overseas.

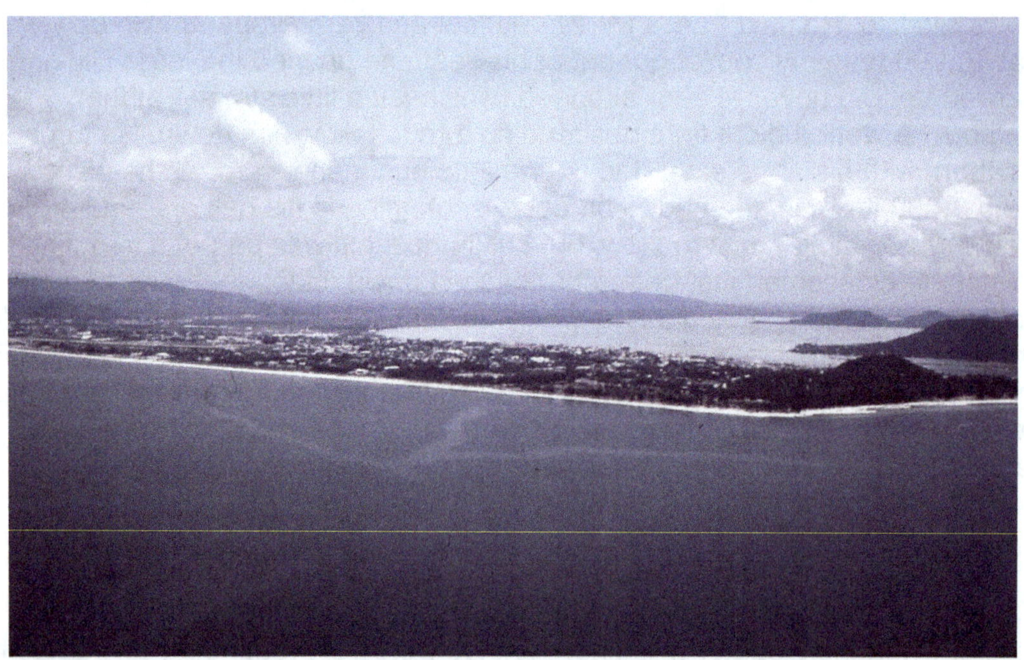

Approaching Songkhla airport

My first away-from-base tour was flying overseas out of Songkhla, Thailand. We were flying to offshore drilling rigs halfway between southern Thailand and Vietnam. The primary contract was to exchange crews on Union Oil drilling rigs. We had a large hangar at the Thai airforce base in Songkhla. Flying overseas and over the water was a great new experience. Flying over the South China Sea with no land in sight took a bit of getting used to. It was always comforting to start seeing the first rigs showing up on our radar screen. I was still in a Sikorsky S-61 but went from fixed to retractable gear. The rigs were 100 nautical miles offshore and located in two different oil fields. This was in March 1983 and the middle of the dry season. It was hot, averaging 36 degrees centigrade each day with very little wind. This required some new procedures when approaching a rig platform. In that kind of heat and no wind, it was necessary to start slowing the aircraft much further back. If you didn't adjust your approach, it was difficult to stop over the platform. If you didn't safely come to a hover over the landing pad, it necessitated a go- around. 1983 was right in the middle of the 'boat people' escaping from Vietnam. They were extremely oppressed, facing capture, torture and death at the hands of the Khmer Rouge. This was an extreme communist party that was formed in Cambodia to create an authoritarian state. So it was very interesting to see the escaping refugees up close and feel empathy for their circumstances. These were very desperate people leaving their country in open and often overcrowded boats. This would be a dangerous crossing in their attempt to reach Thailand, Singapore, Hong Kong or Malaysia.

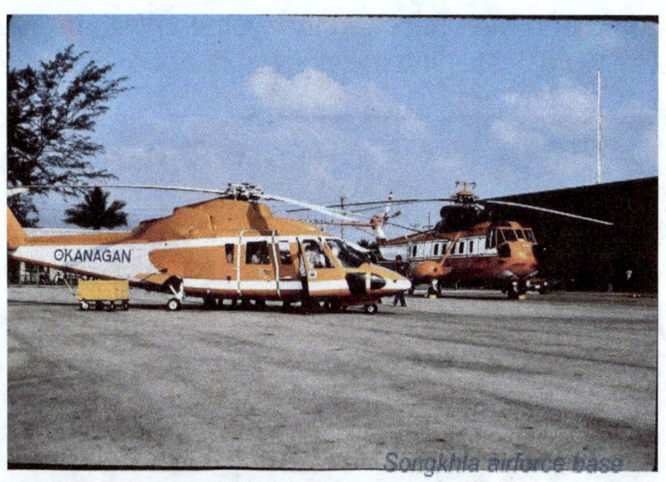

Songkhla airforce base

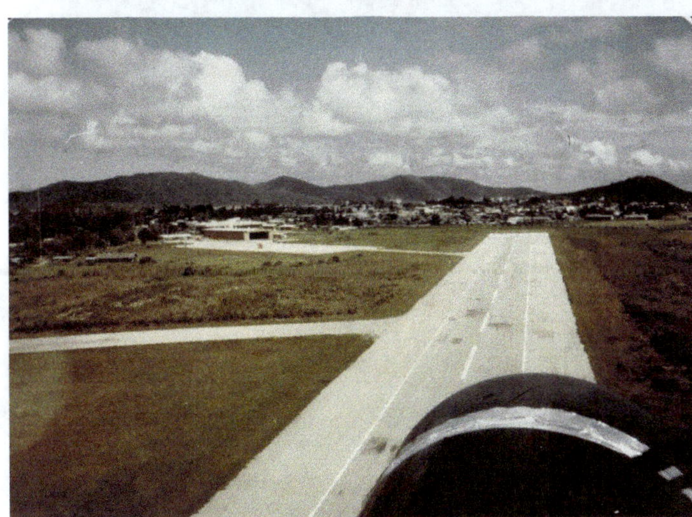
Songkhla airforce base

Many did not make it. Union Oil would allow them to tie up at the base of their platforms to rest up a bit but not board. We landed one day and saw one of their boats tied up to the leg just below the helideck. I leaned over and waved at them. They waved back and seemed genuinely happy, obviously relieved to have gotten this far. They would still have to face the weather, dwindling food and water supplies, plus possible pirate attacks. These 'pirates' were hard for the authorities to apprehend because they were disguised as ordinary Thai fishermen. They attacked the boat people, stealing their fuel, valuables and anything else of value. They often murdered the men, threw them overboard and then attacked the women. With the dangers they faced, they felt that the risk was worth escaping the horrors of not escaping.

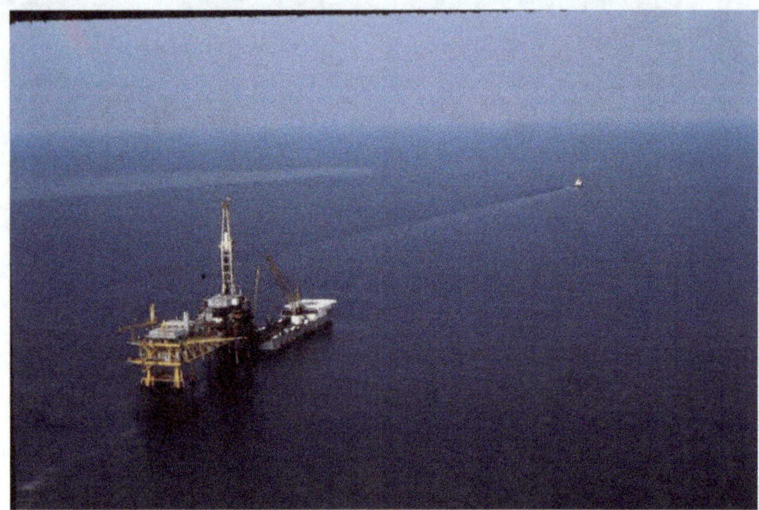

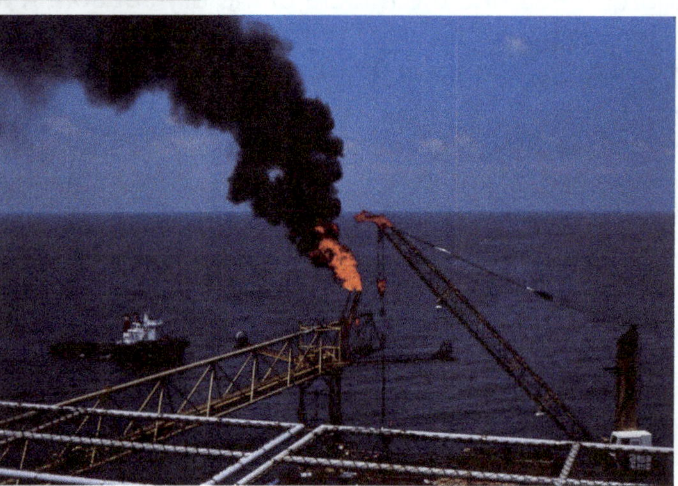

Flaring off gas

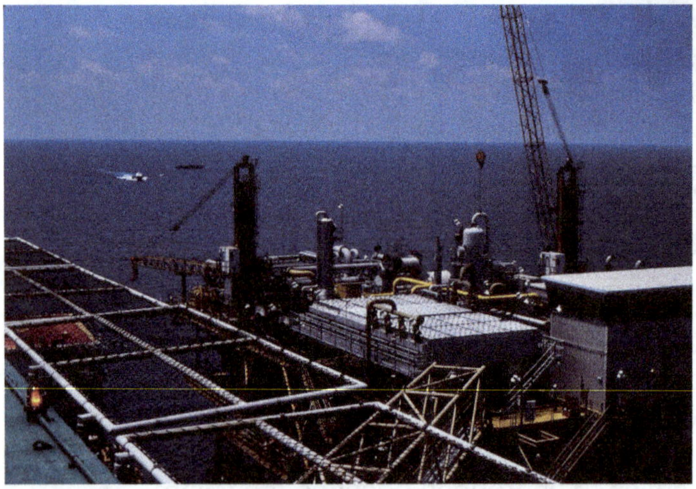

Picking up rig workers

One day

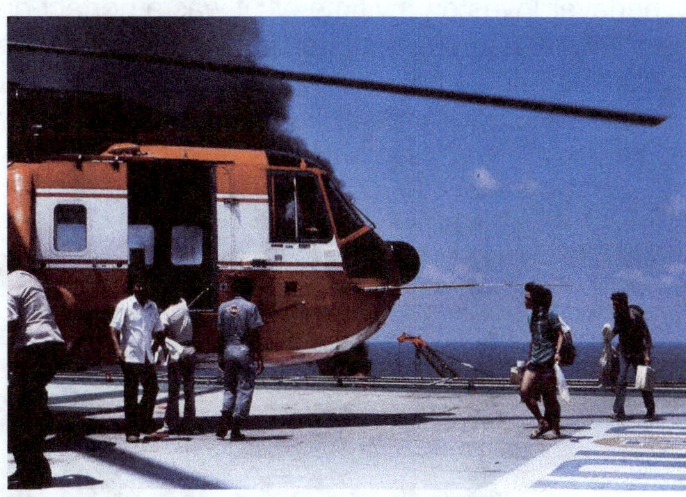

Shift change - Flying workers back to Songkhla

I was on approach to one of the rigs when they radioed us to abort and return to base. This was a very unusual call, and we subsequently found out why. There was a dispute on the rig, which was a type of mutiny. The Caucasian captain was attacked with a fire axe, and they actually fractured his skull. They then turned on each other, Thais versus Malaysians. When we landed back at our base, there was a contingent of four Thai policemen waiting. They were armed to the teeth and were loaded on board. After a one-hour flight, we landed back at the rig, and I was asked to keep the helicopter running. The seas were rough, and the rig was bouncing around as I was waiting on the deck. After about twenty minutes, I radioed down, asking why the holdup. They responded that the police were having trouble rounding up all the troublemakers. They finally paraded them all up and loaded them on board. They were a sullen-looking bunch and knew they were in trouble. There were two cops in the back facing forward and two policemen sitting in the forward seats facing aft. The troublemakers were in the centre. When I looked back, the thing that was a bit disconcerting was that all four policemen went to sleep en route. The prisoners were not handcuffed, and the policemen's guns were very accessible.

Fortunately, nothing happened, and the rest of the flight was uneventful as we landed back in Songkhla. Apparently, the Thais went straight to prison, and the Malaysians were kicked out of the country. Thailand is a fascinating country populated by very gentle, wonderful people. It takes a while for them to trust you, especially in any business dealings, but once they do, you have a friend for life. When I was off--duty, I spent a lot of time with Thai people. The hotel manager where I was staying asked if I would go with her and her husband to visit her sick mother. She was hospitalized in a nearby city and was very lonely. I said that I would and went along. She was so amazed that a 'Westerner' would come and visit her that she broke down in tears. In subsequent visits, when she was able to go back home farther north, I had some great visits. The manager and her husband would do the translating, and this lady and her husband gave me some great insights into their country. They say everyone has a double, and the thing that amazed me was how she resembled my mother. Her facial features, voice and actions were so very similar even though she was Thai. It was interesting because after I became more conversant in the Thai language, I could converse with her without needing a translator.

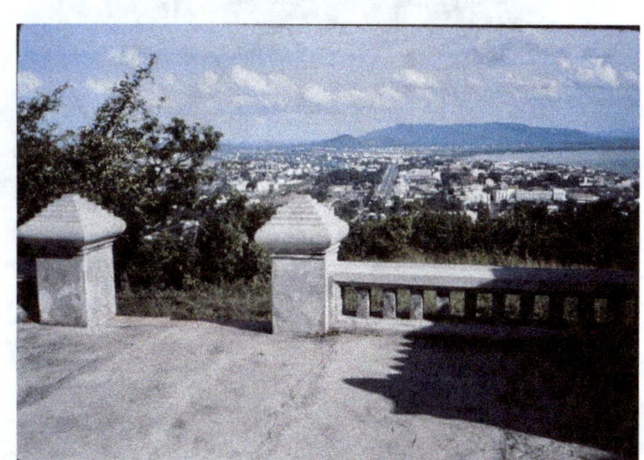

Overlooking Songkhla

Whenever I was on my time off, it was a perfect opportunity to pursue my hobby of catching and mounting butterflies. This had been my passion for 20 years, and tropical butterflies had some amazing colours. There was one variety around the hangar that had a six-inch wing span. There was another rare variety that actually had a diameter of one foot, although I just missed catching one.

Butterfly park, where I could add to my collection

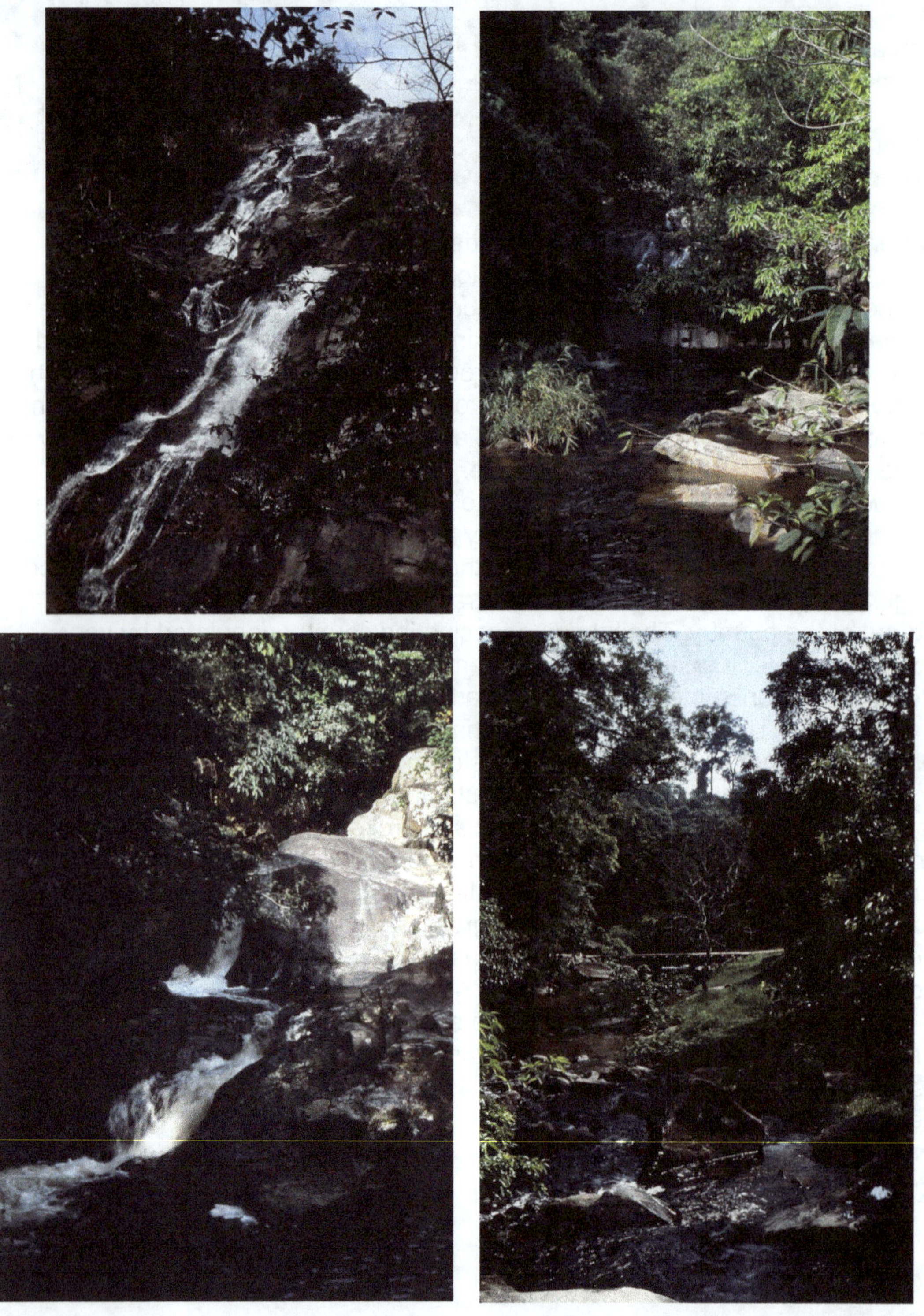

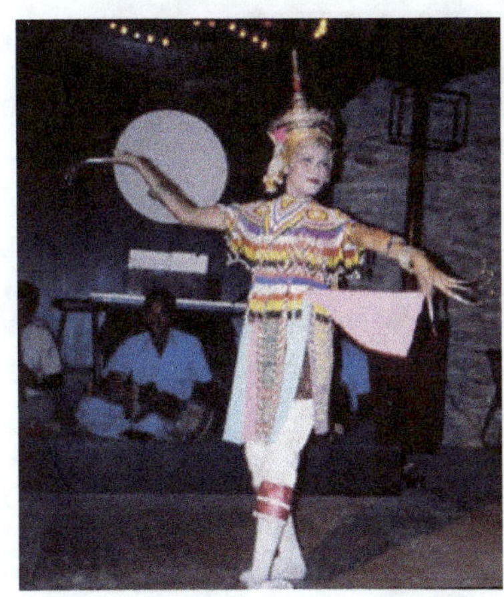

Traditional Thai dancer

One day I was having a bit of a break from the sun and sitting on a rock at the base of a 70-foot cliff. Suddenly, a snake that must have fallen off the cliff landed beside me. I slowly picked up a rock, but he quietly slithered away. The next day I described his colours to our company driver. He said, "Oh, Captain Bill, that's a very bad snake. If he bites you, you die!" There was a joke going around amongst the locals classifying snakes in their country. There were 'One Steppers' and 'Two Steppers.' One step, you die very quickly and 'two steppers,' you take a little longer! Apparently, there are more than 60 varieties of snakes in Thailand, and 40 of them are venomous. Another day I was sitting on a log in the middle of the jungle with my butterfly net. Suddenly a large ape came swinging through the vines. As soon as he saw me, he dropped to the ground and came after me. Apparently, they're quite territorial and have a vicious bite, but I didn't stick around to find out!

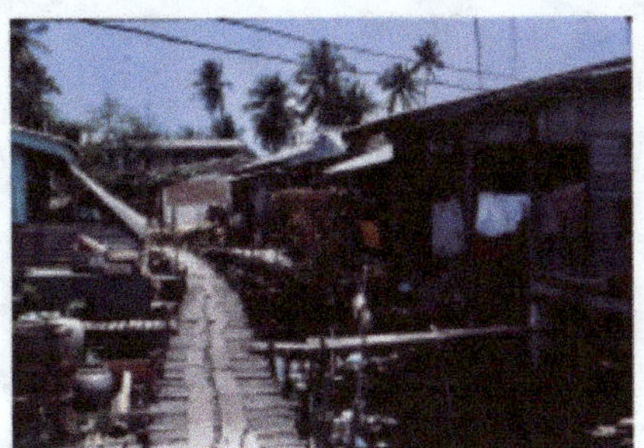

Boardwalk between stilted houses

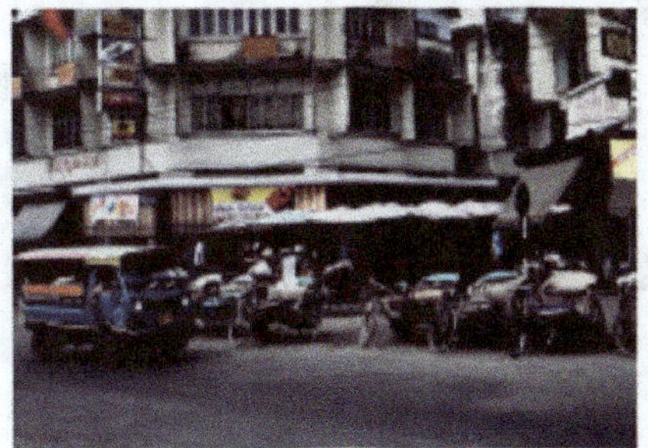

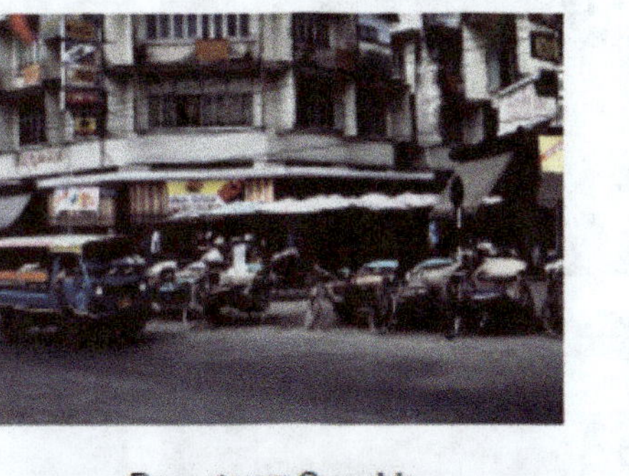

Downtown Songhla

Everyday market

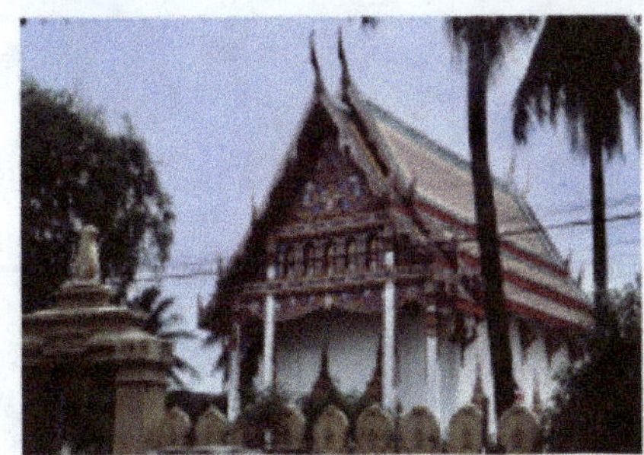

Many...

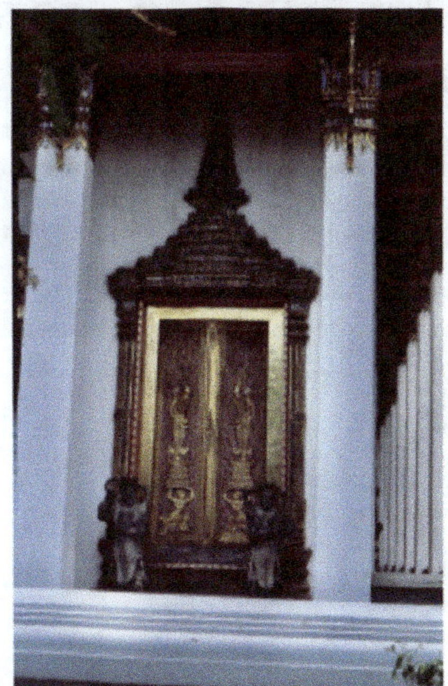

Temples...

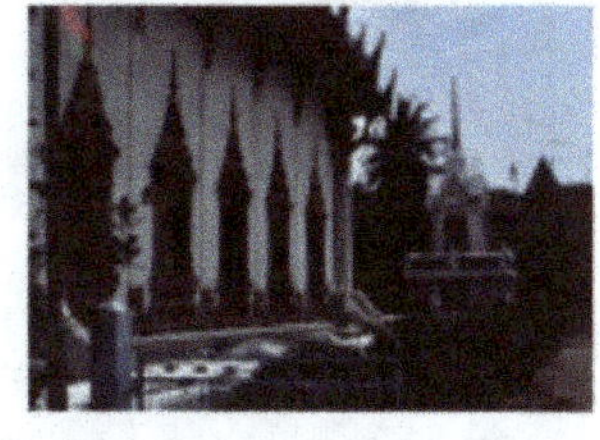

...everywhere

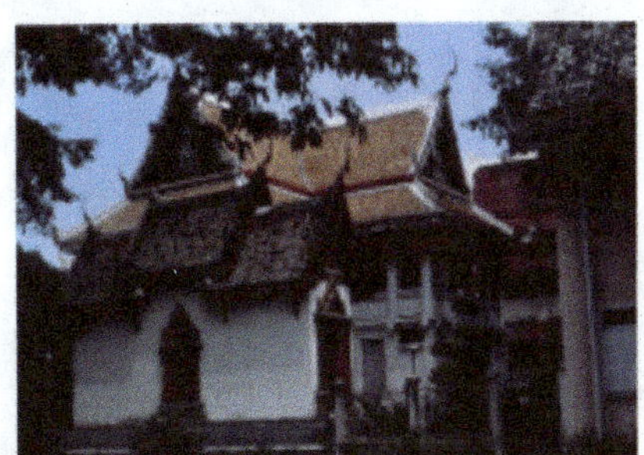

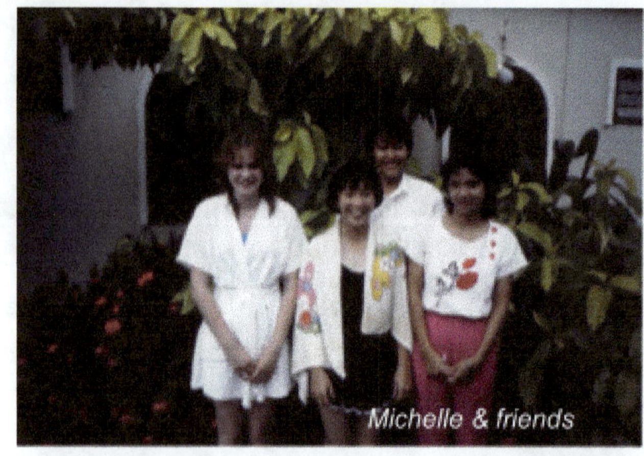
Michelle & friends

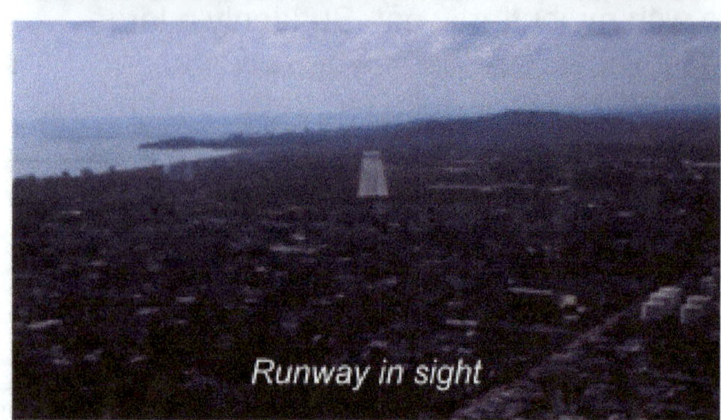
Runway in sight

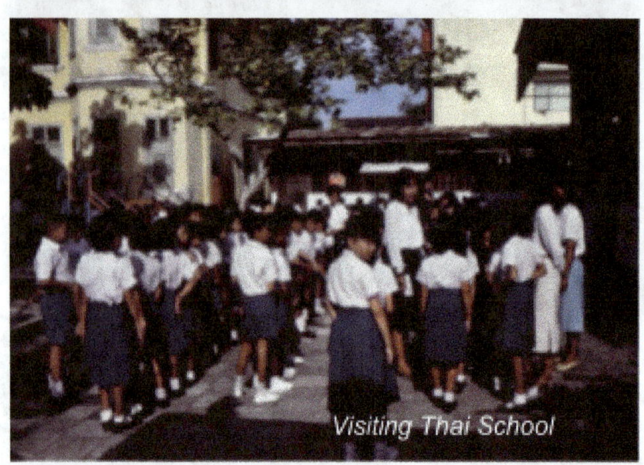
Visiting Thai School

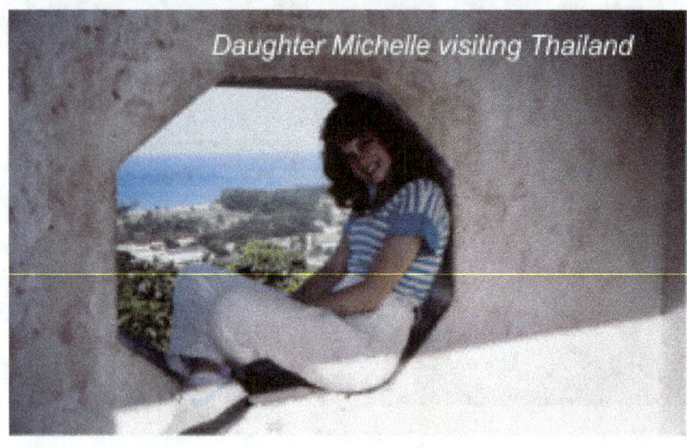
Daughter Michelle visiting Thailand

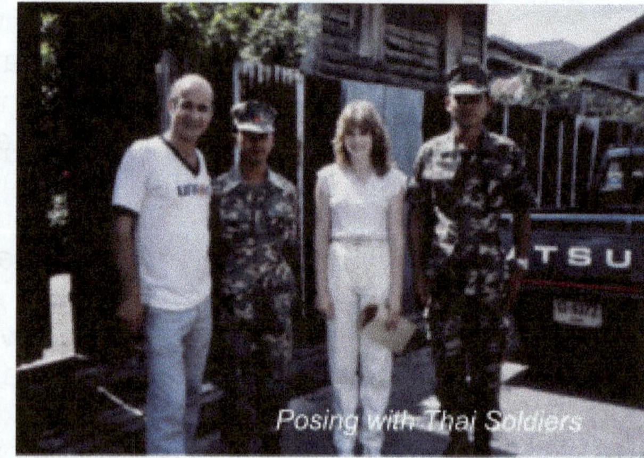

Posing with Thai Soldiers

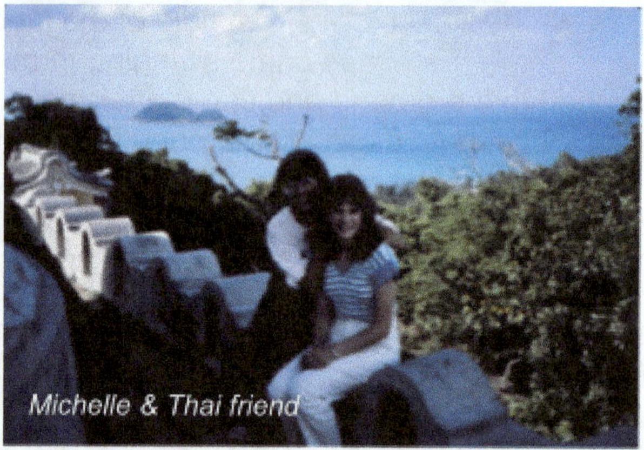
Michelle & Thai friend

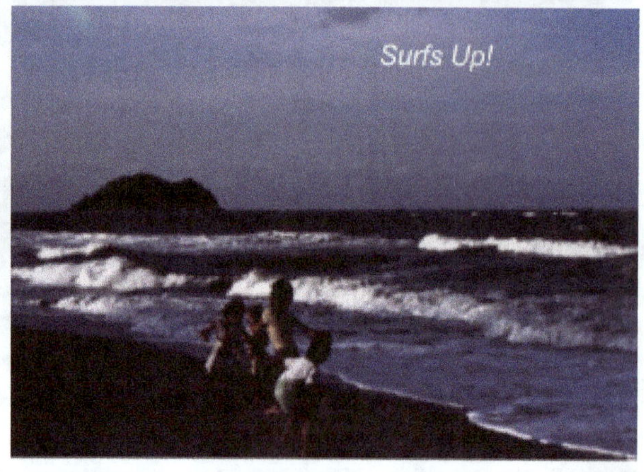
Surfs Up!

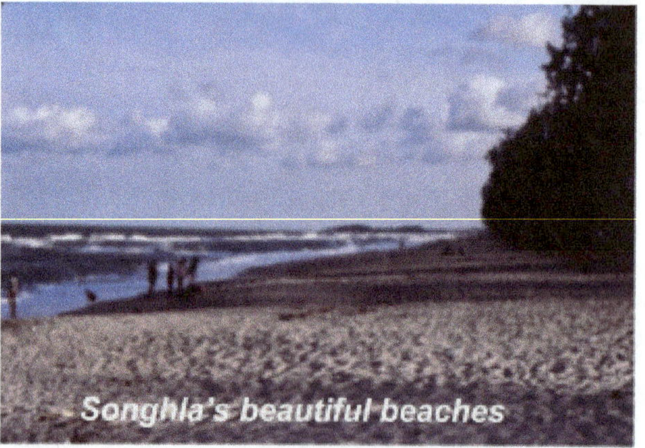
Songhla's beautiful beaches

After two 60-day tours to Thailand,

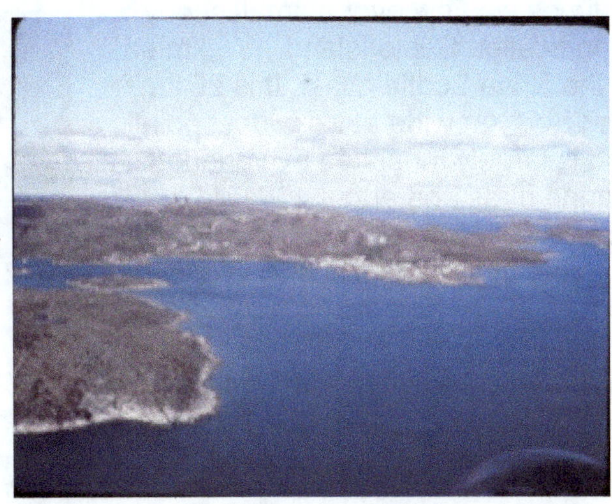

St. John's coast

I was sent to Goose Bay, Labrador still on the Sikorsky S-61. This was a routine tour mainly in support of drilling rigs onshore and offshore. We had an interesting medevac call one night at midnight. There was a driller with a medical condition at a rig about 40 miles offshore north of Gander. The weather was ugly, but the ceiling heights reported at the rig were within our instrument approach limits. It was my turn to fly this trip, and I had a seasoned offshore co-captain in the left seat. I started the descent and set up for approach. We were still in solid cloud, and the ceiling at the rig was holding steady at two hundred feet. We broke out at minimums, and the rig loomed straight ahead. This was a semi-submersible marine vessel that is free to move vertically with the rolling seas.

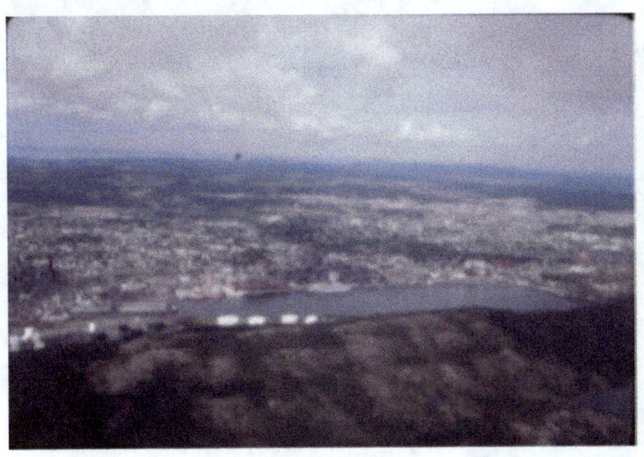

St. John's NL

I was unfamiliar with landing on this type of heaving platform, but my co-captain had no problem talking me through it. The platform was moving up and down approximately 60 feet. Michelle, my experienced copilot, said that the safest procedure was to time your touch-down when it was at its peak travel. If you chased the platform going down, it could come up and wipe out your landing gear. So for short final, it was possible to judge the moment of highest rise, and I 'planted' it. They had the patient ready to go, and we soon had him back at the Gander hospital. For me, that flight was a great learning experience! We returned the aircraft to St. John's Nfld for a crew change and some time off.

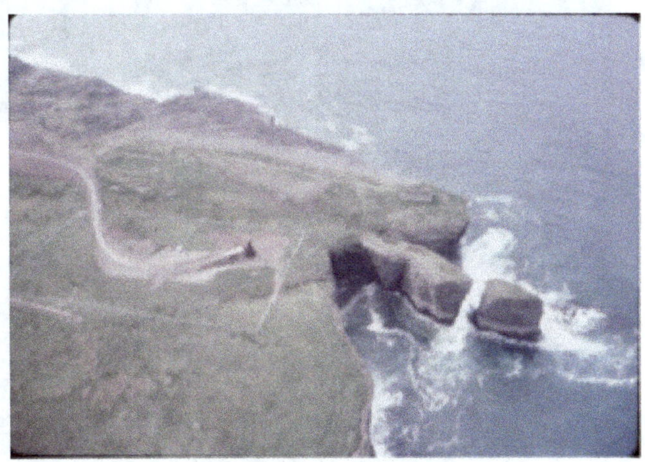

Coastline on way to rig

In a subsequent tour, I was one of the crews supporting offshore drilling operations out of St. John's, Newfoundland. This again was servicing oil drilling platforms offshore well into the Atlantic. Some of the rigs were 200- 300 km one way out from St. John's &
Halifax. This required extra fuel in long- range tanks, so to remain within our gross weight limits, it necessitated a reduction in rig workers.

The extra fuel was needed, especially if we made a missed approach upon returning to St. John's airport. We then had to proceed to our alternate airport, which would add another hour or so to the round trip to the rig.

At times we flew over a small sandy island called Sable Island, 175 km east of the Nova Scotia coast. It is 26 km long by 1 km wide at it's widest point and is largely inhabited by various marine birds and about 400 wild horses. The horses have been roaming this island since the 18th century & are an amazing sight being completely wild. Unfortunately, some of the horses are dying from starvation due to the limited food supply on the Island.

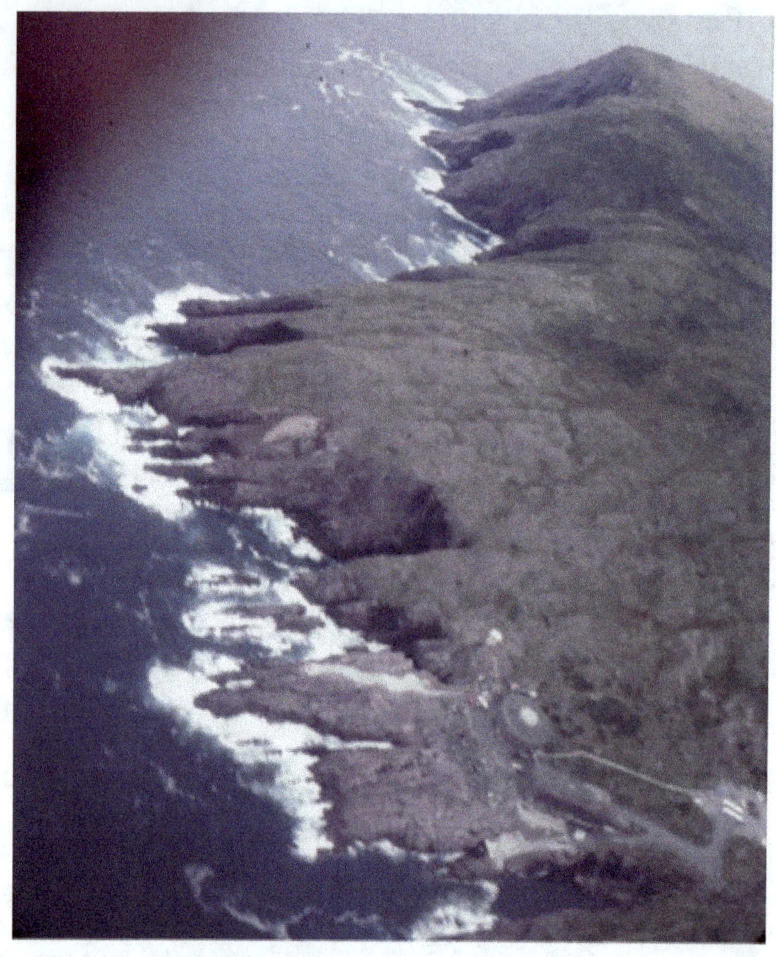

Coastline near St. John's

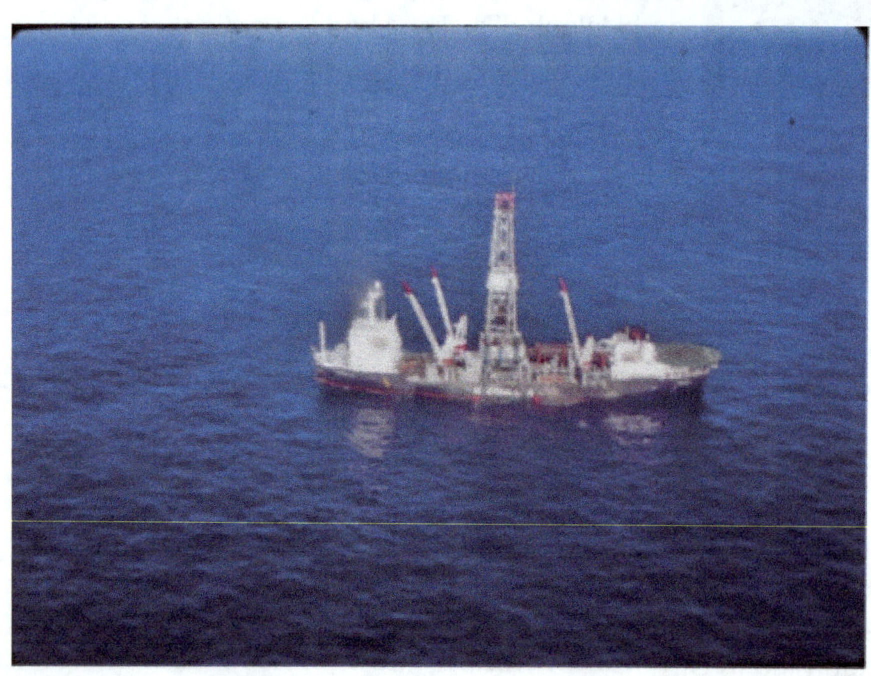

Offshore drillship

Three weeks later, I was off to Bombay, India, in support of their offshore oil fields. Bombay was a culture shock! Masses of people of all different castes and a very large contingent of impoverished people. This included a large population of 'professional ' beggars. They had their own system whereby the beggars at the top got a percentage cut from those below them. It was reputed that some of the head beggars owned entire apartment complexes and were actually quite rich. One of the tragic practices was that some parents would actually deform their babies' limbs at birth. This would enable them to extort more money to play on peoples' pity.

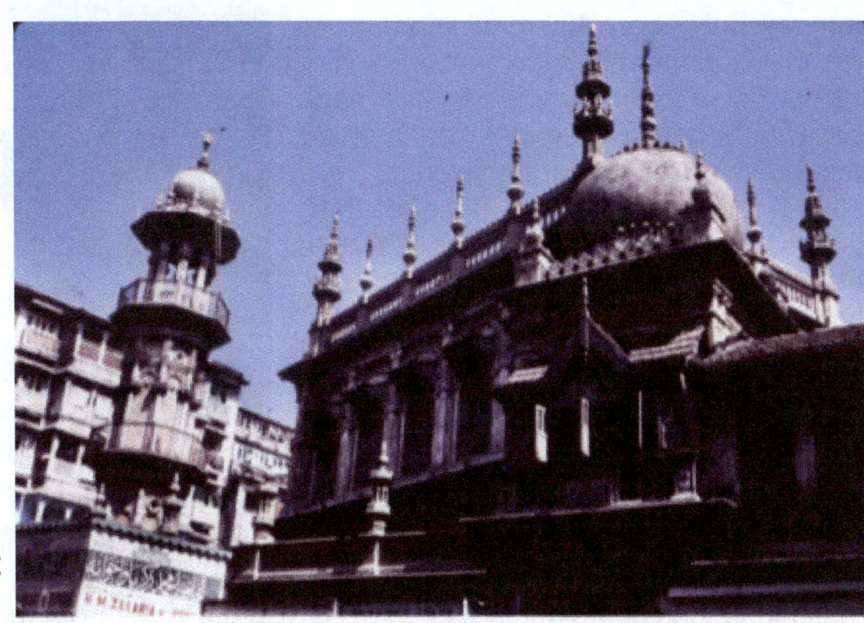

Bombay city centre

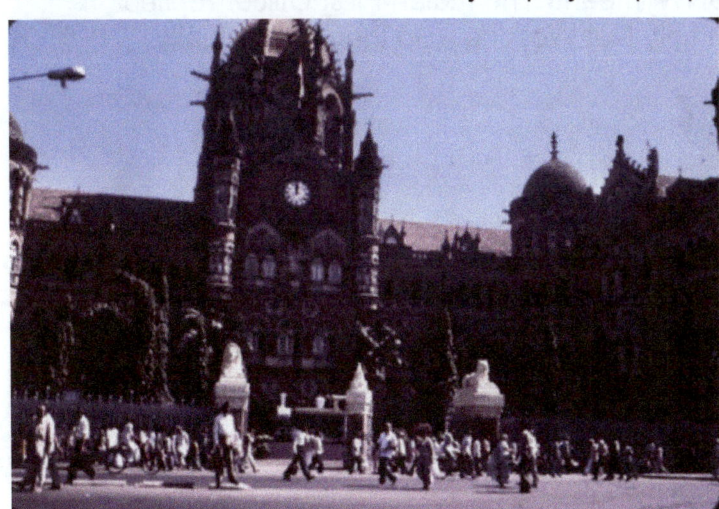

On overseas operations, we were required to wear white shirts, ties and captain or first officer bars. Besides presenting a professional image, it was a good representation by being 'ambassadors' of Canada. Our crews were staying at the Holiday Inn in Juhu, a suburb near Bombay. One day when I was in the dining room, I noticed a very dirty fork beside my plate. I brought this to the waiter's attention, and he was very apologetic. He immediately picked it up, wiped it on his apron and gave it back to me, saying, "Very, very sorry, Captain!" Their international food manager came through later and confirmed this hotel's five-star rating but condemned the kitchen.

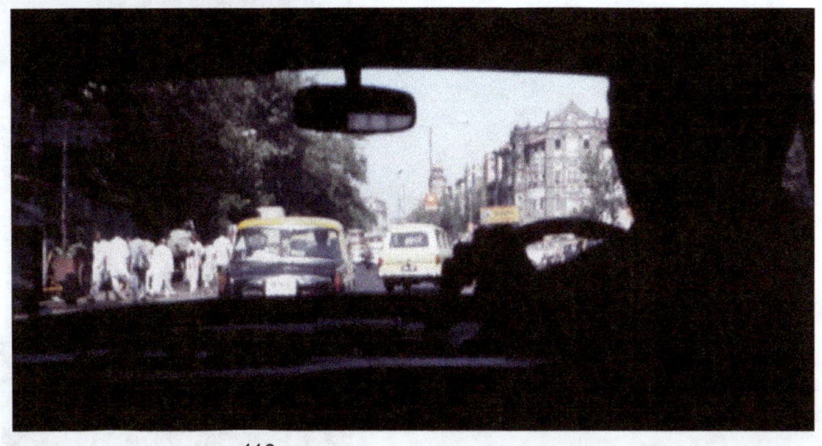

The rigs we flew to were not far from Bombay, only about 40 nm off shore. I was there during monsoon season, and the downpours were phenomenal. It made you wonder how the turbines kept running with the volume of water that went through the engine intakes. But of course, turbines are unaffected by water. We were returning to the airport one day and received an interesting communication from Bombay Tower. He was saying, " Helicopter JSI, you have 'resee-procal' traffic 12:00 o'clock." in a very strong Indian accent. We asked him to repeat and finally realized he was saying "reciprocal" traffic at 12:00 o'clock, which meant oncoming conflicting traffic coming our way. English is the universal language spoken by all controllers, but in India, as in Thailand, it took some getting used to. As you got away from the local ground and tower controllers and into the larger control areas, you often had British controllers. They were always much easier to understand. Quite often, in foreign operations, that country requests you use a locally qualified first officer. One of my co- captains was flying along one day and noticed one of the hydraulic gauges was occasionally erratic. He inquired from his copilot what the placarded letters 'SNW' meant. The Indian First Officer replied in a heavy accent, "Oh Captain, it means "Simply Not Working." So they had actually placarded the gauge that way!

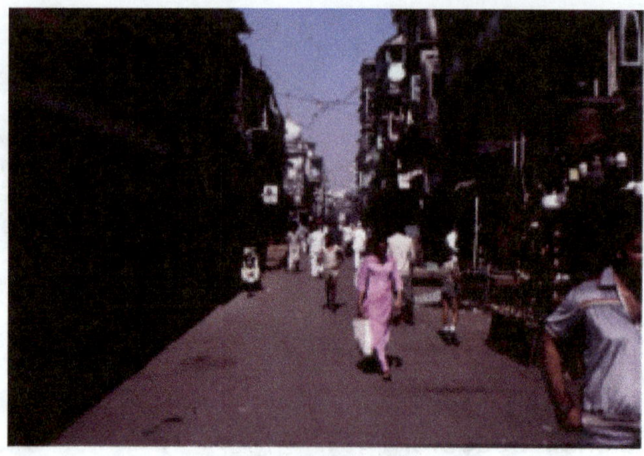

Bombay side street

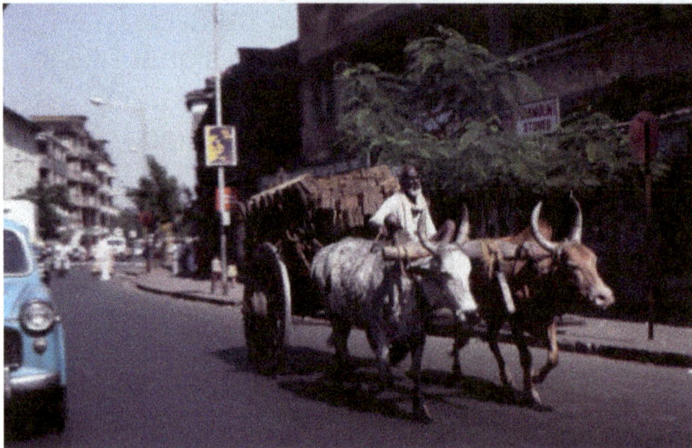

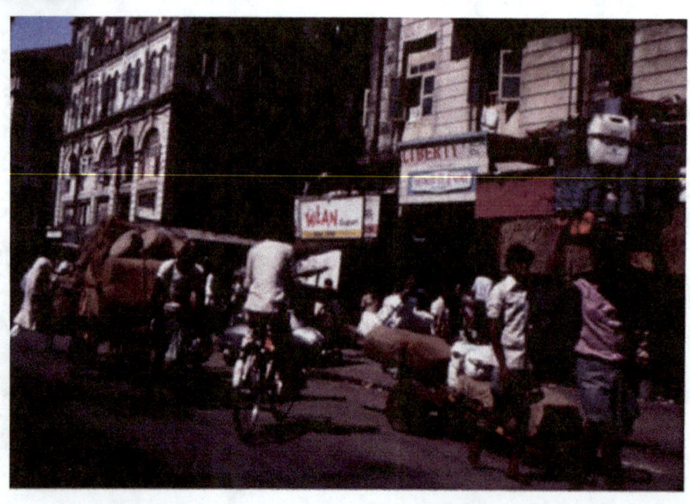

Unfortunately, I started

having some severe back problems, which made sitting in the cockpit very painful. My tour was cut short, and I returned to Canada. Consequently, I lost my medical for five months while I recuperated from my back issue.

When I returned to active duty, I spent the majority of my time in Thailand flying offshore for the next couple of years. I loved the people, and I loved the country; it was starting to feel like home. In 1985 I returned to flying in western Canada and the Arctic. We had offshore contracts with Esso and Shell out of Tuktoyaktuk, Northwest Territories. At the beginning of one tour, I arrived in Tuk for an Esso crew change. That afternoon we flew out to one of the man-made islands where a drilling operation was being staged. It was to be Esso's routine crew change.

However, the weather had moved in with low ceilings and ever-increasing winds. The manager asked us to wait and take refuge in a couple of Atco trailers while they combated the storm. The winds were becoming gale force as the wave action became very threatening. They dumped everything they could on the windward side of the island to stop the wave action, including C-cans and heavy equipment. At around midnight, it turned into an emergency evacuation of all personnel. We didn't have seats for everyone, so out of 12 men, 6 people just sat on the floor without seat belts. The storm was ferocious as the men piled in, and the air stairs door was closed. I picked up very carefully, moved over to clear some obstacles and rotated into forward flight. The S-61 has incredible stability even in those kinds of winds. However, with no forward visibility, the challenge was immediately having to go on instruments from a hover since the visual flight was not possible. This is actually a part of our recurrent training, so it was fairly routine in that emergency situation. It came as a surprise a few months later when Esso presented us with beautiful plaque awards as pictured on Page 151.

This Arctic tour proved to be interesting, with a couple of other incidents. We had a heavy sling load of testing downhole tools for Schlumberger. We were taking them out one night to one of the conical drilling rigs. En route, we were suddenly hit with some severe turbulence and encountered wind shear forces. This caused the sling load to swing out of control. On the third lateral swing, it looked like it might contact the main rotor, so we had to jettison it. The next day we went looking for it and discovered that a 6,000 lb. load makes a very nice hole through the ice! Schlumberger decided that, although awkward, this $20,000 load would be carried internally instead!

A few nights later, we had a trip to Herschel Island, 120 miles west of Tuktoyaktuk. On the way back, we only had a couple of passengers. It was extremely cold outside, so the cabin heater was cycling on a lot, and it was getting hotter and hotter. My co-pilot and I had shed our parkas and were down to shirtsleeves. When we landed in Tuk and opened the cockpit door, it was freezing in the main cabin. What had happened was that one of the half-door emergency exits had blown out en route! Of course, the cabin sensors kept demanding more heat. The two poor passengers were shivering in their heavy Arctic parkas. I asked them why they didn't come up and tell us. They said they were afraid to get out of their seats.

On the same tour, we delivered a sling load of fuel to another rig on a man-made island. The en-route crosswinds were steady at about 40 knots which required a large heading correction to maintain the course. I had a new French pilot from Montreal who was unfamiliar with the area. Halfway to the rig, he casually asked in a heavy French accent, "I wonder what that red light is?" Because of the drift, I quickly saw it on my side as well, at almost eye level. I knew immediately what it was and applied full climb power. There were no other red lights in this area except the one at the top of a 300-foot tower on a small island. To this day, I wonder just how close our sling load was to wrapping around that tower!

After dropping that load at the rig, we landed for fuel. Usually, refuelling was a quick operation, but the rig's pump went unserviceable. So it was necessary for us to pump nine 45-gallon drums of fuel into the S-61 with our hand pump. It was minus 40 degrees C and the usual 30-knot wind blowing. We took turns pumping, and halfway through the fifth drum, my co-captain laughed, saying, "I wonder where is da glory in dis helicopter flying?!" I cracked up as it sounded even funnier with the accent!

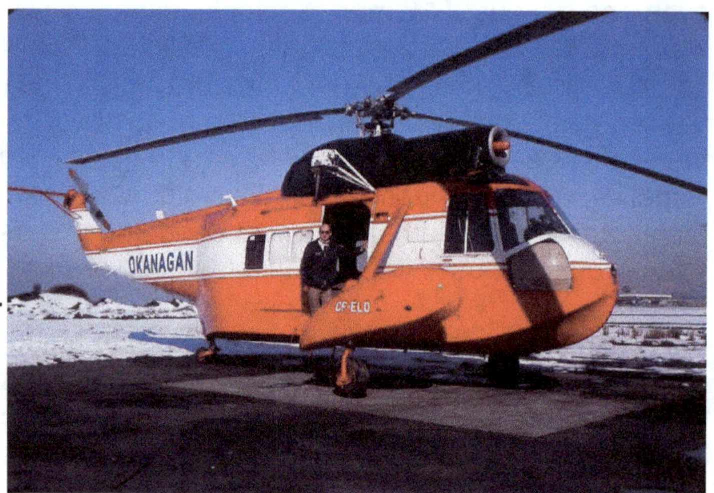

The fire season in BC was at its peak, and forestry needed a heavy lift helicopter in the Whistler area. The S-61 used a water bucket with a 1,000-gallon capacity which was very effective on the fires around Whistler and Squamish. After this, I got a call that took us off the coast in Washington. A quick stop in Vancouver and a crew change. I was teamed up with an old colleague from James Bay days in the 70s. I hadn't seen B Yearwood for 10 years, and now we were both flying for the same company, Okanagan Helicopters. We were contracted by the US Navy to help in the recovery of torpedoes. They would fire off these torpedos on a test range, and they would surface and float vertically. Bill was an expert with a 100-foot-long line and had no trouble snagging these 30-foot weapons. The job was done in a few days, and we had a beautiful direct flight over the Olympic mountains back to Vancouver.

Other than being away from home for 8 months of the year, I loved the variety as a Vancouver pool pilot. You rarely knew what or where you'd be going next.

I received a checkout

on the Sikorsky S-76 recently and had a chance to add to the 50 hours I had on it. This is a 14-place aircraft with retractable landing gear and a cruise speed of 160 mph. Our subsidiary company had a Medevac contract with the Ontario Ministry of Health out of Thunder Bay and Toronto. They used S-76's and I would be filling in on the Thunder Bay base for a month. The whole operation was very well set up, with the helicopter being based right at the airport. The response time was similar to a road ambulance. The crews, pilots and engineers were on standby for their 12-hour shifts and did not leave the hangar. Four minutes after receiving a medevac call from dispatch, we would be in the helicopter being pushed out of the hangar. In the cockpit, we'd be activating all the switches we could, and as soon as the tow bar was disconnected, the engines would be started. This helicopter was on wheels, so as we taxied towards the runway, we'd receive our clearance for takeoff. Throughout your shift, you keep checking the weather for a 200- mile radius. On takeoff, now that the destination is known, you do a final weather check. This seemed very strange to me because, throughout my career, you always checked the weather before a flight. Now, for the sake of expediency, you were required to file a flight plan and receive an IFR clearance once airborne.

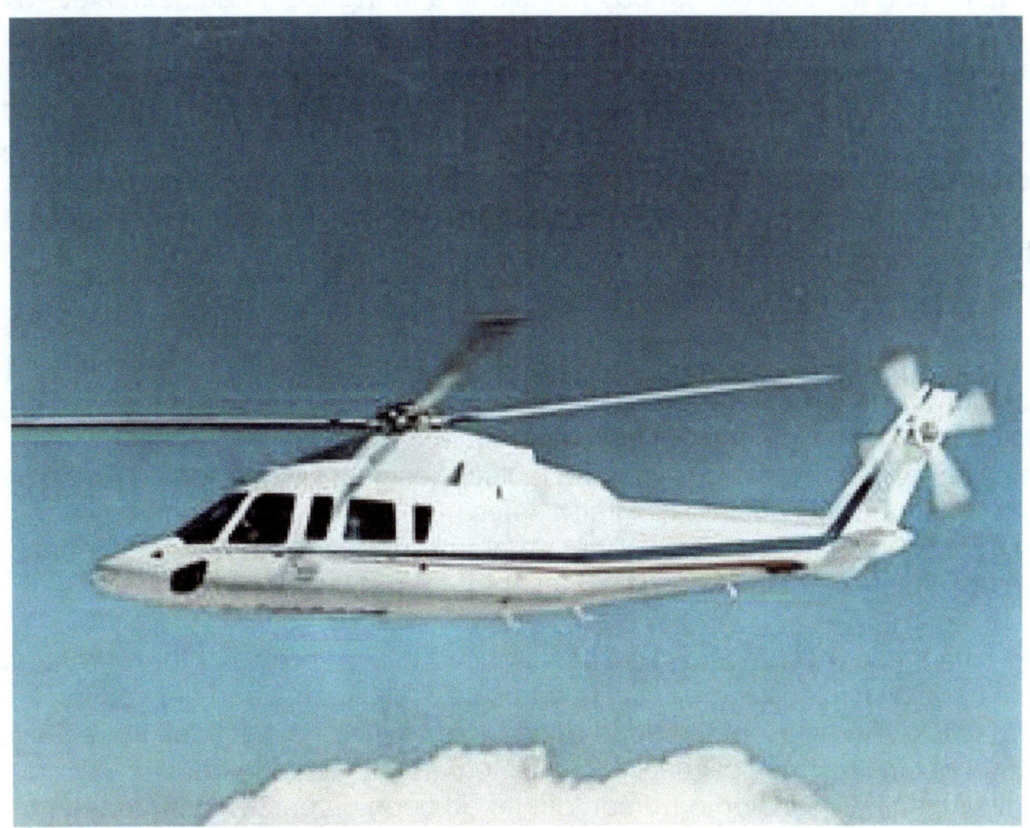

Aircraft used on the medevac program out of Thunder Bay ON

A couple of weeks

after returning home, I was off to Bombay for my second tour to India. I again had a serious medical problem after only a day of operations offshore. This time it was severe dizzy spells and vertigo, which necessitated a return back to Canada. This would result in a loss of my Transport Canada medical and being grounded for the next 7 years. Of course, I was devastated!

My company sent me to a number of specialists to try to determine what was causing this severe vertigo. The dizzy spells were very infrequent, happening only once every couple of months, but they were so debilitating! There was very little warning, and my head would feel like a toppling gyro. It would be impossible to walk, as any object in front of me would turn into numerous duplicate revolving objects, all in perfect clarity. Then, for 2 days after, I would feel very unstable. So our company doctor sent me to a general practitioner for all kinds of tests, then to a neurologist, and finally to a special rotational chair in Winnipeg. This was a special chair that rotated me for a number of sessions. All the tests from all the specialists came up negative. So it was decided by Transport Canada's medical division that I would have to go one-year symptom-free to get my medical back. This was fair and logical but didn't make my grounding any easier.

So what to do now? This would be a very dark period of my life. I was not a young single guy anymore. I had a wife, 3 kids, car payments and a mortgage. I had been a steward on a research ship and a waiter at the Bessborough Hotel in Saskatoon. Other than that, I was not trained for any other kind of job or profession. I won't go into a lot of detail other than I started an import company with children's clothing from Thailand. I imported kids denim clothing and baby shoes to a warehouse in Leduc. The Thai contacts I had made while flying helicopters over there proved to be invaluable. I had learned the language, customs and some business practices of Thailand. Through a commerce lawyer with whom I made contact in Bangkok, I was introduced to the largest Thai trading company called Asoke International.

I formed a company called ThaiCan Imports. I initially gained sole distributorship for 13 styles of baby shoes and marketed them across Canada and California. I then developed lines of denim clothing for kids. This required a trip back to Bangkok every 3 or 4 months. I combined my designs with the factory designers over there. It was quite a learning curve, but I quickly got into it. After a sales meeting with the Sears buyer in Toronto, a certain thing dawned on me. After an hour's meeting with her at their head office, it had absolutely nothing to do with aviation! I missed flying!

I had a long-time friend, K Krueger, who often stopped in at my office at the warehouse in Leduc. He had flown fixed wing all his life and said, "Bill, we have to get you back flying." I kept telling him aviation had dead-ended for me, and I didn't think there'd ever be a chance of getting my medical back. He insisted, so I decided to book an appointment with an MOT doctor in Edmonton. It had been 6 years and more than a year since my last dizzy spell. Fortunately, I had an appointment with a doctor who specialized in tropical medicine. As soon as I mentioned I had flown extensively overseas, he wanted to know if I'd been on certain antimalarial drugs. I confirmed that I had and one of the drugs, Fansidar immediately raised his concerns. He said unequivocally that this was the cause of my vertigo. Apparently, this drug can stay in your fat cells for four years after your last dosage. Since I hadn't taken this drug for 6 years and had no further symptoms of vertigo, he renewed my medical immediately. (Just a note about Keith. I lost him recently, in 2020, when he was killed in a freak accident. He was checking out a colleague in an airplane with amphibious gear. Apparently, they stalled at low altitudes and were unable to recover. Keith had over 30,000 hours of flying time, and his favourite airplane was the Hercules. I miss him very much).

The doctor facilitated me with the perfect timing to get back into aviation and the career I loved! Thai labour had gone up, along with their currency. Plus, shipping costs had increased, and I could no longer compete with the big box stores. I liquidated the remaining stock in my warehouse and started putting out flying applications.

Even with my experience, I was not having much luck with the feelers I had put out. Then my wife noticed an ad in an aviation magazine looking for a medevac pilot. The company was Vancouver Island Helicopters in Victoria, BC, a company I was very familiar with. I didn't realize they had branched out to the medevac business and had gained a contract with the British Columbia Ambulance Service (BCAS).

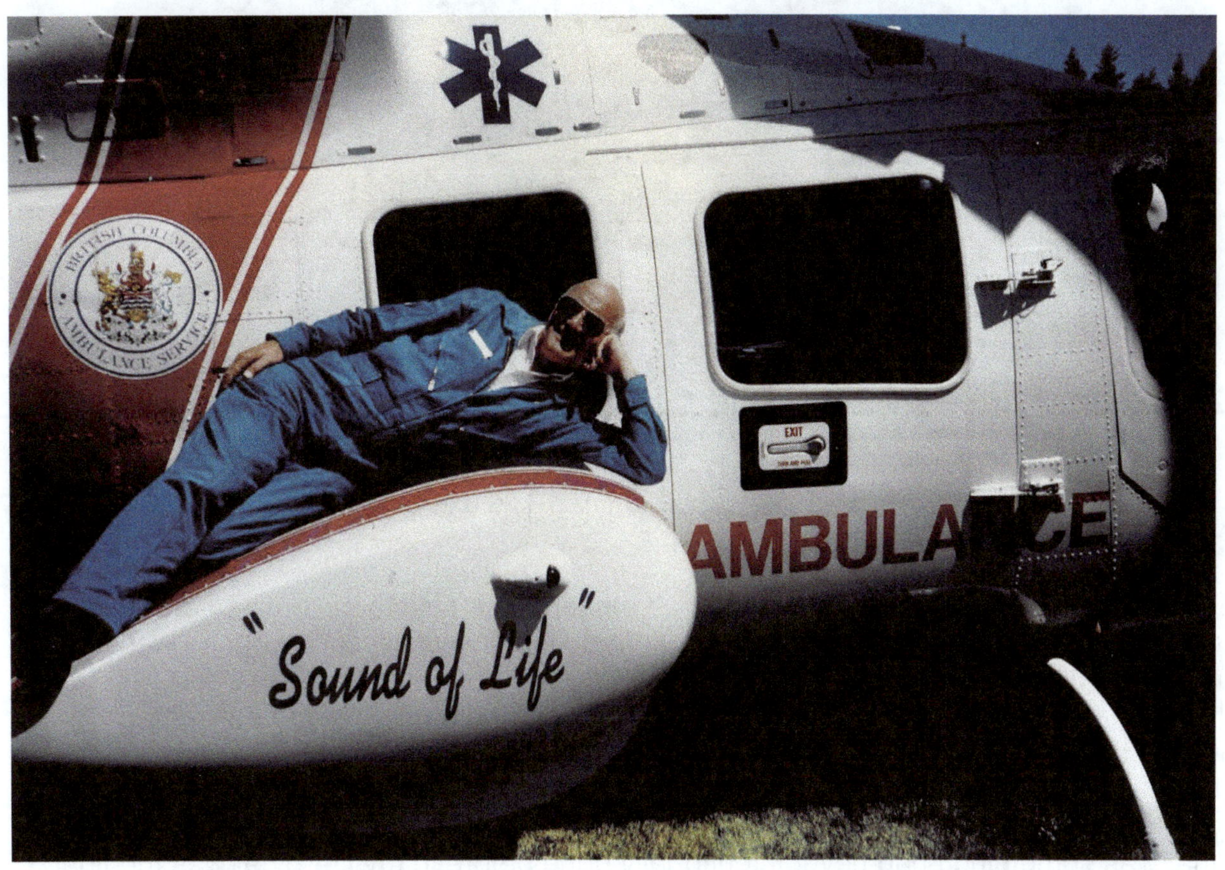

Waiting for paramedics

In 1993 after being grounded for seven years, it was exciting to be back in aviation. After several phone interviews, VIH's chief pilot, B. Reimer, invited me to Victoria for a 'test flight.' I went out on the apron with the senior check ilot, E. Ross. After not having been in a helicopter for seven years, I really wasn't sure what to expect. But it was sort of like the bicycle thing- after a couple of minutes in the cockpit, I felt like I'd never left.

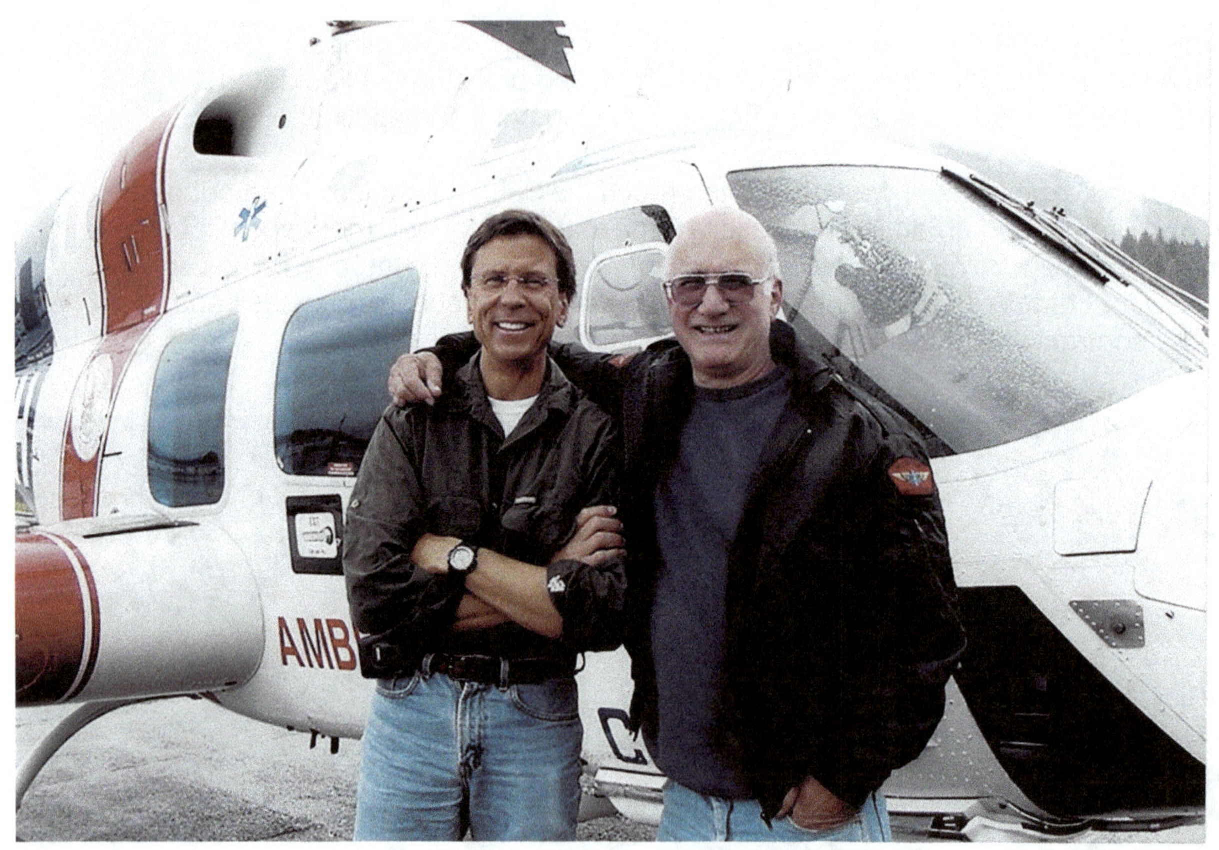

R Bejnar - Many medevacs together - I miss him after he passed!

We flew over to Saltspring Island, and he had me land in a couple of confined areas. A couple of other exercises, and then he took control. I really wasn't sure what he was going to demonstrate as he went into a 70-foot hover in front of a large pine tree. He inched closer and closer until the main rotor blades started nipping at the new green growth at the end of a branch. With a grin, he gave me control and said, "Ok, now you do that."

So that was something I had never intentionally done before in my life! That was the final exercise in precision flying, and we returned to the airport. I was officially hired, and my wife and I started making plans to move from Alberta to Victoria. I was back in the saddle!

I began flying out of that base strictly on the Medevac contract we had with the BC Ambulance Service. The aircraft that we used was the Bell 222. It was specially configured to carry 2 pilots, 2 patients and a combination of 2-3 paramedics, doctors or nurses.

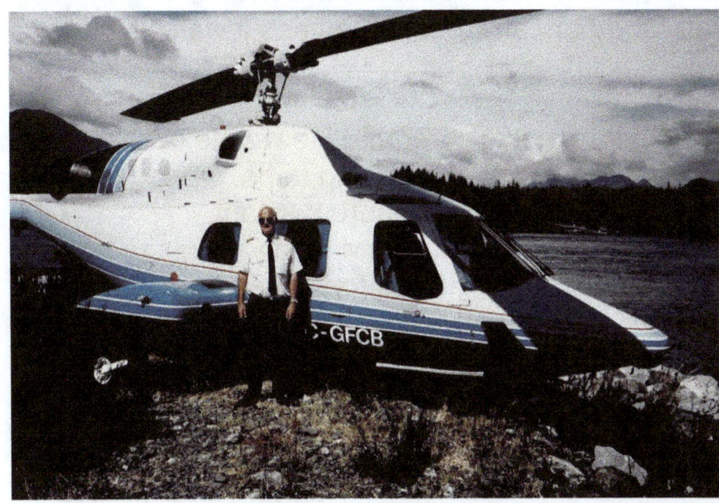

One of the aircraft I was checked out on was one of Donald Trump's personal aircraft. When VIH purchased this 222, it still had gold-plated seat belt buckles and interior door handles. It was fully certified for instrument flight and had retractable landing gear.

We were also on contract with BCAS in Vancouver and Prince Rupert. On the Victoria base, we covered all of Vancouver Island and the lower mainland if the Vancouver machine was tied up on another call. The calls were many and varied throughout our entire area. It could be a heart attack victim in Campbell River, a baby abused from being thrown down the stairs and every other medical trauma you can imagine.

Our shifts ran 12 hours from 6:00 am to 6:00 pm. I will highlight a cross-section of some of the very interesting calls. Late one day, we were called to Ucluelet on the West coast of the Island to pick up two accident victims. They were each the drivers of two cars involved in a head-on collision. We transported both of them to Port Alberni Hospital. An hour later, a car came to a rushed stop at the helipad, and the driver hopped out. He wanted to know how one of the victims was doing. We asked him what his relationship was because we couldn't divulge patient information. He explained that he hoped 'Tommy' wouldn't die because 'Tommy' owed him $3,000!

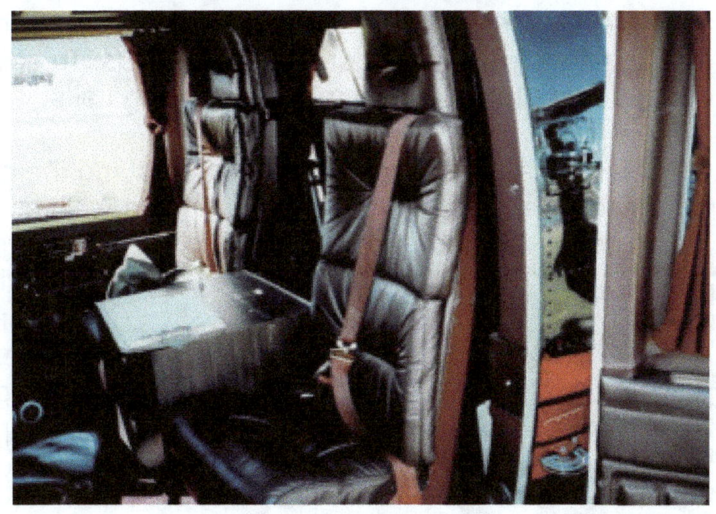

Donald Trump's Executive interior

Another time it was a call to a mountainside east of Powell River. A group of skiers were at the 6,000-foot level when one of the older skiers had a massive heart attack. There was a rock projection for me to land on, but I had to keep running and stay light on the skids for stability. The paramedics tried to resuscitate him, but unfortunately, he didn't make it. Normally we don't transport anybody who has deceased, but in this case, we did because of our proximity to the hospital. In another similar situation, we became involved after a tragic accident at a logging scene north of Pitt Meadows. A limb high up a large pine broke off, killing the faller below. These limbs are often very heavy and can fall as that tree is being felled. They are known as 'widow makers' with good reason. The RCMP helicopter had already landed for the initial investigation but asked us to transport the victim to the New Westminster hospital. The main reason we didn't like to transport bodies is because it ties up the aircraft for other calls, but sometimes it was unavoidable.

Another call was to pick up a patient in Comox having a medical trauma. He was to be transferred to the intensive care unit at VGH in Vancouver. This was going to be interesting for us because of the fireworks going on in English Bay. There was an international competition going on called 'The Festival of Lights.' It was a 'no-fly zone,' so I had to get prior permission to overfly the area and land on the rooftop helipad at VGH. As we landed on the rooftop, it was an incredible view and a different perspective, seeing the panoramic fireworks from above. As we did the cool down, I asked my copilot to take the controls so I could have a better view from the edge of the heliport. When the security guard came rushing over, I had to assure him I was one of the pilots and not a 'psych' patient escaping from the helicopter!

The following day we transferred a patient up Island to the Campbell River hospital. We had just refuelled and were ready to return to Victoria. I was about to start the engines when dispatch called and asked us to stand by for a possible call. There had been an armed bank robbery in Campbell River and a subsequent police chase. This resulted in a rollover by the getaway car with injuries. In the end, they dispatched a road ambulance and cancelled our standby status. To say the least, this would have been right up there in one of the more interesting calls!

On clear days the scenery, the mountains and the ocean were panoramic and made the flights so awe-inspiring. On clear nights as well, all the lights were pristine and carpeted a quiet landscape. On one of those nights, we had to go to Tofino to transport a diver with a condition known as the 'bends.' This always required a flight to be at the lowest level possible so as not to aggravate this type of injury. So we departed the Tofino hospital at midnight, flying just above the waves along the west coast. There was a brilliant full moon splashed across the water, and the West Coast trail was dotted with campfires. This is a very popular hiking trail, with thousands of hikers booking it every year. It was nights like this that made a flight so enjoyable, and you actually felt euphoric.

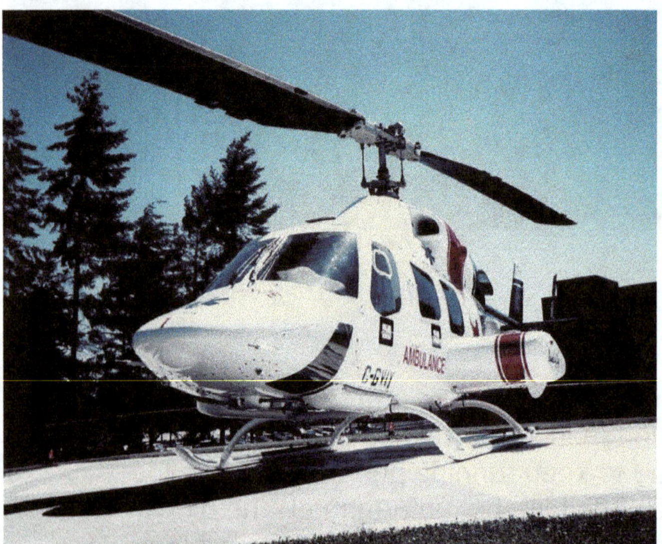

Every once in a while I would be asked to fill in on our Vancouver base. One evening we had a call for a pick-up at the Nanaimo hospital. It was a routine transfer from Nanaimo to the Point Grey University Hospital in Vancouver. It came as a bit of a shock when I received the patient's name, G Frith. J and G Frith were old friends of our family. As I was growing up, they often came out from Saskatoon to our farm to visit. They moved out to Nanaimo when Mr. Frith became the first administrator of the new Nanaimo Regional Hospital. I had heard he was not well, but I didn't realize to what extent. The paramedics told me later that the first thing he asked was if I was one of the pilots. Normally, I wouldn't have been since I was usually based out of Victoria, so this was a bit of a fluke. The paramedics also told me that he had terminal cancer and this would be his last leg. For me, it was very sad when we landed in Vancouver, and I could only think of a final unspoken goodbye.

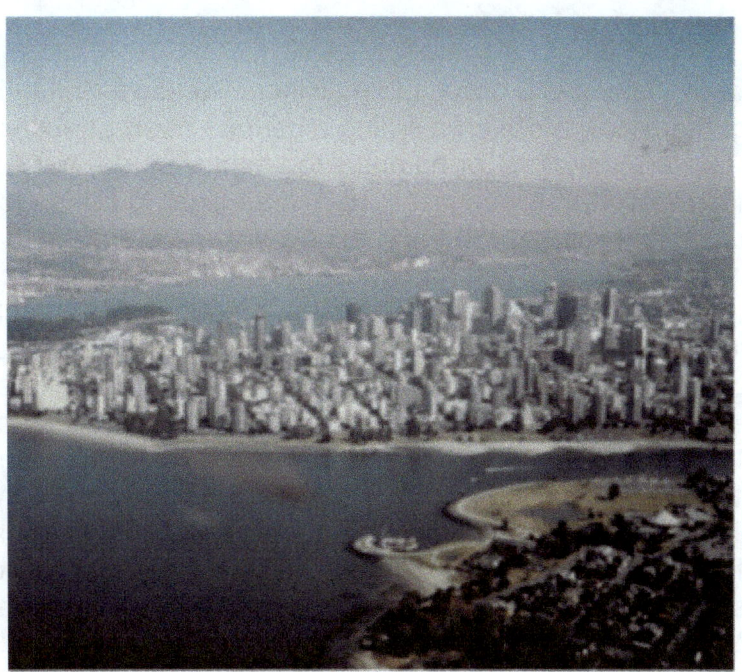

Vancouver

One of the paramedics who regularly flew with us, R Leroux, was a real comedian. He was an excellent example of the ALS (Advanced Life Support) team and head of their Union. We had picked up an elderly patient in Campbell River with heart issues. We landed at Victoria General Hospital and were awaiting the paramedics' return. As they returned, Randy was howling with laughter. I asked him what that was all about? He related this conversation. The patient, as he was being wheeled into the emergency ward, said, "I see you have an old pilot (me) and a young guy up front." With a straight face, R had said, "Yeah, the old guy has lots of experience but doesn't see so good, but the young guy sees great, so that's why they have to fly together." The elderly patient said, "Oh, I didn't know they could do that!" He never corrected him, and I just shook my head.

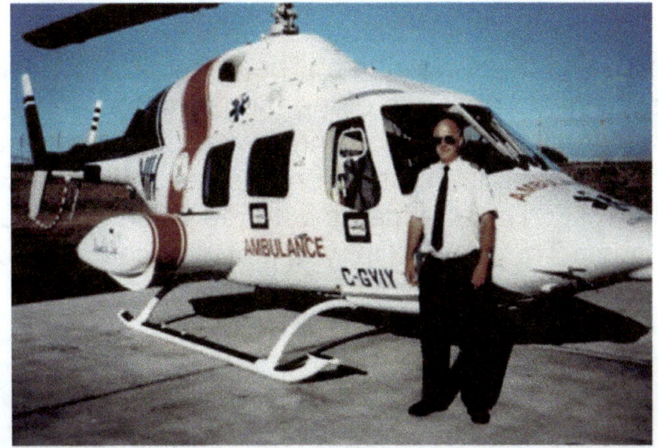

Just east of Victoria is a group of small islands called the Gulf Islands. Early one morning, there was a call concerning a serious heart attack victim on Maine Island. The conditions were just right for potential fog over Victoria, but so far, the two main hospitals were still in the clear. It was just a 10-minute flight to Maine Island to pick up the patient and return to the City. As we approached Victoria General, there was an urgent call from the rear that the patient just had gone into cardiac arrest. They asked to head for the nearest hospital, but Vic General had just fogged in completely. The fog was starting to form over the entire city as I quickly brought up the other hospital in the GPS, the Royal Jubilee. As we arrived at the hospital, it, too, had become obscured.
Just then, I saw a hole on my side, directly over the hospital and had it visual. I told my copilot I had control and did a tight spiral down. I landed in front of Emerg just as the fog completely closed in overhead. We again had R Leroux and his partner on board as they quickly rushed that patient into emergency. When they came back to the helipad, I asked them if the patient was going to make it. R said, "No, I don't think so-he's going to die. " I said, "Oh, that's really tragic. I thought we got him here in time!" Randy said with a grin, "Yeah, he'll probably die, but not for another 20 years." I again shook my head.

Every once in a while, we attended serious highway accidents. Usually, there were police vehicles directing traffic when we landed on the highway. In the lower mainland, I was always amazed at how quickly and how many vehicles backed up in a hurry. They would immediately be bumper to bumper and stopped for 10 kilometres or more. To further complicate things, the opposing traffic would start backing up as well. They would be trying to get a glimpse of the accident scene and, consequently, would rear- end each other as well on occasion. The helicopter was literally a lifesaver at times, as we could deliver critical accident casualties to the nearest hospital very quickly. Medical experts say that life can usually be saved if they can receive critical care in under an hour.

One night we had an emergency transfer of a child over to Children's Hospital in downtown Vancouver. As we were waiting for the paramedics, the Coastguard aircraft from Comox landed beside us with another patient. It was 2:00 am when we landed, and there were a lot of noise complaints across from the hospital. This area west of Oak Street is a very affluent district with high-end houses. The situation worsened when the Coastguard landed, lighting up our switchboard in Victoria. We related this to the Coastguard Captain, and he said something about 'unsympathetic rich people.' They then took off, and hehovered directly over the most lit-up houses while he did his flight planning! Of course, our company was blamed for that as well!

Shortly after joining the company, I was walking our beautiful prairie Collie on the beach. I was keeping an eye on him because of the tangle of logs and slippery rocks. Suddenly, I slipped on a seaweed-covered rock and broke my ankle. I managed to crawl to the top of the bank and caught the attention of a resident. She called an ambulance, which arrived quickly. The attendants laughed when they found out I had flown the ambulance helicopter. They said, "Oh, you just wanted to try out a road ambulance as well!"

In January 1994, the chief pilot decided to have me trained as a check pilot. The Vancouver base manager, K Carswell was the only company medevac check pilot. They needed someone on the Victoria base as well to relieve some of his workload. So K checked me out and covered all the areas I needed to go through with the medevac pilots. To maintain safety and standards, every commercial pilot is required by Transport Canada to go through 6-month recurrent training. This training was broken down into two categories, visual pilot proficiency checks on the aircraft and instrument flight. The main focus of the visual portion was to simulate mechanical aircraft emergencies. This included engine fires, single-engine failures, tail rotor and transmission failures, hydraulic servo problems, jammed controls, etc. It would have been a bit better to do this in a flight simulator because the failures would have been a little more realistic. The only one available to us was in Dallas, Texas, which would have been cost-prohibitive to send all the pilots down. But we could demonstrate the emergencies in the actual aircraft without compromising flight safety.

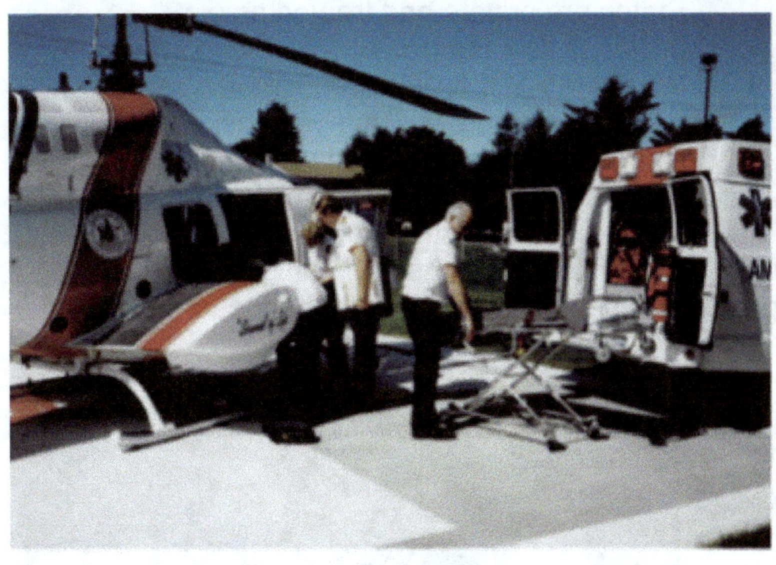

Patient Transfer

The other portion of the PPC's (pilot proficiency checks) entailed flying solely by instruments. The pilot being checked out had to demonstrate flying solely on instruments from point A to B. He was then required to make a full approach, including a missed approach. The flight often included some emergencies: engine fires, lost communications, etc. Throughout the entire flight, conformance to altitudes, tracking, descent and approach parameters had to adhere to Transport Canada's standards. The thing I appreciated as the training captain/first officer was that it kept me current as well. The other benefit was that we could take friends and family along for the ride. The company didn't mind, and there were no insurance issues. Through the years, I was able to take many people up for their first and often only ride in a helicopter. I could isolate their intercoms from us in the cockpit so there was no interference. One interesting note is that the Bell 222 does not have an autopilot. So, for any exercises flying solely on instruments, the pilot has to 'hand fly' the aircraft, which is much more demanding without the aid of an autopilot.

In the Fall of 1994,

there was a medical aircraft convention in Detroit, Michigan. This would prove to be very interesting as all the latest ambulance helicopters and medical equipment would be introduced from around North America. I took off from Victoria with the base engineer. We landed at the Detroit airport the following day. The next morning, ambulance helicopters landed in downtown Detroit. One aircraft at a time was pushed into the famous Joe Louis arena, home of the Detroit Redwings.

During the three-day show, I met a lot of interesting paramedics and pilots from Canada and the USA. One of the crews was tasked to the President's Sikorsky S-61, which is the aircraft you see landing on the Whitehouse lawn. It was great talking to these pilots because they crewed the same type of aircraft I flew in Edson, Alberta.

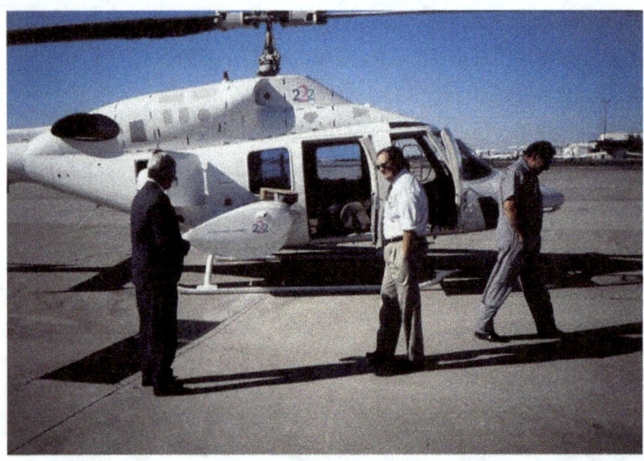

Our Bell 222 was actually up for sale as my company had purchased an updated model. After the show, there were two potential buyers, a hospital in Atlanta, Georgia and another in Abilene, Texas. Some hospitals and helicopters in the States are private and treated as a business. So, the boss asked me to park the aircraft at the Winnipeg airport. On the way to Winnipeg, the company asked me to land at a hospital in Duluth, Minnesota. The hospital administrator wanted a demonstration of the 222 for possible future application. I landed on their rooftop heliport on the edge of Lake Superior. The hospital staff was very impressed with this type of aircraft and thought it would be perfect for their operations.

I completed the remainder of the flight to Winnipeg and hangared it there. I returned to Victoria via commercial airline. Four days later, the hospital in Abilene formally purchased the aircraft, and I was asked to deliver it. Leaving Winnipeg, the weather was perfect, with strong forecast tailwinds at altitude. As I entered the Dallas control area, I was recorded doing ground speeds of 234 mph with that strong tailwind. This was the fastest speed I had ever achieved in a helicopter.

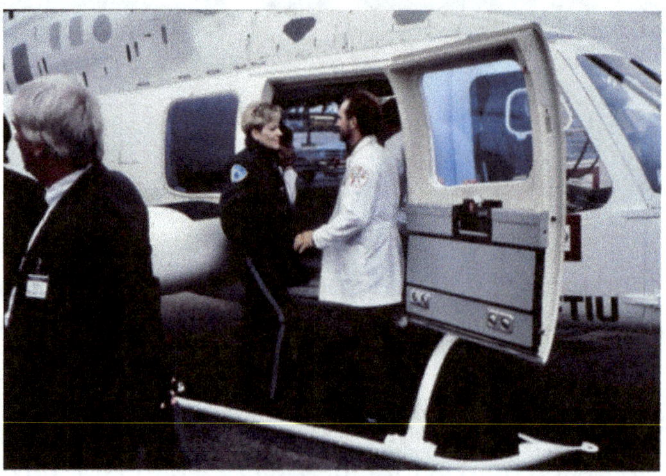

Abilene medical staff

After being tracked on their radar and recognized, I was asked an unusual and informal question by ATC. "Hey, son, just what kind of helicopter are you in?!" I landed shortly after at the Dallas airport in front of Omni Flight's hangar, the company delivering the aircraft to the Abilene hospital. The next morning the chief pilot and I took off for Abilene, 180 miles away. We landed in front of the hospital to the awaiting administration and staff.

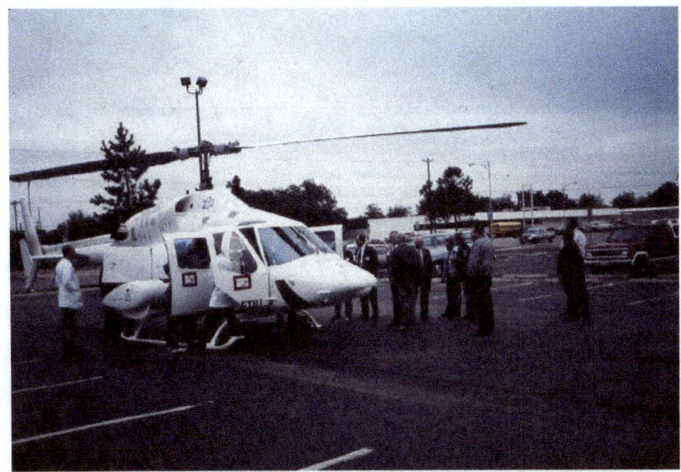

They were all quite excited to see their new medevac helicopter firsthand.

We took off a couple of hours later to Dallas, where the medevac interior would undergo a few alterations. On the way back, we advised the tower we were cancelling our IFR (instrument) flight plan and requested a local visual tour. For years I had watched the TV series 'Dallas,' and I wanted to fly over the ranch, 'Southfork' where most of the filming had taken place. I actually did a low, high-speed pass up the driveway, which was the opening shot for each weekly show.

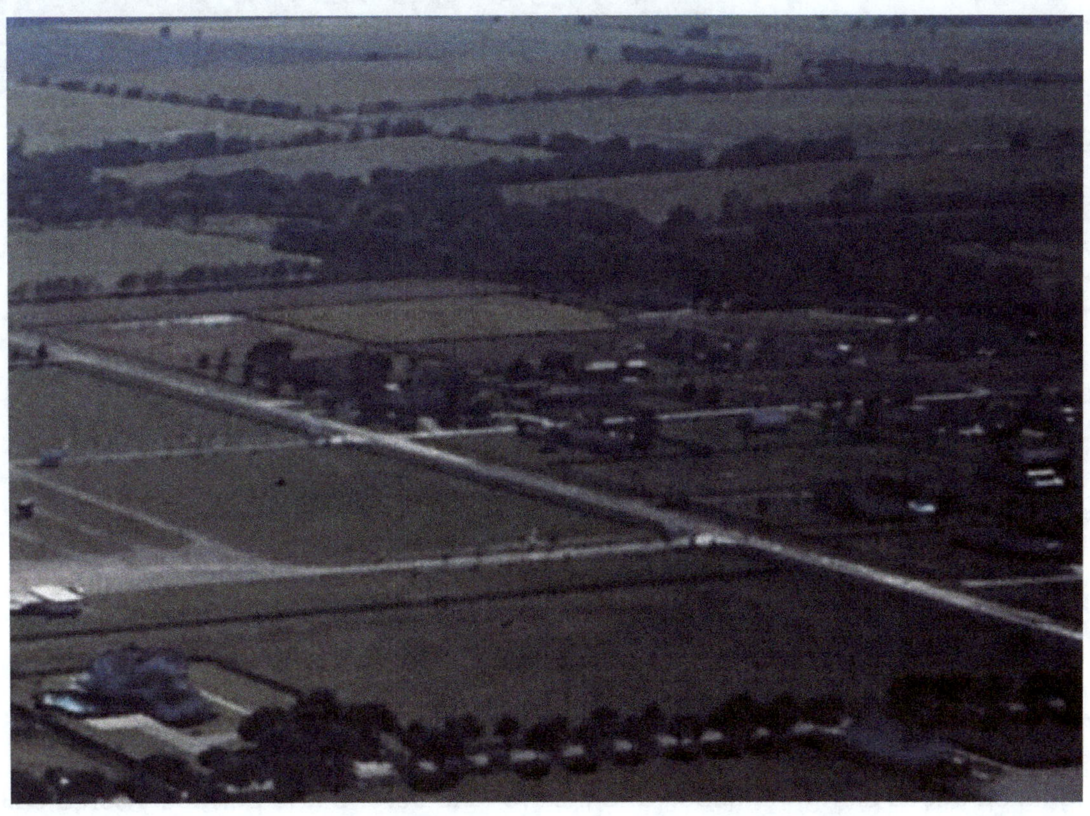

'Dallas' 1978 TV series - Mansion where filming took place - lower left

Returning to Victoria

I was back to some routine patient transfers and not- so-routine medevac calls. One afternoon we got a call to a golf course on one of the Gulf Islands. We landed right beside the 18th hole where a patient was lying unconscious right beside it. Unfortunately, he died of a massive heart attack.

I guess he had died happy doing what he loved if there is such a thing as happily dying!

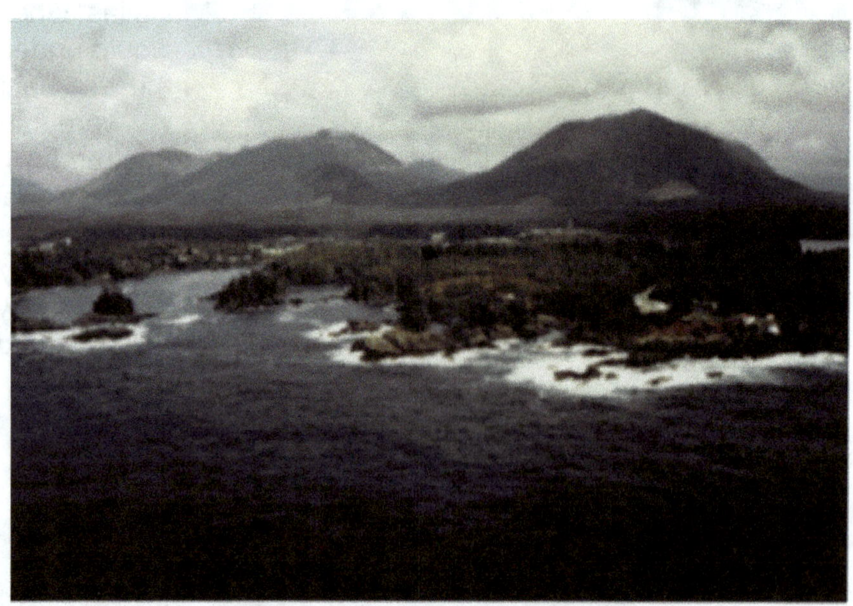

Vancouver Island - west coast

A few days later, we returned to another Gulf Island, where a very traumatic accident had occurred. This faller was limbing some overhead branches with a chainsaw. Apparently, the saw had kicked back and caught him right in the throat. There had been massive blood loss, but the paramedics had him swathed in bandages. We rarely hear about a patient's condition after we've dropped them off at a hospital, but this one was different. A few months later, I was at the Victoria air show watching a Martin Mars water bomber fly past. Out of the crowd, a young gentleman came over and shook my hand. I had no idea, but he was the one who had the chainsaw accident. He had fully recovered and just wanted to express his appreciation that we had come to his rescue.

A lot of our flights were memorable and satisfying just from the spectacular BC scenery.

Night flights were very satisfying in another way. We were returning from Comox one night en route to the Children's Hospital in Vancouver. The skies were perfectly clear, with no winds or turbulence and a full moon. We were filed on airways, and we knew ATC was tracking us. So at times like this, it's easy to slip into a time of reverie. Nostalgia is not out of place as we fly along in this controlled world. The instrument panel is softly glowing, and an unconscious glance at all the gauges in the green is always reassuring. On nights like this, the rotor blades are basically invisible, and with no real sense of movement, you feel as if you're just suspended in space. There are various lights sprinkled along the coast, and the world is serene and perfect. Then a call from Air Traffic Control with an approach clearance and back to reality. There were many memorable flights, and this was one of them.

Royal Roads is a military academy located in the Esquimalt area of Victoria. This was the site to be used by a movie company to shoot a sequel to the horror movie, 'Poltergeist.' They contracted our company to use one of the medevac 222s. They had the helicopter painted completely black with large gold swords on the forward doors. It was a ferocious and imposing-looking aircraft.

I landed on the large lawn area in front of the university. The entire cast and production people were assembled around an enormous table of gourmet foods. Apparently, it's an industry standard to keep everybody well-fed on location. After a lot of scenes were shot inside, it was time for my scene. First, they had wardrobe and makeup attending to me. This involved highlighting facial features and included a full-length wig. I miraculously looked twenty years younger! Then they started the scene with a young couple coming down the main steps from the 'castle.' They were quarrelling as I stood by the open cockpit door. He slid back the passenger sliding door and angrily shoved her in. Then he got into the cockpit and went through the motions of throwing switches and starting the engines. The director motioned to “Cut” and replaced the lead actor with me. Of course, they had already made me to look like this young actor, and I took his place in the cockpit. Now I actually started the aircraft and prepared for takeoff. The only thing I was a little uncomfortable with was the director's request that I immediately retract the gear on liftoff. He wanted to have a sleek-looking aircraft, but this wouldn't have been the time for a dual-engine failure! So, as I flew away, apparently, they blew me up, and I turned into a large fireball! I never saw the production movie, but it must have been quite effective.

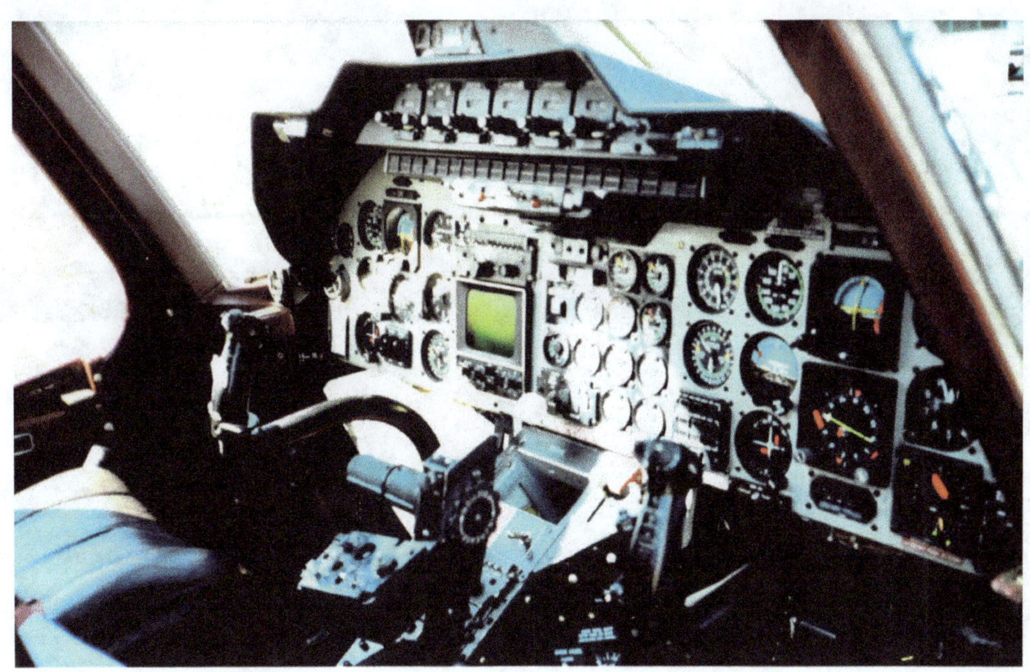

Cockpit - Bell 222A

In 1995 I conducted my first training seminar

with the medevac pilots on our Prince Rupert base. The company rented a conference room in the Crest Hotel, where I held ground school. The next day I began their recurrent flight training, and it was nice seeing some different country. The scenery around Prince Rupert was pretty spectacular, with the coastal mountains, ocean and pristine valleys unspoiled by logging.

The base manager had a beautiful 34-foot powerboat with a wooden hull. Before returning to Victoria, he took a friend and me out for an overnight deep-sea fishing trip. The first night we anchored on the lee side of Smith Island, 14 nautical miles west of Prince Rupert. The next morning we had an early start right on some of the best salmon grounds in the world. Within a couple of hours, I caught my first salmon, which weighed in at 36 pounds. The next day I returned to Victoria with this salmon and freshly caught prawns for a memorable company barbecue. Little did I realize I'd eventually be moving to Prince Rupert permanently.

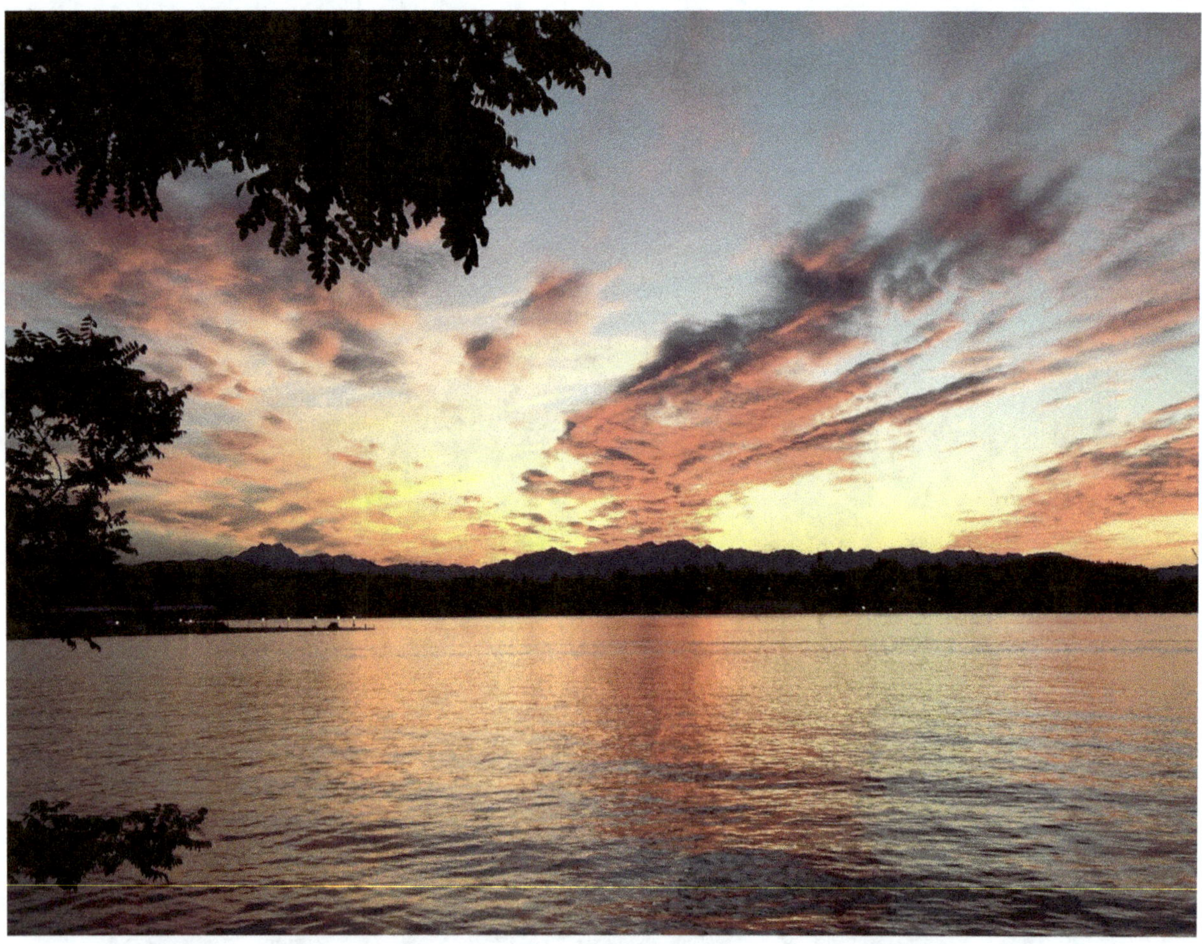

Prince Rupert

Another year had passed

, so I was asked by management to again represent the company at another medevac conference. This one was to be held in Long Beach, California, just south of Los Angeles. The weather was perfect the day I took off from Victoria with strong tailwinds at altitude. Flying along the beautiful California coast, you almost didn't want to get there too quickly because of the scenery, but it did eliminate some fuel stops. The next day, various helicopters from across North America landed one at a time at the Long Beach Convention Centre. It was another successful and well-attended conference. In the space of one year, there had been tremendous developments in new medical equipment and aircraft medical interiors. Our boss, B Hewko, had flown in separately to attend the show. The first night he took us out to the Queen Mary, a luxury cruise ship that has been permanently docked in Long Beach. It's now a major tourist attraction with a formal dining room and luxury accommodations. After dinner, B took us on an 'unofficial' tour of the ship, trying to access the engine room. During the Second World War, the ship was used as a troop transport. It was rumoured that soldiers had left inscriptions to loved ones on the bulkheads in the engine room, and B wanted to see them. We never did find the engine room, but it was an interesting night with the boss!

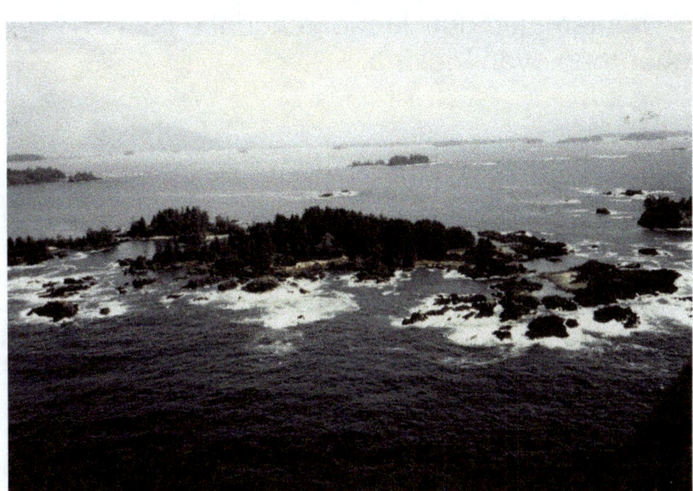

Near Long Beach'

I was especially interested in being in the Los Angeles area because of the infamous O. J. Simpson trial. Simpson, a famous football legend, had previously been on trial for the murder of his wife, Nicole Brown Simpson. The trial had been over for 2 weeks, and Simpson had been acquitted. I had watched the entire trial on TV and found it to be fascinating. One day I had a bit of free time from the convention and happened to come upon some kind of skirmish in the middle of a street. The police had someone down on his stomach and were cuffing him. There was a crowd, and I was a bit closer, leaning up against a lamp post. When he was taken away, a police sergeant noticed me and came right over. He wanted to know what my business was. I assured him I was just a spectator and had just landed a helicopter at their convention centre. That broke the ice, and he said, "Oh, we've been watching you guys land all day! Do you want to go for a coffee?" He introduced me to another cop who had rolled up in a squad car and invited him along as well. These guys looked pretty intimidating in their black uniforms and riot gear. This was the perfect opportunity to get their take on the OJ Simpson trial. Both officers were still furious that Simpson had been acquitted on technicalities. The next day I was able to talk to an African American to get his side of the story. He said in a drawl, "Well, OJ didn't do it, but I'm sure he was there!" An interesting post note is that even though Simpson was acquitted in the criminal trial, he was sued and found to be guilty in a civil trial by Nicole Brown Simpson's family. After three days, the convention was over, and I repositioned the helicopter back to the Long Beach airport. This aircraft wasn't being sold this time but was being leased by a medevac company in Rialto. This was a small town just southeast of Los Angeles. This should have been a quick 30-minute flight, but the fog moved in unexpectedly en route. Soon I was slowed up to 60 knots and needed to land, but there were all kinds of towers and transmission wires in the area. That's when my GPS was invaluable because it was programmed to bring in the 10 nearest airports. It gave me an immediate bearing to a small airport just a couple of miles away called Chino. A quick call to Rialto and the chief pilot drove out to meet me. He was qualified on the Bell 222, so we filed an instrument flight plan. I asked him if he was ok flying as my copilot since he didn't even know me. He said, "With the experience you Canadian guys have flying up there in the mountains, I have no worries." With that vote of confidence, we took off and fifteen minutes later, we broke out on the final approach to Rialto Airport. After inquiring about my overall experience, he offered me a medevac job out of their base in Hawaii. I was tempted until I researched the cost of living in Hawaii and found out it was a lot higher than even Victoria.

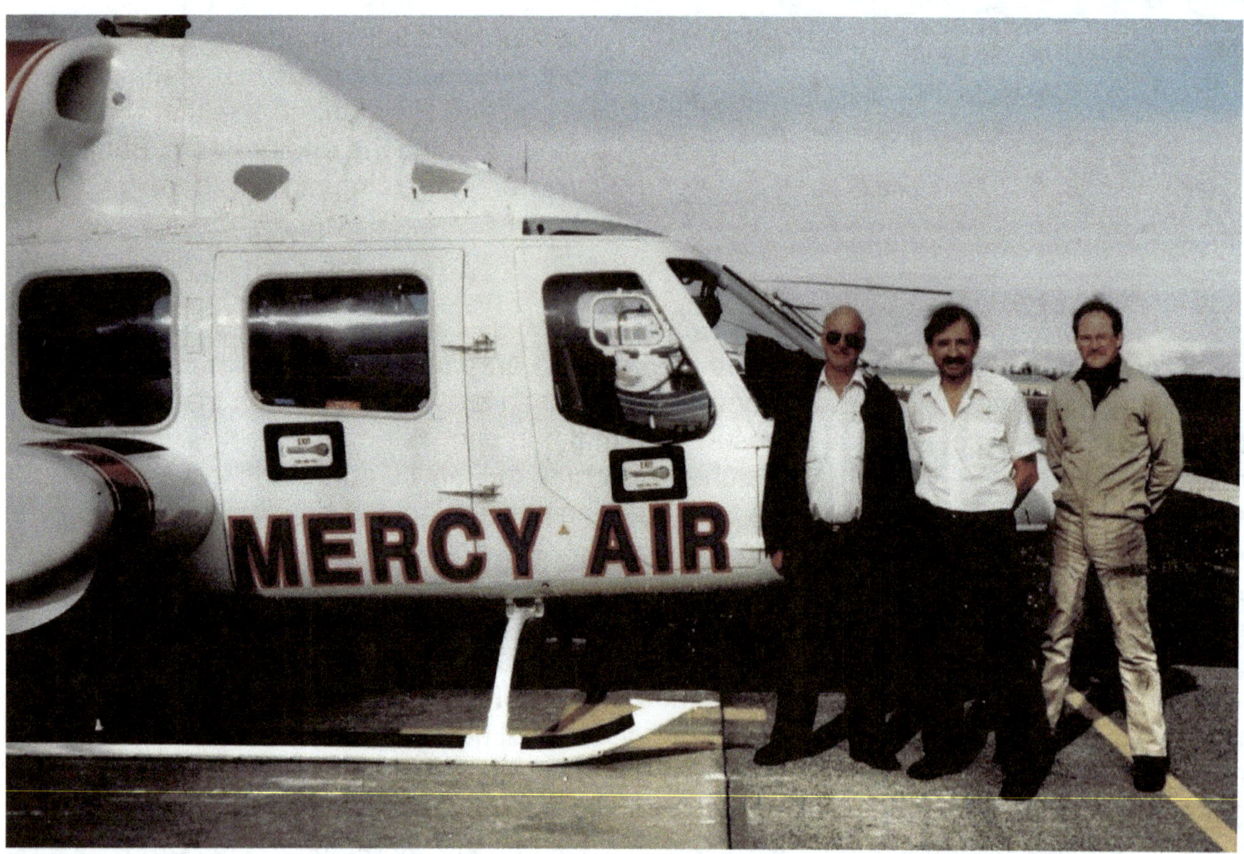

VIH B222 leased to Mercy Air - Rialto CA

In December 1995

, I took a very different direction after receiving a call from C. Fryer, the chief pilot of Abu Dhabi Aviation. It was a position to fly offshore out of Abu Dhabi to the various oilfields in the Persian Gulf. I lived in a compound of crew housing for the pilots and engineers near their heliport. Abu Dhabi Aviation is the largest commercial helicopter company in the Middle East, with a fleet of 57 helicopters. I was checked out on a Bell 412, a 4-million-dollar helicopter that was brand new. Bell had the final assembly of this model done at their plant in Montreal and shipped to the Emirates.

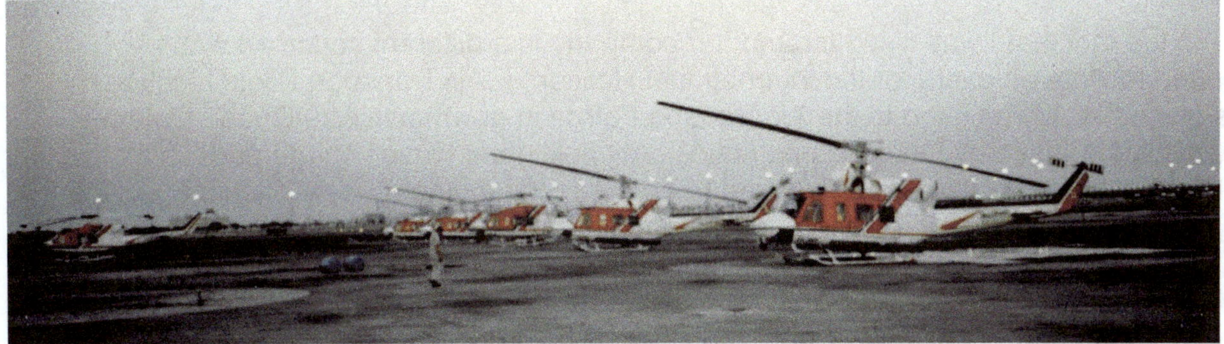

Bell 412 fleet front of hangar

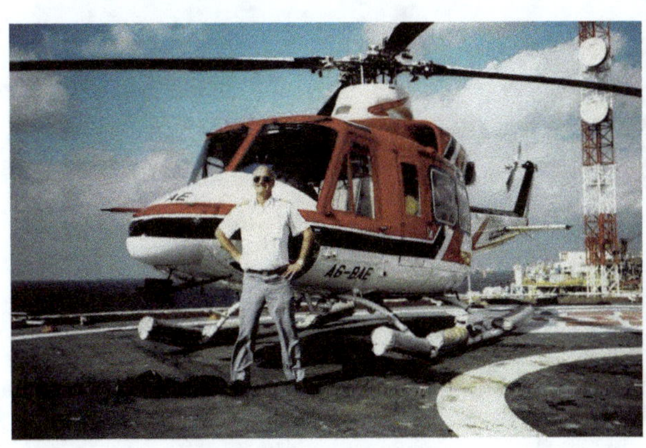

The main oil field we flew to was about 100 nm offshore, halfway between the United Arab Emirates and Iran. Just a few miles from the rigs I landed on, there was an Iranian oil field and rigs just on the other side of the border dividing the Emirates and Iran. There was an international incident involving an ADA (Abu Dhabi Aviation) helicopter mistakenly landing on one of the Iranian rigs. One of the company's pilots landed on one of their rigs largely due to poor visibility. Because of constant tensions in the Gulf area, there was an immediate apology from the Emirates government and the pilot involved. My first officer related another story concerning the same area that was the aftermath of the Six-Day War in 1967. We landed on one of the rigs in the main field, and he pointed out a pattern of 50-calibre bullet holes through the living quarters. During that Arab-Israeli war, a couple of Iranian Mig fighters decided to do a strafing run on this rig. Seventeen oil workers were killed, and they narrowly missed the ADA helicopter. Departures of many helicopters leaving the company airport were systematic and well organized. Each aircraft left from its own parking spot, which was lined up row after row at precision departure times. We would then air taxi over to the main passenger terminal to pick up our crews.

The extreme heat was a bit of a shock. The aircraft starting limitations were predicated on an outside air temperature of a maximum of 45 degrees centigrade. There were some mornings we had to wait for the OAT (Outside Air Temperature) to drop to 45C before we could start the GE engines! The subsequent takeoff was like a hair dryer in your face coming through the outside air vents. Sweat would be streaming from your forehead as you climbed out. Once at an altitude of 3,000 to 6,000 feet over the water en route to the oil fields, it was much cooler. Back at sea level, moving the crews from rig to rig, the temperature was a little more tolerable than on land. I found it irritating that the Arabs would spend millions of dollars buying aircraft but wouldn't install air conditioning units in them.

Due to the fact that I was flying for another company in a different country, I was required to write an exam for the international Helicopter Air Transport Pilots Licence. I was given the day off to go to the Air Transport office in downtown Abu Dhabi. On the way back, I stopped by the base and noticed my helicopter wasn't on the pad. I was told that the helicopter that I normally fly had to do a forced landing on a rig offshore. On the way back from the field, it lost all oil from the main transmission. Just a few days previous, I was inquiring as to why they were going to and from the fields at altitudes of 6,000 feet or higher. My diplomatic advice was that yes, you have two engines, but you only have one gearbox-why go higher than you have to? So taking my advice, they were at only 3000 feet and able to land quickly before there was any damage or even a transmission seizure.

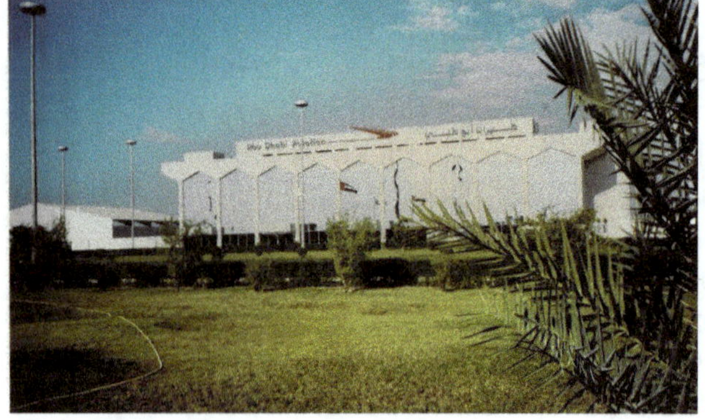

Abu Dhabi Aviation hangar

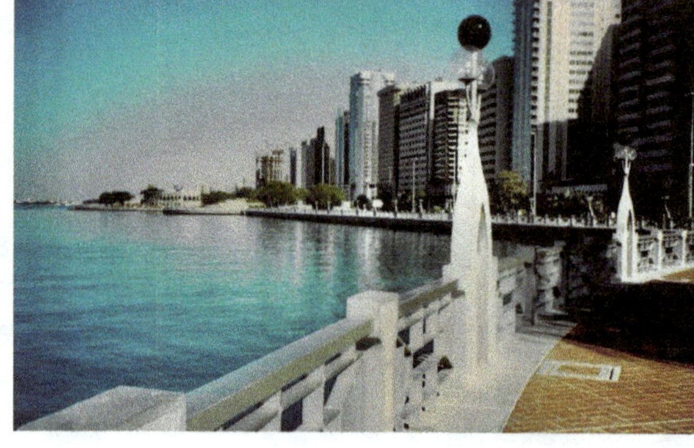

Abu Dhabi waterfront

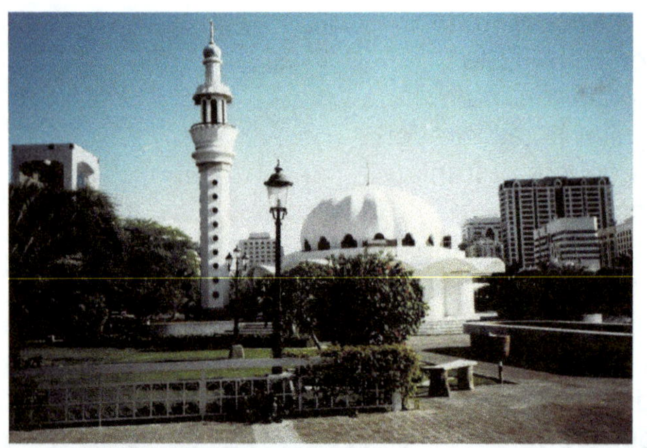

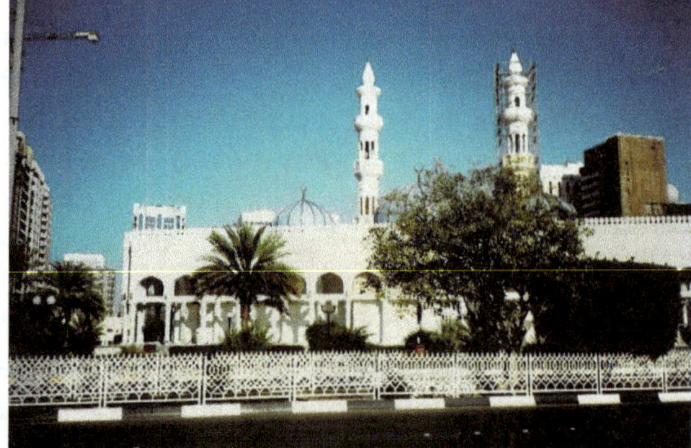

Mosques

The United Arab Emirates is an amazing country

and it's almost like visiting another planet. My experience with the Arabs was not totally pleasant. When you meet them on the street, they have such piercing eyes that seem to look right through you. Perhaps I just hadn't spent enough time there to get to really know them. If you are a national, there is no personal income tax. Also, it seems that they mainly hire workers and professionals from other countries to do the work in their country. In the aviation areas, they mainly hire Canadians, Australians, British and Americans. The country as a whole is very affluent. In one of the general hospitals, there was a two-million-dollar chandelier hanging in a public waiting room. Gasoline was 11 cents/litre at the pumps.

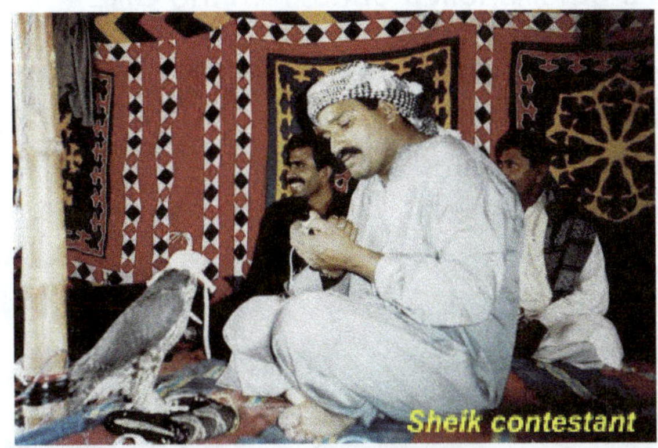
Sheik contestant

The country has a number of sultans with high wealth, stature and political influence. One of the main oil fields I flew to was very large and owned by one of the sultans. It was 300 miles long and 50 miles wide, with many oil wells. It was said that this sheik made millions of dollars per hour from the wells in this one field alone.

A colleague of mine related an interesting experience he had flying for one of the sultans. Most Emirate sultans are extremely wealthy, and my friend P Berling accompanied one of these sultans on a hunting trip. This particular sheik went on annual hunting trips to Pakistan, where he held large tracts of land in the desert. He would take an entourage of people with him, including bodyguards and servants. An important part of his contingent was an accompanying helicopter carrying his blood supply. Captain P and his first officer crewed this aircraft which also stood by for any medical emergencies.

So organizing this trip was quite a process. This sultan owned a fleet of aircraft, from small executive jets to 747s. One of the first loads was bodyguards and servants, followed by the sultan's chefs and food supply. Then the helicopter, a Bell 412, was loaded onto a Russian cargo plane, including the aircrew. The final trip was with a 747 carrying the sultan and his hunting Peregrine falcons. There were 100 of these specially trained falcons. They were not confined to cages in the cargo hold but sat up in the first class section on the seat backs.

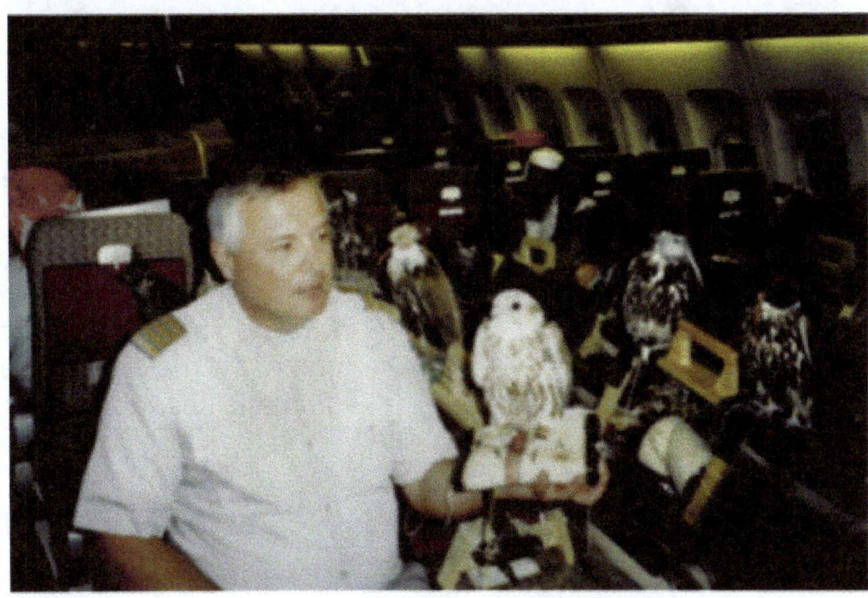
Transporting the peregrines via 747 to Pakistan

An entire hunting camp was set up in this Pakistani desert with the falcons and handlers.

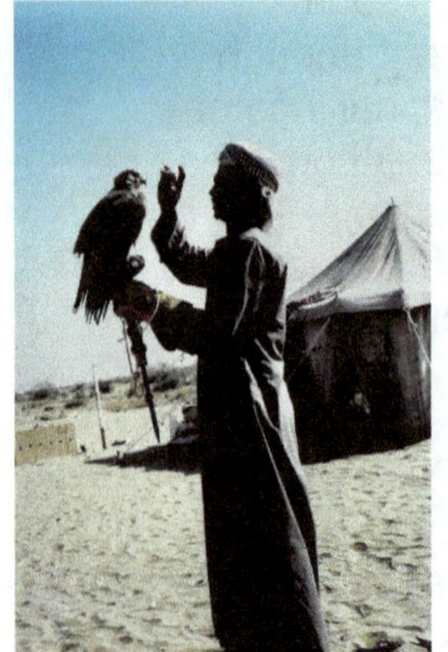

Just a little background on these birds and their extensive training in the United States. To have one falcon trained up to hunting calibre required an average cost of one hundred thousand dollars. On these hunts, the birds are accompanied by 2 medical doctors, each paid about two hundred thousand dollars a year. They were there to patch up the birds if they were injured.

There was a certain species of local Pakistani birds that would be the object prey. The sheik would invite other sheik friends from the UAE kingdom, and they would place bets on whose bird would get the most kills. My friend, Captain P & his copilot were on standby with the helicopter one day. They were in the tent set up in the desert and totally bored. A couple of the sultan's guards came into the tent where P was lying with his elbow resting on a suitcase. One of the guards said, "Hey, Captain, can you please open up that valise." Phillipe had no idea what was in it but was amazed when he opened it to find one million dollars in US currency! This was the sheiks' wagering money on the hunt.

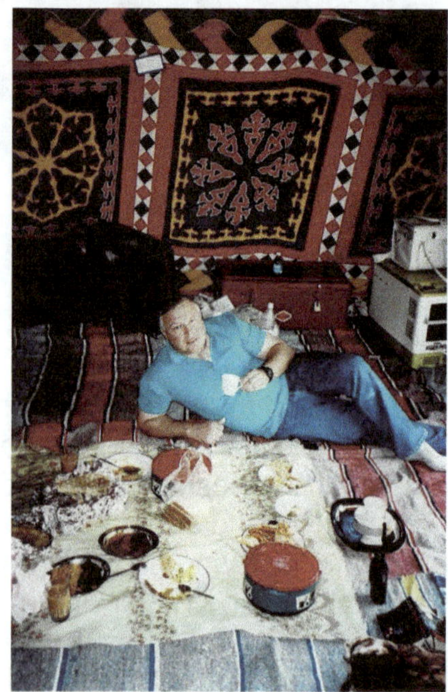

Captain Philippe standing by with helicopter

Whoever got the most kills that day with his bird received a hundred thousand dollars of that cash! When it was all gone, and the suitcase was empty, it was time to go home.

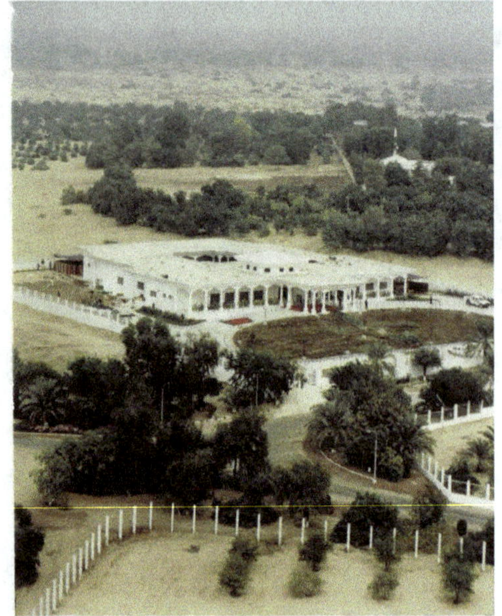

Sultan's desert palace

The Sultan also had a palace nearby the desert camp. Periodically if he had enough 'roughing' it for a while, he would leave the desert and go into one of his palaces to 'freshen up.' After a week, the whole entourage would pack up and head back to one of his main palaces in the UAE. P enjoyed this dramatic change once in a while to the routine of flying to the oil fields.

The United Arab Emirates is a federation

of seven smaller 'Emirates' or states. It's a very interesting country in the Middle East. The crime rate is very low because of the severe punishments. If you're caught stealing, the prison sentences can be very long or even have your hand cut off. In a lot of cases, the prisons are very harsh in that you won't be fed because you committed the crime. So you need to have friends or family to bring you food. There are still public hangings, firing squads or even stoning for crimes of murder or adultery by a wife. An ex-pat can send a young daughter to the corner store at midnight without fear of anything likely to happen to her. Again the punishment for rape or molestation is extremely severe. One of the Canadian captains was the personal lead pilot for one of the sheiks. He mainly flew his Boeing 747 and was well-treated. He and his wife were put up in a luxurious apartment with servants, and everything was paid for. He was supplied with his own Mercedes and driver. His salary was commensurate with senior airline captains. Unfortunately, he became very drunk in public which is something completely frowned upon in this Arab country. He didn't receive a prison term but lost his visa and was kicked out of the country. His wife had been enjoying their life of luxury together and was not impressed! When they returned to Vancouver, she left him! *Expensive lesson.*

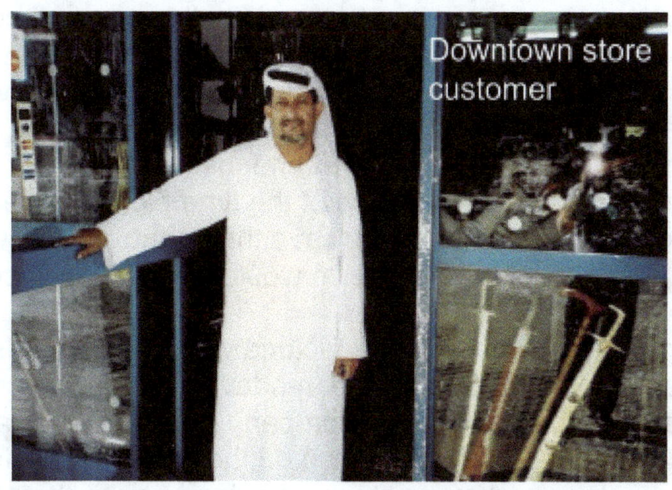
Downtown store customer

Many of the sultans have their own fleets of jet aircraft. They are used extensively for personal travel around the world. Some of them are used during Ramadan to leave the country. Alcohol is absolutely forbidden during this religious observance in Islamic culture. So the sultans fly off with their aides to other countries, leaving all their wives at home, and it's party time!

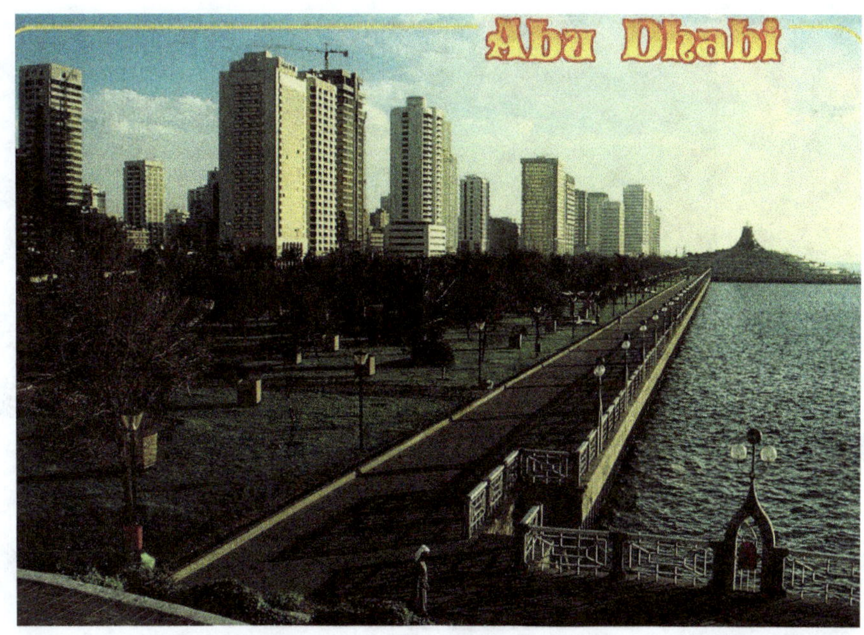

Needless to say,

my flying experiences

were very interesting and challenging at times. The country was fascinating, and I considered moving over there with my wife. However, I'm not sure we could have adjusted to the extreme heat, which was very pervasive. The decision was made after my second tour to the Emirates when I started having severe back problems. On certain days the itinerary involved crew changes at a number of rigs without being able to get out of the helicopter. Because of the time element, we had to 'hot' refuel with the engines running, and I was unable to leave the controls. After six hours of this, the pain in my back became intolerable, which would result in back surgery some years later.

Unfortunately, my position in Victoria with Vancouver Island Helicopters had been filled. However, they needed another medevac pilot in Prince Rupert. By rehiring me, there was an added benefit to the company. I still had my training captain status, so I could conduct all the recurrent training on the medevac pilots in Rupert. This saved the company time and money by not having to bring the pilots down to Victoria for their recurrent training

My wife was not really happy about leaving Victoria but again was so faithful in backing me up and moving. It turned out to be one of the best moves we had ever made! The new friends, experiences and some of the most incredible scenery in the world made it all worthwhile! Prince Rupert is actually only forty miles from the Alaskan Panhandle, and in that NW corner of BC, the scenery is truly breathtaking. Our coverage area was a 200-mile radius around Rupert over spectacular mountains and pristine valleys. The many glaciers were truly spectacular, and each had their own varied formations. Unfortunately, they are receding because of global warming. We could see clear evidence of this as we flew over them over a relatively short time span. In many of the valleys, there were no signs of civilization, hydro wires or logging. From above, we could see salmon spawning in crystal clear streams and large areas of lavender spread like purple blankets.

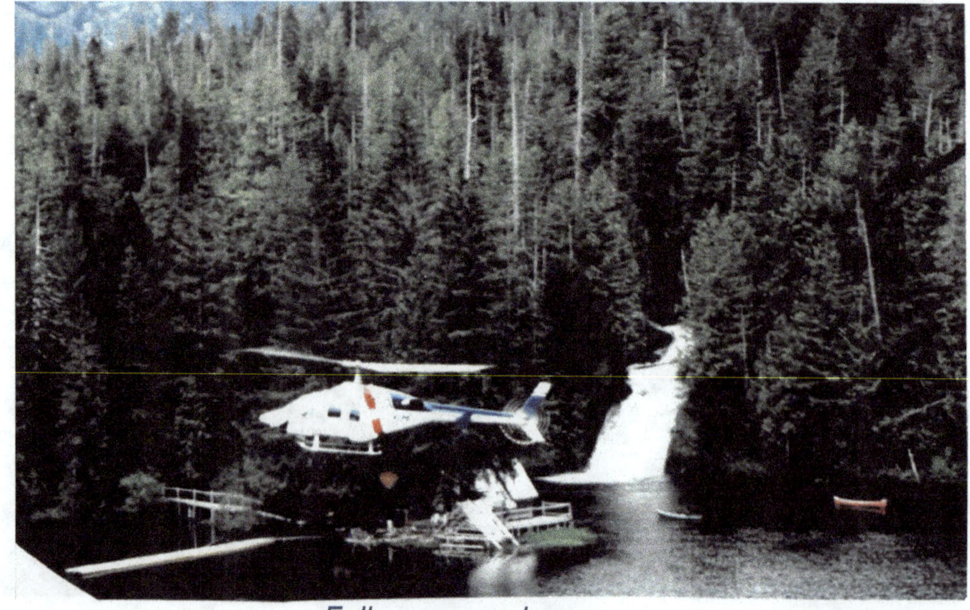

Falls near our home

Most of the medevac flights were varied and seldom routine. Utilizing helicopters was quick and expedient, especially on the Coast. Many of the villages were only accessible by boat or seaplane. Picking up a patient by boat was usually a two to six-hour trip. A helicopter could access the patient much quicker and have them to the emergency or on the operating table in less than an hour. If delivered to a hospital in less than an hour, it was often the difference between life and death.

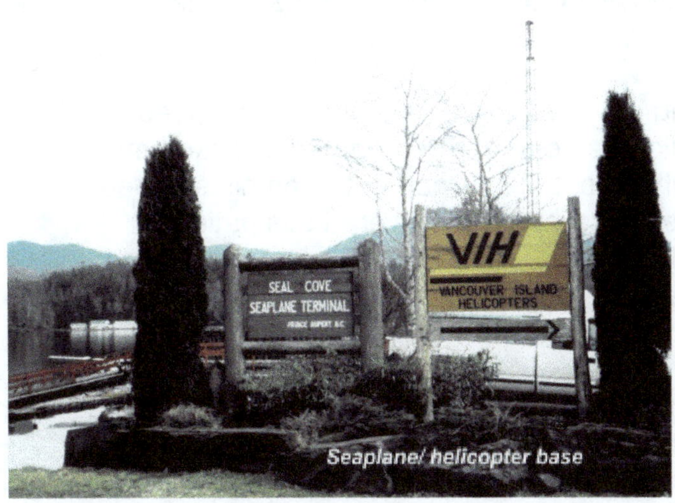

Seaplane/ helicopter base

As that first winter of 1996 set in, it became obvious that the helicopter was even more important and well- utilized. There's only one highway between Prince Rupert and Terrace in the interior, and it can be very treacherous in the wintertime. If there is precipitation, it could be raining in Rupert and snowing in Terrace. Somewhere in between the two cities, the highway can turn from wet to ice and snow. We got a call one day to an accident scene on Highway 16, thirty kilometres east of Prince Rupert. A light pickup truck had hit a semi-truck head-on after being thrown out of heavy ruts in the snow. We landed on the highway, and the pickup truck was wedged under the semi in the ditch. The driver in the half-ton was trapped and died as the paramedics tried attending to him. Often we can transport accident victims to the nearest hospital, but this young driver was not so fortunate.

A few weeks later, on Christmas Day, we received a call to Hartley Bay, south of Prince Rupert. It was a memorable trip for a new paramedic on his first call with the helicopter. The weather was absolutely clear and sunny. The trip down along the Coast was spectacular, with incredible mountain scenery and snow-capped peaks on our left. We landed in Hartley Bay an hour later to a foot of newly fallen snow. I did the normal two- minute cool down on the turbines and shut the aircraft down. To add to an already spectacular day- there was the village church a few blocks in front of us. As we disembarked from the helicopter, there were Christmas carols coming from the steeple on the snow-clad roof. It looked like a Christmas postcard as the new paramedic said, "We're actually getting paid for this !" We were there responding to a young girl having had an experience with a drug overdose. She survived, but the irony is that many of the First Nations' villages were supposed to be drug and alcohol-free.

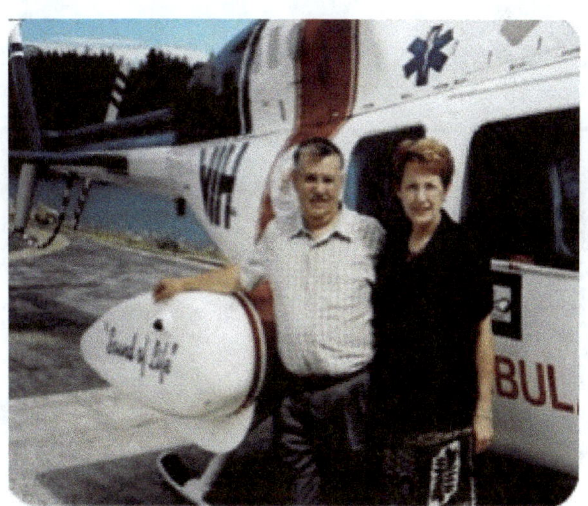
Old school friends

Some of our calls turned out to be non-life threatening and with a certain amount of humour. Early one morning, we picked up a 14-year-old boy in Port Simpson suspected of having seizures. After he was assessed at the Prince Rupert Hospital, he was discharged and went out on the town with his friends.

Apparently, he had fallen off his chair after playing video games for 12 hours. It was simply a case of vertigo, not a seizure.

Another case involved a critical injury to a young guy climbing a tree with an extended rotary saw. As we were loading him into the helicopter, one of the paramedics asked me to hold his bag. I assumed it was personal belongings, but it turned out to be his severed foot! A post note to this call happened 2 months later when we delivered this patient back to his village carrying a small box. I asked him what was in the box. He said that it was his foot and that he was bringing it home. With a smile, he said, "I grew up with that foot, and I'm going to give it a proper burial!"

There were other humorous stories that didn't involve injuries. On the Queen Charlottes, recently named Haida Gwaii, there seemed to be quite a few psychiatric cases. We flew over to pick up an individual scheduled for care at a Terrace psych hospital. When we arrived in Queen Charlotte City, the patient had 'escaped,' and the medical staff couldn't find him. There was another call-up Island in Masset, so it wasn't a wasted trip. Fortunately, we were able to transport that patient back to Rupert in record time since we were already on the Island.

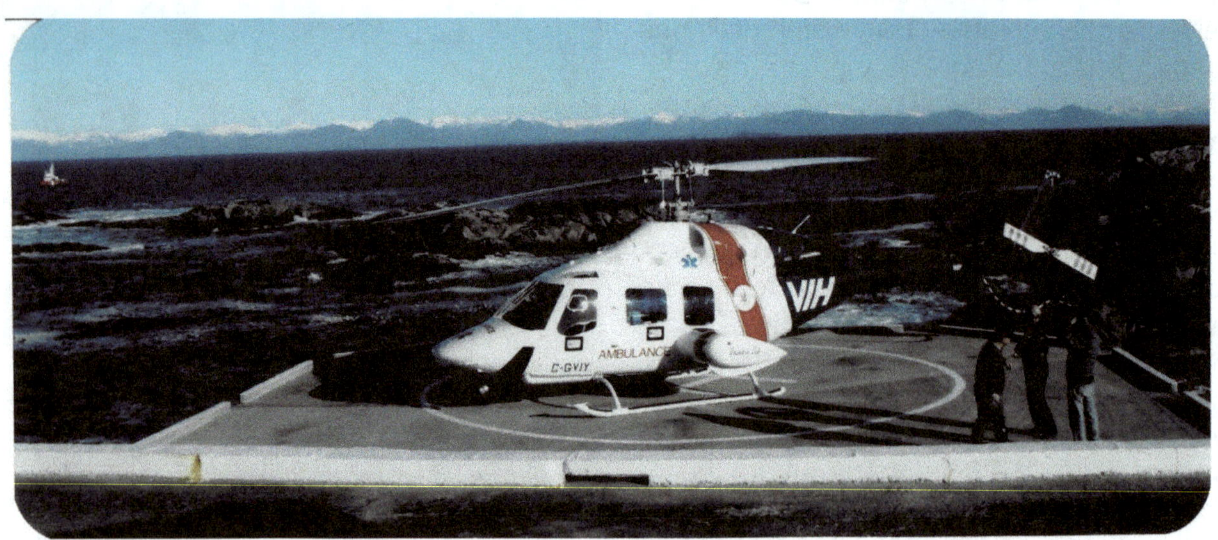

Helipad - Triple Island

There were other interesting psych patient calls

such as a subsequent one to Masset. We were waiting at the airport for the paramedics to return from the hospital with the patient. The ambulance pulled up and parked out of sight on the other side of the terminal. Shortly after, there was a well-dressed young guy wandering around looking at all the parked airplanes. There were scheduled and charter aircraft mainly involved in transporting all the fishermen for the season.

We had a great conversation, but I noticed he wasn't exhibiting any kind of an airport pass. Our paramedics came rushing around the corner looking for their patient! This very normal-looking young guy ended up being in restraints as we transported him back to Prince Rupert. Proof positive you can't always pick out a patient with mental problems.

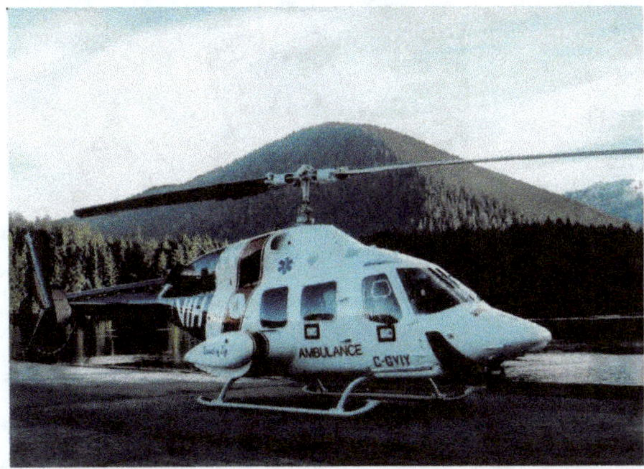

The paramedics took extra precautions with the restraints because of an incident involving another psych patient. A few months previous, a psych patient was being flown along the same route back to Rupert in a Beaver. En route at 3,000 feet, he had managed to open the door and jumped out. He almost dragged the paramedic out with him and tragically fell to his death in the ocean below. They never found his body.

At times, there were other calls when the clinic nurse would call BCAS for the helicopter simply as a precaution. Sometimes it was simply an excuse for the 'patient' and family to hitch a free ride to town. However, the consulting medical staff could never take the chance that it was not a legitimate medical emergency. Sometimes a family member would become irate and antagonistic if you couldn't take them as well. Takeoff weight, at times, could be a determining factor due to fuel considerations and extra medical staff on board. You could often tell the importance of a patient in the village by the crowd turnout. If it was an ordinary family member, just immediate family and friends would gather at the helicopter. If he or she was a Council member, more villagers would gather at the heliport. If it was the Chief or second in command, a large portion of the village would attend. Very interesting hierarchies!

Port Edward - our town

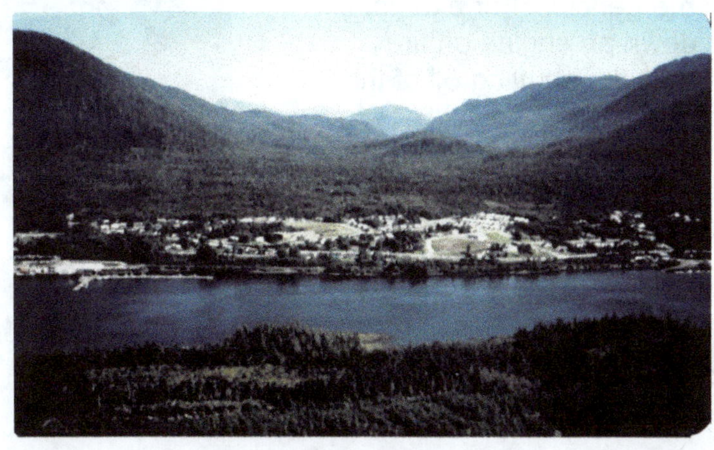

As mentioned previously,

other than being just a line pilot

, I did all the recurrent training of the base medevac pilots as I did in Victoria. This time, I had the advantage of being able to utilize a home computer flight simulator. This was a fixed-place simulator with no motion involved. However, it was very realistic as a procedures trainer. I could plug in any instrument charts and approach plates in North America. It was a great advantage to be able to have the pilots do the instrument work & shoot an approach into an airport they'll never likely go to. Flight simulators are a very important tool for recurrent training and are obviously much cheaper by the hour than the actual aircraft.

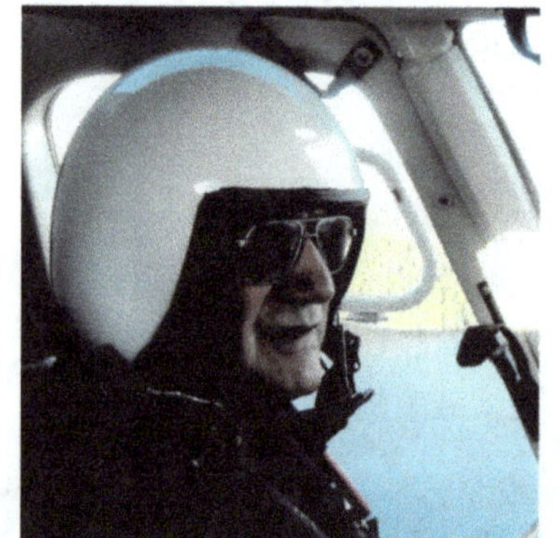

You could also simulate in-flight emergencies in a completely controlled environment without jeopardizing the actual aircraft. Things like engine fires, jammed controls, tail rotor failures, runaway Nicad battery overheating, main rotor and fuselage ice accumulation, electrical failures, transmission failures, etc. The main and tail rotors are run through all the planetary gears in the transmission. If the transmission has a gear failure or complete loss of oil, this in-flight emergency must be dealt with immediately. All emergencies must be dealt with by the use of checklists as if both pilots are in the actual aircraft. This is a standard part of the protocol for exact communication between the captain and the first officer. CRM, or Cockpit Resource Management, has been developed, enabling two pilots to follow standard procedures concerning checklists and flight operations. Consequently, there could be two pilots who have never seen each other before, ending up in the same cockpit and following standard procedures. No longer would you have a first officer trying to 'figure out' what the captain wanted. This resulted in safer and more standardized flight operations.

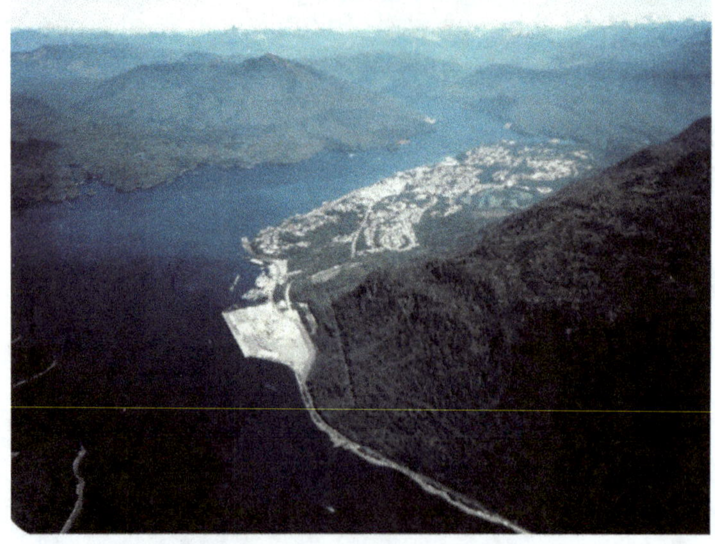

Prince Rupert after a training flight

Checklists are followed by both pilots using the challenge and response method. The co-pilot will read an instruction, and the captain will carry out the action. The 'question and response' method is especially important involving certain emergencies. For example, shutting down an engine on fire also requires the shutting off of that fuel valve. The copilot would physically put his hand on that shut off switch and ask for confirmation. The captain would then check that he had the right engine and say, "Confirm No. 1" (Correct engine No. 1 or No. 2). In the past, there have been occasions in the industry when the remaining good engine was inadvertently shut down by not following this protocol.

There also are other aspects to recurrent training that are critical but non-emergencies in nature. The Bell 222 UT does not have an autopilot, so you are manually hand-flying it at all times. This is just a normal flight skill that doesn't require a lot of concentration. However, when you're completely in the cloud and flying on instruments, a whole new skill set is required. It is critical to keep up a good scan of all the flight instruments when you're in an unstabilized aircraft. If you begin focusing on one or two instruments, such as your artificial horizon, you could quickly succumb to flight vertigo. This disorientation could cause you to get into an extremely unusual attitude, go inverted and possibly crash. So you stress a scan of all instruments, especially if they're experiencing vertigo. If they're feeling this kind of disorientation and can't quickly eliminate it by increased scan- it is imperative that the other pilot takes control.

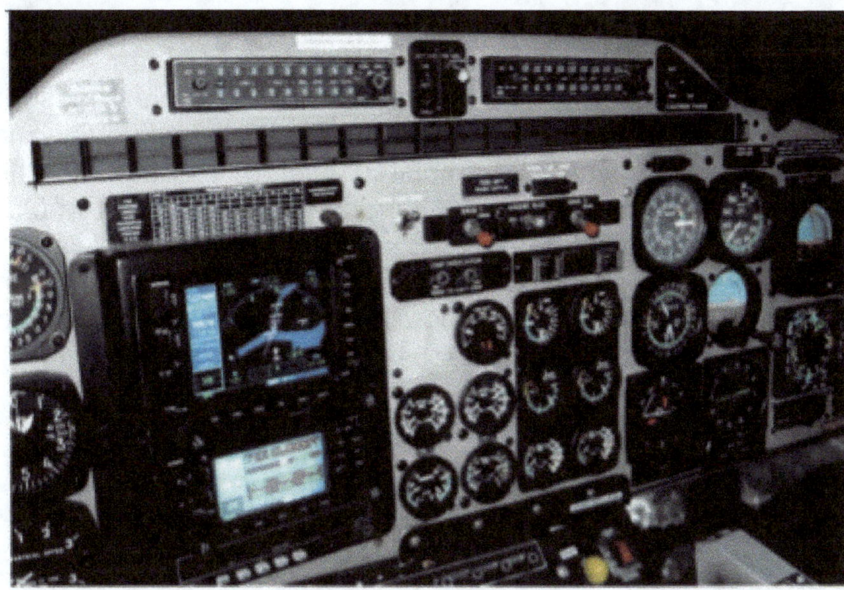

Bell 222 cockpit with new GPS

Another common and potentially dangerous situation is an aircraft's final approach to a landing called CFIT. This is an acronym for Controlled Flight Into Terrain. This can occur on a clear night with the landing area in clear view but no real visual clues on the approach path. This could be over glassy water or snow-covered ground, e.g. The pitfall is that both pilots are looking ahead to the landing area and neither one is monitoring the flight instruments. It's imperative that the two main instruments to be monitored are the altimeter and the radar altimeter. Looking ahead at only the lights of the landing area can be an optical illusion, a feeling that you are at a safe altitude above the terrain. This has often resulted in an aircraft flying into the terrain with engines operating normally. I had a personal experience with this optical illusion one night on an approach to Queen Charlotte City. I had the illusion I was still about a thousand feet above the water as we had a clear sight of the lights on the landing pad area.

Neither of us was monitoring the altitude instruments as we should have been doing. Fortunately, I had bugged the radar altimeter for 200 feet, at which point a ground proximity light illuminates. Suddenly, the light came on, and I pulled up just in time. I almost crashed as a result of the CFIT pitfall. Ironically I had disregarded the safe required approach protocols that I stressed in my training to the other medevac pilots. One of the benefits of being a recurrent training captain is that it kept me current as well. It also reinforced that you still had to be very aware that you could still be vulnerable yourself. Overconfidence or complacency as a training pilot could never be overlooked.

There are some emergencies that can't be demonstrated in a fixed simulator. One would be a tail rotor failure caused by backing into a tree, some other obstacle or a drive shaft failure. I demonstrated this by applying (jamming) a full right pedal to the helicopter in a hover. This simulated a tail rotor failure, and the aircraft would start spinning to the right. To stop it, turning off both engines would immediately stop the spinning. Because of torque, without a tail rotor, the fuselage will spin at the same rpm as the main rotor but in the opposite direction. Turning off both engines eliminates the torque, which immediately stops the spinning. In an actual occurrence, the reaction must be immediate, or you'll roll the aircraft up 'in a ball.'

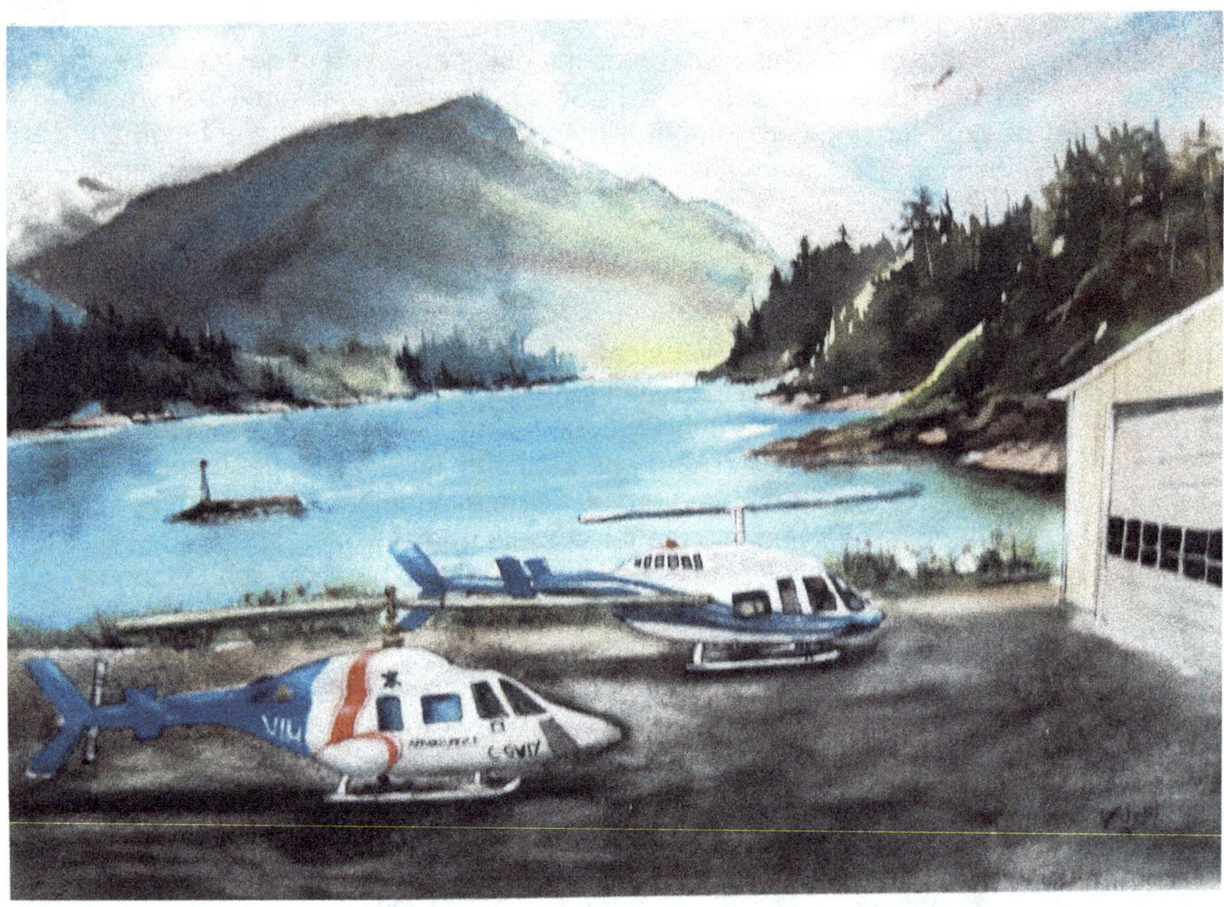

Painted by our friend and artist - Robin Knox

There are

so many perks

to having a helicopter at your disposal in off duty times. The company did not mind the occasional recreational use, such as local sightseeing trips with visiting friends and family. The normal tariff for this Bell 222 was $3,000/hour, but we could simply call it a non-revenue flight or a maintenance check flight if applicable. This way, all air time was still recorded in the aircraft journey log book. At times we could fly over to a favourite fishing spot that was only accessible by helicopter. One of my colleagues tried out something that was very unique and unlikely any other pilot had ever done. He hooked up a crab trap to a 50-foot line attached to the aircraft cargo hook. He then hovered over to the bay beside the hangar and held a hover just above the surface, lowering the crab trap down to the bottom for about 20 minutes. He hovered back to the hangar and set the trap back down with several large Dungeness crabs in it!

Another one of our base pilots was transporting men and materials south of Port Edward, where I was building my two-storey house. The roof trusses, sheathing and shingles were stacked beside the house. I had slings attached to bundles of rafters, and on each return trip from his job site, I would hook up my friend, B. Goddard, to one of the loads. He would lift it up to the second story and return later for subsequent loads. This really aided and accelerated construction and was just another perk of having a helicopter available! After we moved into the house, my son Chad was flying for Air Canada Jazz and on scheduled runs to Prince Rupert. One of my neighbours remarked about Jazz flying low over Port Edward, which was a bit unusual. I said, "Well, that's just my son probably showing a new captain where his parents lived!"

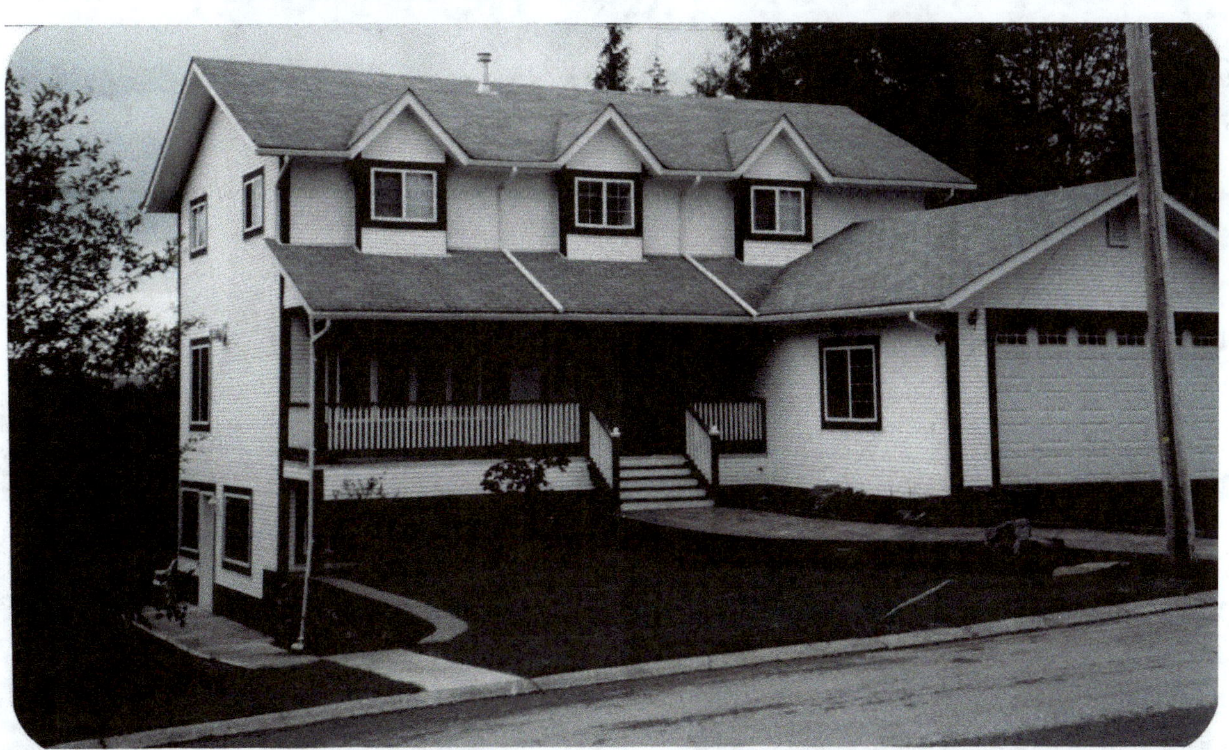

Our new house - Port Edward out side Prince Rupert

I was very proud to have my so

flying for a commercial airline, and we would be on the same frequency when flying in the Prince Rupert area. We both were very conscientious to observe the correct terminology on the radio with air traffic control. We knew the father was listening to the son and vice versa. It was a fun situation!

Flying with my son was like reliving my own earlier climb up the aviation ladder. One day my wife and I were returning from Edmonton to Prince Rupert with Air Canada. There was a stopover in Vancouver to switch airplanes and fly the last leg with Air Canada Jazz. A pleasant surprise was that my son Chad was crewing that flight as a First Officer. It was Chad's turn to fly that leg, so I was fortunate enough to be upfront for the start-up, taxi and takeoff. That was back in the day when you could still be in the cockpit on a jump seat. Throughout the flight, I was completely aware of what was going on, being in the aviation world myself. Needless to say, I was the proud father observing a competent son. He was quietly and professionally anticipating every phase of the flight. His landing in Prince Rupert was smooth and flawless.

Through the years, we have always had a friendly banter back and forth. I would always kid him about not being a real pilot because he wasn't flying helicopters. I would say, "You have to have the propeller on the roof, not on the nose!" One day he got me back when he smiled and said, "Well, Dad, that could be, but I don't see you eating a steak at 30,000 feet either!" That shut me up!

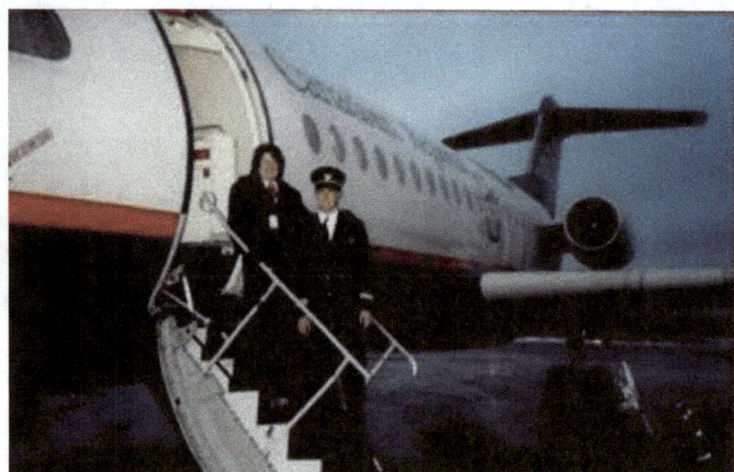

Wife Connie & son Chad

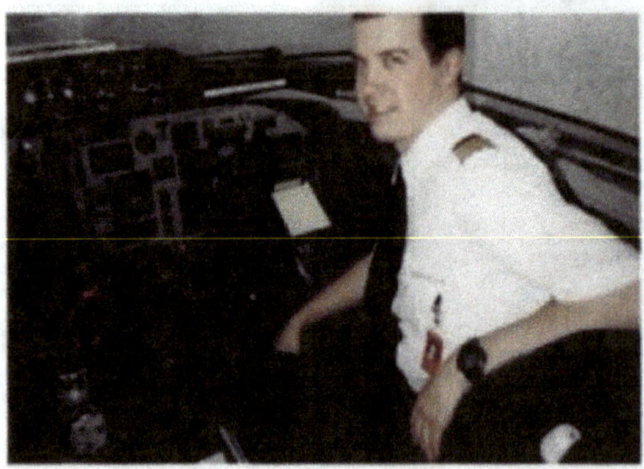

Chad in the cockpit

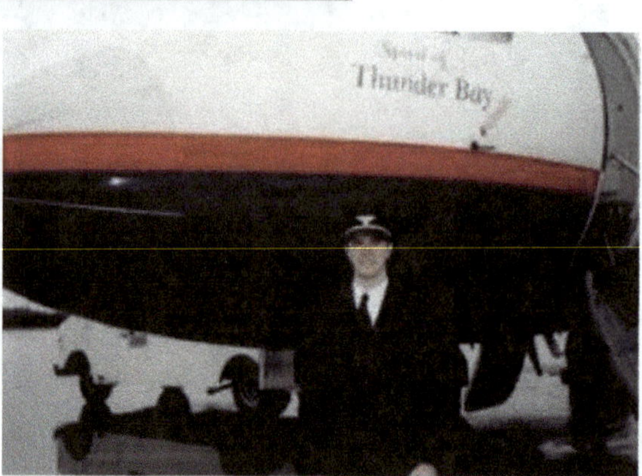

Flying along the northern coast

and over to the Queen Charlottes was fascinating. Not only was the scenery spectacular but there was a lot of marine traffic, as well as wildlife. On occasion, we would see Kermode bears, especially on Prince Patrick Island, just south of Prince Rupert. This is a pure white bear, also known as a 'spirit bear' by indigenous peoples. It looks just like a polar bear but is actually a subspecies of the black bear family. We would often see mountain goats, sheep, moose, deer and timber wolves. Often, a bird's eye view of Humpback and Orca whales, along with porpoises and seals. There was a sand bar just off the north coast of the Charlottes that was generally covered with hundreds of seals and sea lions. They seemed to believe in segregation, as the seals would be at one end of the island and the sea lions at the other. As we slowly overflew with the helicopter, there would be a mass exodus, and the ocean would be churned into a large white froth.

Once a year, the herring went through their spawning cycle, and the water would be filled with large areas of herring eggs or roe. This is also known as a healthy type of caviar, having Omega 3 fatty acids. Entire bay areas would be green or yellowish from trillions of their eggs. The Hooligan, another small fish, is also spawning at relatively the same time of year. This draws the attraction of all the predatory birds, including seagulls and Bald eagles, by the millions. It also became a hazard for helicopters as we tried to navigate around them.

Generally, as we were taking off or landing, the birds would get out of the way, but the odd time they would not or could not veer off. Then we'd have to take, sometimes, an extremely evasive maneuver, utilizing a helicopter's amazing maneuverability. The main rotor blade tips are travelling at 475 mph, just under the speed of sound. Hitting a bald eagle in flight would be like hitting a 15 lb rock. The destructive force on the rotor blades, control rods or windscreen would be catastrophic. On a vertical takeoff from the hangar, one day, we were very fortunate, a seagull not so much. Somehow, just before we transitioned to forward flight, the bird flew into the main rotor blades. At first, we thought the bird had survived as we saw it swimming in the water in front of us. Unfortunately, it was missing one wing, and his carnivorous friends quickly put it out of its misery.

A few days previous, we were on final approach to Port Simpson to pick up a patient after an attempted suicide. As we were passing over a small tree-covered island, there were suddenly hundreds of bald eagles taking off in every direction. After landing in the village, we related this unusual occurrence of such a large number of Bald eagles. We were told that they were feeding on a whale carcass. As a final note to this medevac call, we immediately returned to pick up another attempted suicide. Apparently, a 14-year-old was depressed about her friend's attempt at suicide, so she tried to take her own life as well. Unfortunately, in a lot of these isolated villages, there are not a lot of things for young people to do, and they become very depressed. Often drugs, alcohol or suicide are some of the pursued outlets.

In 2010

I turned 64 and realized I was looking at a major crossroads in my life. Whether to go into full retirement or continue flying for a few more years. I never really regarded my various flying jobs as 'work' but more like, "Oh, I wonder where I'm going next!" It was strangely interesting getting into a medevac and flying since I couldn't even stand the sight of blood! Some of the logging, mountain climbing and highway accidents, to name a few, resulted in some pretty graphic injuries. However, it seemed that if I had to be actively involved in loading and transporting an injured patient, I was ok. Ironically, another interesting fact was that I'd always been afraid of heights. For example, I could not stand being on the top of a tall building and looking down over the side. Also, if I landed on a mountain top with skiers, I would not get out of the helicopter unless I absolutely had to. The guide would get out and remove their skis from the racks. On another occasion, I had a room in a Detroit hotel when I was there for a helicopter medevac convention. My room was on the 53rd floor with floor-to-ceiling glass on the Detroit Riverside. I could not stand at that window looking down. Apparently, 80% of all pilots are afraid of heights, but it's all relative. When you're in an aircraft, there is no real sensation of height, rather it's more like looking down at a map.

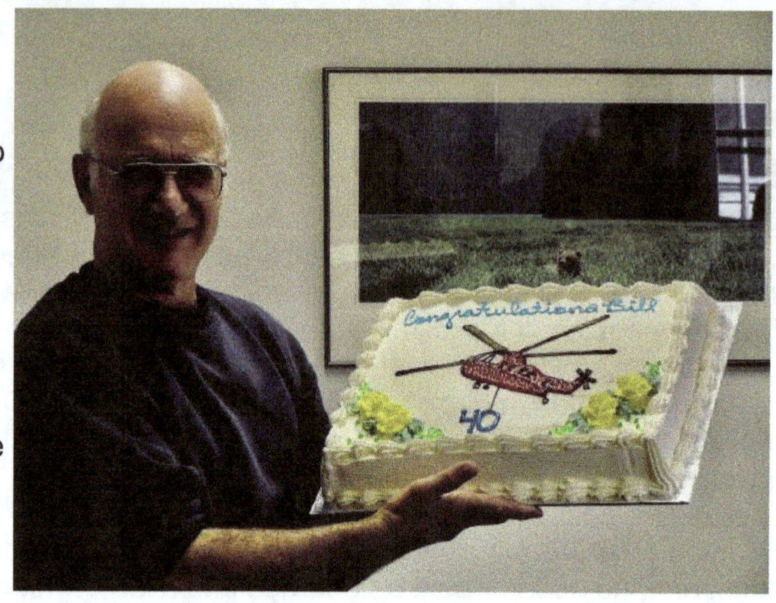

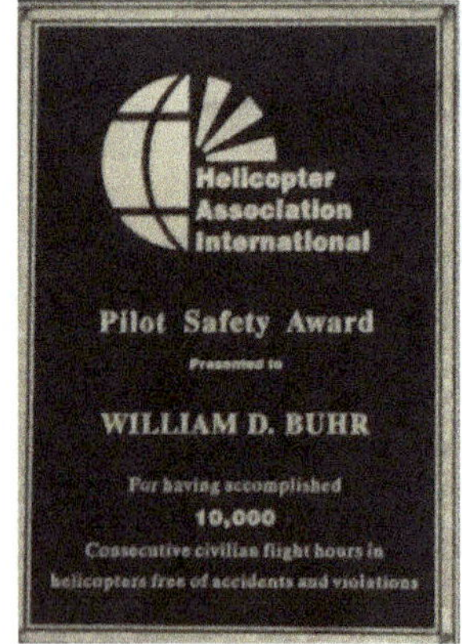

As my retirement was approaching, so was the renewal or possible end of our contract with BC Ambulance Services. The answer to this coming event came about in the Spring of 2011.

The BC government awarded the new contract to HeliJet International on April 1, 2011, after Vancouver Island Helicopters had had it for 20 years.

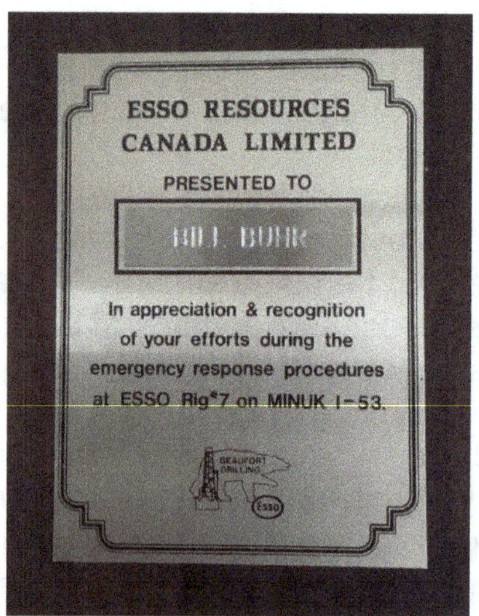

The last few flights did not invoke a frame of mind like some kind of excitement that I would soon be retiring. Rather, it stirred up so many mixed emotions, and so many memories of an amazing career.

Sunsets are often significant in portraying an end or closure to an event in time. We took off for a medevac flight to the Queen Charlottes one beautiful evening. The sun was just setting, and the clouds to the west were illuminated in a kaleidoscope of colours. This turned into a succession of unique atmospheric events quite unlike anything I had seen before. As the sun set, I continued my climb. When I approached the next cloud layer, the sun again became visible and again illuminated those clouds before setting again. As I was nearing our cruise altitude, there was yet one more solid layer of cloud just as the sun, because of our increased altitude, briefly reappeared again. One more time it illuminated the clouds in deep reds and purples before disappearing a final time. This kind of celestial artistry was unforgettable. *You had to be there!*

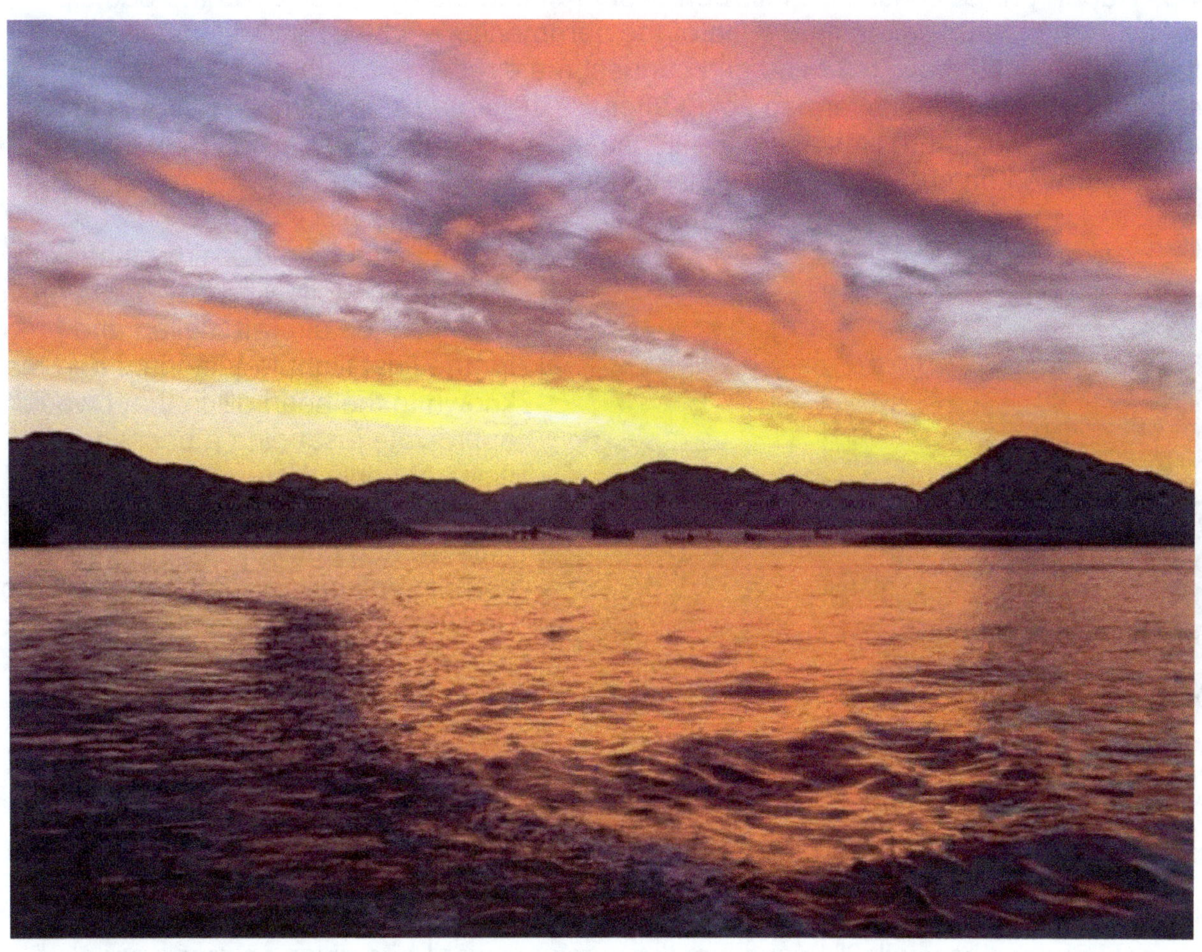

Prince Rupert Harbour

My last medevac flight

was a return to Prince Rupert after delivering a patient to the Terrace Hospital. The paramedics on board were feeling a bit nostalgic as well after flying with VIH crews for so many years. All the paramedics had a large degree of comfort and confidence in our crews. We had carried them through all kinds of weather, flight and patient situations. Throughout the flights, because of our interconnected intercom, conversations were often light and entertaining.

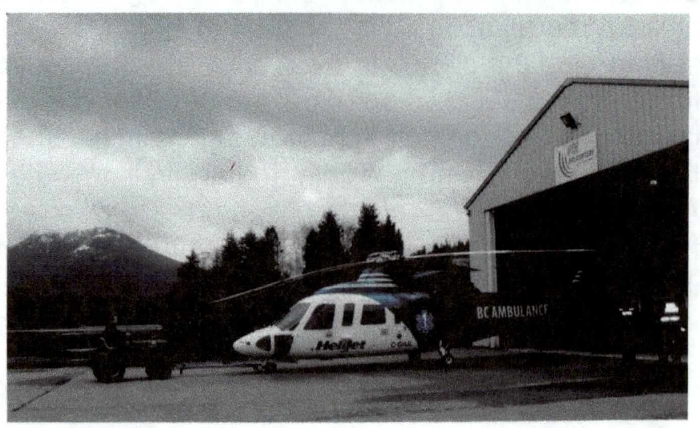

Helijet arriving to take over the contract with BCAS after VIH

At the beginning of that return flight from Terrace, the paramedics requested a low-level flight along the Skeena River. This is a beautiful River winding through the mountains to Prince Rupert on the coast. As I followed every bend in the river, I enjoyed the odd sip from my ever-present coffee mug. One of the paramedics said they should install a coffee canister just above my head and connect me directly to it with an IV! Along the river banks were a lot of fishermen going after the 40-pound king salmon. When I landed back at our hangar, there was a strange sense of closure. The competition's Sikorsky S-76 had arrived on our tarmac in preparation for a seamless takeover.

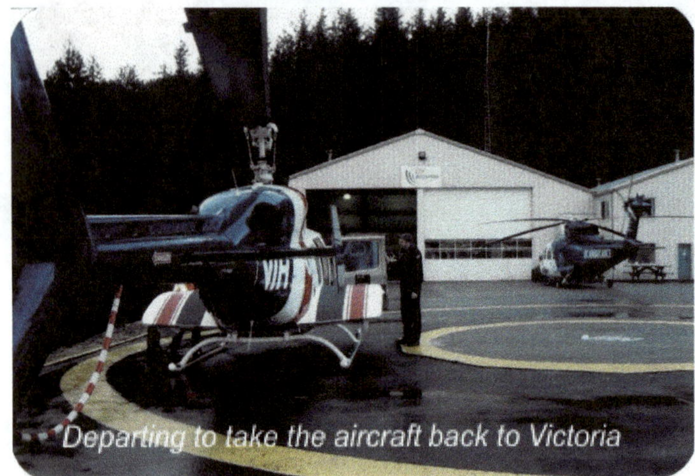

Departing to take the aircraft back to Victoria

Departing to take the aircraft back to Victoria The following day our takeover crew had the aircraft fuelled and prepared for the final flight to Victoria. I had made it known to the head office that I would appreciate just being a passenger on this flight. My only request to the flight crew was if I could fly the last leg into Victoria. This worked out well because we would be dropping off one of the pilots at his home in Duncan, 10 minutes from the Victoria airport.

We took off from Rupert on a beautiful sunny morning. I was comfortably seated in the passenger compartment with my coffee cup and camera. This flight was actually bittersweet. As I looked back on a 44-year career, so many of the almost countless flights came back in complete clarity. I remembered an interesting conversation I had with a pastor from the Baptist church in Prince Rupert. He said, "During all of the years you've been flying, there must have been some very close calls?" I gave him the stock answer I had given so many people." There were a few very close calls, but I've always had God flying as my copilot!" Pastor Andreas kind of cocked his head and said, "Bill, do you think you might have had Him in the wrong seat?" I just roared with laughter, never having had that response before! In other words, I really should have had Him in the Captain's seat on the right!

As we neared the Victoria airport, the crew made a slight diversion and landed in Duncan. The captain had arrived home, and I took his seat at the controls up front. Ten minutes later, I landed at our hangar in Victoria. It was fitting that the weather had moved in, and it was pouring rain. There were no brass bands, no red carpet. Only a forlorn figure, our schedular, Dianne taking a picture of our landing. This was the termination of a 20-year contract, and her little camera recorded it for all posterity.

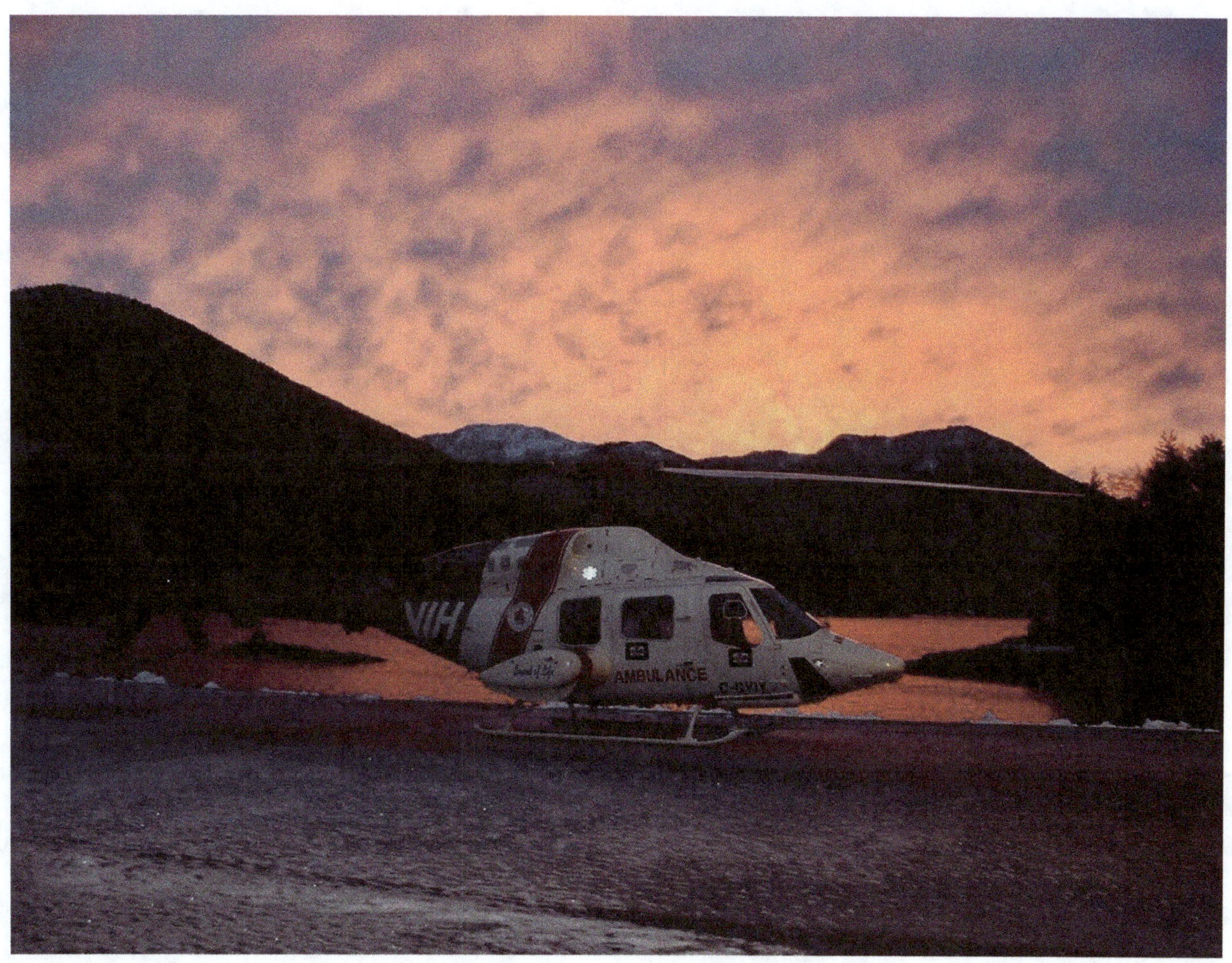

This picture also recorded my final flight.

www.ingramcontent.com/pod-product-compliance
Lightning Source LLC
LaVergne TN
LVHW061246100826
845148LV00008B/1044
* 9 7 8 1 7 3 8 9 7 2 5 0 0 *